the yalta myths

the YALTA MYTHS
an issue in u.s. politics, 1945-1955
athan g. theoharis

university of missouri press, columbia, missouri

Standard Book Number 8262-0088-5
Library of Congress Card Number 70-105269
Printed and bound in the United States of America
Copyright © 1970 by The Curators of the University of Missouri

For my parents, brothers, and sisters

preface

former Secretary of State Dean Acheson remarked during our July 17, 1962, interview: "Yours is not a study in history so much as a study in abnormal psychology." The mere listing of the principal sources for this study — the *Chicago Tribune*, *The Saturday Evening Post*, George Sokolsky, Westbrook Pegler, Fulton Lewis, Jr., David Lawrence, Joseph McCarthy, William Jenner, George Malone, Kenneth Wherry, Everett Dirksen, Patrick McCarran, William Langer, Richard Nixon, Karl Mundt, Styles Bridges, William Knowland, Lawrence Smith, Charles Kersten, Alvin O'Konski, Walter Judd, Paul Shafer, Clare Hoffman, Charles Vursell, Howard Buffett, J. Parnell Thomas, John Rankin, Clare Boothe Luce — tends to support that conclusion.

I have found the postwar decade, 1945–1955, an exciting and critical one: exciting and critical because of the radical change in the popular concept of foreign and domestic policy, which showed the public's underlying frustration and intolerance; exciting and critical because of the lost opportunities for peace and domestic reform that were squandered and emasculated during the Cold War.

An understanding of the period requires a review of both domestic and foreign policy and the realization that they affect each other. The Cold War did not merely influence U.S. foreign policy; it also created a climate that influenced domestic legislation and politics. McCarthyism was not an aberration. It dramatized the acceptance of an anti-Communist rhetoric basic to the Cold War and the shift in focus and tactics of those partisan or conservative Republicans bitterly opposed to the New Deal. Foreign policy gave those Republicans an opportunity to discredit the progressive ideas of the New Deal and a challenge to assail the extended, complex international responsibilities basic to the Truman Administration's containment policy. The responses of those Republicans were negativist, couched in the rhetoric of "victory over communism."

I could never have completed this study without the assistance of numerous friends, associates, and public figures. I gratefully acknowledge the co-operation provided by the many congressmen, senators, and government officials whom I interviewed. Their direct personal involvement afforded otherwise unobtainable insights. I am indebted to John Tagliafero, Dean Kohlhoff, Nikki Feinstein, Richard Kirkendall, Mel Small, and Liza Houston Davey for their literary criticisms and insightful comments. I also express my thanks for the assistance of Bruce Merkle, Research Director of the Republican National Committee; Philip Lagerquist, Archivist at the Truman Library; Philip Brooks, Director of the Truman Library; Erwin Mueller, Research Assistant at the Truman Library; and Joseph Wiewura, Public Relations Director of the Polish-American Congress. A grant from the Truman Library Institute for National and International Affairs afforded the opportunity for research and completion of the study. A Wayne State University grant covered the typing costs. I express my appreciation for photoduplication assistance to Frank G. Artinian, President of the L. G. Haig Shoe Company.

I am most indebted to Professor Walter Johnson, formerly on the faculty of the University of Chicago. His knowledge of the period, his tireless patience, and his interest in the topic were stimulating and invaluable. In addition to serving as an expert critic, he made recommendations on organization and style that finally brought this study into a polished state. I express my gratitude to Lois Johnson, who suffered through my deletions, inked-in corrections, and handwriting while typing the manuscript. Last, I acknowledge the forebearance and confidence of an understanding wife, Nancy, and the financial support and moral encouragement of my parents, brothers, and sisters.

I alone am responsible for the interpretation of the Cold War and the Truman Administration's foreign policy.

A. G. T.

Marquette University
September, 1969

contents

Preface   vii

Introduction   1

1. The Conference and the Myths   10

2. 1945: Co-operation and Compromise   23

3. 1946–1948: The Emergence of Partisan Politics, Part One   39

4. 1946–1948: The Emergence of Partisan Politics, Part Two   56

5. 1949: Subversion and Treason   70

6. 1950: The Repudiation of Bipartisanship   87

7. 1951: Disavowal of Past Commitments   105

8. 1952: Yalta and the Campaign   130

9. 1953–1954: Renunciation of the Campaign, Part One   154

10. 1953–1954: Renunciation of the Campaign, Part Two   180

11. 1955: The Waning of Yalta   195

Conclusion   218

Bibliography   245

Index   256

appendixes

A. House Concurrent Resolution 31   225
B. Memorandum of Secretary of State Stettinius to Secretary   225
   of War Stimson of May 12, 1945
C. Selected Written Questions on the Greek   226
   and Turkish Aid Bill
D. 1948 Republican Foreign Policy Plank   227
E. House Joint Resolutions 444, 74, 36, 111, 63   227
F. House Concurrent Resolutions 102, 13, 56   228
G. House Concurrent Resolution 108   229

H. House Concurrent Resolution 120 229

I. Amendment to the Mutual Security Act of 1951, 230
House Resolution 5113

J. Senate Joint Resolution 67 230

K. Text of the Japanese Peace Treaty 231
Concerning the Kurile Islands and South Sakhalin

L. House Concurrent Resolutions 22, 44 231

M. House Joint Resolution 162 232

N. House Concurrent Resolution 68 233

O. House Joint Resolution 200 235

P. Senate Resolution 75 235

Q. Prominent Congressional Critics of Yalta 236

R. Congressional and Presidential Vote, Polish-American Dis- 238
tricts (or Counties), 1944–1954; Cook County Vote, 1948–
1954 (Congressmen)

the yalta myths

introduction

In 1945, the Yalta Conference was hailed as the dawn of a new era of peace and understanding. Five years later, it symbolized, for many people in the United States, the folly of trusting or seeking to reach accommodation with the Soviet Union; in fact, the postwar communization of Eastern Europe and China were directly attributed to Yalta agreements. Further, during the years from 1948 through 1955, those who wanted the United States to proceed with caution and from a position of strength in any negotiation with the Russians invoked the Yalta experience. Their unquestioned assumption was that Soviet leaders honored their pledges only when they found it expedient or when superior military force coerced them.

This image of Yalta resulted from postwar developments, both international and domestic. The intensification of the Cold War made the assumptions of Yalta suspect. During congressional debates and political campaigns, economic conservatives were able to raise doubts about New Deal and Fair Deal domestic policies by shifting their attack from domestic concerns to foreign policy and internal security matters. These conservatives also cited Yalta in their attempts to justify the need to restrict and investigate the use of executive authority.

Thus, during the late 1940's and early 1950's, they charged that Roosevelt's unilateral and secretive policy making at Yalta had permitted agreements and concessions that were detrimental to national security. Roosevelt's resort to secrecy and his abuse of executive authority, they further charged, was essential to his policy of "appeasing" the Soviet leaders, a policy that had created contemporary problems. Then, centering on the loyalty of federal personnel, these conservatives attributed the conclusion of the specific Yalta agreements either to Communist infiltration of the U.S. delegation and the Roosevelt Administration or to the Administration's being "soft toward Communism."

This focus on national security broadened what had been an essentially conservative critique of the New Deal by providing a less direct, less partisan, or less overtly conservative mode of questioning federal personnel and reformist principles. In this sense, the post-1945 charges of New Deal betrayal and executive abuse of authority differed in substance from the charges that conservatives directed against the Roosevelt Administration between 1933 and 1945. After 1948, these conservatives emphasized primarily international developments; their main criticism of federal personnel involved possible threats to internal security by foreign espionage or subversion.

During the 1930's and the war years, in contrast, their resort to anti-Communist, antiexecutive themes and charges had had a specific, distinctively antireformist purpose. Conservatives then had consistently questioned presidential authority and the advisability of federal reform. During the 1930's, by assailing New Deal priorities and personnel, economic conservatives had sought directly to stymie the enactment of legislation regulating the banks and the securities industry, providing for minimum wages and social security, and creating the Tennessee Valley Authority, the Rural Electrification Administration, and the National Recovery Administration. Anti-New Dealers had represented these measures as alien, subversive, and unconstitutional. Concentrating on Roosevelt's transformation of the office of the Presidency into an agency for initiating legislation and pressuring the Congress to act, they also had claimed that the ramifications of such measures might be dangerous to limited, representative government.

In the late 1930's, these conservatives were able to thwart Roosevelt's attempts to extend the New Deal. They successfully capitalized on the President's attempts to pack the Supreme Court, to purge conservative critics of the New Deal during the 1938 congressional elections, and to reorganize the Federal Government. The resultant stalemate between the Congress and the President derived from not only the failure of the New Deal to bring complete recovery, Roosevelt's shift in priorities after 1938 to foreign policy, and popular concern about the proliferation of federal agencies, but also the structure of the Congress. This structure guaranteed the conservatives a restrictive influence; they could use their congressional prerogatives and the committee system, which was dominated by chairmen whose power was based on seniority.

From 1939 through 1945, conservatives also raised these same criticisms about Roosevelt's methods in foreign policy matters. Challenging his use of executive agreements and powers to extend the United States' international commitments, anti-New Dealers specifically denounced Roosevelt's destroyer deal, his orders to naval vessels to "shoot on sight," the proposal of lend-lease, his assignment of

U.S. convoy coverage to Iceland, and the drafting of the Atlantic Charter. The President had initiated these measures, they charged, in order to bypass congressional prerogatives and lead the United States to war. Roosevelt's subsequent wartime preferences for secrecy and summit diplomacy evoked charges that his actions were undemocratic and contrary to constitutional requirements. This critique, however, had a limited popular impact; the nature of the war undermined the force of these arguments, and Roosevelt's leadership seemingly justified these actions.

After 1945, particularly after 1949, conservative criticisms of New Deal reforms and presidential leadership had a distinctively different impact. Then, the debate concentrated directly on foreign policy and only indirectly involved questions of domestic reform. The subsequent reappraisal of the Yalta Conference and attention it received dramatized the conservatives' shift in tactics from domestic matters to national security and the public's shift in priorities from economic recovery to international peace and internal security. One basis for this interest in Yalta and the resultant spread of domestic conservatism had been the impact of the Cold War on domestic politics. Increasingly after 1947, U.S. politics and values assumed an anti-Communist orientation. An anti-Communist rhetoric that evolved to justify containment policies also served to immobilize reformist politics, to decrease tolerance for dissident ideals and controversial measures, and to legitimate conservative charges of subversion and betrayal. By concentrating on such past foreign policy decisions as the agreements made at the Yalta Conference, conservative critics of the Roosevelt Administration were able to increase their political following and establish the soundness of their earlier critique of New Deal principles and personnel.

Significantly, then, although criticisms of Yalta increased after 1945, and a more suspicious public became concerned about the people who attended the conference and the principles the conferees espoused, the change was not in the agreements. It was in the domestic political climate and the popular assumptions about what constituted a desirable course in foreign policy and the proper limits to executive authority and procedures. Yalta symbolized a policy approach based upon mutual trust and understanding between the United States and the Soviet Union, and with the postwar belief in the folly of trusting the Soviets came the critical reassessment of Yalta. Because Yalta also represented secretive, unilateral presidential diplomacy, this reassessment could directly assail Roosevelt's leadership in foreign affairs and indirectly question his methods in handling domestic problems. National security considerations that were connected with Roosevelt's approach to foreign policy provided the basis for partisan and conservative attacks on the Americanism of New Deal policy makers.

The Truman Administration's adoption of the containment policy amounted to a repudiation of Roosevelt's foreign policy approach; it provided a cover for these conservatives' attacks about Yalta's threat to national security and neutralized the Administration's defense of the conference. Formally, Truman and the other Democratic leaders might defend Yalta, but they did not support the spirit or the assumptions underlying its agreements. Their defense was essentially partisan.

Conservative and partisan Republicans most effectively exploited the symbolism of the conference and the political situation created with the intensification of the Cold War. The ensuing debate was politically irresponsible: Critics charged that past decisions at Yalta had created the Cold War. The implication was that, had the Administration been more forceful, a postwar world more in the U.S. image could have emerged. Although these criticisms and exploitation of the conference contributed to the evolution of a Yalta mythology, they did not follow a consistent pattern in the postwar decade. Domestic concerns determined the timing and nature of the Republican national and congressional leaders' becoming more openly critical of Yalta.[1] Republican criticisms reflected two political phenomena: the

1. It would be appropriate to comment on the selection of the sources for this study of Republican criticisms of the Yalta Conference. Besides reviewing the available literature published by the Republican party during congressional and presidential campaigns and the position formally expressed by Republicans in Congress during congressional hearings and debates, I have examined the editorial position, news reportage, and columnists of the more conservative Republican press.

I have endeavored to give full page citations of newspapers and periodicals wherever possible. Publication citations identified by date only are based on clipping files.

The assessment of the Republican congressional position is based on only those remarks concerning the Yalta Conference. In addition to reading all the major congressional hearings and debates — on questions of both foreign and domestic policy — that referred to or involved Yalta, I have studied the campaign material of the period that the Republican National Committee, the Republican Congressional Campaign Committee, and the Republican Senate Policy Committee have in their files and that the Library of Congress or the Truman Library possess. (The records of the Democratic National Committee were particularly valuable, because they contain an extensive file of Republican campaign literature.)

To ascertain the position of the conservative Republican press, I had to be selective. I chose to concentrate on the editorials and news reports of the *Chicago Tribune*. The *Tribune*, because it consistently criticized Roosevelt and the

factional split on questions of foreign and domestic policy within the Republican party, and the opportunities provided by the intensification of the Cold War for a more critical Republican response to Yalta.

The conflicting positions of different Republicans concerning Yalta and the direction of general foreign policy reflect, I would argue, a threefold factional division within the Republican party. I call these factions "extremists,"[2] "partisans,"[3] and "moderates."[4] By this classification, I do not mean to suggest that these factions were monolithic. In part, this description arbitrarily ignores substantive nuances and the basic differences in political philosophy and policy position among those individuals and media classified as "extremist,"

New Deal and expounded Taft Republicanism, is an invaluable and representative source of the conservative press. I also reviewed the columns written by David Lawrence, George Sokolsky, Westbrook Pegler, and Fulton Lewis, Jr., and the three major conservative periodicals — *Time*, *U.S. News and World Report*, and *The Saturday Evening Post*. This list is representative, not of public opinion (for this study is not of public opinion), but of the post-1945 conservative assessment of Yalta. *Newsweek*, the *New Republic*, and *The Nation* counterbalance *Time*, *U.S. News and World Report*, and *The Saturday Evening Post*. The editorials of *The New York Times* serve as a counterweight to the *Tribune* and a representative of moderate Republicanism.

In my selective research on the Polish-Americans, I have concentrated primarily on the Chicago Polish community for a variety of reasons. First, the Chicago Polish community generally reflects the political position on Yalta expressed by the leaders of other such communities, be they in Buffalo, Detroit, or Milwaukee. Second, the *Chicago Tribune*'s anti-Roosevelt proclivities resulted in its providing extensive coverage to the criticisms of Yalta voiced by Chicago Poles. Third, Chicago is the center of the Polish-American Congress and the residence of its president, Charles Rozmarek. As such, it does represent and influence the national political position adopted by organized Polish groups.

2. As "extremists," I would list the following: the *Chicago Tribune*, *The Saturday Evening Post*; columnists George Sokolsky, Westbrook Pegler, David Lawrence, Fulton Lewis, Jr.; Republican Senators Joseph McCarthy, Styles Bridges, Robert Taft, William Jenner, George Malone, William Langer, Everett Dirksen, Kenneth Wherry, John Bricker, Bourke Hickenlooper; Democratic Senator Patrick McCarran; Republican Congressmen Paul Shafer, Clare Hoffman, Lawrence Smith, Daniel Reed, Carl Curtis, Charles Vursell, William Lemke, Howard Buffett, Noah Mason, George Dondero, Arthur Miller, John Wood; Republican Congresswoman Clare Boothe Luce; and Democratic Congressman John Rankin.

3. As "partisans," I would list the following: *U.S. News and World Report*, *Time*; columnists Raymond Moley, Arthur Krock; Republican Senators Richard Nixon, Karl Mundt, William Knowland, George Bender, Homer Capehart, Homer Ferguson, Arthur Watkins, James Kem; Republican Congressman Alvin O'Konski, Walter Judd, Joseph Martin, B. Carroll Reece, John Jennings, Charles Kersten, Timothy Sheehan, Charles Halleck, Alvin Bentley; former Ambassador to Poland Arthur Bliss Lane; and former President Herbert Hoover.

4. As "moderates," I would list the following: *The New York Times*; Republican Senators Alexander Wiley, Arthur Vandenberg, H. Alexander Smith, Henry Cabot Lodge, Eugene Millikin, Edward Thye, Irving Ives; Republican Congressmen John Vorys, Robert Hale, Chester Merrow, Kenneth Keating, Hugh Scott, and John Lodge; Republican leaders Thomas Dewey, Harold Stassen, John Foster Dulles; and former President Dwight Eisenhower.

"partisan," or "moderate." George Sokolsky and Westbrook Pegler, for example, were critical of Roosevelt and the New Deal, but they differed in their reasons for supporting or opposing particular policy decisions. The classification has merit in generally outlining shared political views and tactics. In this section, I intend to describe only cursorily the main characteristics that I rely on to determine the membership of these factions, leaving documentation of this classification to the text of the study. The reader, moreover, has the additional recourse of reviewing the primary sources — campaign literature, newspaper coverage, and the congressional debates.

In 1945, only the "extremists" forthrightly criticized the conference. By 1949, although they had different reasons, the "moderates" and "partisans" also voiced this bitter criticism of Yalta. This post-1949 "alliance" between these three Republican factions was a hesitant, short-lived, and uneasy one. As critics, these Republicans shared only a common negativism and commitment: to defeat a Democratic Administration. Apart from this objective, the "moderates," "partisans," and "extremists" differed strikingly in their purposes for criticizing Yalta, however blurred these differences seemed between 1949 and 1952.

The "extremists" consistently depicted Yalta as the symbol of New Deal and Fair Deal appeasement or procommunism. Espousing a verbally assertive anticommunism, these conservatives demanded total victory, emphasized U.S. omnipotence, and thus generally opposed all of the Administration's foreign policy responses. Moreover, they usually attacked past policy decisions, partly for strictly political reasons. Because they were an opposition, they were not required to consider the responsibilities of power but could offer attractive, if unrealizable, alternatives. When advocating either retrenchment or confrontation, however, they assumed that the United States, by itself, could impose U.S. ideals on the postwar world. The "extremists," whose main goal was to discredit the New Deal, were either for isolation or indifferent to the possibly dismembering effect that their critique might have on popular support or understanding of the Truman Administration's allegedly internationalist foreign policy. Despite the aggressive tone of their rhetoric, the "extremists" opposed measures involving overseas military and economic commitments, even when those measures were anti-Soviet.

In contrast to the "extremists," both the "partisans" and "moderates" at least supported an internationalist foreign policy. In their critique of Administration policy, the "partisans" and "moderates" concentrated primarily on *past* Administration decisions, and thus on Yalta, while supporting the contemporary Administration's policy. The "moderates" tempered their criticisms and sought to avoid discrediting internationalism or bipartisanship. In addition, the "moderates" accepted some New Deal reforms but tried to prevent further changes. The "partisans," however, differed from both the "extremists" and "moderates" less over policies than politics. Their principal objective was to defeat the Democrats. Their post-1948 critique of Yalta and the bipartisan foreign policy was as guarded as their pre-1948 support of Yalta and the bipartisan foreign policy had been.[5]

The relationship among these three Republican factions, and the basis for their co-operation, encompassed three chronological periods: 1945–1949, guarded and somewhat hesitant support among most "partisans" and "moderates" for the Truman Administration's foreign policy; 1949–1952, the "moderates'" and "partisans'" adoption of the "extremists'" tactic of concentrating on foreign policy for partisan purposes; and 1953–1955, the "moderates'" tacit break with the "extremists" and the "partisans." The shift in tactics reflected both new political developments — Truman's 1948 victory and Eisenhower's 1952 election — and a changed domestic climate created by the intensification of the Cold War and the legitimation of an anti-Communist foreign policy that advocated confrontation.

From 1945 to 1949, the "extremists" were virtually the sole Republican critics of Yalta. The Republican party, they argued, should make the Democrats' foreign policy a campaign issue and support particularly the repudiation of Yalta. Republican congressional leaders, however unsympathetic they were to the Roosevelt Administration's policy toward the Soviet Union, did support the Truman Administration's containment policies. When they were critical of Administration foreign policy, the leaders concentrated on present decisions and only obliquely referred to decisions made in the past. Accordingly, the "moderates" and "partisans" were sharply at odds with the "extremists." The "extremists'" reaction to the strategy adopted by Thomas Dewey, the Republican presidential nominee in 1948, dramatized this rift. Dewey had expressed support for the bipartisan foreign policy and had concentrated on arguments about

5. Since the partisan debate about the Yalta Conference during the postwar period is the center of this study, a sketchy description of the congressional districts of the people who criticized Yalta is essential. In Appendix Q, I have briefly described the main political orientation and concerns of the congressmen and senators whose views are discussed in the text.

domestic matters. The "extremists" denounced him for failing to condemn the foreign policy of past Democratic administrations, and after Truman's victory, they attributed Dewey's defeat to this failure.

After the 1948 election, the "moderates" and "partisans" changed their political strategy. They increasingly resorted to the "extremists'" concentration on past foreign policy decisions, which they termed erroneous, and the allegedly subversive personnel who were formulating policy. Despite this shift in tactics, both groups still disagreed fundamentally with the "extremists" and continued to espouse bipartisanship and internationalism. The "moderates'" and "partisans'" decision to stress foreign policy and anticommunism, however, indirectly helped to restore the "extremists'" respectability and to increase their influence in the Republican party and in the nation.

This post-1948 shift in Republican strategy profited from a series of significant international and domestic developments that occurred between 1948 and 1950. These included the Soviet explosion of an atomic bomb, Chiang Kai-shek's retreat to Formosa, Alger Hiss's trial and conviction for perjury, and the outbreak of the Korean War. These developments made more people doubt past policies and federal personnel.

Specifically by exploiting Yalta, Republican leaders sought to increase their national influence and following by discrediting Administration foreign policy makers. The 1948 presidential election had answered a critical, tactical question for the Republicans: Could the party defeat the Democrats nationally by ignoring foreign policy and concentrating solely on domestic issues? Thus, during the 1952 presidential campaign, the Republican party sought to gain popular support by pledging to repudiate Yalta, to eliminate from the State Department the men who had supported Yalta, and to preclude future Yaltas by curbing the use of executive authority in making foreign policy.

After the 1952 election, the "moderates" reverted to their pre-1949 position. The Eisenhower Administration, faced with the responsibilities of power, gradually broke with the "extremists" by overtly or tacitly rejecting their earlier charges and promises. Its 1953–1955 actions — House Joint Resolution 200, the Bohlen nomination, opposition to the Bricker Amendment, publication of the Yalta papers, and attendance at the Geneva Conference — indirectly renounced the "extremists'" tactics in order to restore a semblance of normality to U.S. partisan politics and the consideration of foreign policy.

By late 1954, the disparity between the "moderates'" and the "extremists'" positions on policy matters — and the "moderates'" effectiveness in undercutting the "extremists" — led even the "partisans" to reappraise the desirability of a negativist, simply anti-Communist stance. Senate censure of McCarthy dramatically reflected the "partisans'" attempts to distinguish their position from that of the "extremists." The basis for their disassociation from the "extremists," however, was expediency. The "partisans" realized that the "extremists," because of their rift with the Eisenhower Administration, had become a political liability.

In sum, gradually after 1945 Yalta had become an important issue in U.S. politics, a symbol of Cold War distrust and suspicions. This study will review the shifting attitudes toward Yalta that stemmed from the Cold War and the partisan context for the changed assessment of the conference in the period from 1945 to 1955. Specifically, the study shall examine the variety of seemingly unrelated debates involving Yalta: the Truman Doctrine, the Marshall Plan, resolutions supporting the liberation of the satellite countries and the repudiation of Yalta, hearings on General MacArthur's dismissal, the Japanese peace treaty, Alger Hiss's perjury conviction, the Korean War, Far Eastern policy, Polish national anniversaries, House Joint Resolution 200, the Bohlen nomination, the Bricker Amendment, the publication of the Yalta papers, and the Geneva Conference of 1955. The study will appraise these debates in terms of how the Yalta mythology evolved and how it was used to affect policies and to further partisan objectives. Also, the study will assess the nature of the foreign policy debate and its effect on domestic reform.

chapter 1
the conference and the myths

the wartime military alliance between the United States, the Soviet Union, and Great Britain posed formidable political problems for these countries in the event of an Axis defeat. Primarily because Allied wartime unity had been based on the commitment to defeat the Axis Powers and not on commonly shared objectives or mutual trust, major and potentially divisive differences among these Allies remained. If they continued to be unresolved, these differences could frustrate attempts to attain a durable peace. The potentiality for a future break in Allied unity could also enable Germany or Japan to exploit these differences to regain power and influence. Further, from the U.S. point of view, postponing political and military considerations until a future peace conference and thereby allowing the military situation to determine postwar developments was strategically unwise, since such actions would surely permit the development of spheres of influence.

In part, the desire to avoid the post-World War I experience led Roosevelt, Churchill, and Stalin to support summit diplomacy. Thus, the Big Three, at times only Two, at Casablanca, Moscow, Quebec, and Teheran, sought to co-ordinate military strategy and delineate areas of agreement toward future wartime and postwar developments in Germany, Eastern Europe, the Balkans, and the Far East. At these earlier conferences, however, the Big Three had avoided binding commitments, except on pressing military matters. Discussions that involved their fundamental policy differences and their conflicting political objectives were postponed until the future. By 1944, with the successful establishment of the Second Front and the continuous military reversals suffered by Germany and Japan, this procedure was no longer desirable. The certainty of military victory made it imperative for the wartime Allies to reach a common understanding on peace aims and postwar objectives.

Intending to resolve these policy differences through negotiation and concession, Roosevelt suggested another Big Three meeting to Stalin and Churchill. On July 17, 1944, Roosevelt advised the Marshal, "Things are moving so fast and so successfully that I feel there should be a meeting between you and Mr. Churchill and me in the reasonably near future." The President proposed that such a meeting take place in northern Scotland around the tenth through the fifteenth of September.[1] In his reply, Stalin expressed an interest in the idea of a summit conference but indicated that military considerations precluded his attendance at that time or place. He offered to send Molotov to represent him. Roosevelt, however, continued to press for a meeting of the Big Three. In January, 1945, after protracted correspondence between Roosevelt, Churchill, and Stalin, they agreed upon the specific time and place. The Big Three would convene at Yalta in the Crimea in early February, 1945.[2]

At the Yalta meetings of February 4–11, Roosevelt, Churchill, and Stalin sought to resolve the complex military and political problems. They hoped to defeat the Axis Powers quickly and to avert postwar divisions that might otherwise frustrate the basis for a durable peace. They worked specifically to determine a common policy toward liberated Europe (Germany, the Balkans, and Eastern Europe), to develop guidelines for a permanent international organization, to co-ordinate Allied military efforts for the final attack on Germany, to conclude an agreement on postwar occupation zones in Germany, and to establish a specific commitment on the timing of Soviet entry in the Far Eastern war.

Roosevelt recognized that if the Big Three failed to agree, the military and geographic status of the Soviet Union could determine postwar political developments that would virtually set up Soviet spheres of influence in Europe and Asia. Indeed, the position of Soviet armies in 1945 created distinct natural advantages for the Soviet Union; they occupied Eastern Europe, they could dominate North China and Manchuria, and they could exercise continuous in-

1. President Roosevelt to Marshal Stalin, July 17, 1944, in U.S. Department of State, *The Conferences at Malta and Yalta, 1945*, 3.
2. Marshal Stalin to President Roosevelt, July 22, 1944; President Roosevelt to Marshal Stalin, July 27, 1944; Marshal Stalin to President Roosevelt, October 19, 1944; Prime Minister Churchill to President Roosevelt, October 22, 1944; President Roosevelt to Prime Minister Churchill, October 22, 1944; Prime Minister Churchill to President Roosevelt, October 23, 1944; President Roosevelt to Marshal Stalin, October 24, 1944; Marshal Stalin to President Roosevelt, October 29, 1944; President Roosevelt to Prime Minister Churchill, November 14, 1944; President Roosevelt to Marshal Stalin, November 18, 1944; Prime Minister Churchill to President Roosevelt, November 19, 1944; Marshal Stalin to President Roosevelt, November 23, 1944; President Roosevelt to Prime Minister Churchill, November 26, 1944; President Roosevelt to Prime Minister Churchill, December 23, 1944; Ambassador to the Soviet Union (Harriman) to President Roosevelt, December 27, 1944; President Roosevelt to Ambassador Harriman, January 6, 1945, in *The Conferences at Malta and Yalta*, 4–5, 8–12, 14–18, 21–23, 30, 551.

fluence in both Eastern Europe and the Far East. Roosevelt also realized that the failure to mitigate East-West distrust and mutual suspicions could harden prewar divisions. A policy of accommodation, however, could possibly avert or minimize Soviet intervention and lay the basis for an independent world order.

The people who attended the Yalta Conference could not resolve these basic differences or ensure a lasting peace. The conflicting aspirations of the Big Three made a willingness to compromise and to accept legitimate Allied strategic interests a requisite for agreement, and even if all were willing to fulfill that requisite, they could only outline possible solutions and try to establish a framework for future co-operation. There was no assurance that the inevitably vaguely worded agreements would be implemented or mutually understood.

Roosevelt confronted an additional problem, namely the readiness of the U.S. public and congressional leaders, particularly the Republican opposition, to accept the unilateral character of his diplomacy and the limits within which the U.S. delegation had operated at the conference. In view of prewar isolationism, he did not know whether the public was prepared for the magnitude of the wartime changes that determined the character of the agreements or whether it would accept the new responsibilities basic to international co-operation and involvement. Moreover, he did not know whether the congressional leaders, particularly the Republican congressmen and press, would accept either his leadership or Yalta's spirit of compromise and concession.

Thus, when preparing for the conference, President Roosevelt had to deal both with an international problem, that of Soviet security and political objectives in Eastern Europe and the Far East, and a domestic one, that of popular or congressional suspicions about his priorities and the conduct of executive diplomacy. Because of these considerations, the President had both to respond to the realities of the postwar political situation in Eastern Europe and Asia and to make sure that the composition of the U.S. delegation could at least neutralize a partisan attack on the principles of this meeting and its necessarily secretive and unilateral character.

To achieve the latter objective, Roosevelt selected an expert, nonpartisan delegation. It included Secretary of State Edward Stettinius, Special Assistant to the President Harry Hopkins, Fleet Admiral William Leahy (Chief of Staff to the President), Ambassador to the Soviet Union Averell Harriman, James F. Byrnes (Director, Office of War Mobilization), General George Marshall (Chief of

Staff, U.S. Army), Fleet Admiral Ernest King (Chief of Naval Operations and Commander in Chief, U.S. Fleet), Vice-Admiral Wilson Brown (Naval Aide to the President), Stephen Early (Secretary to the President for press affairs), Lieutenant General Brehon Somervell (Commanding General, Army Service Forces), Vice-Admiral Emory Land (War Shipping Administrator), Brigadier General Andrew McFarland (Secretary of the Joint Chiefs of Staff), Major General Laurence S. Kuter (Staff of Commanding General, U.S. Army Air Force), Major General John Deane (Commanding General, U.S. Military Mission in Soviet Union), H. Freeman Matthews (Director of European Affairs, Department of State), Alger Hiss (Deputy Director, Office of Special Political Affairs, Department of State), Charles Bohlen (Assistant to the Secretary of State), Edward Page (interpreter and assistant to Bohlen), and some minor military and technical advisers.[3]

This delegation was designed to meet the major military and political issues that would be considered at the conference. The military advisers would provide expert advice on military strategy and have the opportunity to co-ordinate future military operations. Harriman's knowledge of Soviet affairs, Matthews' expertise as head of the European desk at the State Department, and Stettinius' responsibilities as Secretary of State warranted their participation. Bohlen and Hiss served as invaluable aides and technicians. Because of his knowledge of Russian, Bohlen served as the U.S. delegation's translator. Hiss was responsible for collating the various preconference briefing papers drafted by the State and War departments. In addition, his earlier involvement with the planned international organization and his expertise concerning it justified his inclusion in the delegation. Byrnes and Land were invited because military decisions made at Yalta would necessarily involve considerations of supply and lend-lease. Byrnes's close political relations with Senate leaders and his shrewd political sense made him an excellent liaison man for Roosevelt. Because he was a participant at Yalta, Byrnes could more successfully undercut congressional sensitivities about not having been consulted or invited to participate in policy making. (Indeed, after returning from Yalta, he lobbied the Congress to develop support for the agreements and to quiet doubts about them.)

Although it distinctly was not bipartisan or reflective of all sectors of public opinion, the delegation was an expert working party. Roosevelt could rely upon the delegates' experience and skill to dis-

3. *The Conferences at Malta and Yalta*, 30, 36, 553, 968.

arm possible criticisms of the conference's decisions and procedures. Moreover, he did retain the option of appointing a bipartisan delegation to the forthcoming formal peace conference, and he followed that procedure when he selected the members of the U.S. delegation to the San Francisco Conference, where the United Nations Charter was drafted.

Roosevelt recognized that his delegation would have to operate within the limits imposed by wartime developments, the specific strategic objectives of the Soviet Union, and the available opportunities internationally for exercising U.S. influence. Above all, the Big Three had to resolve problems relating to the postwar Soviet role in Eastern Europe and Germany, the boundaries of Poland, a joint occupation policy toward Germany, the initial membership and voting rights in the proposed United Nations, the timing of Soviet entry into the Far Eastern war, and the political role that this entry guaranteed the Russians in the Far East. These questions had been considered earlier within the Administration, dominating the formal preconference discussions. The principal objective, then, was to attain unity among the Allies, unity that would be the basis for an effective, stable peace. The Administration did adopt a firm bargaining position, but it was willing to make concessions that were essential and realistic.

At Yalta, Roosevelt accepted the inevitability of radical changes between the prewar and postwar Eastern European governments. He also accepted the inevitability of increased Soviet influence in Eastern Europe based on military and geographic considerations. In addition, he understood the Soviet intent, and ability, to prevent the re-establishment of the kind of *cordon sanitaire* that the West had imposed after World War I.

Wartime developments had guaranteed that the defeat of Germany would enhance Soviet influence in Eastern Europe. The war had created in that area a domestic political vacuum in which native Communists could operate in the guise of nationalists. Anti-German national resistance movements, dominated by Communists and supported in some cases by the Allies and in others by the Soviet Union, had been able during the war to capitalize on the occupation role of the Germans. These movements, which were committed to liberating their countries from German control, were in a strong military and political position to challenge the prewar regimes for control. Formerly exiled to the Soviet Union because of repressive policies instituted during the prewar period by right-wing military governments, the leaders of these movements had been native to these countries and could claim to represent democratic, antifascist forces.

Further, all of the prewar Eastern European and Balkan regimes except Czechoslovakia were rightist dictatorships relying on the support of their armies to remain in power. The economic impact of the war not only required radical economic reforms but also had made such reforms popular. Although the prewar governments were capable of becoming more democratic and of instituting limited reforms, they were not likely to provide the leadership to resolve these problems or to capitalize on discontent aggravated by the war.

Also, the Germans had created a vacuum in power by first displacing the prewar governments and their bureaucratic and military structures and then retreating in 1944 and 1945. Soviet troops, supporting the native Communists, had filled this vacuum and could exploit their position. Thus, radical political change was inevitable unless the Western Powers provided arms or threatened to intervene to restore the exiled or — in Hungary, Rumania, and Bulgaria — Axis-allied governments to power.

The absence of potentially workable democratic institutions in Eastern Europe prior to the war further complicated the restoration of normal political processes. During the 1920's and 1930's, governments of Eastern Europe (Czechoslovakia again excepted) had outlawed all opposition parties. This lack of operational political parties having a national political base forestalled automatic use of democratic procedures after liberation. Broadly based interim governments would have to preside until elections could be held. In view of the Soviet military position and strategic interest in this area, satisfactory determination of the character of these governments required trust and understanding between the West and the Soviet Union.

Considering these conditions, the Yalta provisions for Allied concurrence in the selection of interim provisional governments, the commitment to hold free and democratic elections, and the establishment of a tripartite (Russian, U.S., British) commission to supervise political developments represented a realistic solution to the complex Eastern European problem. In essence, though, the agreement on Liberated Europe tacitly conceded a dominant role to the Russians but offered the United States and Britain the opportunity for involvement and pressure.

The nature of Allied diplomatic objectives and the differences in them compelled secrecy about the conference proceedings. Reasons of strategy also prohibited the immediate release for publication of the Yalta agreements concerning voting rights in the proposed United Nations organization, the Soviet commitment to enter the Far Eastern war, the release of Allied prisoners held by the Germans, and the specific reparations payments that Germany would be required to pay. The UN voting agreements were released to the press in March, 1945; the Far Eastern agreements, on February 11, 1946; and the protocols concerning Allied civilians and troops imprisoned by the Germans, on March 8, 1946, and March 24, 1947.[4]

Roosevelt and the other conferees did not initially release the agreements determining voting rights in the proposed United Nations for two reasons. First, they wished to consult the French and Chinese. Also, by not publishing the agreements ceding the Soviet Union and indirectly the United States three votes each in the General Assembly, the Yalta conferees precluded France, or any other state, from championing the rights of the smaller states so strongly that it would subvert the planned conference at San Francisco.

Not only international but also domestic considerations influenced Roosevelt's decision not to publish these agreements. Internationally, a veto was consistent with the power and independence of the countries involved; domestically, this provision would serve to answer charges that U.S. participation in an international security organization would unduly restrict national sovereignty. He persuaded Stalin to agree that the veto not apply to votes on procedural matters. Roosevelt wanted this agreement because it would create an effective organization that guaranteed a voice for the smaller states and because it would disarm criticisms of the proposed organization by "isolationists" and "perfectionists." He also anticipated a possible domestic furor about the three votes given the Soviets and guarded against it by reserving the right for the United States to receive three votes as well.

Roosevelt maintained silence about the Far Eastern agreements because military strategy called for it. U.S. military leaders believed at the time of the conference that Soviet military aid was essential for an early victory over Japan; they did not know how long the war would last or how effective the atomic bomb would be. The announcement of these agreements might have precipitated a Japanese attack on the Soviet Union that would have weakened the Soviet military effort against Germany. Such an announcement would also have per-

4. Protocol of Proceedings, Protocol of German Reparations, Agreement Regarding Entry of Soviet Union into the War Against Japan, Agreement Between the United States and the Soviet Union Concerning Liberated Prisoners of War and Civilians, in *The Conferences at Malta and Yalta*, 975–87.

mitted the Japanese government to prepare its people for Soviet involvement and thereby offset any psychological impact that a surprise entrance might have incurred. Thus, the communiqué of February 11 did not disclose the existence of the Far Eastern agreements, and Roosevelt denied that the Far East had been a topic at Yalta when he made his March 1, 1945, report on the conference to the joint session of the Congress.

In 1945, the Roosevelt Administration, particularly members of the State and War departments, thought the Far Eastern concessions a diplomatic success for the United States. The Administration's policy makers believed that Soviet military aid was vital, and they feared that in return the Soviet Union might demand occupation rights in Japan and a sphere of influence in Manchuria and North China. They also feared that the Soviet Union might provide military and diplomatic support for the Chinese Communists that would frustrate the resolution of the civil war in China and contribute to continued instability. At Yalta, however, the Soviet Union not only accepted a definite timetable, agreeing to enter the Far Eastern war three months after the conclusion of the war in Europe, but also in effect recognized the Nationalist Government by pledging to conclude a treaty of mutual friendship and alliance. The Soviets limited their demands to joint operation of the Chinese Eastern Railroad and the South Manchurian Railroad; the return of South Sakhalin and the Kurile Islands, territories held by the Japanese, to Soviet control; the grant of "lease" rights to Port Arthur; and acceptance of the "preeminent interests" of the Soviet Union in the internationalized port of Dairen.

Specific details about Allied occupation policy toward Germany and the exact level of reparations charged to that country could not be published immediately after the conference because the conferees had postponed such details for future discussions. At Yalta, they did generally outline the decisions to disarm Germany, to rid her institutions of nazism, and to require her to pay for the destruction of the territory and resources of the Allied Powers. In the published communiqué of February 11, they enunciated the basic guidelines for the occupation policy toward Germany and the economic obligations she would face. The Three Powers then declared the intent of their German policy: "Germany will never again be able to disturb the peace of the world."

In addition, the February communiqué set forth the spirit and conditions of harmony that had characterized the Yalta meetings. It announced the Three Powers' commitment to establish a permanent international organization and their invitation to other states to participate in the formal drafting of a charter. It detailed the principles agreed upon for founding "free and democratic" institutions in Eastern Europe and the Balkans and declared that the Curzon line would be Poland's eastern territorial boundary. Stressing the important function of the foreign ministers at the conference, the communiqué also reported the Big Three's intent to hold regular meetings of their foreign ministers. The communiqué concluded:

> Our meeting here in the Crimea has reaffirmed our common determination to maintain and strengthen in the peace to come that unity of purpose and action which has made victory possible and certain for the United Nations in this war. . . .
> Only with continuing and growing cooperation and understanding among our three countries and among all peace-loving nations can the highest aspiration of humanity be realized — a secure and lasting peace. . . . [5]

Because most people in the United States were interested in continued Allied co-operation and because they recognized the important role of Soviet troops in defeating the Axis Powers, they initially acclaimed the Yalta agreements. Criticisms of the agreements were minor. At this time, most critics belonged to a conservative minority skeptical of Roosevelt's leadership and internationalism. Only after 1949 were the Yalta agreements and procedures extensively denounced, and by the 1950's, many people in the United States believed they symbolized treason, betrayal, and the folly of trusting the Soviets. Yalta was not the only secretive conference at which key decisions had been reached, but the others — Teheran and Potsdam — received criticism only when they were linked with Yalta. Those people who hated Roosevelt attacked Yalta and Teheran. Those who opposed what they considered the Administration's harsh policy toward Germany and those who wished to associate the Truman Administration directly with Roosevelt's policies denounced Yalta and Potsdam. This emphasis on Yalta and the distinction between it and these other wartime conferences came from the development of the Yalta mythology.

Several political developments contributed to the evolution of this mythology. The postwar international crises between the United States and the Soviet Union, the impact of the Cold War on domestic politics, and the shift after 1948 in Republican campaign strategy

5. Communiqué Issued at the End of the Conference, February 11, 1945, in *The Conferences at Malta and Yalta*, 969–75.

had changed popular perceptions about Yalta. Doubts about the se-
crctive conduct of the conference, the composition of the U.S. delegation, and the controversial Eastern European and Far Eastern
agreements began to spread. Gradually, more and more people en-
tertained these doubts and came to believe the myths. By 1950, these
myths provided one basis for partisan criticisms of the use of executive authority, loyalty procedures, and policy recommendations.

The most prevalent criticism of Yalta cited the secrecy of the
conference proceedings and the Administration's failure to disclose
all the agreements immediately after the conference. Although military strategy was a successful justification for secrecy in 1945, it
became a less meaningful explanation as the war became history
and ncw secret agreements were disclosed. Critics could then effectively suggest that the Administration had intentionally kept these
agreements from the public in order either to cover up errors in
judgment or to set up an unalterable policy of appeasement.

The manner in which the Administration had represented the
conference's commitments intensified these suspicions. The February,
1945, communiqué did not state or imply that additional understandings had been concluded. Roosevelt hinted during his March 1,
1945, report to the Congress that unpublished agreements had been
reached, but he specifically denied that he had discussed the Far
East at Yalta. Moreover, following publication on March 29, 1945,
of the "three votes" agreement, Secretary of State Stettinius assured
the press that no further Yalta secret agreements remained undisclosed, "with the exception of military decisions and related matters."
Roosevelt's and Stettinius' denials, with the subsequent disclosure of
the Far Eastern agreements, cnabled critics to rebut the Administration's contentions that no further agreements existed.

Conservative Republicans had instinctively distrusted Roosevelt's resort to executive agreements and secretive diplomacy. They
opposed his transformation of the Presidency into an institution that
made policy and attempted to form public opinion, and they suspected his motives and priorities. They also opposed in principle his
attempt to commit the United States to collective security and internationalism, but they did not simply denounce his policy of co-operat-
ing with the Soviet Union and restricting German power and influence. Rather, they concentrated on the inherently elitist nature
of his sccret, personal diplomacy at Yalta.

The intimations about the Yalta Far Eastern agreements made
by James F. Byrnes in January, 1946, buttressed this critique of execu-

tive procedures. At that time, Byrnes, who had attended Yalta as an adviser to the President, publicly expressed ignorance about both the existence of the Far Eastern agreements and the location of the formal text. Byrnes's role at Yalta had principally been that of an astute political adviser who was knowledgeable about congressional sensitivities and the possible partisan ramifications of decisions reached or considered at the conference. Because he had been a member of the delegation and because he had been Truman's Secretary of State since July 3, 1945, his remarks created the impression that Roosevelt had made far-reaching agreements at Yalta, agreements unknown to even his main advisers. Thus, a declaration of ignorance from a man of Byrnes's position seemed to document charges that additional secrets existed.

Security and loyalty considerations also called forth ghosts of Yalta. Since the late 1930's and early 1940's, opponents of the New Deal had charged that the Roosevelt Administration had been infiltrated by Communists. During the late 1940's and early 1950's, Senators McCarthy, Nixon, Mundt, and the Republican National Committee refined these charges, focusing on the existence of "Communists in the State Department" and other sensitive federal agencies. Alger Hiss's attendance at the Yalta Conference and his conviction of perjury in 1950 linked this concern about national security with Yalta and its agreements. Having attended Yalta as an adviser to Secretary of State Stettinius, having participated in the drafting and collating of position papers for the use of the U.S. delegation, and having served as secretary at the San Francisco Conference, Hiss seemingly represented a subversive who had risen to an important policy-making position. His attendance at the conference, in view of the secrecy surrounding the discussions and the agreements, could be exploited to confirm subversion and betrayal. Indeed, the Yalta mythmakers identified Hiss as one of the architects of the conference and its agreements.

Associated with this portrayal of Hiss's subversive influence at Yalta was a concern over Roosevelt's mental abilities. Roosevelt had appeared tired and worn during 1944. When addressing the Congress on March 1, 1945, he had delivered his report while seated. The President apologized, explaining that he was tired from the strains of a long trip. His death, one month later, provided one basis for subsequent charges that he had not been in command of his faculties at Yalta. Critics affirmed that a tired, enfeebled, and incompetent President, unduly sympathetic to leftist ideas, had been incapable of resisting the pressures of either Marshal Stalin or the "Communist" Alger Hiss at Yalta.

Other allegations of Roosevelt's presumed lack of mental alertness, which supposedly created the opportunity for Hiss and Stalin to determine policy, came from William Bullitt, a former ambassadorial appointee of the President, and James Farley, Roosevelt's campaign manager during the 1930's and Postmaster General from 1933 to 1940. In 1948, Bullitt questioned Roosevelt's health and mental competence at Yalta, and in 1951, Farley contended that since 1940 Roosevelt had not been in good health and could easily have been influenced by sycophants at Yalta. Their former policy-making positions, their associations with Roosevelt, and, more importantly, Farley's Democratic credentials made their allegations effective material for anti-New Dealers to cite as supportive, objective confirmation of Roosevelt's incompetence.

The spirit of the conference further contributed to the evolution of the Yalta mythology. Postwar international developments — the communization of Eastern Europe and China, the confrontation with the Soviet Union, and the efforts to rebuild Germany and Japan — made more convincing the charges that the Yalta concessions were harmful, stupid, and possibly subversive. Critics then specifically denounced the Far Eastern and Eastern European concessions to the Soviet Union and the restrictions imposed on Germany and Japan.

The frustration and bitterness of ethnic groups, particularly the Polish-Americans, maximized the political impact of the mythmaking about Yalta. These groups accepted the charge that the conference had ceded Eastern Europe to the Russians. They were willing to believe that the communization of Eastern Europe had been the result of the leeway the Soviet Union received at Yalta. This frustration over the alleged sellout was effectively exploited by appeals to "liberate the satellite countries" and "repudiate Yalta."

Similarly, the development of the myth that the Far Eastern agreements had ceded China to the Russians happened only after the defeat of the Chinese Nationalists, the communization of China, the outbreak of the Korean War, and the subsequent Chinese Communist involvement. This accusation had not been popularly voiced, or accepted, in 1945 or 1946. The Truman Administration's later defense that these agreements had been based on the military importance of Soviet aid was unconvincing. The Yalta critics pointed to the Administration's awareness of the success of the atomic bomb, the timing between Soviet entrance on August 8, and Japanese

surrender on August 14 as contradicting the need for Soviet involvement. They attributed the agreements either to Roosevelt's "soft-
ness toward Communism" or to the influence of "Communists in
Government."

The acceptance of these myths about the nature of the Yalta
agreements and the character of the personnel provided the foundation for a new political setting and new tactics. Increasingly after
1949, foreign policy and internal security became all-absorbing. The
symbolism and mythology of Yalta provided seemingly conclusive
support for charges that past decisions had caused contemporary difficulties and Communist infiltration of the Federal Government had
caused the "sellout" and "betrayal" of Eastern Europe and China.

chapter 2
1945: co-operation and compromise

The tone of U.S. politics in 1945 was distinctly favorable toward a policy of détente toward the Soviet Union. Most people in the United States, including the Republican leaders in the Congress and the Republican National Committee, supported Roosevelt's broad foreign policy objectives of continued Allied co-operation in peacetime, the unconditional surrender of the Axis Powers, and the establishment of a permanent, international, collective-security organization. They especially welcomed the Yalta Conference because it seemed to provide hope for Allied unity and co-operation after the war.

In 1945, only the "extremists" openly denounced the Yalta Conference. Their criticism stemmed from their skepticism of any policy proposed by President Roosevelt that involved co-operation with the Soviet Union or that required international commitments by the United States. This criticism reflected the idealistic tenor of popular values by presenting its arguments in terms of opposition to power politics and cynical realism.

The important question to most U.S. citizens in 1945 was not whether the Soviet Union would play a major role during the postwar world. They wanted to know what the form and nature of the Soviet role would be and whether the United States could avert Allied disunity or confrontation. The issue, in short, was whether power politics and military action would determine the course of events and thereby obviate a stable peace. Thus, most of the public supported Roosevelt's diplomatic efforts to reach an understanding with the Soviet Union and to create an effective world organization capable of resolving international crises and averting the development of spheres of influence. They thought summit diplomacy and international co-operation essential for a lasting peace. For these reasons, they welcomed the Yalta Conference and its announced agreements. Roosevelt's resort to secrecy and his failure to involve the Congress or the public in the determination of policy were not viewed suspiciously or condemned except by a small minority.

Nonetheless, Roosevelt could not rely on continued popular tolerance and acquiescence. He faced the prospect of a debunking critique of his unilateral policy making, the character of compromise in the commitments and understandings, and the secretiveness of the conference. Critics might also contrast the loftiness of the ideals expressed in the Atlantic Charter and the cynical realism of the Yalta agreements. Such possibilities forced the President to try to influence the public, and through them the Congress, to accept the necessity for these procedures and concessions.

Cognizant of the realities of this political situation, the President, both before and after the conference, attempted to prepare the public for the new role that the United States would have to play in international politics and to appreciate the limits to U.S. influence and diplomatic options. He stressed the need for the public and Congress to accept the legitimacy and diversity of interests between states and to understand that international agreements, such as those reached at Yalta, were inevitably compromises dealing with possible, not necessarily desirable, situations.

In his January 6, 1945, State of the Union address, Roosevelt directly sought to undercut isolationist and anti-Soviet sentiments. Accordingly, he praised "our active and indomitable allies" Great Britain and the Soviet Union and the "heroic resistance movements" in the occupied countries.[1] Peace would not resolve all wartime problems. "Nations like individuals," he observed, "do not always see alike or think alike, and international cooperation and progress are not helped by any nation assuming that it has a monopoly of wisdom or of virtue." [2]

In addition, Roosevelt attempted to keep congressional leaders fully abreast of diplomatic discussions. On January 11, 1945, he held a special bipartisan meeting with Senators Tom Connally (Democrat, Texas), Alben Barkley (Democrat, Kentucky), Elbert Thomas (Democrat, Utah), Arthur Vandenberg (Republican, Michigan), Wallace White, Jr. (Republican, Maine), Warren Austin (Republican, Vermont), and Robert La Follette, Jr. (Progressive, Wisconsin). At this meeting, Roosevelt discussed with these congressional leaders the Administration's plans for the proposed world organization, the differences between the United States and the Soviet Union, and Eastern European developments. On January 17, 1945, Secretary of

1. U.S. House of Representatives, House Documents, 79th Cong., 1st sess., 1945, I, 3.
2. *Ibid.*, 10.

State Edward Stettinius, Jr., briefed the full Senate Foreign Relations Committee on the Administration's policy toward the liberated areas and other questions later dealt with at Yalta.[3]

The mood of U.S. politics was sympathetic to this stress on co-operation and mutual understanding, on the limits to U.S. power, and on the unsuitability of a policy that sought confrontation. The U.S. press, covering the political spectrum from *The Saturday Evening Post* to the *New Republic*, stated hope for the continuation and perfection of United Nations co-operation.[4] Conferences among the Big Three were deemed desirable and necessary, and fears were expressed as much about British imperialism as about Soviet aspirations. In February, a letter to President Roosevelt from the newly elected Democratic members of Congress recommended that the United States provide the leadership necessary for achieving co-operation and an enduring peace.[5] Similarly, Senator Arthur Vandenberg, after admitting the existence of differences among the Allied Powers, argued that no nation could have its way. He called for co-ordinated consultations through an international organization.[6]

The reservations expressed prior to the conference in 1945 pertained to Roosevelt's tactics, not his policies. Arthur Krock's criticisms of secret diplomacy centered on Roosevelt's "parental theory of administration."[7] Thomas E. Dewey emphasized the importance of the Yalta Conference, which was then in session, and his general support for it. The 1944 election results, Dewey observed, reflected differences over who would constitute the United States delegation rather than differences over foreign policy. He quickly affirmed the differences between the parties' domestic policies.[8]

This tolerant tone provided the background for the formal February 11, 1945, communiqué announcing the Yalta Conference agreements. The communiqué enumerated, in glowing terms, the conference results and emphasized the determination of the Big Three to co-operate in achieving and maintaining the peace.

3. U.S. Senate, *Review of Bipartisan Foreign Policy Consultation Since World War II*, Senate Document No. 87, 82d Cong., 2d sess., 1952, 5.

4. *The Saturday Evening Post*, 217 (February 3, 1945), 100; *The New York Times*, February 3, 1945, 10; *Washington Post*, February 3, 1945, 2; *The Nation*, 160 (February 3, 1945), 120–22; *Newsweek*, 25 (February 5, 1945), 108.

5. U.S. *Congressional Record*, 79th Cong., 1st sess., 1945, XCI, Part 10, A460.

6. *Ibid.*, A490.

7. *The New York Times*, February 9, 1945, 14.

8. U.S. *Congressional Record*, 79th Cong., 1st sess., 1945, XCI, Part 10, A547.

President Roosevelt developed this theme in his March 1, 1945, formal report to the joint session of Congress on the conference's objectives and decisions. Intended to silence conservative criticisms that he had usurped legislative prerogatives, Roosevelt's personal and prompt report emphasized the Congress' responsibility for the achievement of peace. By indirectly recalling the Senate's role in defeating the Versailles treaty, Roosevelt underlined Congress' co-responsibility and power. He warned:

> . . . the question of whether it [Yalta] is entirely fruitful or not lies to a great extent in your [Congress'] hands for unless you here in the Halls of the American Congress, with the support of the American people, concur in the general conclusions reached at that place called Yalta, and give them your active support, the meeting will not have produced lasting results.[9]

In 1945, at least, Roosevelt could not be effectively assailed for bypassing Congress. The public doubted the Congress, not the President. In fact, many constitutional amendments had been introduced providing for the House to share with the Senate the responsibility for ratifying treaties. The justification advanced for these amendments was the need to prevent the repetition of the 1919 experience.

In addition, Roosevelt's speech and the February 11 communiqué had been warmly received by the news media and by both Republican and Democratic senators and congressmen. *The New York Times, New Republic, The Nation, Newsweek, Time, U.S. News,* Senators Alben Barkley and Wallace White (majority and minority leaders, respectively), Joseph Guffey (Democrat, Pennsylvania), Alexander Wiley (Republican, Wisconsin), Congressmen George Mahon (Democrat, Texas), Luther Johnson (Democrat, Texas), Jerry Voorhis (Democrat, California), Walter Granger (Democrat, Utah), John McCormack (Democrat, Massachusetts), Chester Merrow (Republican, New Hampshire), Homer Ramey (Republican, Ohio), and Congresswoman Helen Douglas (Democrat, California) had praised Yalta as an important step toward world peace and security. Welcoming this spirit of co-operation and compromise as the best prospect for a lasting peace, they hoped that the same method would characterize the Allies' approach to future international problems. None criticized the agreement to designate the Curzon line as the eastern boundary of Poland, and most of them commended the Yalta compromises as illustrative of the range of agreement among the

9. U.S. House of Representatives, *Journal of the House of Representatives of the United States,* 79th Cong., 1st sess., 1945, 157.

Big Three. *The New York Times*, in fact, concluded that Roosevelt deserved a strong congressional endorsement of the agreements. *Time* magazine, in characteristic prose, reported the "breathless enthusiasm" that Yalta, "the most important conference of the century," received in the United States, adding that no citizen of the United States, Great Britain, or the Soviet Union could claim that his nation's interests had been "sold down the river."[10] Even former President Herbert Hoover described the Yalta agreements as a solid foundation for postwar reconstruction. He stated, "If the agreements' promises and ideals which are expressed shall be carried out it will open a great hope in the world."[11]

Only warnings by some commentators that the Yalta agreements had yet to receive each country's approval tempered this enthusiastic reception. Whether the Congress would accede to the agreements or whether it would sacrifice Yalta's principles because of political expediency was as much doubted as whether the British or Russians would actually accept the agreements. Other commentators feared that Yalta might fail because the U.S. public might reject the responsibilities associated with international involvement. Most observers concluded that the agreements reached at Yalta were no guarantee of world peace. Conceding that the conference marked a hopeful beginning, they argued that future developments would determine its success. Common to all these guarded appraisals was the hope that the spirit of Yalta — continued Allied co-operation — would not be dissipated or proven groundless.[12]

The main criticism of the February 11 communiqué and Roosevelt's March 1 report came from Polish-Americans and the "extrem-

10. U.S. *Congressional Record*, 79th Cong., 1st sess., 1945, XCI, Parts 1 and 10, 1026, 1044, 1046, 1050–52, 1094, 1119, 1168, A663–64, A675, A706, A718, A722–23, A937, A1019, A1054, A1067–68, A1109. Indicative of this concern, Walter Judd, a Republican congressman from Minnesota, inserted into the *Congressional Record* an article by Ernest Lindley praising Republican statesmanship and support of Roosevelt's international objectives. *Ibid.*, Part 10, A670. *The New York Times*, February 13, 1945, 22; February 14, 1945, 18; February 15, 1945, 18; February 16, 1945, 22; March 1, 1945, 20; March 2, 1945, 18; March 4, 1945, 3E. *Newsweek*, 25 (March 5, 1945), 24; March 12, 1945, 42, 54. *U.S. News*, 18 (February 23, 1945), 32; March 2, 1945, 14. *New Republic*, 112 (February 19, 1945), 243–44. *The Nation*, 160 (February 17, 1945), 169–70, 173–75. *Time*, 45 (February 19, 1945), 15, 23.
11. *Chicago Tribune*, February 13, 1945, 2.
12. *Time*, 45 (February 26, 1945), 15, 23–24. *The New York Times*, February 18, 1945, 3E; February 27, 1945, 18. *U.S. News*, 18 (February 23, 1945), 11–12, 27. *The Nation*, 160 (February 24, 1945), 201. *New Republic*, 112 (February 26, 1945), 278–80. *Newsweek*, 25 (February 26, 1945), 24, 40–42, 44, 50, 68. U.S. *Congressional Record*, 79th Cong., 1st sess., 1945, XCI, Part 10, A875.

ists," who attacked the agreement about the Polish boundary. Polish-American Congressmen Alvin O'Konski (Republican, Wisconsin), Thaddeus Wasielewski (Democrat, Wisconsin), Joseph Ryter (Democrat, Connecticut), the Polish-American Congress, and other Polish-American fraternal and religious organizations denounced the use of the Curzon line as the fifth partition of Poland. Bitterly anti-Russian, narrowly nationalistic, and decidedly unrealistic, these Polish-Americans tried to force the President and the Congress to support the Government-in-Exile, which was located in London, and Polish territorial interests. In an address delivered before the announcement of the Yalta decisions, O'Konski summed up these expectations when he argued, "It is most important that should Poland lose this diplomatic battle with Russia [over the Curzon line] all Europe, yes all the world, loses just as heavily. Without a free Poland there can be no free Europe or a free world. The fate of Poland will determine whether the war has been won or lost." [13]

This Polish-American reaction created a situation ripe for Republican political exploitation. In 1945, the only Yalta agreement the Republicans criticized was the decision to use the Curzon line. The March 27 issue of the *National Republican Club Bulletin* commended the Yalta Conference but denounced this boundary decision.[14] To counter this kind of appeal, on February 26, Congressman William Barry (Democrat, New York) had introduced House Concurrent Resolution 31 urging congressional disapproval of the agreement about the Curzon line. The resolution, referred to the House Foreign Affairs Committee, was not reported to the Congress or acted upon by it.[15] Significantly, Barry's resolution did not urge repudiation. It tacitly assumed that the Soviet Union could be trusted to adhere to the Eastern European agreements and that Roosevelt had not exceeded his constitutional authority.

In contrast to the Polish-Americans, "extremist" Congressmen Lawrence Smith (Republican, Wisconsin), William Cole (Republican, Missouri), Daniel Reed (Republican, New York), Paul Shafer (Republican, Michigan), Clare Hoffman (Republican, Michigan), Senator Hugh Butler (Republican, Nebraska), Congresswoman Clare

13. *Ibid.*, Parts 1, 3, 10, and 11, 1072, 1326, 3394, 3621, A396, A669–70, A746, A748–49, A810, A985–86, A1059, A1064, A1092, A1744, A1769, A1823, A1831, A1876. Polish-American Congress, *Memorandum to the Senate of the United States on the Crimea Decisions Concerning Poland; Polish-American Congress Bulletin*, I, 2 (March–April, 1945).
14. U.S. *Congressional Record*, 79th Cong., 1st sess., 1945, XCI, Part 11, A2042.
15. For the text of the resolution, see Appendix A.

Boothe Luce (Republican, Connecticut), columnists George Sokolsky and David Lawrence, and the *Chicago Tribune* attacked Yalta as a sellout to the Soviet Union and as confirmation of Roosevelt's sinister ambitions. Their criticism emphasized Roosevelt's abuse of presidential authority and his pro-Soviet leanings. They denounced the cession of Polish territory to the Soviet Union and, most pointedly, the harsh treatment of Germany and cession of German territory to Poland. Besides being anti-Soviet, their rhetorical emphasis was idealistic in its criticism of the secrecy of the conference and the conferees' violation of the principles expressed in the Atlantic Charter. To these critics, Yalta was sinister because it sacrificed principle for realism. Underlying this criticism was a definite bias against Roosevelt and the New Deal.[16]

The Roosevelt Administration's disclosure on March 6 of the agreement about vetoes in the UN Security Council elicited a few Republican protests, but the "extremists," when criticizing the disclosure, assailed this agreement as a resort to power politics. Their stand, which seemed to be principled and idealistic, again revealed their antipathy to Roosevelt and a policy involving international commitments. While denouncing the veto as a concession to power politics, the "extremists," at the same time, argued that this provision favored Soviet interests and that it would effectively compromise the United Nations. Accordingly, they counseled the need to reappraise the U.S. commitment to the United Nations.[17]

A similar alignment followed the March 29 release of the Yalta agreement that gave the Soviet Union three votes in the UN General Assembly. The intention of this unprecedented agreement was to placate the Soviet Union. No valid defense could then be given

16. *Chicago Herald-American*, January 9, 1945, 6; March 2, 1945, 6; October 31, 1945, 19. *Chicago Tribune*, February 13, 1945, 4; February 14, 1945, 6, 7, 14; February 15, 1945, 1; February 16, 1945, 12; February 19, 1945, 10; February 20, 1945, 10; February 27, 1945, 10; March 1, 1945, 7,14; March 2, 1945, 2, 4, 9; March 3, 1945, 10; March 5, 1945, 5. *U.S. News*, 18 (February 23, 1945), 28–29; March 9, 1945, 28–29. U.S. *Congressional Record*, 79th Cong., 1st sess., 1945, XCI, Parts 2 and 10, 1425, 1700–1702, A605–6, A666–67, A679–80, A696, A730–31, A737, A912–13, A938, A965, A977. Republican Congressman George Bender, championing the public's right to be fully informed, expressed apprehension over Roosevelt's admission that not all of the Yalta agreements had been disclosed. In contrast, Republican Senator Harlan Bushfield conceded that the Soviet Union's military position would enable it to extend its influence over Eastern Europe. Bushfield opposed any Administration move to stem Soviet influence or to force U.S. allies to accept the U.S. form of democracy. *Ibid.*, 1769–70, A933.

17. *U.S. News*, 18 (March 16, 1945), 28–29. *Chicago Herald-American*, March 6, 1945, 15; March 19, 1945, 6. *Chicago Tribune*, March 6, 1945, 1, 10; March 13, 1945, 4, 10; March 15, 1945, 16; March 17, 1945, 12; April 1, 1945, 16.

for granting India but not White Russia or the Ukraine a vote in the General Assembly. Although he was concerned over domestic ramifications, Roosevelt, who was unwilling to press the issue, secured a similar right for three U.S. votes. To preclude arousing sensitivities of the small powers, and thus to promote maximum attendance at San Francisco, the agreement was kept secret until invitations had been sent out and accepted. The Big Three sought to avoid the impression that the small powers were invited only to ratify decisions already agreed upon.

The nature of the objections to the "multiple vote" agreement reveals much about the political situation in the United States in 1945. Neither *Time, U.S. News,* nor *The New York Times* challenged the agreements per se. These publications attacked only the methods of the Roosevelt Administration's diplomacy. They criticized the secrecy of the conference and the length of time that this agreement had been kept secret. None depicted the agreement as an unwarranted concession to the Soviet Union. They accepted the need for compromise and concession as necessary and desirable. When they expressed concern, they usually voiced fear that the possible adverse ramifications of the agreement might inhibit the establishment of a United Nations organization.[18]

Those who had objected to the veto agreement adopted a moralistic tone about the "multiple vote" agreement, assailing the cynicism and betrayal of the smaller nations that underlay this power-political decision by the Big Three. Inherently anti-Roosevelt and anti-Soviet, they pointed to this secret concession to the Soviet Union as confirmation of Roosevelt's deceit and pro-Soviet tendencies. Because there had been two disclosures within a month, they further hinted that there might be other secret agreements. At the same time, they stated that this disclosure should cancel the proposed international organization.[19]

In their condemnations of both the veto and "multiple vote" agreements made at Yalta, the "extremists" were not basically interested in a more democratic and representative international organization. None of them expected or would have supported a perfectly

18. *The New York Times,* March 31, 1945, 18; April 1, 1945, 3E; April 2, 1945, 18; April 4, 1945, 20; April 5, 1945, 22. *U.S. News,* 18 (April 6, 1945), 24; April 13, 1945, 11–12. *Time,* 45 (April 9, 1945), 23–24; April 16, 1945, 19–20. *Newsweek,* 25 (April 9, 1945), 22, 52.

19. U.S. *Congressional Record,* 79th Cong., 1st sess., 1945, XCI, Part 11, A1569–70, A1609, A1684. *Chicago Tribune,* March 30, 1945, 1; April 2, 1945, 1; April 3, 1945, 10; April 4, 1945, 11; April 5, 1945, 14. *Chicago Herald-American,* April 7, 1945, 9; April 9, 1945, 8; April 10, 1945, 8.

equal world organization. They had previously charged that U.S. participation in an international organization circumscribed the national sovereignty and unduly extended U.S. commitments; they would use the same charges in the debate about the Bricker Amendment. In 1945, however, they sought to capitalize on the initial secrecy and power-political aspects of these agreements to discredit both Roosevelt's leadership and this internationalist policy.

Although the "extremists" had little political impact, the disclosure of formerly secret agreements had raised doubt and concern about the possibility of further secret agreements concluded at Yalta. During a press conference following the release of the "multiple vote" agreement, Secretary of State Edward Stettinius, Jr., was asked whether other secret agreements had been made at Yalta and, if so, when they would be published. At the time, Stettinius deferred answering the question. On April 3, however, he declared that all secret agreements had been published except the "military plans agreed to at Yalta *and related matters* connected with the defeat of the enemy [which] can be made known only as they are carried out."[20]

The Administration, for political reasons alone, would have found it convenient to release the Far Eastern agreements in April, but Stettinius could not release them or even admit their existence. Germany had not been defeated, the Soviet Union had yet to declare war on Japan, the Japanese were not defeated, and no one knew how long the war would last. Although the public would have welcomed a Soviet pledge to intervene in the war against Japan,[21] Stettinius could only cryptically assert that all secret agreements were disclosed except military decisions and related matters — and the Far Eastern agreements clearly fell in this category. (Indeed, publication of the agreements in April could have compromised the subsequent denunciations of the Far Eastern concessions as unnecessary and undesirable.)

Nor was this wish to have Soviet assistance in the war against Japan confined to April. In February, Soviet involvement was the goal most discussed by the press. Military analyses in the *Army and Navy Journal* and by Hanson Baldwin, the military correspondent for

20. U.S. Department of State, *The Department of State Bulletin*, XII, 302 (April 8, 1945), 600. Italics mine.
21. This concern appeared in the responses of columnist Arthur Krock and *Time* magazine to the April, 1945, Soviet renunciation of her neutrality pact with Japan. Krock and *Time* affirmed that the Far East had been discussed at Yalta and emphasized the inevitability and correctness of Soviet involvement in the war against Japan. *The New York Times*, April 6, 1945, 14. *Time*, 45 (April 16, 1945), 25.

The New York Times, then stated that the Yalta conferees had discussed the Far East and that the Soviet Union had promised its involvement. These analysts also accepted Soviet political influence as the inevitable result of this involvement.[22]

Moreover, the press response to the Soviet declaration of war on August 8 — exactly three months after the German surrender — was equally favorable. *Newsweek* and *The New York Times* attributed this Soviet action to a Yalta agreement and called it one of Roosevelt's great triumphs. *Time* magazine simply reported, without comment or interpretation, rumors that a Yalta agreement had earlier secured a Soviet promise to enter the war in return for concessions similar to those embodied in the Sino-Soviet treaty.[23] The press also welcomed the August 14 announcement of the terms of the Sino-Soviet treaty. Even people in the United States who supported Chiang Kai-shek considered the treaty a Chinese victory that also benefited the United States. They expressed hope for China's future and called the treaty a confirmation of Soviet good faith.[24]

Only the "extremists" assailed this sympathetic view of the Soviet Union and Administration policy. Although they were consistently skeptical about Soviet aspirations and the Administration's Soviet policy, the "extremists" were not prescient; they simply opposed any internationalist policy suggested by the Roosevelt Administration. They claimed in 1945 that Soviet aid was unnecessary, but they never implied that Roosevelt could have averted Soviet intervention. Their main point was that the Soviet Union might have exacted concessions from the Roosevelt Administration at Yalta. This criticism originated more from their antipathy toward Roosevelt than from their consideration of the options open to the U.S. delegation to Yalta.[25]

The essential negativism of these "extremist" criticisms revealed their primary goal — discrediting the New Deal. Before the announcement of the conference results, they had concentrated on Roosevelt's domestic policies and had only indirectly attacked his foreign policies. They had then intended to discredit Roosevelt's leadership, particularly his use of the Presidency to bring about domestic reform. Either

22. *The New York Times*, February 11, 1945, 7; February 14, 1945, 10.
23. *The New York Times*, August 9, 1945, 20; August 13, 1945, 18. *Newsweek*, 26 (August 20, 1945), 56. *Time*, 46 (August 20, 1945), 20.
24. *Ibid.*, July 20, 1945, 13. U.S. *Congressional Record*, 79th Cong., 1st sess., 1945, XCI, Parts 7 and 8, 9545, 10863–64. Congressman Walter Judd, speech, March 15, 1945 (printed privately by U.S. Government Printing Office).
25. *Chicago Tribune*, April 6, 1945, 2; April 7, 1945, 8; April 13, 1945, 12; August 10, 1945, 5; August 13, 1945, 18. *Chicago Herald-American*, April 19, 1945, 11; April 23, 1945, 9; May 3, 1945, 13; August 25, 1945, 9.

they suggested that in 1944 the public had supported Roosevelt's foreign policies but had expected changes in his domestic policies or they argued that the aim of the Roosevelt Administration's foreign policy was to implement a policy of centralization and regimentation. Later, they sought to raise doubts about Roosevelt's political loyalties by referring to concessions made at Yalta. By late 1945, they no longer distinguished between New Deal domestic and foreign policies; they attacked both as disastrous and mistaken.[26]

Although the "extremists'" criticisms had focused on Roosevelt's role at Yalta, Roosevelt's death on April 12, 1945, did not terminate this assault. A poorly prepared Harry S Truman, then elevated to the Presidency, encountered these continued efforts to use Yalta's symbolism in order to debunk New Deal policies. Truman was a good politician, but he had little knowledge of the complexities of international politics and specifically of Eastern European developments. Because he had not been involved in foreign policy decisions or discussions during the Roosevelt Administration, he found it difficult to lead the public at a time when enlightened leadership was imperative. His vacillation caused public confusion about the rationale for the Administration's foreign policy and Soviet actions in Eastern Europe. His ignorance of prewar Eastern European politics and his lack of sympathy for Soviet objectives in that area adversely influenced his presentation of the Administration's foreign policy to the public and to the Soviet Union. His suspicions unnecessarily caused Soviet doubts about U.S. good faith and the U.S. public's doubts about Soviet good faith. Truman's distrust, coupled with political developments in Eastern Europe, contributed to a shift in the popular concept of the Yalta Conference. Originally, people in the United States had recognized Yalta as a hopeful beginning for peace, but gradually they came to attribute postwar difficulties to the Soviet Union's violations of its Yalta pledges.[27]

Nonetheless, qualified trust in the Soviet Union and support for future Big Three conferences to resolve differences remained. Despite

26. U.S. *Congressional Record*, 79th Cong., 1st sess., 1945, XCI, Parts 4, 5, 10, and 11, 5040, 6020, A554, A1811, A1868–69. *Chicago Herald-American*, March 16, 1945, 3. *U.S. News*, 18 (February 2, 1945), 28. *Chicago Tribune*, October 26, 1945, 16.

27. U.S. *Congressional Record*, 79th Cong., 1st sess., 1945, XCI, Parts 3 and 11, 3995, A1899–1900, A1902, A2043. *The New York Times*, April 25, 1945, 22. *Newsweek*, 25 (April 30, 1945), 48. *U.S. News*, 18 (April 27, 1945), 13–14. In fact, Ernest Lindley contended that the U.S. public, had it doubted Soviet intentions to fulfill her international commitments, would not have accepted the Yalta compromises. *Newsweek*, 25 (April 30, 1945), 44.

the frustrating failure to reach agreement at the meetings of the Council of Foreign Ministers, the public continued to believe in the possibility of Allied co-operation. They assumed that the Soviet Union would fulfill its obligations and that its aspirations were legitimate. The news media and congressmen, both Republican and Democratic, showed understanding of the Soviet position and of the limits to what the United States could do. The Republican leaders pointedly disassociated the party from the "extremists'" anti-Soviet, pro-German position. They supported continued consultations between the United States and the Soviet Union and praised the results of the Potsdam Conference.[28]

Although people in the United States did not welcome Potsdam's results as enthusiastically as they had welcomed Yalta's, they did recognize that the results conformed to the realities of international politics. *The New York Times* asserted, "Undoubtedly compromise was made, but the American people are confident that he [Truman] did what was best and possible. His reception will be warm." [29] Even the Polish-American Congress accepted the Yalta "free election" agreement as basic U.S. policy. Roosevelt's commitment to joint consultations with the Soviet Union and his trust of that country received no criticism then. When elections were not held in 1945, domestic conservatives and Polish-Americans denounced the Soviet Union for not abiding by this Yalta agreement.[30]

The characteristic response from Republicans was a hesitancy to malign Yalta openly. As late as May, even Styles Bridges (Republican, New Hampshire), Robert Taft (Republican, Ohio), Karl Mundt (Republican, South Dakota), and Everett Dirksen (Republican, Illinois) did not directly debunk the conference. Bridges did condemn Yalta's "injustice" to Poland and the "immorality" of the veto agreement. Taft simply criticized the public relations efforts of the State Department and suggested that the glowing press releases on Yalta, Dumbarton Oaks, and other international conferences were exceed-

28. *U.S. News*, 18 (May 25, 1945), 13–14, 28–29; 19 (October 8, 1945), 29; October 12, 1945, 15–16; October 19, 1945, 88. *The New York Times*, May 25, 1945, 18; June 30, 1945, 16; July 29, 1945, 10E; August 3, 1945, 16; September 26, 1945, 22. *Time*, 46 (July 16, 1945), 13–14; September 17, 1945, 29. *Newsweek*, 26 (July 23, 1945), 96. U.S. *Congressional Record*, 79th Cong., 1st sess., 1945, XCI, Part 13, A4297.

29. *The New York Times*, August 8, 1945, 22.

30. *Time*, 46 (July 16, 1945), 15; July 23, 1945, 40–42. *The New York Times*, July 7, 1945, 12. U.S. *Congressional Record*, 79th Cong., 1st sess., 1945, XCI, Parts 6 and 12, 7743–44, A3745, A3347–48, A3571. *Polish-American Congress Bulletin*, I, 3 (June–July, 1945).

ingly "biased." Dirksen and Mundt, however, appraised the positive aspects of international diplomacy. Dirksen said that Yalta and the other wartime conferences represented the cause of freedom. Mundt cited Yalta, Quebec, Hot Springs, and Bretton Woods to support the establishment of an international office of education.[31]

In 1945, this reluctance to launch an open attack on Yalta distinguished these Republicans from the "extremists" who even manufactured incidents in their efforts to discredit the conference. The *Chicago Tribune*, in fact, periodically reported additional secret Yalta agreements. Among these alleged Yalta "secrets," as reported by the *Tribune*, were agreements ceding Korea to the Soviet Union,[32] promising to the Soviet Union control of the Dardanelles,[33] providing for the United States to secretly deliver 90 to 100 convoy ships to the Soviet Union,[34] and assigning Egypt to the British sphere of influence.[35]

The "extremists," moreover, simply called Potsdam a benefit to the Soviet Union and focused their most biting criticism on the Administration's German policy. Congressmen Paul Shafer, Lawrence Smith, Roy Woodruff (Republican, Michigan), Dewey Short (Republican, Missouri), columnists George Sokolsky and David Lawrence, and the *Chicago Tribune* denounced as "harsh," unhumanitarian, and un-Christian the provisions for German reparations and, in this same moralistic tone, warned against the repetition of the Versailles "errors." [36]

Certain decisions related to the termination of the war in the Pacific renewed interest in Yalta during August and September, 1945. When the Japanese surrendered, Soviet troops were allowed to replace U.S. troops that had liberated the Kurile Islands. Inevitably, the "extremists" decried this development, and on August 28, Congressman Paul Shafer demanded that Congress investigate whether some secret agreement had ceded the Kuriles to the Soviet Union.

31. U.S. *Congressional Record*, 79th Cong., 1st sess., 1945, XCI, Parts 3, 5, 11, and 12, 3936, 4093, 4128, 5845, A2413, A3204–6.

32. *Chicago Tribune*, May 7, 1945, 1; May 10, 1945, 9; May 16, 1945, 7; May 17, 1945, 6; June 3, 1945, 4; June 23, 1945, 3.

33. *Ibid.*, March 20, 1945, 12.

34. *Ibid.*, September 28, 1945, 2.

35. *Ibid.*, July 17, 1945, 4; July 22, 1945, 10.

36. U.S. *Congressional Record*, 79th Cong., 1st sess., 1945, XCI, Parts 12 and 13, A3144–45, A4083, A4731–32, A4776–77. *Chicago Herald-American*, September 22, 1945, 9. *U.S. News*, 19 (August 10, 1945), 36–37. *Chicago Tribune*, April 27, 1945, 14; May 11, 1945, 16; June 18, 1945, 12; August 3, 1945, 10; August 4, 1945, 6.

Shafer then emphasized the strategic importance of the islands for U.S. security.[37]

James F. Byrnes, who succeeded Stettinius as Secretary of State on July 3, 1945, cleared up this mystery during a September 3 press conference. Byrnes then told the press that Soviet occupation did not result from any agreement concluded at Potsdam. The disposition of the Kuriles and South Sakhalin, Byrnes noted, had been discussed at Yalta, but after affirming that he "remembered well" the Yalta "discussions" on the Kuriles and South Sakhalin, he denied that the conferees had agreed to cede these areas to the Soviet Union. Such an agreement, Byrnes asserted, was the subject of a peace conference. He confirmed the Soviet right to these areas and his intention to discuss the matter with Soviet Foreign Minister Molotov at the forthcoming London Conference. Cagey and evasive in his remarks, Byrnes left the impression that additional, more significant understandings — particularly concerning China — had been reached at Yalta.[38]

Byrnes's September announcement evoked surprisingly little comment in either the press or Congress. Perhaps this Yalta disclosure was ignored or quickly forgotten because of its seemingly un-newsworthy character or because of the greater interest in the Pearl Harbor investigation, which was then in session. George Sokolsky, Raymond Moley, David Lawrence, *Time*, and *Newsweek* did not even report Byrnes's remarks; *U.S. News* only briefly reported his comments on the last page of its September 14 issue.[39] The *Chicago Tribune*, however, criticized this new "Roosevelt secret agreement." The *Tribune* claimed that Soviet possession of the Kuriles threatened U.S. security, and it deemed this loss of safety the price that the people of the United States had to pay "for having presidents who put their personal interest and their egotism above the true interests of their country."[40]

The year closed on an explosive note: In December, Patrick Hur-

---

37. *Ibid.*, August 29, 1945, 2.

38. The *New York Herald-Tribune* correspondent, in fact, ascribed the Soviet "renunciation'" of the Chinese Communists, referring to Soviet recognition of the National Government, to an earlier agreement concluded at Yalta, later embodied in the Sino-Soviet treaty. *New York Herald-Tribune*, September 5, 1945, 1. *Chicago Tribune*, September 5, 1945, 1. *The New York Times*, September 5, 1945, 1, 9. This *Herald-Tribune* story led reporters to ask Charles Ross, presidential press secretary, if such an agreement had been concluded at Yalta. Ross replied that he knew nothing about any of the Yalta agreements. Transcript of press conference, September 6, 1945, Record of White House Official Reporter, Ross Papers, Truman Library.

39. *U.S. News*, 19 (September 14, 1945), 104.

40. *Chicago Tribune*, September 6, 1945, 18. Responding to this *Tribune*

ley resigned as U.S. Ambassador to China and denounced both "Communist" and "imperialist" (that is, pro-British) influence in the State Department. In the Senate Foreign Relations Committee hearings on his resignation, Hurley did not attack the Roosevelt and Truman administrations' Far Eastern policy decisions, not even those made at Yalta. He assailed only the actions of State Department personnel and condemned the secrecy and insubordination of career officers. Affirming his support for the Administration's Far Eastern policy, he argued, "Our policy and the Russian Chinese policy are in accord. Russia, I believe, is adhering to the policy which she agreed to in the Sino-Soviet treaty in August, 1945." Hurley also praised the Sino-Soviet treaty, expressed trust in the Soviet Union, and denied that the Chinese Communists were "real" Communists.[41] When Republican Senator Styles Bridges asked whether any agreement concerning China had been concluded at Yalta, Hurley replied that he had not attended the conference. He advised Bridges to question Secretary of State Byrnes.[42]

Apparently, Bridges had learned about the Yalta Far Eastern agreements. He may have received his information from a State Department leak or from Hurley. The next day, when Secretary of State Byrnes appeared before the committee, Bridges asked him whether any agreement concerning China had been concluded at Yalta. Caught offguard, Byrnes first attempted to skirt Bridges' question and then replied evasively and embarrassedly. He finally admitted:

I do not recall the various agreements [of the Yalta Conference]. It is entirely possible that some of the agreements arrived at Yalta affected China in some way or another, and I have told you that I would gladly furnish you the communiqué and then you could decide whether or not they affected China. If they were made they certainly were made by the heads of government, and certainly only the three Governments were represented there.[43]

Bridges' questions and his tone of assurance made it impossible for Byrnes to deny point-blank that any agreement on China had

charge, *The New York Times* editorially affirmed, "It is to their [the Soviet Union's] paramount strategic interest, and not ours, that they should have such bases. . . . In Russian hands they [the Kuriles] will bring an ally no nearer to the United States than she already is, and interpose an effective bulwark against any new Japanese advance." *The New York Times*, September 9, 1945, 8E.

41. U.S. Senate, Committee on Foreign Relations, *Hearings on the Investigation of Far Eastern Policy*, 79th Cong., 1st sess., 1945, 3, 6–7, 9, 12, 14–15, 19–24, 31–32, 40L, 40M, 178.

42. *Ibid.*, 123–24.

43. *Ibid.*, 233.

been concluded at Yalta. (In December, Byrnes was fully aware of the Yalta Far Eastern agreements. His July, 1945, communications with U.S. Ambassador to the Soviet Union W. Averell Harriman on the Sino-Soviet treaty negotiations documented his awareness. In addition, he admitted in January, 1946, that he had read the full text of the Yalta agreements in August, 1945.) Not fazed by Byrnes's evasiveness, Bridges noted the importance of any agreement concerning China and observed that had any such agreement been made, Byrnes would have been aware of it.[44]

In 1945, Hurley's charges were virtually ignored. Few people defended him after he was attacked by Congressman Hugh DeLacy (Democrat, Washington) and Congresswoman Frances Bolton (Republican, Ohio). Even Congressman Walter Judd, who would later forthrightly support Hurley and attack the State Department, was silent.[45] Only the "extremists" championed Hurley: The *Chicago Tribune* and Congressmen Carl Curtis (Republican, Nebraska) and Ross Rizley (Republican, Oklahoma) deplored Hurley's resignation and demanded a housecleaning of Communists in the State Department.[46]

By December, 1945, Yalta was still considered, perhaps not as enthusiastically as in February, a hopeful beginning to peace. Although U.S.-Soviet relations had worsened, no one portrayed the Yalta Conference as sinister or harmful to the national security. The "extremists" assailed the conference, but few people seriously listened to their denunciations. Moreover, the "extremists" were interested more in discrediting Roosevelt and the New Deal than in condemning the results of Yalta. A quote from the *Chicago Tribune*'s farewell to 1945 is indicative:

> The American people must disown these faithless men who spurn our interests and give them away to nations who owe their survival to us. Let America do away with the hyphenates, the little and small Americans who betray the splendor of their country.[47]

44. *Ibid.*, 231–32.
45. U.S. *Congressional Record*, 79th Cong., 1st sess., 1945, XCI, Part 13, A5177, A5166, A5210–11.
46. *Ibid.*, A5159, A5175. *Chicago Tribune*, December 6, 1945, 2; December 10, 1945, 16.
47. *Ibid.*, December 31, 1945, 8.

chapter 3
1946–1948: the emergence of partisan politics, part one

From 1946 through 1948, the "moderates," the Republican National Committee, and the "partisans" did not attack the past Administration's foreign policy as part of a conscious political strategy to discredit the Truman Administration. Although they became increasingly more critical of the Yalta agreements, these Republicans co-operated with the Truman Administration and supported its proposals to implement a containment policy. In their criticisms of the past Administration's foreign policy decisions, these Republicans did not demand the repudiation of such agreements as those made at Yalta. They simply expressed their commitment to a positive course on future policy. As an opposition, they argued that they could provide the needed improvements of a basically sound foreign policy.

In contrast, the "extremists" consistently criticized what they called New Deal foreign policy, but their denunciations of this policy varied considerably. They called every Administration effort to negotiate or co-operate with the Soviet Union too soft and appeasing; at the same time, they assailed the containment policy as too aggressive and threatening. Throughout, they blamed Yalta for existing international problems. All of their divergent criticisms showed their commitment to discredit the New Deal and to inhibit any form of international involvement for the United States.

In this period, the Administration generally was able to assume leadership and initiative. The Republican leaders and most of their followers remained quiescent, even after the potentially controversial Administration decision of January, 1946, to recognize the Bulgarian and Rumanian governments. In a press conference on January 8, President Truman had asserted that recognition of these Balkan governments and the Yugoslavian Government was contingent upon their acceptance of the Yalta agreements and specifically upon their having free elections. In his State of the Union address, Truman described the "free election" agreement as basic U.S. policy. He expressed pleasure that the "common effort of the United Nations to learn to live together did not cease with the surrender of our enemies."[1]

The main criticisms of Administration policy during 1946 concerned the probability of the Administration's enforcing the Yalta provisions. Republican leaders urged Truman to adopt a more forceful approach, but they never demanded the repudiation of Yalta. Their principal criticism pointed out Truman's vacillation and his failure to make the Soviets fulfill the Yalta guarantees.[2] Public appraisals of the Administration's policy seldom questioned the desirability of continued co-operation with the Soviet Union. The "extremists" assailed this policy, but their criticism was more anti-Roosevelt than anti-Yalta. They attributed the recognition of the Balkan governments and other policies that they said benefited only the Soviet Union to pro-Communists in the State Department.[3]

The domestic political importance of Polish-Americans gave developments in Poland great political significance in the United States. Although some "extremists" and certain prominent Polish-Americans had been upset when the United States recognized the Polish Provisional Government, few other people criticized the Yalta provisions until the promised early elections were postponed to later in 1946 — and postponed again to 1947, when they were finally held. Even so, most critics in 1946 protested Soviet violations of the Yalta provisions rather than the actual agreements. The more bitter Polish-American Congress, however, demanded that the Truman Administration repudiate Yalta.[4]

Echoing these denunciations of Yalta, the "extremists" charged that the Yalta agreements had reduced Poland to a Soviet puppet state. Although they had criticized the Roosevelt and Truman administrations for appeasing the Soviet Union, the "extremists" now denounced the Truman Administration's protests over the Polish Pro-

1. Transcript of press conference, January 8, 1946, Records of White House Official Reporter, Truman Papers, Truman Library. U.S. *Congressional Record*, 79th Cong., 2d sess., 1946, XCII, Part 1, 138.

2. *Ibid.*, Parts 1, 9, and 10, 224, A234, A333–34, A2261. Ernest Lindley specifically recommended that a stronger military defense be developed in order to back up U.S. words with force. *Newsweek*, 27 (March 11, 1946), 26. *The New York Times*, February 3, 1946, 8E. *Time*, 47 (February 4, 1946), 29. *The Saturday Evening Post*, 218 (February 2, 1946), 100.

3. *Chicago Herald-American*, February 4, 1946, 9. *Chicago Tribune*, February 7, 1946, 20. U.S. *Congressional Record*, 79th Cong., 2d sess., 1946, XCII, Part 1, 1182–83.

4. *Ibid.*, Parts 1, 9, and 10, 1163, A1193, A1254, A1402, A2264; *Ibid.*, 1947, XCIII, Part 12, A3217. *The New York Times*, June 19, 1947, 20; September 5, 1947, 18. *Newsweek*, 30 (September 1, 1947), 32. *Polish-American Congress Bulletin*, II, 5 (January, 1946), 12, 21, 50.

visional Government's failure to hold early elections. They said that the protests were tantamount to a declaration of war and that the protests were too late because of concessions earlier concluded at Yalta.[5]

Developments in Asia, however, caused the most controversy about the Yalta Conference in early 1946. The Truman Administration decided to cede to an international trusteeship formal control over those islands in the Pacific that U.S. troops had captured from Japan during World War II and had occupied since that time. This decision led to questions about whether the Soviet Union would also follow this policy of internationalization with the Kurile Islands, which had come under Soviet control after Japan's surrender in August, 1945. These questions led to the formal publication of the Yalta Far Eastern agreements in February, 1946, and the subsequent furor.

The Truman Administration's decision about islands occupied by the United States was already known when Acting Secretary of State Dean Acheson held a press conference on January 22. At that time, reporters asked him about Soviet control of the Kuriles and whether the Soviet Union would cede these islands to an international trusteeship. He replied that Soviet control of the Kuriles had been agreed to at Yalta. This agreement, he disclosed, permitted Soviet occupation of the islands as a military operation but did not give the Soviets permanent possession. He added that the final result might be the Soviet Union's retention of full control.[6]

The question of Yalta secrets recurred when, on January 26, Moscow Radio contradicted Acheson and argued that Yalta agreements had clearly given the Kurile Islands and South Sakhalin to the Soviet Union upon the defeat of Japan.[7] The "extremists," and others who opposed the decision to cede the Pacific islands occupied by the United States, attacked this disclosure of a Yalta agreement on the Kuriles. They pointedly recalled Roosevelt's and Stettinius' denials that agreements concerning the Far East had been concluded at Yalta.[8]

In a press conference on January 29, 1946, Secretary of State James Byrnes attempted to clarify the matter. He had disclosed on

5. In addition, the *Chicago Tribune* accused President Truman of favoritism when he denounced Soviet, but not British, imperialism. *Chicago Tribune*, March 2, 1946, 10. *Chicago Herald-American*, April 13, 1946, 6; July 17, 1947, 17; July 18, 1947, 13. U.S. *Congressional Record*, 80th Cong., 1st sess., 1947, XCIII, Part 8, 9890–92.
6. *Chicago Tribune*, January 23, 1946, 12.
7. *Ibid.*, January 27, 1946, 1. *Newsweek*, 27 (February 4, 1946), 46.
8. *Ibid.* (January 28, 1946), 32–34. *Chicago Tribune*, January 29, 1946, 10.

September 4, 1945, that the United States had acceded to Soviet occupation of the Kuriles and South Sakhalin but that the final status of these territories would be decided at the peace conference. The remarks he made on January 29 helped create another Yalta myth and provided material that Yalta critics would effectively use to confirm Roosevelt's sinister and secret personal diplomacy. Byrnes stated that the Kuriles and South Sakhalin were ceded to the Soviet Union at Yalta but that he had not known of these Yalta agreements until a few days after the surrender of Japan on August 14, 1945. He had not known about them because he had not attended the February 11 session: He had left the conference the previous day. Whether Stettinius was aware of this particular agreement, Byrnes did not know. Neither the text nor a copy of the text was in the State Department archives, but the text might be in the White House files. He then disclosed that agreements on Port Arthur and Dairen had been reached at Yalta but that these and the other Far Eastern agreements would not become final or binding until they were ratified by a peace treaty with Japan.[9]

Byrnes's contention of ignorance sharply contrasted with his assertion, made in September, 1945, that he "remembered well" the Yalta discussions on the Kuriles. His own admission that he had read the full text of the Yalta agreements in August, 1945, made meaningless his explanation in January that he had not attended the final conference meeting. He was, in September, fully aware of the conference's results, even by his own qualified admission that he had learned of the agreements only when reading the full text in August. Byrnes's knowledge of the agreements had not changed, but his willingness to be associated with them had.

Byrnes's tortured and evasive replies to Bridges' questions during the December, 1945, Senate hearings on Hurley's resignation had compromised Byrnes politically. His earlier equivocation and hazy memory had left him open to criticisms of deliberate deception or refusal to co-operate with Congress. His testimony in December determined this tactical political maneuver of January, 1946. By reiterating his ignorance, Byrnes could preserve good relations with congressional Republicans and contrast his seeming openness with Roosevelt's secrecy. Moreover, by shifting the onus of the blame to Roosevelt, he would not have to explain the Truman Administration's failure to publish the agreements earlier, in August or Septem-

    9. *Ibid.*, January 30, 1946, 5. U.S. Department of State, *The Department of State Bulletin*, XIV, 345 (February 10, 1946), 189–90.

ber, 1945. The anti-Roosevelt prejudices of many congressional Republicans gave Byrnes one means of disarming those Republicans who would have been his bitterest critics. (By 1958, Byrnes's memory was even more faulty. Then, in his memoirs, he contradicted both his September, 1945, and his January, 1946, statements by asserting that he did not learn of the Far Eastern agreements until February 10, 1946.)[10]

Byrnes's comments about Stettinius and about the repository of the Yalta text were even more dissembling. In January, Byrnes could definitely have stated that Stettinius, and the State Department, knew about the agreements and the location of the Yalta text. A May 12, 1945, State Department memorandum to the War Department confirms that Stettinius knew of the Far Eastern agreements and also that the text was not deliberately hidden in Roosevelt's private files. In this memorandum, which concerned future U.S. policy toward Soviet entry in the Far Eastern war, Stettinius asked Secretary of War Henry Stimson whether the War Department felt that the Far Eastern agreements ought to be carried out or reconsidered. Stettinius reported the State Department's belief that definite Soviet commitments on certain points were necessary before the United States should agree to implement the Yalta concessions.[11]

Having at least read the text of the agreements in August, 1945, Byrnes must have known its location. Yet, he refused to state affirmatively that the text was then — and always had been — in the White House files except when the State Department reviewed it. He left the impression that no one but Roosevelt had made the agreements or knew about them. Byrnes had learned about the Far Eastern agreements at least by July 3, 1945, when he became Secretary of State. From June to August, 1945, the Chinese Nationalists and the Soviets were consulting about a proposed pact of friendship and alliance based on the Yalta terms. As Secretary of State during this period, Byrnes was fully aware of these discussions. His knowledge of the existence of the Yalta agreements, if not of their formal terms, can be documented as early as July 4, 1945. On that date, President Truman instructed Byrnes to send a telegram to W. Averell Harriman, U.S. Ambassador to the Soviet Union, affirming that the United States

10. James F. Byrnes, *All in One Lifetime*, 266, 268.
11. Memorandum of Secretary of State Stettinius for the Secretary of War, May 12, 1945, Stettinius Collection, University of Virginia Library. See Appendix B for text. The memorandum was the focus of a serious policy re-evaluation in Cabinet circles during May, 1945. The War Department, in its reply of May 23, argued against any formal move to reconsider these concessions and urged instead a more informal approach.

would not then offer its interpretation of the Yalta terms concerning China. Again on July 6, Byrnes informed Harriman that the United States, as a signatory of the Yalta terms, expected to be consulted before any Sino-Soviet agreement was reached. [12]

Acheson and Byrnes were not the only people questioned in January, 1946. Asked about the Yalta agreements at his press conference on January 31, President Truman reported having first learned of the Kuriles agreement when he was reviewing the text of the Yalta agreements in preparation for the Potsdam Conference. The text of the agreements, Truman asserted, had never been lost but had always been in the President's private files. He stated that although he had known its location all along, he simply had not looked at the text earlier. To a question about when the full text of the Yalta agreements would be made public, Truman replied that he must first consult with the Soviet Union and Great Britain and obtain the approval of those countries. The Yalta Conference, Truman maintained, had provided a body of agreements, not a treaty. He contended that most of the agreements had already been made public and that the others would be disclosed at the proper time.[13]

Undoubtedly, Truman knew the details of the Yalta Far Eastern agreements before July. When he had assumed the Presidency, he had been briefed by Stettinius, Byrnes, and Bohlen about the Yalta agreements and the Roosevelt Administration's Far Eastern policy. Stettinius had also given Truman a full account of U.S. diplomacy.[14] Truman, as well as Byrnes, found the Yalta Far Eastern agreements a controversial, unwanted legacy. Uncommitted to their enforcement, the Truman Administration had to justify its failure to release the agreements for publication in August or September, 1945, with Soviet entrance into the Japanese war or the formal surrender of Japan. By remaining silent about the rationale for this delayed publication, Truman tacitly catered to the intense anti-Roosevelt prejudices of his potentially bitterest critics in the press and Congress.

The admission in January, 1946, of a Yalta agreement about the Kuriles and the February 11 publication of the entire text of the Far Eastern agreements elicited concern and protest. The major critique, voiced by columnist Arthur Krock, *U.S. News, The New York Times, Newsweek, Time*, Republican Senator Arthur Vandenberg, the Republican Senate Policy Committee, and the Republican National

12. Harry S Truman, *Memoirs*, Vol. I, *Year of Decisions*, 315–19.
13. Transcript of press conference, January 31, 1946, Records of the White House Official Reporter, Truman Papers, Truman Library.
14. Harry S Truman, *Memoirs*, Vol. I, *Year of Decisions*, 14–17, 22–23.

Committee's *Republican News*, centered solely on the Truman and Roosevelt administrations' tactic of secrecy rather than the terms or wisdom of the agreements. In fact, these commentators conceded that the military situation justified secrecy until the close of the war. Only *U.S. News* and *Time* intimated that further agreements remained undisclosed.[15]

The "extremists" Congressmen Frederick Bradley (Republican, Michigan), Robert Grant (Republican, Indiana), Karl Mundt, B. Carroll Reece (Republican, Tennessee), William Pittenger (Republican, Minnesota), Roy Woodruff, Joseph Martin (Republican, Massachusetts), John Rankin (Democrat, Mississippi), Congresswomen Clare Boothe Luce, Edith Rogers (Republican, Massachusetts), Governor Dwight Green (Republican, Illinois), the *Chicago Tribune*, columnists George Sokolsky and David Lawrence never directly denounced these Yalta concessions. Rather, they attacked Roosevelt personally and, through their attacks on Roosevelt, the New Deal. This new disclosure revealed more of Roosevelt's "deceit and duplicity," both of which were characteristic of the New Deal. Martin charged:

> We will have the same crushing bureaucracy, arrogance and waste; the same deceit and trick phrases; the same distortion and weird construction of law; the same kind of secret government at home and secret diplomacy abroad that we have suffered under for these 12 and more long years.

Extending this theme, Mrs. Luce maintained:

> The reason is that they [the New Dealers] will not, dare not, tell the American people the plain truths and solid facts of the European and Asiatic situations that have developed as a result of Teheran, Yalta, London, and Potsdam. They will not, or dare not, tell us the commitments that were overtly or secretly made in moments of war's extermination by a mortally ill President, and perhaps mortally scared State Department advisers.[16]

15. Even the *Chicago Tribune* and Senator Taft conceded that the Administration had no alternative but to adhere to the terms of the agreement. They recommended, however, a reversal of Administration trusteeship policy and U.S. annexation of the islands captured from Japan during World War II. *U.S. News*, 20 (February 8, 1946), 27, 28, 68; February 15, 1946, 15–16. *Newsweek*, 27 (February 11, 1946), 24. *Time*, 47 (February 11, 1946), 20; February 18, 1946, 28; March 4, 1946, 25–26. *The New York Times*, February 5, 1946, 22; February 12, 1946, 24. U.S. *Congressional Record*, 79th Cong., 2d sess., 1946, XCII, Part 2, 1692–94. *Chicago Tribune*, February 1, 1946, 1; February 3, 1946, 10; February 4, 1946, 1; February 17, 1946, 13. Republican Senate Policy Committee, *Chronology of Secret Agreements at Yalta; The Republican News*, March, 1946.

16. *Chicago Tribune*, February 2, 1946, 6; February 13, 1946, 5; Febru-

These criticisms were neither representative nor effective. More importantly, the anti-Soviet bias of the "extremists" did not influence many people, although the public had become increasingly more skeptical. Soviet actions in Manchuria in February, 1946, while arousing U.S. doubts about Soviet good faith, illustrated how differently people appraised Yalta in 1946 than they would in 1949. Congressman Walter Judd, far more critical of the Yalta conferees' betrayal of Chiang Kai-shek in the Far Eastern agreements, did not espouse repudiation. In fact, Judd demanded that the Administration enforce the Yalta terms. *Newsweek, U.S. News,* and *The New York Times* also demanded the enforcement of the Yalta provisions and portrayed Yalta as limiting Soviet expansion.[17] Thus, while rumors and attacks on Yalta proliferated, the conference had not become an effective political issue. *Time* magazine wrote of these rumors, "Every day brought a new one. An international rumor not ascribed to Yalta was no more respectable than a resident of Boston's Back Bay whose ancestors had not come over in the Mayflower." [18]

Time's charge had a basis. The *Chicago Tribune* had been busily discovering new Yalta secrets. On April 27, the *Tribune* reported that Italian and German reparations terms had been secretly fixed at Yalta.[19] In July, the *Tribune* charged that a secret Yalta agreement had authorized Stalin to maintain a German slave-labor force of two million men for twenty years. The British and the French, the *Tribune*

---

ary 24, 1946, 4; March 1, 1946, 7; March 15, 1946, 16; March 19, 1946, 2; March 20, 1946, 20. *U.S. News,* 20 (February 8, 1946), 30–31. *U.S. Congressional Record,* 79th Cong., 2d sess., 1946, XCII, Parts 2, 9, and 10, 1827, 2348, A411, A479–80, A617–18, A648, A684, A688–89, A710, A724, A916–17, A925–27, A2010. *Chicago Herald-American,* February 12, 1946, 10; February 19, 1946, 9; February 28, 1946, 15.

17. *U.S. News,* 20 (March 1, 1946), 22–23. *Newsweek,* 27 (February 25, 1946), 52. *The New York Times,* February 14, 1946, 24; February 18, 1946, 20. *U.S. Congressional Record,* 79th Cong., 2d sess., 1946, XCII, Part 11, A2763–64. In 1947, as well, *The New York Times, Time* magazine, *The Saturday Evening Post,* George Sokolsky, Congressmen Walter Judd and Chester Merrow were critical of the Yalta Far Eastern agreement, but they simply reaffirmed the need for assuring its implementation. They did criticize the Administration's secrecy and its failure to consult Chiang Kai-shek in advance; the thrust of their argument was that these actions all the more required that the Administration secure Soviet compliance with the terms of the agreement. *The New York Times,* March 12, 1947, 24; July 24, 1947, 20. *Time,* 49 (March 17, 1947), 20–21. *The Saturday Evening Post,* 219 (March 29, 1947), 156. *Chicago Herald-American,* April 1, 1947, 13; June 12, 1947, 18. *U.S. Congressional Record,* 80th Cong., 1st sess., 1947, XCIII, Parts 3, 5, 10, and 11, 3311–13, 6553, A1431–32, A2578–80.

18. *Time,* 47 (March 11, 1946), 27.

19. *Chicago Tribune,* April 27, 1946, 1. In fact, the Yalta conferees did not finally establish reparation terms, but they did accept the figure of twenty billion dollars as a "basis for discussion."

noted, had made the same "iniquitous" use of German slave labor.[20] On May 17, *U.S. News* reported a Yalta secret agreement permitting each military commander full control over and use of property in his occupation zone. *U.S. News* observed that this agreement allowed the Soviet commander in Manchuria to justify the Soviets' stripping Manchurian industry.[21]

On March 8, the State Department released to the press the text of a far more controversial, and misrepresented, Yalta agreement. This bilateral agreement, which Soviet and U.S. military leaders had concluded, provided for the exchange of those citizens of Allied countries who had been held as prisoners of war. Under this agreement, the Allies would return these prisoners of war to their native lands. The controversy about this agreement resulted from its provision that all Soviet citizens who had fought on the Axis side would be turned over to the Soviet Union and that these war prisoners would be treated as Soviet nationals.[22]

The Vatican was quick to protest this decision. A ranking Vatican prelate, Cardinal Tisserant, charged that a still-secret Yalta agreement had defined as Soviet citizens all those who had left the Soviet Union after 1929. Confronted by a State Department denial of this charge, Cardinal Tisserant contended that he had seen an "authentic" copy of this agreement. The Cardinal refused, however, to disclose the source of his information and further insisted that those Russians who had voluntarily fought with the Germans should not be returned to the Soviet Union.[23]

The "extremists'" reaction to this issue revealed one central target of their anti-New Deal stance: Roosevelt's willingness to co-operate with the Soviet Union in order to contain Germany. Distinctly pro-German and anti-Soviet, the "extremists" stated that the Roosevelt Administration's policy that called for unconditional surrender was leading to Soviet domination of Europe by removing the German bastion. They demanded the repudiation of the unconditional-surrender policy and the policies of co-operation with the

20. *Ibid.*, July 21, 1946, 18. Contrary to these charges, Yalta had provided only for the use of labor and material as a form of reparations payment. This form of payment was not the same as "slave labor."

21. *U.S. News*, 20 (May 17, 1946), 76. No such agreement was concluded, although military jurisdictional control had been established.

22. U.S. Department of State, *The Conferences at Malta and Yalta, 1945*, 985–87.

23. *Chicago Tribune*, February 25, 1946, 6; March 6, 1946, 4. In reporting these Vatican charges, the *Chicago Tribune* asserted that more than 50,000 men had been turned over to the Soviet Union under this provision. February 26, 1946, 12; March 3, 1946, 11.

Soviet Union against Germany because they believed that a strong Germany would be a vital counterweight to Soviet influence in Europe. Furthermore, they decried the rationale for the Nuremberg trials, and reparations, as well as the Morgenthau Plan, which proposed stringent restrictions on the postwar German economy in order to deny Germany a war-industry potential. A revised policy toward Germany, the "extremists" averred, was essential to prevent the communization of Europe.[24]

The "extremists" exhibited these sympathies most openly during Senate debate on a proposed amendment to the Third Supplemental Appropriation Act of 1948. The subject of that debate was the appropriateness of a formal congressional repudiation of German reparations. Senator Henry Dworshak (Republican, Idaho), criticizing the provisions about German reparations that were established at the Teheran, Yalta, and Potsdam conferences, sarcastically expressed his sympathy for Senator Arthur Vandenberg's having to reconcile the "stupid and inconsistent" foreign policy decisions of "New Deal" administrations. In reply, Vandenberg denied that he was embarrassed when he defended State Department policy and added that he always expressed his disagreement when he opposed policies, such as "certain" Yalta agreements. He then retorted that since the debate concerned German reparations, the speakers should concentrate on that topic.[25]

But the debate did not solely involve German reparations. Senator Joseph Ball (Republican, Minnesota) later questioned Vandenberg about the extent of his commitment to support, through appropriations and authority, the Yalta agreements and other executive commitments. Ball also asked whether the United States was bound by the Yalta agreements or whether repudiating them would be helpful.

Vandenberg declined to comment on Roosevelt's legal right to conclude the Yalta agreements. After expressing personal disagreement with many of these agreements, he stated that the United States was bound by what had happened at Yalta. Senator Eugene Millikin (Republican, Colorado) then observed that the Senate clearly had

24. *Chicago Herald-American*, July 20, 1946, 7; March 6, 1947, 17; June 16, 1947, 11. *Chicago Tribune*, March 21, 1946, 18; April 29, 1946, 14; August 8, 1946, 20; December 20, 1946, 22; January 29, 1947, 9; March 19, 1947, 1, 7, 18; March 20, 1947, 8, 20; December 12, 1947, 24. *The Saturday Evening Post*, 219 (April 5, 1947), 156. U.S. *Congressional Record*, 79th Cong., 2d sess., 1946, XCII, Part 2, 1949, 2052–54.
25. *Ibid.*, 80th Cong., 1st sess., 1947, XCIII, Part 9, 11685–86.

the right to repudiate executive agreements. The question did not center on the Senate's right, Millikin asserted, but whether this right should be exercised as an act of policy. He attributed the offensiveness of Yalta to the Administration's violation of its promises to the people of the United States and to the Congress, and he cited the Atlantic Charter and previous Administration denials concerning secret Yalta agreements. To ensure peace, Millikin maintained, the United States must keep its word. He added:

> We made an agreement, I do not like it, and I should like to see it ended; but let us not end it in this glancing way. If it is to be ended, let us approach it frontally, in an issue to come before us and raised primarily for the purpose. . . . I think we may have to come to the repudiation of some of our wartime Executive agreements, but there is no need to go into that now.

Vandenberg and Democratic Senator Tom Connally concurred.[26]

A shift in U.S. policy concerning German reparations did occur in 1947. During a conference of the Council of Foreign Ministers, held in Moscow in March, the Soviet Union had insisted that the Yalta conferees had set German reparations payments to the Soviet Union at ten billion dollars. The United States, however, contended that this figure had been proposed only as the basis for future discussions.[27] By 1947, the Administration had come to support German recovery as an imperative part of the containment policy. The seeming failure of Yalta's spirit of co-operation had increased opposition to Soviet demands for reparation from Germany.[28]

Formally, a spirit of Allied co-operation and unity had persisted throughout 1946, despite a growing skepticism about Soviet actions. Accordingly, Winston Churchill's March, 1946, speech in Fulton, Missouri, elicited limited popular support. Only after the intensification of the Cold War did the "iron curtain" reference secure popular acclaim. In 1946, Administration policy, and congressional support for that policy, remained formally committed to negotiations and co-

26. *Ibid.*, 11690–91.
27. U.S. Department of State, *The Department of State Bulletin*, XVI, 404 (March 30, 1947), 564.
28. U.S. *Congressional Record*, 80th Cong., 1st sess., 1947, XCIII, Parts 10 and 11, A1354–55, A1953. *Time*, 49 (March 24, 1947), 27. *The New York Times*, April 25, 1947, 20. In marked contrast, the *Times* had maintained in 1946 that a reparations policy would help preserve peace by preventing the resurgence of an aggressive Germany. Allied unity was essential to the implementation of this policy; Yalta and other wartime conferences had thereby safeguarded peace by providing the basis for continued postwar co-operation. *Ibid.*, May 1, 1946, 24.

operation with the Soviet Union through the United Nations or foreign ministers meetings.[29]

The "extremists," despite their former criticisms of Yalta's "appeasement" of the Soviet Union, denounced Churchill's demand for a firmer Anglo-American policy. They also opposed the proposed loan to Great Britain and other policies entailing political or economic commitments to other countries. They simply criticized Roosevelt's leadership and policies for failing to create a perfect world, but they never proposed how such a world could have been created. Because they attributed postwar developments to Roosevelt's policies rather than Soviet actions, they questioned a policy of confrontation and instead demanded the repudiation of Roosevelt's leadership. They had little sympathy for substantive anti-Soviet policies. On the one hand, they asserted that the Administration should have stood firm at Yalta. At the same time, they decried the conclusion of a formal anti-Soviet alliance with Great Britain. Moreover, only the *Chicago Tribune* and George Sokolsky welcomed Churchill's strong anti-Soviet speech. Congressmen Hubert Ellis (Republican, West Virginia), Frederick Smith (Republican, Ohio), Everett Dirksen, Ralph Church (Republican, Illinois), Howard Buffett (Republican, Nebraska), William Blackney (Republican, Michigan), Walter Horan (Republican, Washington), and John Rankin (Democrat, Mississippi) condemned the "aggressive" tone of the speech. They said that it posed the threat of war and that it was a disguised British attempt to secure financial aid by using the U.S. anti-Soviet concern.[30]

Exploited repeatedly to undermine other policies, Yalta appeared in debates that had no relationship to its conferees' decisions. It became a symbol and a standard used by the "extremists" to attack Administration policy in general. Thus, Senator William Langer (Republican, North Dakota), in a June 7 speech opposing the extension of selective service, blamed Yalta for postwar problems.[31] During the debate in May on State Department appropriations, Congressman John Jennings (Republican, Tennessee), a prohibitionist, proposed the elimination of the $800,000 fund for foreign service

29. U.S. *Congressional Record*, 79th Cong., 2d sess., 1946, XCII, Parts 2 and 3, 1970, 1971, 1974, 3066–67.

30. *Ibid.*, Parts 2, 3, and 10, 1972, 1973, 2265, 2266, A1300–1301, A1532, A1562–63. *Chicago Herald-American*, March 9, 1946, 7; March 16, 1946, 7; March 18, 1946, 8; April 19, 1946, 16; May 3, 1946, 23. *Chicago Tribune*, March 7, 1946, 18; May 16, 1946, 16; May 26, 1946, 20; June 15, 1946, 12; July 7, 1946, 18. *The Saturday Evening Post*, 218 (March 30, 1946), 120.

31. U.S. *Congressional Record*, 79th Cong., 2d sess., 1946, XCII, Part 4, 6216–17.

officers, since some of the money was used to purchase liquor. To justify this deletion, Jennings attributed the U.S. failure at Yalta to excessive drinking.[32]

Despite these criticisms, the Republican National Committee and Republican congressional leaders continued to support the Administration's foreign policy, and they did not attempt to undermine public confidence in it. Indeed, Senator Arthur Vandenberg stressed the need for responsible criticism of the Administration's policy and support for it. Although he considered the Yalta agreements too power-political, Vandenberg demanded the enforcement of the conference's provisions. During discussion of the proposed loan to Great Britain, Vandenberg argued that Congress should base its support for foreign loans on the recipient nation's adherence to treaty obligations. Thus, he argued, the United States should not aid the Polish Provisional Government because it had defaulted on the Yalta provision for free elections. Vandenberg noted:

> We have underwritten the Yalta agreement and the Potsdam agreement and subscribed our integrity to their promises. It seems to me that we are entitled to use every influence at our command, including our fiscal resources, in insisting upon the faithful execution of those agreements.[33]

The "extremists" and other members of the Republican party shared an anti-New Deal bias, but they split on the use of foreign policy as a campaign tactic. Republican strategy in the 1946 congressional election distinguished between New Deal foreign and domestic policies. It called for attempts to discredit the loyalty of the Democrats, based upon their stand on domestic issues. Republican National Committee Chairman B. Carroll Reece argued that the Democratic National Committee Chairman's statements on domestic policy bore

> a definite made-in-Moscow label. That is why I believe I am justified in saying that from a long-range viewpoint the choice which confronts Americans this year is between communism and republicanism. I am sure that all of you [Republicans]

32. *Ibid.*, 4361. Prohibitionists and the "extremists" persistently developed this theme. Jennings reiterated the charge in 1948. *Ibid.*, 80th Cong., 2d sess., 1948, XCIV, Part 2, 2149. In 1949, the president of the Woman's Christian Temperance Union blamed postwar problems on drinking at Yalta. *Chicago Tribune*, August 22, 1949, 28. Both Westbrook Pegler and the *Chicago Tribune* emphasized that drinking at Yalta was one cause for the conference's disastrous results. *Chicago Herald-American*, November 14, 1947, 3. *Chicago Tribune*, January 11, 1948, 20; August 26, 1949, 10.

33. U.S. *Congressional Record*, 79th Cong., 2d sess., 1946, XCII, Parts 3, 7, 8, and 9, 3841, 9060–63, 10534, A1199–1200.

will agree that no taint of communism attaches to the Republican Party. The same cannot be said of our opposition.[34]

The "extremists" argued that the New Deal's foreign policy was also communistic. The *Chicago Tribune* expressed opposition to moderate Republicans by noting that adoption of men like Vandenberg or Harold Stassen as Republican standard-bearers in the 1948 campaign would preclude the use of such foreign policy decisions as those made at Yalta. Congressman Charles Vursell (Republican, Illinois) developed this theme when he charged:

> Every American knows that those "four freedoms" were sacrificed for many peoples in many lands at Yalta. What has the New Deal offered the people of the United States in place of the "four freedoms"? The New Deal offers the four C's, confusion, control, corruption and communism. . . . When the home, the church, the fireside, and the flag replace the four C's, the American people will enjoy the freedom they so richly deserve and are entitled to enjoy.[35]

In 1946, Republican tacticians rejected the approach advanced by the "extremists" and used the issue of Yalta only in Polish-American districts. In those areas, voters resented the decision to use the Curzon line as the eastern boundary of Poland, and they had become increasingly concerned about the lack of free elections in Poland. Accordingly, Republicans had a chance to capture the Polish-American vote. In a nationally distributed handbook, the Chairman of the Cook County (Illinois) Republican Committee urged Republican precinct workers to campaign in Polish districts. He stated that Polish-American resentment about Yalta provided the opportunity to divert Polish-American loyalty from the Democratic party.[36] Congressman Alvin O'Konski also helped his party by campaigning in Chicago [37] and other cities with large Eastern European and Baltic populations. His theme was the "Democratic betrayal" of Poland, other Eastern European countries, and the Baltic states at the Yalta Conference.[38]

These Republican tactics brought limited success. Some Polish-

34. *Ibid.*, Part 11, A3441.
35. *Ibid.*, Part 12, A4801. *Chicago Tribune*, June 11, 1946, 14.
36. John Leonard East, *Republican Precinct Workers Handbook*, 76.
37. *Chicago Tribune*, November 1, 1946, 3; November 2, 1946, 3; November 3, 1946, 7.
38. Alvin O'Konski, interview, July 10, 1962. Congressman Zablocki confirmed that the Republicans had used Yalta during the campaign. He felt that their use of this issue was one factor that led to the Democrats' 1946 defeat in Milwaukee. Congressman Clement Zablocki, interview, July 24, 1962.

American leaders who had been Democrats became Republicans. The most dramatic switch was that of Charles Rozmarek, president of the Polish-American Congress. In April, the President of the Wisconsin Young Democrats, a Polish-American, joined the Republican party,[39] and in October, the officers of the War Veterans Committee for a Free Poland urged Chicago Poles to vote Republican. These officers favorably contrasted Republican criticisms with Democratic non-disavowal of Yalta.[40] On October 28, Chicago Republican leaders were invited, reportedly for the first time, to meetings of important Polish groups. At these meetings, Republican candidates and party leaders vehemently assailed Yalta.[41]

The Republicans were unable to capture the Polish-American vote permanently, but they did try to utilize Polish disaffection over the "injustices" to Poland that the Yalta conferees allegedly perpetrated at the conference[42] and the formal protests enunciated by prominent Polish-Americans.[43] In the 1947 mayoralty election in heavily Polish-populated Chicago, the Republicans again attempted to capitalize on this resentment over Yalta. The *Chicago Tribune*, Senator Wayland Brooks (Republican, Illinois), and Congressman Alvin O'Konski campaigned for the Republican candidate, Russell Root, and emphasized the "Democratic betrayal" of Poland at Yalta. They urged Polish-Americans to support Root as one means of "wiping the slate clean" of such secret agreements as those made at Yalta. Indeed, the *Tribune* charged that a vote for the Democratic candidate, Martin Kennelly, was "an encouragement to continue the policies of loot, starvation, and exile that have brought despair to the peoples of Poland, Hungary, Czechoslovakia, Yugoslavia, and the Baltic states, as well as to Germany, and are laying the foundation for another war. That is what Mr. Kennelly stands for in the campaign and what Mr. Root is against."[44]

These efforts of 1946 and 1947 eventually failed. Besides not being able to match the organizational structure of urban Democratic

39. *Chicago Tribune*, April 25, 1946, 18.
40. *Ibid.*, October 14, 1946, 5; October 27, 1946, 8.
41. *Ibid.*, October 28, 1946, 1; October 31, 1946, 8.
42. U.S. *Congressional Record*, 80th Cong., 1st sess., 1947, XCIII, Parts 4 and 11, 4542, 4544, 4546–47, A2102, A2115, A2156.
43. *Ibid.*, Parts 2, 4, 9, and 10, 2180, 1808–9, 5205–11, A63, A116, A1257, A1125, A1489–90, A1635, A1694, A2739–40, A2873. Stanislaus Mikolajczyk, *The Rape of Poland.* Arthur Bliss Lane, *I Saw Poland Betrayed. Chicago Tribune*, April 5, 1948, 16.
44. *Ibid.*, March 24, 1947, 1, 18. See Appendix R for a breakdown of the Polish-American vote in congressional and national elections during the period 1944–1954.

machines in Polish areas, the Republicans had been defeated by the frontal response of the Democratic National Committee and local candidates, as well as anti-Polish, pro-German stands of the "extremists" and "partisans" on the Oder-Neisse line and the liberalization of immigration policy. The Democratic National Committee answered the Republican charges by openly and positively championing Yalta. The Teheran, Yalta, and Potsdam conferences, the committee insisted, confirmed the Democratic party's role in achieving Allied unity. Striking at Republican isolationism and obstructionism, the committee observed, "The Democratic Administration did not wait for the end of the war to start preparing for peace; and today the whole effort of the Administration is centered on fulfilling the promises which were held out to the world in the Atlantic Charter and at Yalta." [45] The Republican efforts were also doomed by the stated positions of some Republicans. Independent of their championing the Polish cause over the decision to use the Curzon line, the "extremists" and "partisans" disagreed with the Polish-Americans about the question of the Oder-Neisse line and President Truman's proposed displaced persons bill. In debates on these issues, the "extremists" and "partisans" simply castigated Yalta, but they called the prospect of establishing the Oder-Neisse line as Poland's western boundary a "grave injustice" to Germany. They also opposed liberalizing the immigration policy and blamed the problem of displaced persons on Roosevelt's private decisions.[46]

The Administration's constructive, bipartisan outlook was the norm in early 1947. Most Republicans, either on principle or for expediency, praised the postwar Administration's foreign policy because it was bipartisan. Republicans as diverse as Senators Styles Bridges, Arthur Vandenberg, and Congressman John Lodge (Connecticut) demanded that the Administration fulfill its responsibility to see that the Yalta Far Eastern and Eastern European agreements were enforced. Democratic Congressmen Michael Feighan (Ohio), John McCormack (Massachusetts), Charles Melvin Price (Illinois), and Thomas Gordon (Illinois), *Time* magazine, *The New York Times*, and even the Polish-American Congress agreed with these Republicans. They did not directly question the rationale or the essence of these Yalta agreements; they portrayed enforcement as an action that would lead to peace by reducing distrust and suspicion. Indeed, John Foster Dulles virtually apologized for the conference:

45. Democratic National Committee, *Campaign Issues . . . 1946: A Handbook for Candidates, Speakers and Workers of the Democratic Party*, 92–102.
46. *Chicago Tribune*, June 14, 1947, 2; June 16, 1947, 16.

It was vital that the war unity of these three [the United States, Great Britain, and the U.S.S.R.] be preserved and Soviet leadership relied on that to bargain at Teheran and Yalta. As a result, Soviet land policy was further extended in Europe and in the Pacific.[47]

This Republican commitment to bipartisanship and support in matters of foreign policy inevitably frustrated the "extremists." They had hoped, as the *Chicago Tribune* reported, that the Republican congressional majority would investigate the "secret" history of the Roosevelt Administration's "treacherous years," particularly the Yalta Conference. The *Tribune* specifically urged the new Congress to repudiate the bipartisan foreign policy and, as a necessary first step, to adopt a resolution declaring that the United States was not bound by the Teheran, Yalta, and Potsdam agreements. When, instead, the Senate voted to confirm George Marshall as Secretary of State and the House Committee on Foreign Affairs limited its investigation of the State Department to the conduct of the war, the *Tribune*'s editors reacted vehemently. The *Tribune* again emphasized the importance of repudiating Yalta, particularly those provisions concerning the "exploitation" of Germany, and the necessity for publishing all of the Yalta "secrets." [48]

Prior to the announcement of the Truman Doctrine, the Yalta Conference was involved in controversy not because the nature of its agreements seemed wrong but because their disclosure had been delayed. The "extremists'" attacks on Yalta and the Administration's foreign policy carried little weight in Republican congressional or national strategy. Although Republican spokesmen, both "partisans" and "moderates," had become more critical of the conference, they demanded the implementation of the Yalta agreements, not their repudiation. Diplomatic pressure, many people hoped, would achieve Soviet compliance with the Yalta pledges.

---

47. U.S. *Congressional Record*, 80th Cong., 1st sess., 1947, XCIII, Parts 1, 2, 10, and 11, 144–45, 641–42, 734, 990, 994–95, 1575–78, A80–81, A262, A343, A378–79, A565, A1970. Polish-American Congress, *Memorandum on Poland to Honorable George C. Marshall*, 8. *Polish-American Congress Bulletin*, III, 6 (February, 1947). Joseph Kania, telegram to President Truman, April 17, 1947, Truman Papers, OF 463, Truman Library. *The New York Times*, January 7, 1947, 26; January 9, 1947, 22; January 27, 1947, 22; February 22, 1947, 12. *Time*, 49 (January 20, 1947), 54.

48. *Chicago Tribune*, November 8, 1946, 16; November 18, 1946, 18; November 28, 1946, 26; December 3, 1946, 20; December 18, 1946, 22; December 20, 1946, 22; December 31, 1946, 8; January 5, 1947, 1, 4; January 8, 1947, 18; January 9, 1947, 20; January 16, 1947, 18; February 6, 1947, 18.

chapter 4

1946–1948: the emergence of partisan politics, part two

The "partisans" and "moderates" became more critical of Yalta in late 1947 and 1948, but they still wanted to be associated with internationalism and to avoid the stigmas of isolationism and partisanship that marked the "extremists'" position. The "extremists" persisted in their efforts to discredit the New Deal and the Truman Administration's continuation of New Deal reforms as well as its internationalist approach. In spite of their persistent and bitter criticism of the Administration's foreign policy, they were basically not interested in foreign policy matters as such. The congressional debates on the Truman Doctrine and the Marshall Plan confirmed this difference: The "partisans" attempted, within a bipartisan, internationalist framework, to discredit Roosevelt and thereby embarrass the Truman Administration; the "extremists" were fundamentally interested in obstructing any form of internationalism.

President Truman's March 12, 1947, and Secretary of State Marshall's June 5, 1947, requests for aid to reconstruct Europe marked a radical change in postwar U.S. foreign policy. On the one hand, these actions committed the United States to the defense and support of lands that did not belong to it and thus extended the definition of those interests affecting the national security. In a different sense, these policies marked a sharp break from Roosevelt's conciliatory, noninterventionist policies toward the Soviet Union and the underdeveloped countries. Aid to Europe, more specifically to the royalist Greek government and the equally conservative Turkish government, indicated not support for democracy but opposition to communism. With the Truman Doctrine, the Administration formally broke from Yalta's spirit of co-operation with the Soviet Union and reliance on the United Nations and adopted the containment policy of negotiating from military strength and promoting political stability.

Although many liberals and internationalists in the United States criticized it, the Truman Doctrine did receive popular support. The U.S. public, increasingly more suspicious of Soviet aspirations, had become disillusioned by the Soviet Union's refusal to comply with the U.S. interpretation of the Yalta agreements. Most people welcomed this new policy of military and economic aid to Greece and Turkey because it showed the Administration's intention to resort to more than mere verbal protests.

During congressional consideration of the Truman Doctrine, the Administration, recognizing the need for Republican support, sought to avoid the semblance of partisanship. To justify this policy of confrontation, Democratic spokesmen emphasized the postwar experiences that had necessitated this change in policy from co-operation to containment. Congressmen James Richards (Democrat, South Carolina), William Whittington (Democrat, Mississippi), and Senator James Eastland (Democrat, Mississippi) denied that past Administration policies had been weak or had failed, but they conceded that those policies had not yielded expected results. They blamed this failure on the Soviet refusal either to adhere to its commitments or to reach agreement.[1]

For the "partisans" and "extremists," who had accused the Truman Administration of appeasing the Soviet Union, the Truman Doctrine posed a dilemma. Here was a hard-line policy, but it involved both economic and military international commitments. They could not summarily assail Administration appeasement; consistency alone required that they support this policy. The "extremists" and "partisans" resolved this political dilemma in different ways. Both groups used the Truman Doctrine to denounce past policy, particularly the Yalta agreements. The "partisans" supported the Truman Doctrine as a welcome change from what they termed mistaken policies of co-operation, and took credit for this shift. The "extremists," however, opposed the Truman Doctrine and called it an aggressive policy that would possibly weaken the United States.

The "partisans" and "moderates" had to support the Truman Doctrine. As members of the majority party in Congress, they could not simply criticize or oppose; they had to take affirmative action. Moreover, these Republicans were eager to escape the isolationist stigma given the party by Republicans who had defeated the League of Nations and blocked Roosevelt's efforts during the 1930's. As members of the majority party, however, they were in a good bargaining position — the Administration was dependent upon their support.

Congressman Karl Mundt attempted to capitalize on the Ad-

1. U.S. *Congressional Record*, 80th Cong., 1st sess., 1947, XCIII, Parts 3 and 4, 3324, 3327, 4689–91, 4793–94.

ministration's dependence. On March 20, during the House Foreign
Affairs Committee's hearings on the Truman Doctrine, Mundt specifically asked Acting Secretary of State Dean Acheson why the complete texts of the Yalta, Teheran, and Potsdam agreements could not
be made public. In reply to Mundt's question, Acheson stated that
all the items of the Yalta and Potsdam protocols had already been
made public. He added that he would look into the matter and let
the committee have his judgment on publication of the formal texts.[2]
Addressing the House later in the day, Mundt argued:

> I think it especially important that the administration make
> available to Congress and the country photostatic copies of
> the agreements which were made and signed at the conferences
> held in Cairo, Teheran, Yalta, and Potsdam. It is quite ap-
> parent to us all that the implications of the present situation
> in Greece and Turkey and the vast ramifications flowing from
> the proposals cannot be divorced from the agreements and
> commitments made at these historic conferences.[3]

At a session of the hearings on March 21, Mundt again pressed
Acheson about the existence of any further agreements. He asked
whether Acheson felt that the country was entitled to this information. Acheson stated that at that moment he lacked the information
to reply but hoped to have it before the end of the day. Congressman
John Davis Lodge (Republican, Connecticut) then asked Acheson
if the Yalta, Teheran, and Potsdam agreements were binding on the
United States. Action on some of these conferences' subjects (military matters), Acheson asserted, was within the constitutional powers
of the President, while action on others was within his negotiating
powers and would have to be ratified by Congress or by the Senate.[4]
When the State Department released the formal texts of the
Yalta and Potsdam agreements three days later, Mundt praised the
department's performance,[5] but his concern for these texts seemed
to come more from partisan motives than from any impartial desire
for information. His request had no relation to any of the Yalta agreements. Although he and other "partisans" may have hoped to find a
Yalta agreement concerning Greece, they apparently intended to
find new grounds for critically contrasting the agreements with the

---

2. U.S. House of Representatives, Committee on Foreign Affairs, *Hearings
on H.R. 2616: A Bill to Provide Assistance to Greece and Turkey*, 80th Cong.,
1st sess., 1947, 8.
3. U.S. *Congressional Record*, 80th Cong., 1st sess., 1947, XCIII, Part 10,
A1155.
4. *Hearings on H.R. 2616*, 60–61.
5. *Ibid.*, 94.

Administration's shift to an anti-Soviet policy. The committee members' written questions to the State Department exemplified the nature of their concern. The answers to these questions, which were possibly designed to embarrass the Administration, would have revealed nothing about the basis for the Truman Doctrine.[6]

Congressmen John Vorys (Republican, Ohio), Walter Judd, Robert Hale (Republican, Maine), Karl Mundt, Chester Merrow, and Jay LeFevre (Republican, New York) also welcomed the Doctrine's firmer policy toward the Soviet Union and contrasted it to Yalta's "weak" approach. Mundt averred that the Truman Administration had been forced to change its foreign policy because of the Republicans' 1946 electoral success and their demands for a firmer policy. Merrow and Hale criticized Soviet expansion into Eastern Europe as a violation of Yalta agreements, and Merrow further demanded that the Soviet Union be pressured into compliance with the Yalta and other agreements.[7] In a more partisan vein, Congressmen Alvin O'Konski and Frank Mathews (Republican, New Jersey) questioned the sincerity of the Administration's anti-Communist credentials. Ascribing current problems to Yalta, these congressmen deemed the Doctrine simply a political maneuver by the Administration to regain lost popularity.[8]

The "extremists" opposed the Truman Doctrine's far-reaching economic and political commitments. They demanded that U.S. commitments be limited and suggested that the Congress repudiate the Yalta agreements instead of implementing the Doctrine. According to Congressmen Clarence Brown (Republican, Ohio), John Robsion (Republican, Kentucky), Marion Bennett (Republican, Missouri), Frederick Smith, Lawrence Smith, Charles Vursell, William Lemke (Republican, North Dakota), George Bender (Republican, Ohio), Howard Buffett (Republican, Nebraska), John Bennett (Republican, Michigan), Senator Hugh Butler (Republican, Nebraska), and the *Chicago Tribune*, the Yalta conferees had already sown the seeds of World War III, and the Truman Doctrine might do nothing but precipitate this conflict. They wanted fuller knowledge of the Doctrine's commitments because, they hinted, those commitments might set a precedent for future aid to other nations. Their primary fear,

6. See Appendix C for a list of these questions.
7. U.S. *Congressional Record*, 80th Cong., 1st sess., 1947, XCIII, Parts 3, 4, 10, 11, and 12, 3784, 4623–24, 4635–37, 4947, A1305–6, A1391, A2192, A3050, A1197. Judd initially had criticized the Truman Doctrine for bypassing the UN, but later, in May, he contended that Roosevelt had been outtraded at Yalta because of his hope of creating an effective UN.
8. *Ibid.*, Parts 2 and 4, 2460, 4798.

however, was that this policy would so weaken the U.S. economy that socialism would ensue. Indeed, Buffett said, "So, besides involving the United States in bankruptcy commitments abroad, a communist drive would divert suspicion and attention from Stalin's agents in the New Deal."

Buffett, Marion Bennett, and the *Tribune* reiterated this concern about internal security. Bennett argued that the place to fight communism was in the United States rather than Greece. Implying that both the Truman Doctrine and Yalta benefited communism, Buffett stated his doubts that the New Deal, after promoting communism for years, could suddenly become anti-Communist. In fact, he suggested, Stalin might want U.S. intervention in the Balkans, and he added that a Communist could pursue no more effective course in 1947 than to appear to be anti-Communist. The *Tribune* expressed suspicion of any policy proposed by Truman, Vandenberg, and the "New Dealers." [9]

The "extremists" and the "partisans" had, in conflicting ways, deprecated the New Deal, but they had not convinced Republican leaders that the Democrats could be defeated only by undermining public faith in the Administration's direction of foreign policy. Most Republicans tempered their criticisms and usually confined them to specific proposals. Even Mundt's criticisms did not imply that the Administration was untrustworthy.

The Marshall Plan debates of late 1947 and early 1948 further highlighted the "partisans'" political exploitation of the Administration's changed position on foreign policy and the "extremists'" basic negativism. The rhetoric of both factions was anti-Communist, but the "partisans" emphasized the Soviet threat and the need for a more hard-line approach, while the "extremists" impugned the New Deal and domestic radicalism.

The "partisans" commented on Yalta during the debates on the Marshall Plan only when they thought it would help their party. They supported the present Administration's foreign policy but denounced that of the past and blamed the country's problems on the

9. *Ibid.*, Parts 2, 3, 4, and 10, 2215–17, 2335–37, 2783–85, 2833, 2849, 3369–70, 4598–99, 4600, 4606, 4685–86, 4731–32, 4611, 4621, 4628, 4924, A1123–24, A1195–96. *Chicago Tribune*, March 13, 1947, 18; March 14, 1947, 16; March 21, 1947, 9; March 22, 1947, 1; March 26, 1947, 14; April 10, 1947, 18. Indeed, Republican Congressman Noah Mason opposed any form of foreign aid. Simply castigating Yalta for existing international problems, Mason expressed this "extremist" obsession with domestic developments by suggesting that only a general "house-cleaning" was needed. U.S. *Congressional Record*, 80th Cong., 2d sess., 1948, XCIV, Part 10, A1635.

Yalta Conference. Congressman Karl Mundt and Senator Henry Cabot Lodge stated that Yalta's weak policy had increased Soviet postwar strength. They noted that pressure from the Republican Eightieth Congress had forced the Administration to adopt a firmer policy.[10]

The "extremists" used the debate to charge that past Administration policy had caused the current European economic crisis. *The Saturday Evening Post*, the *Chicago Tribune*, George Sokolsky, Senators Robert Taft, Edward Martin (Republican, Pennsylvania), Congressmen George Bender, Frederick Smith, Clare Hoffman, John Phillips (Republican, California), Charles Vursell, William Lemke, Charles Halleck (Republican, Indiana), Howard Buffett, and Hubert Ellis all blamed Yalta's appeasement for Western Europe's economic problems. Except the *Post*, they simultaneously denied that any amount of economic aid could correct Yalta's disastrous results and argued that such aid would undermine the U.S. economy and precipitate another world war. The Plan, they further implied, was an attempt to regiment the U.S. economy and to divert public attention from the internal Communist threat. As one step toward a more effective foreign policy, they advocated the displacement of Truman, Marshall, and other "New Dealers." Buffett also proposed repudiation of the unconditional-surrender policy because this policy had ruthlessly destroyed Japan and Germany — the "natural" bastions, strategically and politically, against the spread of communism. Developing this theme, Vursell insisted upon the continuation of U.S. aid to Austria and Germany and the termination of Soviet occupation of Eastern Germany. He contended:

> If we lose the peace, the responsibility for losing the peace shall be placed on the doorstep of the Yalta conference, and the failure to allow British and American troops to go on and take Berlin. . . . I cite the record of the past major mistakes of the State Department and the administration leaders, that we may better determine in the light of past performances the Congress is justified in trusting the judgment of our leaders in their new plan for rebuilding western Europe.[11]

10. U.S. *Congressional Record*, 80th Cong., 1st sess., 1947, XCIII, Parts 4 and 13, 5233–35, A4794–95. Similarly, Congressman Judd, while introducing an amendment that extended economic aid to Greece, Turkey, and China, assailed the Yalta betrayal of Eastern Europe and China. Judd did not, however, advocate repudiation. His criticism of Yalta was confined to berating past mistakes or weakness. *Ibid.*, 2d sess., 1948, XCIV, Part 3, 3331–33.

11. *The Saturday Evening Post*, 220 (November 22, 1947), 168. The *Post* did support the Marshall Plan but demanded the removal of the controls imposed upon Germany at Yalta and after the war. This German bias constituted

Confident that the Soviet Union was intent on communizing the world, an assessment seemingly confirmed by the Czechoslovak coup in February, 1948, the Truman Administration steadily increased its reliance on military power. In March, the Brussels Pact was ratified, and the U.S. Senate paved the way for the formation of NATO by approving the Vandenberg Resolution. This action marked a shift from the Truman Doctrine's and Marshall Plan's policies of predominantly economic aid. From policies first of seeking co-operation and then of promoting stability through economic aid, the United States Government had become committed to a policy that relied on military alliances and military aid.

President Truman defended the correctness and necessity of this change in policy. In an address to the American Society of Newspaper Editors on April 17 and in a press conference on April 23, he praised the Yalta and Potsdam conferences as noble efforts to achieve understanding and trust with the Soviet Union. Truman attributed the failures of these conferences to produce lasting results to Soviet bad faith and wondered whether the Soviet Union simply made agreements with the intention of later violating them. After stressing the need to rely on force, he stated that U.S. policy goals had not changed but that the means of achieving them had.[12]

Independent of the militarization of the Administration's policy, in 1948 the political climate in the United States remained forward looking and responsible. Most Republicans, when criticizing foreign policy, cited past decisions to show the kind of commitment they would avoid. They did not propose to repudiate past policy nor did they try to discredit the Truman Administration by decrying past

---

a central plank of the "extremists'" assault on not only the Marshall Plan but also the Administration's German policy in general. The "extremists" specifically demanded the end of all postwar restrictions on Germany. *Chicago Tribune*, June 7, 1947, 12; October 30, 1947, 16; April 5, 1948, 18; June 30, 1948, 16; July 11, 1948, 18; July 12, 1948, 18; July 17, 1948, 6; August 11, 1948, 18; November 18, 1948, 7; December 22, 1948, 18. *Chicago Herald-American*, May 1, 1947, 22; May 2, 1947, 19; August 1, 1947, 15; November 12, 1947, 20. U.S. *Congressional Record*, 80th Cong., 1st sess., 1947, XCIII, Parts 7, 9, and 13, 8985–88, 10645, 10656–60, 10804–8, 10872–74, 10929, 11198–99, 11283–84, A4003, A4251, A4501–2, A4748; *ibid.*, 2d sess., 1948, XCIV, Parts 2, 3, 9, and 10, 2549, 3241, 3626, 3659–61, A55, A933–34, A2105.

12. Harry S. Truman, speech, April 17, 1948, Washington, D.C., Records of White House Official Reporter, Truman Papers, Truman Library. Transcript of press conference, April 23, 1948, Records of White House Official Reporter, Truman Papers, Truman Library. *The New York Times*, in a series of editorials during 1948, echoed this view of postwar developments, defending Yalta and the necessity for a firmer policy. *The New York Times*, February 26, 1948, 22; March 3, 1948, 22; April 16, 1948, 22; April 20, 1948, 22, 26; May 13, 1948, 24; May 19, 1948, 26; May 24, 1948, 18.

policy decisions. Republican leaders wished, above all, to avoid the image of partisanship and to free the party of any stigma of the "extremists'" negativism.

Approaching the 1948 campaign, both major parties called for unity and co-operation on foreign policy. Both President Truman and Republican Congressman Chester Merrow endorsed this view. Although he had been critical of former policy for not being firm enough, Merrow hoped that both national conventions would adopt "an identical bipartisan foreign policy platform. It would be an announcement that the United States faces the world with a solid united front. It would be clearly understood that we intend to approach international issues in bipartisan unity and not in partisan dissension."[13]

In the presidential primaries, only the "extremists" criticized the bipartisan foreign policy and the past Administration's foreign policy decisions. Prior to the Republican National Convention, the "extremists" pressured the Republican party to adopt foreign policy as a campaign issue. Westbrook Pegler, George Sokolsky, and the *Chicago Tribune* proposed Yalta, and New Deal foreign policy in general, as the principal issue in the forthcoming campaign. They argued that the Republican party could safely repudiate all of Roosevelt's and Truman's concessions to the Soviet Union. The party would certainly lose, they averred, if it supported the bipartisan foreign policy, the policy of the "New Deal and of professed Republicans who have sold out their party." Their particular targets were Republican Senator Arthur Vandenberg, the symbol of the bipartisan foreign policy, and Franklin Roosevelt, who they identified as the "greatest friend" the Communists ever had.[14]

The tone of the 1948 campaign as well as the tenets of the 1948 platform and the tenor of the remarks of speakers at the Republican National Convention indicated the Republican leaders' tacit rejection of this argument. In their speeches Charles Halleck, Kenneth Wherry, Clare Boothe Luce, and Dwight Green mainly criticized New Deal domestic policies and principles. Even their critical references to Yalta portrayed the conference as an example of New Deal leadership.

13. U.S. *Congressional Record*, 80th Cong., 2d sess., 1948, XCIV, Part 3, 3998.

14. *Chicago Herald-American*, June 19, 1947, 21; June 27, 1947, 7; March 27, 1948, 3. *Chicago Tribune*, September 19, 1947, 22; December 15, 1947, 3; March 29, 1948, 20; April 21, 1948, 20; April 22, 1948, 3; April 27, 1948, 1; May 9, 1948, 24; May 11, 1948, 14; May 19, 1948, 6; June 15, 1948, 16; June 21, 1948, 20.

The Republican Eightieth Congress, they said, had partially corrected these mistaken and burdensome agreements.[15]

The Republican presidential candidate and the Republican National Committee never identified these past decisions as New Deal policies. Although they referred to "Communists in Government" and criticized the foreign policy of the Roosevelt and Truman administrations, the Republicans chose to accentuate their greater administrative expertise. They could do a better job. They pointed to Democratic mistakes and pledged a spotless, efficient Administration. This condescending temperateness partially came from their confidence of success: They did not want to alienate the Democrats, whose congressional support they would need. Even Herbert Hoover, who asserted that many of the "past mistakes" could have been avoided, said that the Republican party and the nation faced a world situation requiring action, not regrets.[16]

The Republican platform reflected this attitude. It criticized secret agreements, not because they were harmful, but because the public had not been informed. It expressed opposition to appeasement but stressed the need for co-operation. In short, the platform urged a firm policy toward the Soviet Union rather than withdrawal into Fortress America and nonrecognition of the Soviet government. It pledged to make all foreign commitments public and subject to constitutional ratification. It did not demand the repudiation of Yalta or pledge to publish the Yalta proceedings, but it did prescribe the future Republican course of action. The Republicans did not simply castigate Democratic policy; they propounded a foreign policy of their own. The platform's statement on foreign policy closed with a plea to the Democrats to join with them to stop politics in foreign policy.[17]

The Republicans' commitment to a bipartisan foreign policy did not mean the absence of criticism. They contended that they were obligated to criticize policy constructively. Thus, B. Carroll Reece, chairman of the Republican National Committee, said:

> Our Party, by its record over the past few years . . . has demonstrated its willingness to cooperate with the present Administration on vital issues of foreign policy. *But that does*

15. *Official Report of the Proceedings of the Twenty-fourth Republican National Convention, 1948*, 46, 57–59, 69, 173–74.

16. Herbert Hoover, speech before the Republican National Committee, June 22, 1948.

17. "The 1948 Platform of the Republican Party." For text of plank on foreign policy, see Appendix D.

NOT mean that we are foreclosed from criticizing policies which have resulted in our involvement in our present difficulties. We have been willing to clean up the mess, but we have NOT condoned policies which have got us into the mess.[18]

Republicans would attack the vulnerable results of Yalta agreements, but they would not cite those agreements as evidence of Democratic treason or blundering. In 1948, Republican strategy dictated that the party's candidates point to the mistakes of Yalta as examples of actions to shun in the future. After stating that concentration on mistakes of the past accomplished nothing and then listing those mistakes, Republican candidates advocated a policy of firmness.[19] They pledged support for the bipartisan foreign policy, emphasized the role of the predominantly Republican Eightieth Congress in promoting such a policy, and criticized the Administration only for not acting more quickly and firmly.[20]

National Republican leaders did try to influence two groups of voters by specifically attacking Yalta. The Republican National Committee directed a set of pamphlets at veterans groups, presumably the most militantly patriotic groups in the United States. In these pamphlets, the committee pointed out that, while the veterans won the war, the Administration had lost the peace at Yalta and Potsdam. The committee berated Yalta for its secrecy and the Administration for its appeasement of Russia.[21] Presidential candidate Thomas Dewey, vice-presidential candidate Earl Warren, and the Republi-

18. B. Carroll Reece, "United We Win," *The Republican News*, June, 1948.

19. Thomas Dewey, address, Salt Lake City, Utah, September 30, 1948. News Release, Republican National Committee. Earl Warren, address, Louisville, Kentucky, September 22, 1948. News Release, Republican National Committee. Earl Warren, address, Spokane, Washington, October 13, 1948. News Release, Republican National Committee. Arthur Vandenberg, address over CBS, October 4, 1948. News Release, Republican National Committee. Eugene Milliken, address, New York City, New York, October 21, 1948. News Release, Republican National Committee.

20. Republican National Committee, *Dewey in '48: He Gets Things Done*. During the 1948 campaign, Dewey expressed support for a bipartisan foreign policy, advocated the inclusion of China in the Marshall Plan, opposed a policy of appeasing the Soviet Union, and demanded a firmer stance toward the Soviet Union. Although Charles Halleck indicated his support for the UN in his report on the 80th Congress, he criticized the Administration's former reliance on secrecy and the "New Deal President's" abuse of power when concluding executive agreements "detrimental to our interests." Republican National Committee, *The 80th Congress Delivers!* 44–45.

21. Republican National Committee, *Veterans . . . Look! Before You Vote*. Republican National Committee, *The Veterans Case Against the Democrat-New Deal*. Republican National Committee, *Veterans the Peace for which You Fought*.

can National Committee also used Yalta in their appeals to Polish-Americans. None of these Republicans demanded repudiation of the Yalta agreements or the liberation of Eastern Europe, but they did connect Poland's "tragic" fate to the Administration's "secret" diplomacy at Yalta, and they called for a firmer policy toward the Soviet Union. The isolated partisan references to Yalta were moderate in tone. They were used to win votes rather than to undermine public confidence in the Administration or the bipartisan containment policy.[22]

As one result of this Republican strategy, Charles Rozmarek, president of the Polish-American Congress, formally supported national and Illinois Republican candidates in the 1948 election. He charged that Roosevelt had betrayed Poland at Yalta and that Truman had not corrected the situation.[23] The effect of Rozmarek's remarks and the Republicans' 1948 Yalta appeal was minimal. Although many Polish-Americans in Chicago voted for Dewey, Truman carried the city.

The "extremists" persistently attacked New Deal foreign policy. Westbrook Pegler, George Sokolsky, and the *Chicago Tribune* reviled Roosevelt's leadership. According to them, Roosevelt's appeasement policy at Yalta had enabled the Soviet Union to expand its territory and increase its strength. They suggested that Roosevelt had made the concessions partly because he had secured the Communist vote of New York State in the 1944 election. During the 1948 campaign, none of these "extremists" argued that Dewey's failure to adopt foreign policy as a major campaign issue was tactically disastrous. (They would develop this theme only after Truman's surprising success.) The *Chicago Tribune*, however, emphasized the needlessness of the Yalta, Teheran, and Potsdam concessions, and in September, 1948, it asked why Dewey had failed to develop the charges made by William Bullitt.[24]

22. *Chicago Tribune*, May 31, 1948, 13; June 4, 1948, 4; October 24, 1948, 7. Earl Warren, address, Buffalo, New York, September 25, 1948. News Release, Republican National Committee. Earl Warren, address, Chicago, Illinois, October 6, 1948. News Release, Republican National Committee. Thomas Dewey, address, Chicago, Illinois, October 26, 1948. News Release, Republican National Committee. Both Illinois Republican candidates for re-election, Senator Wayland Brooks and Governor Dwight Green, sought to capture the Polish-American vote by regularly assailing the Yalta betrayal of Poland. *Chicago Tribune*, October 13, 1948, 1; October 21, 1948, 5, 7.

23. *Ibid.*, June 7, 1948, 15; October 31, 1948, 7.

24. *Ibid.*, July 14, 1958, 18; July 26, 1948, 18; September 10, 1948, 20; September 28, 1948, 15; October 5, 1948, 6; October 18, 1948, 3; October 19, 1948, 6; October 23, 1948, 10; October 27, 1948, 22. *Chicago Herald-American*,

Bullitt's charges had appeared in *Life* magazine on August 30 and September 6, 1948, at the inception of the 1948 campaign. Before becoming *Life's* foreign correspondent in 1944, Bullitt had served as an ambassador under Roosevelt.[25] In these articles, Bullitt charged that Roosevelt's and Truman's errors at Teheran, Yalta, and Potsdam had "lost" the peace. Roosevelt had erred when, because of poor advice from the State Department and his own and Harry Hopkins' "wishful appeasement" of the Soviets, he failed to secure definite written pledges from the Soviet Union during the war.[26] Roosevelt's inordinate faith in his ability to deal with Stalin had led to Yalta's results. At Yalta, Roosevelt had been "more than tired" and had had difficulty in "formulating and expressing his thoughts." Recalling that certain Yalta agreements were kept secret from Byrnes, Bullitt noted that the U.S. public, unaware that it had been "bamboozled," had initially applauded Roosevelt's return from Yalta.[27] Not having personally attended Yalta, Bullitt could not have known whether Roosevelt had trouble expressing his thoughts, was more than tired, or whether Roosevelt had difficulty in formulating his thoughts.

These attempts to discredit Roosevelt's foreign policy failed in 1948. The public believed that isolationism had caused World War II, and they considered a policy of international involvement — a responsible and reasonable, fair yet peaceful foreign policy   essential. Such a policy seemingly had been implemented by Truman over opposition by conservative Republicans. The Eightieth Congress' support for the Administration's foreign policy, moreover, had limited Dewey's and the Republican National Committee's use of foreign policy. Criticizing the past would have left them open to charges of attempting to undermine the foreign policy that "moderate" and "partisan" Republicans had helped establish. In addition, the House Un-American Activities Committee's charges of "Communists in Government" carried little weight in the campaign. Most people considered communism an external threat, and the Un-American Activities Committee's quest for publicity and its obvious partisanship reduced its

---

July 9, 1948, 16; August 19, 1948, 22; August 22, 1948, 10; September 10, 1948, 32; September 16, 1948, 3; October 7, 1948, 34; November 3, 1948, 3; November 9, 1948, 3.

25. Bullitt served as U.S. Ambassador to the Soviet Union (1933–1936), France (1936–1941), at-large (1941–1942), and special assistant to the Secretary of Navy (1942–1943).

26. William Bullitt, "How We Won the War and Lost the Peace, Part One," *Life*, 25, No. 9 (August 30, 1948), 91–94.

27. William Bullitt, "How We Won the War and Lost the Peace, Part Two," *Life*, 25, No. 10 (September 6, 1948), 86–90.

effectiveness. Also, President Truman's establishment of a loyalty program for federal employees and the Attorney General's prosecution of domestic Communists temporarily neutralized these charges.

During the campaign, the Democrats defended Yalta and Potsdam as realistic efforts to achieve peace, efforts frustrated by Soviet intransigence and bad faith. They maintained that when co-operation failed, the Administration then shifted to a policy relying on military and economic strength. They contrasted their support for the Truman Doctrine, Marshall Plan, Berlin blockade, the Vandenberg Resolution, and their role in formulating and sustaining the United Nations with the obstructionist tactics of the "extremist" Republicans. The Democrats used the "extremists'" irresponsibility to question Republican dedication to the bipartisan foreign policy, and they argued that not attempting to co-operate with the Soviet Union in 1945 would have impaired the war effort.[28]

The Republicans were the vulnerable party in 1948. The Administration's persistent protests to the Soviet Union about developments in Eastern Europe and Manchuria pointed to Soviet culpability rather than laxness in the Administration. Truman's handling of the Berlin crisis,[29] in which he retained the U.S. position in Berlin by resorting to the air lift, also helped him in the campaign. His action matched forcefulness with the dominant public concern to avoid war. Further, after wartime co-operation failed to endure, the Administration had instituted a hard-line foreign policy represented by the Truman Doctrine and U.S. support for the unification of West Germany. The Roosevelt and Truman administrations' foreign policy seemed correct and reasonable, especially when it was contrasted with that of the "extremist" Republican opposition. Finally, discussion of Yalta or any other event involving foreign policy could not be effective because the real issue in 1948 was domestic. The Republicans' success in 1946 had partially been a result of the public's

28. *Democracy at Work: Being the Official Record of the Democratic National Convention, 1948* (Philadelphia: Local Democratic Political Committee of Pennsylvania, 1948), 8, 9, 35, 43, 44, 46, 99. "The 1948 Platform of the Democratic Party." Democratic National Committee, *Fact Sheet No. 10.* "Files of the Facts. IX: Foreign Policy, 1948 Campaign," Research Division, Democratic National Committee. Harry S Truman, speech, Garrett, Indiana, October 13, 1948, Records of the White House Official Reporter, Truman Papers, Truman Library. Harry S Truman, speech, Boston, Massachusetts, October 27, 1948, Records of the White House Official Reporter, Truman Papers, Truman Library.

29. Significantly, both Ernest Lindley and *The New York Times* assailed the Soviet blockade of Berlin as a violation of the Yalta agreements. *Newsweek*, 32 (August 2, 1948), 24. *The New York Times*, July 16, 1948, 18; July 23, 1948, 18; August 13, 1948, 14; September 10, 1948, 22; October 2, 1948, 14.

reaction to wartime controls and to the number of labor strikes; the Democrats' success in 1948 was due to the policies of the Eightieth Congress.

By showing the popularity of domestic reform and New Deal politics, the 1948 campaign results indicated the need for a revised Republican campaign strategy, and the "extremists'" criticisms of foreign policy portended the future Republican attack. As long as co-operation with the Soviet Union and suspicions of Germany were the norms, the "extremists'" political effectiveness would remain minimal, but the U.S. attitude toward the Soviet Union was increasingly less amenable to compromise. Developments in Germany exemplified the ever-widening breach between the United States and the Soviet Union. The Soviet policy toward Germany had not changed, but Western interests had, and the unification of the Western zones of Germany symbolized this shift. The emergence of new tenets about foreign policy and internal security, and this changed view of Germany and the Soviet Union, abetted the international Cold War. It also fostered a domestic cold war that McCarthyism symbolized and that the House Committee on Un-American Activities and the "extremists" perpetuated. Thus, the "extremists" had introduced the themes that became basic Republican strategy after 1949: the irrelevance of a strong foreign policy without an effective policy for internal security and the need to reassess and repudiate past commitments in order to have a more dynamic foreign policy.

chapter 5
1949: subversion and treason

The year 1949 marked a transition from nominal bipartisanship to outspoken partisanship in the debate on U.S. foreign policy. The "moderates" and "partisans" modified the "extremists'" charges, which they had formerly belittled or ignored, and incorporated them into Republican strategy and tactics. Although Republican leaders tacitly supported the Truman Administration's containment policy, they increased their attacks on earlier foreign policy decisions and gradually abandoned their stance of restained, constructive criticism.

Three events in 1949 — the Soviet explosion of an atomic bomb, Alger Hiss's trial for perjury, and Chiang Kai-shek's military defeat — seemed to substantiate the "extremists'" warnings about threats to internal security. The "extremists," joined by the "partisans," traced the relationship of these events to Yalta and contended that Communist infiltration of the Roosevelt and Truman administrations had created a real danger to internal security, a danger that was the basis for current difficulties. An anti-Communist political rhetoric, which was ostensibly anti-Soviet, came to characterize the domestic political debate. The emphasis was less on the need for a more effective diplomacy than on the importance of improved safeguards for internal security and investigations of loyalty.

The Soviet explosion of an atomic bomb in September, 1949, far ahead of Administration predictions, shattered public confidence. This loss of the U.S. monopoly on atomic weapons increased anxieties about Soviet aims and helped to create a new political climate. Tolerance for radical ideas and for a détente with the Soviet Union decreased. At the same time, support for loyalty investigations and for a deterrent, primarily military foreign policy increased.

The explosion also raised concern about internal security. Had Communist spies made possible this Soviet atomic development? Were more effective security precautions needed? In this context, the Alger Hiss trial assumed particular importance. Because Hiss was an important and respected New Deal official, his trial for perjury made many people in the United States reassess Administration loyalty procedures and the nature of the Communist threat. Hiss's association with New Deal foreign and domestic policies and his important role in helping formulate and popularize the UN inevitably brought these policies into focus. Was Hiss's presumed treason symptomatic? Were other seemingly trustworthy officials spies?

Chiang Kai-shek's military defeat established the possibility that pro-Communists in the State Department had betrayed the Nationalist Chinese. China's territorial expanse, the myths of China's invincibility, Chiang's purported popularity, the delayed disclosure of the Yalta Far Eastern agreements, and the post-1945 policy of aid to China provided vulnerable points for criticisms of the Administration's Far Eastern policy. In 1949, the "extremists'" denunciations of appeasement and charges of a sellout no longer seemed irrational and absurd. Their definite accusations convinced many people who were seeking an explanation for these unexpected developments.

The concurrence of Hiss's trial and Chiang's defeat intensified this reaction. Both were related to Yalta; Alger Hiss had attended, and agreements concerning China had been concluded there. The secrecy of the conference's proceedings and its agreements permitted allegations about Hiss's role and the rationale for the Far Eastern agreements. In 1949, some Republicans would effectively portray the former secrecy surrounding the Yalta Conference as the Administration's deliberate attempt to conceal the results from public review.

Moreover, the nature of President Truman's leadership contributed to this change in public sentiment. Truman's justification in 1947 for his loyalty program had legitimized internal security investigations, and his partisan rejoinder during the 1948 campaign to charges made by the House Committee on Un-American Activities eventually undermined his own credibility. Further, Truman's distrust of the Soviet Union made his defense of Roosevelt's policies seem shallow, apologetic, and partisan. His firm stance in Greece and Western Europe, the announced intention of which was the stemming of Communist expansion, had seemingly confirmed the advantages of a resolute foreign policy. In comparison, the Truman Administration's Far Eastern policy, particularly the efforts of the Marshall mission in 1946, appeared mistaken, stupid, or treasonous.

Finally, the Republican national leaders, whose candidates had lost the 1948 presidential election and the 1949 special U.S. Senate election in New York, had re-evaluated their tactics on foreign policy. The Republican candidates in those elections, Thomas Dewey and John Foster Dulles, had formally supported the bipartisan foreign policy before and during their campaigns, and they had denounced the "extremists'" tactics. In the 1948 campaign, the "extremists" had deplored Dewey's failure to attack past Administration foreign policy, and they later blamed his defeat on this omission. They ascribed Dulles' defeat in 1949 to "me-tooism" and "Deweyism." Blaming Yalta for the Cold War, they urged the adoption of not only a more resolute campaign stance but also new, more conservative leadership in the Republican party.[1] These defeats seemed to corroborate the "extremists'" political advice.

After deciding that not criticizing the Administration's foreign policy would lead to defeat in subsequent national elections, congressional Republicans, and then their national leaders, markedly changed their strategy on foreign policy. Although they never directly attacked the Administration's foreign policy, the congressional Republican leaders after 1949 questioned, within the context of bipartisanship, the more controversial ways in which the Administration implemented it. They declared that the Administration had not pursued a bipartisan foreign policy because it had not consulted the Republicans before it made decisions. The Administration, they charged, expected uncritical Republican support of disastrous policies formulated by Democrats. More than any others, the Yalta agreements symbolized the kind of decision that, the Republicans stated, had been made without their knowledge. For those agreements and all other decisions about which they had not been consulted, they abjured all responsibility.

In this changed milieu, wartime and postwar foreign policy decisions came under searching review. Ill-prepared for the complexities of foreign policy and the limitation on it, many people in the United States had come to regard the Soviet Union almost as the Antichrist. Anticommunism emerged in the United States virtually as a secular religion. People viewed the world situation in rigid moral terms of right and wrong, Christian democracy and atheistic communism.

Moreover, the burdens of foreign aid and international involvement seemed not to have accomplished the stated objectives of achieving peace and making international politics democratic. Apparently, only the Soviet Union had profited from World War II. To a conservative, optimistic public, which viewed communism as oppressive and atheistic, Soviet postwar successes were incomprehensible. Accustomed to immediate, easy solutions and expecting world acclaim, many people in the United States sought a scapegoat, a

1. *Chicago Tribune*, November 9, 1949, 1, 2; November 10, 1949, 16.

ready explanation. They retained a naïve faith in the ability of the United States, should it so will, to create the world in its image.

The term *un-American* became respectable. The vagueness and indefinable nature of this concept favored the critics and those unscrupulous people who used the term for political purposes. The "extremists'" more subtle reformulation of their charges of "Communist influence" during and after 1949 at least contributed to its more effective use. Their persistent repetition of these more sophisticated charges, the adoption of "un-American" by many Republican spokesmen, and the use of the term by many members of the U.S. press finally made the charge and the term appear to be legitimate.

The changed fortunes and tactics of the House Committee on Un-American Activities showed the changed focus. From 1946 to 1948, the committee had not been primarily interested in espionage activity. Its definition of subversion involved Communist infiltration of New Deal agencies and Communist influence in the formulation of New Deal domestic policies. It considered the reform ideas of the New Deal subversive and sought to equate communism and the New Deal. Its various friendly witnesses stressed the importance of the Communist movement during the 1930's. In their questioning, committee members stressed the past associations and beliefs of New Deal officials, as an exchange between committee members John Parnell Thomas (Republican, New Jersey) and John Rankin (Democrat) indicated. Justifying the committee's refusal to include the testimony of a witness, William Remington, Thomas denied that the committee was trying to "whitewash" anyone but had in fact been "unearthing your [sic] New Dealers for 2 years, and for 8 years before that."[2] Further, Whittaker Chambers' original testimony in August, 1948, claimed only that Alger Hiss had been a Communist party member in the 1930's. Chambers then specifically denied that Hiss's party function had been subversion. Following the committee's line, Chambers charged that Hiss's role was to help other Communists infiltrate the Administration, and he confirmed the Communists' successful infiltration of New Deal agencies.[3]

In 1948, the committee virtually ignored the Administration's foreign policy, and it was only superficially concerned about Hiss's role at Yalta. Congressmen Karl Mundt, John McDowell (Republi-

2. U.S. House of Representatives, Committee on Un-American Activities, *Hearings Regarding Communist Espionage in the United States Government*, 80th Cong., 2d sess., 1948, 548.
3. *Ibid.*, 1202.

can, Pennsylvania), and Committee Counsel Robert Stripling merely noted that Hiss had attended the Yalta Conference.[4] At that time, no committee member or Republican congressman charged in committee or on the floor of Congress that Hiss had been an influential adviser at Yalta.

In its *Interim Report*, issued on August 28, 1948, the committee defined its primary interest as ascertaining Communist espionage in the United States Government. The committee emphasized espionage in its report, but its conception of espionage was limited to only the presumed infiltration of Communist employees into the New Deal. After describing its intentions to publicize this "subversive conspiracy," the committee further stated, "this Communist penetration in the Government began as early as 1934." Its investigations, according to the committee, confirmed the existence of "Communist espionage groups composed of Government employees and Government officers in Washington, D.C."[5]

As long as the committee criticized individual beliefs and associations and attacked New Deal domestic reforms as un-American or subversive, its appeal and impact were limited. The committee became important only when it switched the emphasis of its investigations from domestic infiltration to foreign espionage. In September, 1948, the committee held hearings on espionage activities in the atomic program. In its report of September 27, the committee demanded the immediate indictment of five persons for alleged wartime

4. *Ibid.*, 656–57, 1175, 1202, 1297.
5. U.S. House of Representatives, Committee on Un-American Activities, *Interim Report on Hearings Regarding Espionage in the United States Government*, 80th Cong., 2d sess., 1948, 4–8, 11, 14. The absence of the term "Communist" from the title of the committee's August report reflected its different concept of espionage before the so-called pumpkin papers were uncovered. These committee charges, which appeared before December, 1948, were championed primarily by the "extremist" press. They focused on Roosevelt; their straw man was Roosevelt, not Alger Hiss. Interestingly, these "extremists," although highlighting Chambers' testimony, did not wholly align with Chambers. Instead, they emphasized Roosevelt's and the New Deal's pro-Soviet proclivities and averred that Roosevelt's policies, not spying efforts by Elizabeth Bentley or Whittaker Chambers, had aided the Soviet Union. Summing up this view, the *Washington Times-Herald* argued, "There was a perfect understanding between Roosevelt and the Reds — which is the largest single reason why the Communists and Fellow Travelers are so thick and powerful in our government today that only a Dewey-Warren administration can root them out." This *Times-Herald* statement was quoted in Thomas Sancton, "The Case of Alger Hiss," *The Nation*, 167 (September 4, 1948), 251–52. *The Saturday Evening Post*, 219 (May 3, 1947), 152; 221 (October 2, 1948), 132. *Chicago Herald-American*, August 14, 1948, 3; October 5, 1948, 3; October 6, 1948, 3; October 7, 1948, 3; October 12, 1948, 3; October 13, 1948, 3; October 15, 1948, 3. *Chicago Tribune*, September 2, 1948, 20; September 4, 1948, 2, 8; September 5, 1948, 1, 2; October 15, 1948, 1.

atomic espionage. The committee presented no factual evidence to document this conclusion; it had based its report on hearsay testimony. President Truman and Attorney General Clark effectively belittled the demand because of the lack of evidence.[6]

In December, 1948, after the presidential campaign, the committee presented its first tangible evidence for its allegations of "espionage." In contrast to its earlier anti-New Deal tone, the committee then justified its function on the need to ascertain whether an "espionage ring" threatened national security by still operating in the Administration.[7] Similarly, Whittaker Chambers asserted that, although the "pumpkin papers" (documents that Chambers allegedly had received from Hiss in 1938) had never reached the Soviet Union, a great deal of material had.[8] In December, 1948, and again in March, 1949, Chambers altered his previous testimony and described Hiss as one of the "most zealous" Russian spies in Washington.[9] Chambers' changed position corresponded to the committee's changed approach. The breaking of this new evidence in the Hiss-Chambers case, well staged for maximum publicity, came at a critical juncture for the committee.

Before the "pumpkin papers," the committee's partisanship and intemperateness had enabled President Truman to disparage its charges. Indeed, in a press conference in August, 1948, Truman had argued that the committee served "no useful purpose" and that it had revealed nothing new. He had accused the committee of violating the Bill of Rights, of slandering innocent people, and of attempting to create a "red herring" to divert public attention from the record of the Eightieth Congress. Truman had also dismissed Congressman Mundt's "manufactured" charge that a spy ring then operated in Washington. For these reasons, Truman had reiterated his refusal to release classified information to the committee. Truman, however, had defended the necessity of loyalty and security investigations. He had reported having initiated an F.B.I. investigation "to be on the safe side" and noted that such an investigation would be more judicious than that of the committee and would not sacrifice the Bill of Rights.[10]

6. *The New York Times*, September 28, 1948, 1, 22, 23; September 29, 1948, 1, 17; September 30, 1948, 1, 14, 15; October 1, 1948, 1.

7. *Hearings Regarding Communist Espionage in the United States Government*, 80th Cong., 2d sess., 1948, 1379.

8. *Chicago Tribune*, December 5, 1948, 1.

9. *Ibid.*, November 22, 1949, 1.

10. Transcript of press conference, August 5, 1948, Records of White House Official Reporter, Truman Papers, Truman Library.

At another press conference in August, Truman had restated his doubts that any significant wartime subversion had occurred, but he did acknowledge the need for a new statute on loyalty and security. Any investigations of federal employees on loyalty or security grounds, Truman had maintained, should avoid the House Un-American Activities Committee's violations of freedom of speech.[11] Truman had assailed only the committee's methods. Implicit in his charge was the assumption that past associations and controversial ideas were valid grounds for judging an individual's loyalty. He never challenged the committee's right to judge what constituted un-American activities.

In the 1948 campaign, Truman had assailed Dewey's reference to the need to eliminate Communists from government as really an attempt to eliminate Democrats from government. He had confirmed his Administration's vigilance and pointed to his initiation of a loyalty program in 1947. Truman had then challenged the failure of the House Committee on Un-American Activities to investigate German and Japanese spies.[12]

Far more committed and dynamic leadership was needed. Truman's narrow partisanship would soon hurt him politically. His success in 1948 had stemmed more from the intemperateness and anti-New Deal commitment of the committee than from his rebuttal. In a sense, Truman had allowed the committee to define the rules of the game. His stress on the need to preserve freedom of speech and his denial of wartime subversion conflicted with his demand for F.B.I. investigations and for a new statute on loyalty and security. If he saw no threat, he did not need a revised statute or new investigations. Truman was far too much the pragmatic politician who was intent on preventing the partisan use of subversive investigations. His loyalty program indirectly admitted past guilt and added respectability to the nature of the House Committee on Un-American Activities. Moreover, the intensification of the Cold War, due both to U.S. and Soviet policies, created the milieu wherein safeguards for internal security seemed imperative.

Chambers' disclosure about the "pumpkin papers" completely changed the political situation. Confronted by this striking new development, Truman emphasized the Attorney General's vigilance

11. Transcript of press conference, August 19, 1948, Records of White House Official Reporter, Truman Papers, Truman Library.
12. Transcript of press conference, September 2, 1948, Records of White House Official Reporter, Truman Papers, Truman Library.

and denied that security leaks existed within his Administration. Reiterating his "red herring" charge, he dismissed this new development as simply partisan politics. He further stated that, if the committee were sincerely interested in prosecuting these charges, it
should submit its evidence to the Attorney General. Truman then
referred to the 1948 election results as evidence of public confidence
in his Administration and his security program.[13] This partisan rejoinder, so typical of the President, made him appear to be attempting to hide possible security risks for partisan reasons.

The lameness of Truman's defense of the Bill of Rights and his
dismissal of the new evidence as partisan in motivation sharply contrasted with the "extremists'" confident, patriotic tone. The Pearl
Harbor investigation and earlier investigative activities by the House
Committee on Un-American Activities had failed to discredit the
New Deal, but for once, the "extremists" seemingly had definite evidence of disloyalty within the New Deal. Capitalizing on existing
doubts, they demanded further investigations of the Roosevelt and
Truman administrations.

For the "extremists," the Hiss trial was a formality; the charges
alone were sufficient for conviction. They never questioned the au-
thenticity of the documents or whether anyone could prove that Hiss
actually gave them to Chambers. Because they were committed to
continued investigations, they questioned the adequacy of existing
safeguards, and their critique principally aimed at past Administration policies of co-operation with the Soviet Union. Therein, Yalta
assumed a major symbolic role. Indeed, after 1948, the "extremists"
played up Hiss's presence at Yalta, even describing him as the "archi-
tect" of the conference. To them, the New Deal was on trial. For
their purposes, Hiss's acquittal could not exonerate the Roosevelt
Administration. They could use the conviction of this man who had
become important in the State Department to incriminate the New
Deal policies and personnel.

More specifically, Chambers' new documentary evidence provided the basis for a renewed but indirect assault on the New Deal
through attacks on the State Department. To the "extremists," Communist infiltration of the State Department had been conclusively
proven and the New Deal's integrity discredited. They thus affirmed
that, had Alger Hiss not passed these secrets on to Chambers, someone else in the State Department had. Their demands for a house-

13. Transcript of press conference, December 9, 1948, Records of White
House Official Reporter, Truman Papers, Truman Library.

cleaning of the State Department were in fact directed at the New Deal.[14]

The "extremists'" reaction to Truman's nominations of Dean Acheson as Secretary of State and W. Walton Butterworth as Assistant Secretary of State dramatized this partisan commitment. A former associate of Hiss and a student of Supreme Court Justice Felix Frankfurter, Acheson had also helped formulate earlier Administration foreign policy. The "partisan" Senator William Knowland (Republican, California) and the "extremist" Senators Styles Bridges, Kenneth Wherry (Republican, Nebraska), Congressman John Sanborn (Republican, Idaho), columnist Westbrook Pegler, and the *Chicago Tribune* deemed the appointment tantamount to nominating Hiss. They also concentrated on the Yalta Conference when justifying their opposition to the nomination. Acheson, they averred, was part of a "pro-Soviet" bloc in the State Department that had used its influence to draft policies — the Yalta agreements, the UN Charter, the Morgenthau Plan, and the plans drafted at the Bretton Woods Conference — that undermined the national interest. Wherry condemned the Yalta agreements on Germany and said that a vote for Acheson would mean "condoning of the administration's program to destroy German industry and keep her forever an agricultural state."[15]

During the Senate Foreign Relations Committee's hearings on Acheson's confirmation, supporters of the bipartisan foreign policy tried to undercut this tactic of guilt by association. Tom Connally, H. Alexander Smith (Republican, New Jersey), and Arthur Vandenberg pressed Acheson on his relationship to Hiss. Their questioning enabled Acheson to state that Hiss had never been his assistant, that Hiss had been only a State Department associate, and that he had not, and did not know who had, appointed Hiss to the Yalta delegation. Connally, after affirming his own anticommunism in the Senate debate on confirmation, did observe, "it seems that the only argument some persons can present is to holler about Alger Hiss and then refer to Yalta. They seem to have to dig up something about

14. *Chicago Tribune,* December 7, 1948, 20; January 13, 1949, 13; June 3, 1949, 1; June 4, 1949, 1; June 19, 1949, 1; June 25, 1949, 3; July 8, 1949, 12; July 12, 1949, 20. *Chicago Herald-American,* December 16, 1948, 18; December 17, 1948, 22; August 2, 1949, 8. *The Saturday Evening Post,* 221 (December 25, 1948), 72. U.S. *Congressional Record,* 81st Cong., 1st sess., 1949, XCV, Part 12, A174.

15. *Ibid.,* Parts 1 and 12, 464, 709, A158. The six senators who voted against Acheson's confirmation were Bridges, Capehart, Jenner, Knowland, Langer, and Wherry. *Chicago Herald-American,* January 13, 1949, 3. *Chicago Tribune,* January 10, 1949, 26; January 15, 1949, 8.

the dead President of the United States, and then go back to Yalta."[16] This debate and these questions that implied guilt by association reflected both the tenor of the period in 1949 in which Hiss was tried and the obvious political ramifications of his conviction.

A Soviet invitation in January, 1949, for joint U.S.-Soviet consultations further revealed the deep anti-Soviet and anti-New Deal suspicions of the "extremists." On the basis of the Yalta experience, Westbrook Pegler, George Sokolsky, the *Chicago Tribune*, Senator Pat McCarran (Democrat, Nevada), and Congressman Thomas Jenkins (Republican, Ohio) questioned the value of any conference with the Soviet Union. They then argued that such policies as those promoted at Yalta could only have resulted from Communist infiltration of the New Deal because they were so inimical to U.S. interests. In their criticisms of Yalta and other policy decisions, particularly lend-lease, the distinction between "Communists in Government" and the New Deal became blurred. The problem, they asserted, was not simply an historical one, for a "pro-Russian" group still operated in the State Department.[17]

The Senate debate in September, 1949, on W. Walton Butterworth's confirmation as Assistant Secretary of State again revealed this negativist strategy.[18] Senator William Knowland, who opposed Butterworth's confirmation as he had earlier opposed Acheson's, cited Butterworth's association with the Administration's earlier policy toward China. Attributing Chiang Kai-shek's defeat directly to Yalta, Knowland then implied that Hiss had been influential in drafting the Yalta Far Eastern agreements. He further suggested that former Vice-President Henry Wallace might have been influential in formulating the Administration's policy toward China.[19]

16. U.S. Senate, Committee on Foreign Relations, *Hearings on the Nomination of Dean G. Acheson to be Secretary of State*, 81st Cong., 1st sess., 1949, 6–9, 11–13. U.S. *Congressional Record*, 81st Cong., 1st sess., 1949, XCV, Part 1, 709.
17. *Chicago Herald-American*, January 20, 1949, 3; April 8, 1949, 32; May 13, 1949, 20; May 16, 1949, 12. *Chicago Tribune*, February 2, 1949, 18; February 3, 1949, 5; May 6, 1949, 4. U.S. *Congressional Record*, 81st Cong., 1st sess., 1949, XCV, Parts 13 and 14, A2072, A2104, A3108.
18. Republican partisanship was reflected in the fact that all 27 negative votes against Butterworth's confirmation were cast by Republicans. U.S. *Congressional Record*, 81st Cong., 1st sess., 1949, XCV, Parts 1 and 10, 468, 13294.
19. *Ibid.*, Part 10, 13264–67. In a similar strategic effort to capitalize on the Hiss disclosure, the *Chicago Tribune* affirmed that during World War II, the New Dealer Harry Hopkins had given U.S. war secrets and uranium to the Soviet Union. These secrets, the *Tribune* added, had expedited Soviet explosion of an atomic bomb. Earlier in the year, the *Tribune* had demanded an investigation by the House Committee on Un-American Activities to determine whether the information received by the Joint Chiefs of Staff during the war, upon which

The 1949 reappraisal of Administration Far Eastern policy was also directly related to the concern about loyalty and security that the Hiss trial elicited. Even the "extremists" and other people who supported Chiang Kai-shek had not consistently blamed the Administration's Far Eastern policy for his problems. Although they had been bitterly critical of the Yalta Far Eastern agreements, Congressman Walter Judd, George Sokolsky, the *Chicago Tribune*, and *The Saturday Evening Post* had never directly stated in 1948 that these agreements undermined Chiang's position. They had condemned post-Yalta decisions, particularly George Marshall's mission to China in 1945 and 1946, more than Yalta policy. In 1948, their main concern had been to get a definite U.S. commitment to support Chiang and thus to enforce the Yalta agreements. Their critical references to Yalta had been oriented to the domestic situation; they averred that the conference revealed the naïveté of the Roosevelt and Truman administrations. They had not charged that these policies indicated Communist subversion or a pro-Communist State Department.[20]

As Chiang Kai-shek's position in China became less tenable, Republican criticism of Yalta and the Truman Administration increased. Formally responding to these attacks, in August, 1949, the State Department published a White Paper on China. The White Paper was intended to silence criticisms that the Administration's conduct of foreign policy had been secretive and to discount charges that the Administration had no set China policy but merely responded to events as they happened. The paper set forth the guidelines for past decisions, defended those decisions, and attributed the Chinese Communists' success to Chiang's failure to institute necessary reforms and his resultant loss of popularity.

The White Paper failed, however, to quiet the charges made by critics of Yalta and the Truman Administration. By 1949, a more critical assessment of the Administration's past China policy had evolved, and it was no longer confined to the "extremists." Although modifying the "extremists'" anti-New Deal charges, the "moderates" and "partisans" stated that the Yalta Far Eastern agreements were par-

---

it based its judgment to secure Russian intervention in the Far Eastern war, had been censored. "Proven evidence" of Communist infiltration of the New Deal, the *Tribune* argued, necessitated such an investigation. *Chicago Tribune*, January 3, 1949, 12; January 14, 1949, 2; December 5, 1949, 20; December 15, 1949, 24.

20. U.S. *Congressional Record*, 80th Cong., 2d sess., 1948, XCIV, Part 12, A4555–62. *The Saturday Evening Post*, 221 (November 27, 1948), 156. *Chicago Tribune*, December 6, 1948, 6; December 13, 1948, 2. *Chicago Herald-American*, December 6, 1948, 10; December 8, 1948, 32.

tially responsible for Chiang's defeat. At this time, they did not renounce the bipartisan foreign policy or the policy of containment.
Instead, they denied that the Administration's Far Eastern policy
had been bipartisan. The communization of China, they further argued, could have been prevented had the Administration pursued
the same resolute containment policy in Asia that had proven successful in Europe. The "extremists" and certain "partisans" affirmed that
Chiang's problems and defeat stemmed directly from decisions made
by the Roosevelt and Truman administrations at Yalta and after. They
asserted that Truman, Roosevelt, and the "State Department crowd"
had betrayed Chiang by appeasing the Soviet Union. Some blamed
Truman more than Roosevelt and suggested that this development
resulted from the Truman Administration's failure to implement the
Yalta agreements. The more standard view, however, held Roosevelt
responsible.

The "extremists" suggested that developments in China proved
the bankruptcy of a bipartisan foreign policy and the necessity for
congressional investigations of the executive branch and of earlier
policy decisions. Yalta and the Far Eastern policy were evidence of
Communist subversion. Chiang's defeat had been engineered by
pro-Communists in the State Department — Alger Hiss had been at
Yalta. They extended this attack to Roosevelt personally and implied
further that Roosevelt might have sought to "communize the
world."[21]

Republican Congressman Walter Judd and Senator William
Knowland used the congressional debate on the extension of the
European Recovery Program to criticize the Administration's failure
to provide a similar program for China. Shocked that aid to Chiang
Kai-shek would be terminated, Judd emphasized Nationalist China's
importance for U.S. security by arguing that acceptance of Chiang's
defeat would eventually result in the communization of Japan, South-
east Asia, and the Philippines. Blaming the "loss" of China on the Yalta

21. *Time*, 54 (August 15, 1949), 11–13. *The Saturday Evening Post*, 221
(January 29, 1949), 10; 222 (September 3, 1949), 10; October 15, 1949, 10.
The New York Times, August 12, 1949, 16; November 29, 1949, 28. *Chicago
Tribune*, February 14, 1949, 24; June 20, 1949, 2; June 25, 1949, 2; July 18,
1949, 17; July 27, 1949, 3; August 9, 1949, 14; August 10, 1949, 3. *Chicago
Herald-American*, January 31, 1949, 8; June 23, 1949, 30; April 7, 1949, 22.
U.S. *Congressional Record*, 81st Cong., 1st sess., 1949, XCV, Parts 2, 4, 5, 8, 9,
11, 12, 13, 14, 15, and 16, 1450–51, 5237–41, 6390–91, 10941–42, 10958,
10961–62, 11810–13, 11882, 14341, A458, A1129, A1344–45, A2187–89, A2871,
A5114, A5216, A5451–52, A5456, A5696, A5704, A6302, A6631. Democratic
Congressman Thomas Gordon also denounced past Administration foreign policy
as mistaken and charged that it was responsible for Chiang's defeat.

Far Eastern agreements he demanded an investigation to determine who was responsible for them.[22] Knowland similarly emphasized the Administration's responsibility for Chiang's defeat. He inserted into the *Congressional Record* the text of the Yalta Far Eastern agreements and the list of the conference delegates. When Senator Tom Connally asked him the reason for these insertions, Knowland replied that they provided necessary information about the past Administration's China policy. In reply, Connally expressed support for Knowland's proposed amendment extending the European Recovery Program, which had been set up by the Economic Cooperation Act of 1948, to give aid to those areas not under Communist domination. Connally, however, charged that Knowland's speech was simply "a partisan attack" because of its unnecessary reference to Yalta.[23]

Senators George Malone (Republican, Nevada), Homer Ferguson (Republican, Michigan), and Kenneth Wherry developed a similar assault on the Administration during the debate on appropriations for foreign aid. Malone and Ferguson noted that George Marshall had advised Roosevelt at Yalta to support Soviet involvement in the Far Eastern war. They pointed out that Marshall had also advised Roosevelt when Berlin was "given" to the Soviets at Yalta without provisions for U.S. access rights. Both doubted that Marshall knew anything about China or communism.[24]

Although they were virulently anti-Communist and demanded a more resolute foreign policy, the "extremists" did not support the North Atlantic Treaty Organization, the Mutual Defense Assistance Act, the extension of the European Recovery Program, or any other of the Administration's policies of economic or military aid. They described such aid as useless and as potentially dangerous because it extended U.S. involvement and commitment. Their arguments against NATO, the Mutual Defense Act, and the European Recovery Program paralleled their earlier opposition to the Truman Doctrine and the Marshall Plan.

George Sokolsky, Senators William Jenner (Republican, Indiana), William Langer, and Arthur Watkins (Republican, Utah) opposed NATO because it involved increases in the size and scope of U.S. foreign commitments. They re-emphasized the Yalta conferees' responsibility for the problems in Europe and attacked the secrecy of the Yalta agreements. Neither the Congress nor the U.S. public

22. *Ibid.*, Part 3, 3827.
23. *Ibid.*, 3767–71.
24. *Ibid.*, Part 8, 10958, 10961.

had assented to these terms. The use of executive authority should be restricted, and NATO might permit further executive encroachments upon legislative prerogatives as well as bankrupt the United States. Besides, NATO would not deter war and might precipitate it. In addition, Jenner questioned how anyone could trust the Truman Administration, which suffered from strong "Communist" influence, to implement an anti-Communist program.[25]

During debate about the Mutual Defense Assistance Act, Congressman William Lemke and Senators George Malone and Arthur Watkins attributed U.S. international involvement to mistakes made at Yalta. This aid program, Malone warned, would be directed by the same men who "dictated" U.S. policy at Yalta. Lemke, Malone, and Watkins doubted that the United States could provide sufficient military aid to deter a Soviet attack and recommended concentrating on domestic affairs. Lemke characterized internationalists as "betrayors of our Nation," and Watkins expressed his fears that the act might make the President the "greatest war lord of all times." Assailing Yalta and the bipartisan policy, he noted:

> This so-called bipartisan policy has made it difficult, if not impossible, to present to the people of the United States the real truth about what has happened in the diplomatic field during the war and immediately following it. Many of the advisers in the State Department, including the Secretary of State, were partly responsible for what happened at Teheran, Yalta, Quebec, and Potsdam, and, of course, the present President of the United States is responsible for Potsdam and what has happened since that time.[26]

The "extremists'" denunciations of these containment policies sharply distinguished them from the "moderates" and "partisans."

25. Although he was critical of NATO, Sokolsky also decried the establishment of NATO's defense line on the Elbe as an abandonment of the "enslaved peoples." Similarly, the "extremists" criticized the containment policy as being both too aggressive and too defensive. *Chicago Herald-American*, March 8, 1949, 10; April 21, 1949, 22; April 27, 1949, 22; May 5, 1949, 10; June 21, 1949, 8; August 22, 1949, 10. *Chicago Tribune*, November 3, 1949, 20; November 19, 1949, 12. *The Saturday Evening Post*, 221 (February 26, 1949), 12; 222 (September 10, 1949), 12. U.S. *Congressional Record*, 81st Cong., 1st sess., 1949, XCV, Parts 1, 3, 4, 7, and 12, 1341–42, 3266–67, 5029–34, 9092–94, 9106, 9553–61, A734.

26. *Ibid.*, Part 10, 13160–61. The "extremists" voted against not only military assistance but also the extension of E.R.P. They denounced both measures as wasteful and unnecessary, recommending that the Administration concentrate on internal security. *Ibid.*, Parts 3, 8, and 9, 4147–48, 9916, 13168. Westbrook Pegler voiced this protest about executive authority in his condemnation of Yalta, Potsdam, Roosevelt's domestic reform leadership, and Roosevelt's 1940 actions in support of Great Britain. *Chicago Herald-American*, March 15, 1949, 3; March 16, 1949, 3.

Although the "moderates" and "partisans" had shifted to the right, they strictly limited their criticisms of the Administration's foreign policy to such past decisions as those concluded at Yalta. Moreover, their criticisms were more temperate. *The New York Times* and Senators Arthur Vandenberg and John Foster Dulles, who held an interim appointment as Senator from New York until that state's special U.S. Senate election in November, 1949, described the Yalta Conference as simply mistaken. At the same time, these Republican spokesmen supported NATO and other U.S. international involvements because they were means for preserving the peace and because they were consistent with the principles underlying the United Nations.[27]

Predictably, the Yalta conferees were blamed also for sacrificing Poland. Republican Congressmen Kenneth Keating (New York), John Lodge, Joseph Martin, Hugh Scott, Jr. (Pennsylvania), Senators Homer Capehart (Indiana), Joseph McCarthy (Wisconsin), and Democratic Congressmen Harold Donohue (Massachusetts), Thomas Gordon, Edward Garmatz (Maryland), and Chester Gorski (New York) used Polish national observances — Polish Constitution Day, the anniversary of Pulaski's death, and the German attack on Poland — as occasions to say that Yalta had contributed to Poland's loss of freedom. Some demanded the termination of U.S. recognition of the Polish Government; others, the repudiation of Yalta. Capehart formally announced his opposition to any treaty incorporating the Yalta decisions on Poland.[28]

This changed domestic climate and anti-Communist rhetoric, moreover, provided the cover for an "extremist" and "partisan" assault on the Administration's former policy toward Germany. According to Westbrook Pegler, George Sokolsky, the *Chicago Tribune*, *Time* magazine, Congressmen Richard Nixon (Republican, California), William Lemke, and Senator William Langer, Yalta's unjust, discriminatory treatment of Germany harmed the national interest and, as expressed by Sokolsky, unwisely removed the German barrier to "Slavic expansionism" into Europe.[29] *The New York Times*'s position on the German question gave further evidence of this change. Noting

27. U.S. *Congressional Record*, 81st Cong., 1st sess., 1949, XCV, Part 7, 8892, 9275. *The New York Times*, April 2, 1949, 14; April 13, 1949, 28.

28. U.S. *Congressional Record*, 81st Cong., 1st sess., 1949, XCV, Parts 4, 9, 11, 12, 13, and 16, 555–63, 12584, 14200, A587–88, A6208–9, A6687.

29. *Ibid.*, Parts 10, 12, and 14, 13036–38, A548, A3342. *Chicago Tribune*, May 23, 1949, 20; June 19, 1949, 22; December 28, 1949. *Time*, 54 (November 28, 1949), 20–26. *Chicago Herald-American*, March 15, 1949, 3; March 16, 1949, 3; May 6, 1949, 32.

that Yalta's policy of collaboration with the Soviet Union had failed, the *Times* called for a reassessment of the Administration's past German policy and for the construction of a strong, democratic Germany. Pursuing this theme, the *Times* stated that the acceptance of the

> Soviet-fixed frontiers in Germany under the changed conditions since Yalta could transform the permanent military frontier of Russia from the Curzon line to the Oder. And that would convert Paris [the site of the 1949 Council of Foreign Ministers] into a Super-Yalta under which Western Europe could never live in either security or a stable peace.[30]

Consistent with this more sympathetic view toward Germany, the "extremists" Congressman Lawrence Smith, Senator Pat McCarran, George Sokolsky, and the *Chicago Tribune* demanded a reappraisal of U.S. policy toward Franco's Spain and Marshall Petain, former President of Vichy France. Singling out the Yalta agreements as examples of the Roosevelt Administration's sympathies for the Soviet Union, they demanded a more forthright anticommunism that involved U.S. recognition of Franco's Spain and the release of Petain from prison. They contrasted the Administration's recognition of the Eastern European Communist governments and its defense of Roosevelt's collaborationist policy at Yalta with its refusal to recognize Spain and its opposition to Petain. Sokolsky further noted, "Many of the archcollaborationists still are in high office and no one even asks them what happened to their conferences at Teheran and Yalta and even Potsdam."[31]

The Truman Administration's defense of past policies was lame and apologetic in contrast to the bitterness of these charges. In an attempt to exonerate his earlier willingness to negotiate with the Soviet Union, President Truman blamed the Cold War completely on Soviet bad faith. The Soviet Union, Truman contended, made agreements, only to break them at a later date. He argued that the Yalta agreements had been unilaterally broken by the Soviet Union.[32] Other defenders of the Administration's foreign policy of co-opera-

30. *The New York Times*, April 29, 1949, 22; May 5, 1949, 26; May 22, 1949, 8E; May 23, 1949, 22; May 30, 1949, 12.

31. U.S. *Congressional Record*, 81st Cong., 1st sess., 1949, XCV, Part 14, A3168. *Chicago Herald-American*, February 24, 1949, 10. *Chicago Tribune*, May 6, 1949, 4; February 23, 1949, 12; May 20, 1949, 10. Indeed, McCarran attempted to amend foreign aid appropriations to include aid to Spain.

32. Transcript of press conference, April 22, 1949, Records of White House Official Reporter, Truman Papers, Truman Library. Harry S Truman, speech to the Committee for Economic Development, Washington, D.C., May 12, 1949, Records of White House Official Reporter, Truman Papers, Truman Library.

tion no longer supported the spirit of Yalta but weakly defended
the conference agreements, particularly the more controversial Far
Eastern agreements, on military grounds. They emphasized the pressure exerted by the Joint Chiefs of Staff for Soviet involvement in the
war against Japan and suggested that the military had erred in over-
estimating Japanese strength and resistance. Their main reaction to
Republican criticisms was to assail the partisan motivations of Yalta
critics, to denounce Soviet bad faith, or to stress the limitations confronting the Administration and the spirit of the time when the agreements were concluded.[33]

By 1949, Yalta was no longer examined on the basis of the needs
and limitations of 1945. Both Democratic supporters and Republican
critics had ceased to view it as a diplomatic conference that tried
to achieve peace through compromise and understanding. Instead,
it had become a symbol of a mistaken or treasonous course of action.
Truman's contrasting U.S. good faith with Soviet bad faith set the
tone for Democratic justifications of Yalta. Defenders and critics of
Yalta, who were basically unconcerned about the conference as
such and who had partisan motives, ignored or bitterly assailed
this spirit. Democrats denounced Stalin as the devil, the "extremists"
assailed Roosevelt and the New Deal, and the "partisans" and "moderates" criticized the naïveté of the participants in this Democratic
conference.

Although Yalta had not changed, its spirit and agreements were
no longer consistent with the negative anticommunism of postwar
U.S. politics. The Truman Administration's anti-Communist rhetoric
and its containment policy, combined with developments in the Far
East and in the Alger Hiss case, had served to legitimate both an
anti-Soviet, pro-German policy and an obsession about "Communists
in Government." This newly created political climate influenced
subsequent decisions that affected internal security and foreign
policy as well as the general tone of the political debate on dissent
and reform.

33. U.S. *Congressional Record*, 81st Cong., 1st sess., 1949, XCV, Parts 9,
10, 12, and 15, 12584, 12757, A1047–48, A4298–99, A5211. Owen Lattimore
and Admiral Ellis Zacharias concurred in this view of Yalta and Far Eastern
criticisms. Owen Lattimore, "Our Failure in China," *The Nation*, 169 (September 3, 1949), 223–26. Admiral Ellis Zacharias, "The Inside Story of Yalta,"
United Nations World (January, 1949). *Newsweek*, 34 (August 15, 1949), 38;
September 19, 1949, 22. *The New York Times*, June 15, 1949, 28. *The Nation*,
168 (June 18, 1949), 685; 169 (October 1, 1949), 315–17.

chapter 6

1950: the repudiation of bipartisanship

The Republican opposition to the Yalta agreements and other earlier foreign policy decisions intensified in 1950. Alger Hiss's formal conviction for perjury and the outbreak of the Korean War were both catalysts and pretexts for Republican contentions that the earlier foreign policy had failed to protect U.S. interests. Hiss and Korea seemingly confirmed the basic weaknesses of the Administration's policy, added credence to Republican declarations that Yalta policy and policy makers must be repudiated, and made it feasible for the Republicans to concentrate on Yalta and other past decisions. These events provided cover for a wide-ranging attack, within a bipartisan framework, on presidential appointments, policy recommendations, and justifications of past policy decisions.

References to Yalta appeared during congressional debates and in the 1950 congressional campaign, the main topic of which was national security from both internal and external threats. The "extremists" and the "partisans" no longer concentrated on New Deal personnel and reforms. Their main criticism was that the Roosevelt and Truman administrations, by mistakenly, naïvely, or traitorously trusting the Soviet Union, had undermined national security and had created current international problems. Senator McCarthy would perfect this approach, directly blaming Communist influence for these problems. Because his criticisms were confined to the State Department and were not overtly partisan or anti-New Deal, they were especially effective.

The rejection of the bipartisan foreign policy accelerated. Critics of foreign policy stressed the past Administration's decisions rather than existing policies, and in 1950, the first resolution proposing that Congress repudiate Yalta as one means of rectifying past wrongs was introduced. The foreign policy views of Senators Robert Taft and Styles Bridges were increasingly adopted by other Republican leaders.

Both critics and defenders of the earlier foreign policy had come to believe that the Soviet Union could not be trusted to keep its promises unless it was confronted by superior military force. They eventually believed that the Yalta spirit was unrealistic, and the conference became the symbol of undue or unwise trust. Inevitably, the "extremists" gained respectability and influence. Their critique of Yalta and their demand that the Republican party concentrate on questions of foreign policy were similar to what they had been in 1945. In 1950, however, the "moderates" and "partisans" supported these views, though in a more temperate form.

A statement of Republican principles and objectives, adopted on February 6 by Republican members of the House and Senate with the concurrence of the Republican National Committee, clearly showed this shift. The statement expressed Republican support for "peace and justice in a free world while maintaining independence and rights of the American people." It noted that, while the war had been won in 1945, peace had not been attained. It denounced secret agreements, presidential failure to furnish adequate and accurate information to the Congress, and abuse of executive agreements. It supported executive and legislative consultation in the formulation and development of foreign policy. The statement expressed outrage about "the tragic consequences of the Administration's failure to pursue these objectives, in many fields, particularly in the secret agreements of Yalta." It then emphasized the need for constructive criticism and set forth the Republicans' commitment to see that the Administration complied with these policy guidelines and to preclude infiltration by Communists, fellow travelers, or sympathizers into the Federal Government. The statement defined the major domestic issue confronting the nation as "liberty against socialism."[1]

A congressional debate on the Korean Aid Bill in January demonstrated this renewed partisanship. Republican Congressmen John Vorys and Arthur Miller (Nebraska) cited Yalta to justify their opposition to the bill. Both contended that Korea had been divided by a Yalta or Potsdam secret agreement. They considered the economic provisions of the bill wasteful and of no benefit. As Miller argued, economic aid would indirectly help the Soviet Union, since the absence of a program providing primarily military aid would make the fall of South Korea "inevitable."[2]

The vote on the Korean Aid Bill underscored this partisan ob-

1. U.S. *Congressional Record,* 81st Cong., 2d sess., 1950, XCVI, Part 2, 1541.
2. *Ibid.,* Part 1, 572, 635.

structionism of congressional Republicans and the more general political objectives of Southern Democrats. The bill was defeated by a vote of 191–192. Voting against it were 132 Republicans and 47 Southern Democrats.[3] Although an amended version passed the House in February, by a vote of 240–134, those opposed included 91 Republicans and 32 Southern Democrats.[4] The Administration's foreign policy requests were no longer divorced from partisan considerations. Conservative Southern Democrats and Republicans co-operated to curb executive initiatives in foreign policy and to force the Administration to cater to the congressional establishment.

The debate about foreign policy sustained the focus on Yalta. Thomas Dewey, John Foster Dulles, *Life*, *Time*, *The Saturday Evening Post*, *U.S. News and World Report*, and columnist Raymond Moley criticized Yalta for sacrificing principle for expediency and the conferees for trusting the Soviet Union. The delegates to the conference had erred in their outlook, and their decisions had caused current world problems. The conferees' weakness, undue trust, and naïveté showed the need for a more forceful approach. No administration could institute such an approach if it did not at least recognize these past errors. *Time* stated, "Stalin might have taken Manchuria and Poland without the Yaltese benison; but at Yalta he got something more than territory: proof that the West did not have enough good sense to distrust him."[5]

Dulles developed a more sophisticated version of this moralistic theme while justifying his criticisms within a bipartisan approach to foreign policy. He denounced the Roosevelt and Truman administrations' orientation toward military objectives and their disregard for political, moral, and material power in their conduct of U.S. diplomacy. At the same time, he criticized them for not being sufficiently assertive and for failing to recognize that the Soviet Union respected only power. Formally committed to bipartisanship — because such a commitment was politically expedient and because bipartisanship promoted U.S. and international security — Dulles reinterpreted the term. He maintained that certain past policies, such

3. *Ibid.*, 656.
4. *Ibid.*, Part 2, 1749.
5. *U.S. News and World Report*, 28 (March 3, 1950), 14; April 28, 1950, 31–33. *Time*, 55 (January 2, 1950), 40. *Life*, 31 (July 24, 1950), 26. *The Saturday Evening Post*, 222 (February 11, 1950), 10. *Newsweek*, 36 (August 7, 1950), 80. In contrast, columnist Ernest Lindley assailed Soviet actions after Yalta. Postwar events, Lindley argued, confirmed the worthlessness of Soviet promises and the necessity for relying on military strength. *Ibid.*, 35 (February 20, 1950), 22.

as the Yalta Far Eastern agreements, could be criticized within a bipartisan framework because they had not been bipartisan.[6]

The "extremists" remained to the right of these Yalta critics. In addition to assailing the conference more bitterly, they attempted as well to emphasize Roosevelt's personal culpability. Existing world problems could be attributed directly to Yalta, according to George Sokolsky, Westbrook Pegler, the *Chicago Tribune*, Congressmen Carl Curtis, Harold Lovre (Republican, South Dakota), George Dondero (Republican, Michigan), Senators George Malone, Kenneth Wherry, Arthur Watkins, Karl Mundt, Edward Thye (Republican, Minnesota), and James Eastland. This mistaken, foolhardy conference had betrayed U.S. interests, and a more dynamic foreign policy was demanded. Summing up, Sokolsky argued that these mistakes were being perpetuated because the same policy makers continued in power. He added:

> The United States has become so befuddled by a domestic struggle for the continuance in office by the New Deal group, that Stalin could utilize situations to his advantage. *The most useful situation for him was the absolute political necessity for the State Department to cover up the mistakes made by Roosevelt at Teheran and Yalta.*[7]

Sokolsky and his colleagues were not alone. Yalta dominated congressional debates on foreign policy and the State Department. No longer viewed merely as a diplomatic conference, it had acquired symbolic significance; its critics emphasized the Administration's responsibility for international problems, and its proponents blamed the Soviets. This new anti-Yalta rhetoric reflected the anti-Communist assumption of the containment policy and the debate on the contemporary foreign policy: Confrontation was the way to pressure the Soviet Union to become more conciliatory.

Consistent with this emphasis, on March 28, 1950, Republican Congressman Robert Hale introduced House Joint Resolution 444. Hale justified U.S. "withdrawal" from the Yalta agreements because of repeated Soviet violations. The repudiation of Yalta, he argued, would reaffirm the U.S. commitment to the principles of the Atlantic

6. John Foster Dulles, "Korean Attack Opens New Chapter in History," *Department of State Bulletin*, XXIII, 579 (August 7, 1950), 208–9. John Foster Dulles, *War Or Peace*, 16, 122, 137, 174, 179.

7. *Chicago Herald-American*, January 5, 1950, 22; January 17, 1950, 10; January 24, 1950, 3; February 22, 1950, 14; March 20, 1950, 3; June 2, 1950, 16; July 3, 1950, 3; July 13, 1950, 18. *Chicago Tribune*, March 20, 1950, 22. U.S. *Congressional Record*, 81st Cong., 2d sess., 1950, XCVI, Parts 4, 5, 7, 10, 14, and 17, 4578, 5758–60, 8622–23, 13658, A815–17, A2063–64, A6058–60.

Charter and give the "subjugated" peoples of Eastern Europe new hope. Hale did not refer to Asia.[8] Although it was never acted upon, the resolution highlighted the altered Republican conception of Yalta and the new Republican approach to foreign policy, which proposed to resolve alleged past Administration errors by congressional resolutions. This first resolution to repudiate Yalta had been introduced by a supporter of the bipartisan foreign policy. Although the emphasis of Hale's resolution was on Poland and former U.S. Ambassador to Poland Arthur Bliss Lane collaborated in the drafting, Hale did not represent a large Polish-American constituency. Hale's justification for the resolution and the language used in it belied its real intent: a formal expression of opposition to certain past policies.[9]

Alger Hiss's conviction for perjury precipitated even more intense attacks by the "extremists" and "partisans" on the Yalta Conference and the State Department. The *Chicago Tribune, Time* magazine, *The Saturday Evening Post*, George Sokolsky, Westbrook Pegler, Congressmen Richard Nixon, Clare Hoffman, Ralph Gwinn (Republican, New York), and Senators Styles Bridges, William Knowland, Homer Capehart, and James Eastland said that the Hiss case vindicated their suspicions of the New Deal's and the Yalta conferees' great betrayals. Hiss's influence at Yalta, they noted, emphasized the need for greater congressional scrutiny and continued investigations of the Administration as one means for ascertaining the extent of "Communist infiltration" of the New Deal and the Fair Deal. Articulating this anti-Roosevelt bias, Bridges pointedly asked:

> How long must we go on attempting to justify Mr. Roosevelt's mistake at Yalta? That was the original error. Let us assume for the sake of debate, as his New Deal adherents claim, he was the greatest President of all time. Can we not admit that even he could make a mistake, instead of trying to cover up anything.[10]

Hiss's conviction also enabled the "extremists" and "partisans" to use Hiss and Yalta as symbols that justified the revision of some decisions and the repudiation of others. They insisted that certain policies reflected Communist influence or communistic ideas. Republican

8. See Appendix E for the text of the Resolution.
9. Congressman Robert Hale, interview, July 16, 1962.
10. *Chicago Tribune*, January 22, 1950, 3, 18; February 15, 1950, 20; May 23, 1950, 20; May 29, 1950, 2. *Chicago Herald-American*, January 25, 1950, 3; January 26, 1950, 32; February 15, 1950, 3; March 7, 1950, 3. *Time*, 55 (January 30, 1950), 11–12. *The Saturday Evening Post*, 222 (February 25, 1950), 10. U.S. *Congressional Record*, 81st Cong., 2d sess., 1950, XCVI, Parts 1, 6, 13, and 14, 755–57, 817, 999, 1007, 1146–47, 7890, A550, A896, A2510–11.

Senator George Malone raised the symbols of Yalta and Hiss to support his demands for an investigation of Michael Lee, repudiation of the Trade Agreements Act of 1934, termination of all U.S. trade with the Communist countries, and the establishment of a tariff on copper. Congressman Donald O'Toole (Democrat, New York) also used these symbols when he assailed the proposal for giving economic and military aid to Yugoslavia.[11]

Republican Senator Karl Mundt most pointedly developed this tactic. He had made a national reputation during the investigation of Hiss by the House Committee on Un-American Activities. Because he had recognized the partisan potential of this forum, his principal objective was to buttress the committee's influence and respectability. He first emphasized the committee's role in securing Hiss's conviction. He then described Hiss as a member of an underground group that engaged in espionage activities, tried to infiltrate the Administration, and attempted to subvert the national interest. Hiss, Mundt charged, had numerous opportunities to exert his "pro-Communist" influence during the various discussions and meetings at Yalta because Roosevelt had been in poor health and had been unable "to think things through himself." Mundt noted, "It was thought necessary to have on the advisory staff someone who thought communism a noble thing." He then asserted:

> Perhaps a more alert and critical attitude by the Republican Party would have compelled the Democratic administration, and Presidents Roosevelt and Truman to clean house more thoroughly. . . . Perhaps if we Republicans had insisted sooner and more ardently on a disclosure of the secret agreements made at Yalta we would have discovered much sooner that there must have been influence at work at that unfortunate conference which had other causes to serve and other motives to fulfill than a consideration of American interests and world security and integrity.

In concluding, Mundt maintained that the Hiss case confirmed the need for continued vigilance, which a strengthend committee could provide.[12]

In this Senate speech, Mundt quoted liberally from recently published books by James Byrnes, Henry Stimson, James Farley, and

11. *Ibid.*, Parts 2, 10, 13, and 17, 1891, 2551, 2564, 14211–12, A1063, A5919.
12. *Ibid.*, Parts 1, 13, and 14, 890, 894, 900–905, A843–44, A1199–1200, A1961–62.

Edward Stettinius, Roosevelt's Secretary of State. Mundt especially drew from Stettinius, and in so doing, he distorted Stettinius' main themes. His purposeful efforts to use Stettinius' account to document his own assertions were primitive in comparison with those of the junior Senator from Wisconsin, Joseph McCarthy. In his famous Lincoln Day address in Wheeling, West Virginia, on February 9, McCarthy employed a similar pseudo-scientific approach, which he later perfected. McCarthy charged that 205 known Communists were in the State Department. He emphasized Alger Hiss's recent conviction and then stressed Hiss's important advisory role at Yalta to the "physically tired and mentally sick Roosevelt."[13]

By resorting to themes of guilt by association, the "extremists" and "partisans" linked past policies and individuals associated with Alger Hiss or the Yalta Conference. The thrust of their critique was that the main threat to U.S. security was internal, that U.S. interests had been betrayed by Communists or pro-Communists, and that the Yalta experience necessitated a critical re-examination of past policy decisions and the loyalty of policy makers. They singled out Dean Acheson, George Marshall, Owen Lattimore, Philip Jessup, Harry Hopkins, and Franklin Roosevelt. They demanded the repudiation of such policies as those followed at Yalta, and the exclusion from public office of men associated with them.

One target for their attacks was Secretary of State Dean Acheson. Congressmen Alvin O'Konski, Hugh Scott, Jr., Charles Potter (Republican, Michigan), W. Sterling Cole (Republican, New York), Lawrence Smith, Senators James Kem (Republican, Missouri), Styles Bridges, Kenneth Wherry, William Jenner, Edward Martin, Karl Mundt, George Malone, Owen Brewster (Republican, Maine), and Joseph McCarthy denounced Acheson's association with Alger Hiss and his defense of Hiss and the Yalta Conference. Wherry ascribed existing problems to a "leadership tainted by a concept of government that does not square with the American heritage." Jenner noted that the "Alger Hiss group" had "engineered the Yalta sellout" and had turned "Communism loose around one-half of the world." McCarthy summarized this view:

> We know that at Yalta we were betrayed. We know that since Yalta the leaders of this Government by design or ignorance have continued to betray us. . . . We also know that the same men who betrayed America are still leading America. The traitors must no longer lead the betrayed.

13. *Ibid.*, Part 2, 1952–81.

On a more partisan note, O'Konski charged that the United States was threatened in 1950 because the Democrats, having gained national control in 1932, had "nurtured and supported" the Soviet Union. O'Konski concluded, "We must make it clear to the American people that if a thing is good and sound and wholesome for the welfare of the American family, then the Republican Party is for it and will fight for it and that it is the only truly American party today."[14]

Yalta provided one point for Senators William Jenner, George Malone, and Homer Capehart to attack George Marshall's nomination as Secretary of Defense.[15] During the congressional debate on confirmation, Marshall's association with Yalta and the Administration's earlier policy toward China were cited as grounds for disqualification. Although it was confirmed by a sizable majority — 220–105 in the House and 47–21 in the Senate — the nomination encountered decided "partisan" and "extremist" opposition. There were 32 senators and 105 congressmen who were not recorded on this vote. Many Democrats simply abstained, while the Republicans constituted the major opposition to confirmation; 20 Republican senators of a total of 42 and 101 Republican congressmen of a total of 109 were against it.[16]

The concern about internal security that enabled the "extremists" to challenge Marshall's and Acheson's loyalty could more indirectly be carried over to castigate Franklin Roosevelt. The "extremists" identified the main threat to national security as the result of domestic acceptance of communistic ideas that appeared in Harry Hopkins' description of the Soviet Union as a peace-loving nation. The Yalta agreements were the basis for current international problems and an indication of the general lines of New Deal thinking. The remedy lay, they argued, not in a militaristic foreign policy but in the repudiation and exclusion from office of the "Yalta-men."[17]

This denigration of Soviet power and the emphasis on internal

14. In contrast, Democratic Congressman James Davis, who was critical of the conference decisions and advocated the appointment of a new Secretary of State, never assailed Acheson personally. *Ibid.*, Parts 3, 6, 8, 9, 12, 13, 14, and 18, 3416, 4120, 7742, 10761, 10791, 10843, 11359, 11991–94, 12077, 16057–58, 16178, 16238–39, 16309, 16489, A758, A995, A1017–18, A1175, A1692–94, A2052, A2131–32, A4965, A7325, A7517, A5773.

15. *Ibid.*, Parts 11 and 18, 14913–15, 14923, A7216–17.

16. *Ibid.*, Part 11, 14931, 14972–73.

17. *Ibid.*, Parts 8, 16, and 17, 10461, 10643, A5111–12, A5391, A5488–89, A5891–92. *Cleveland Plain Dealer*, September 5, 1950. *Chicago Herald-American*, July 21, 1950, 3; July 25, 1950, 11; August 4, 1950, 13; December 6, 1950, 3, 42; December 11, 1950, 18. *Chicago Tribune*, May 1, 1950, 2; May 5, 1950, 14; October 30, 1950, 14; December 12, 1950, 18. *The Saturday Evening Post*, 222 (May 6, 1950), 10.

security underlay the "extremists'" demands for a more dynamic policy and their opposition to any anti-Soviet policy that involved foreign commitments. Thus, they might demand a bolder approach, but their criticism always returned to the theme of the Administration's weakness or naïveté in counseling negotiations with the Soviet Union. They simultaneously decried past Administration "appeasement" policies and current efforts to ensure U.S. involvement overseas; they supported the defense of the "Western Hemisphere as the Gibraltar of western civilization," the withdrawal of U.S. troops from Korea, and the cessation of military aid to Europe.[18]

The "extremists" and "partisans" also criticized Yalta's harsh treatment of Germany and welcomed the Truman Administration's more conciliatory German policy. The *Chicago Tribune*, Republican Senators Robert Taft, William Jenner, Congressmen William Lemke, and Walter Judd condemned the policy of unconditional surrender, the agreements on German reparations, the dismantling of German plants, and the division of Germany. Lemke pointedly described Yalta and the Roosevelt Administration's wartime policy toward Germany as the "revengeful and hateful doctrine of intellectual pygmies." In addition, the *Tribune* sympathetically reported a German expatriate committee's demands that the Sudentenland be returned to Germany, and it represented the electoral showing of a German refugee party as a protest against the loss of German lands and lives in Eastern Europe. These results confirmed, the *Tribune* suggested, "how from Korea to Germany the world was experiencing the folly of agreement with the Soviet Union."[19]

Despite the outspoken bitterness of these criticisms, the State Department and other proponents of the Administration's foreign policy did not defend Yalta's spirit of compromise, co-operation, and tolerance because they were unsympathetic to it. When discussing Yalta, they simply contrasted Soviet bad faith with U.S. honor and trust. President Truman's statements expressed this feeling of injured innocence and U.S. altruism. Truman noted how the United States had attempted to co-operate with the Soviet Union and had sought to

18. U.S. *Congressional Record*, 81st Cong., 2d sess., 1950, XCVI, Part 12, 16478–79, 16513, 16553–59, 16874–75. In contrast, the "partisans," who attributed contemporary problems to the past Administration's China policy and Yalta, supported military commitments. They assailed the past and demanded the repudiation of Yalta. *Ibid.*, Parts 4, 7, 9, and 12, 4804, 9631, 12183–87, 12743, 16047–50.

19. *Ibid.*, Parts 3, 11, and 14, 3299–3301, 4142–43, 14397, A2642. *Chicago Tribune*, March 9, 1950, 18; March 27, 1950, 20; June 11, 1950, 16; June 13, 1950, 18; August 8, 1950, 10; November 2, 1950, 16.

conciliate existing differences. These efforts, which were made at Teheran, Yalta, and Potsdam, had failed because the Soviet Union had violated its agreements. When peace was not achieved by these means and when it became obvious that the Soviet Union had no intention of abiding by its agreements, his Administration responded forcefully. His own anticommunism was documented by his establishment of a loyalty program for federal employees in 1947. McCarthy's charges not only lacked foundation but were partisan in motivation. These political tactics, Truman added, would not succeed, but they might endanger the bipartisan foreign policy. For these reasons, he deemed McCarthy the "greatest asset the Kremlin has." [20]

Senators Scott Lucas (Democrat, Illinois), Robert Kerr (Democrat, Oklahoma), Tom Connally, Brien McMahon (Democrat, Connecticut), Congressmen Walter Lynch (Democrat, New York), Adolph Sabath (Democrat, Illinois), John Kee (Democrat, West Virginia), *Newsweek, The New York Times, New Republic,* and *The Nation* also stated that the more critical Republican attacks on Yalta were partisan in motivation. In turn, they denounced Soviet violations of Yalta as the basis for current problems and called for a policy of firmness and strength. Concerned about the possibly dismembering effect that Republican criticisms might have on public support for the bipartisan foreign policy, they counseled the need for unity and for a concern about present developments. The *Times* summed up this view when it expressed fear about the use of the public's shocked reaction to the Korean War by Republicans who wanted the United States to abandon international commitments. Withdrawal from an international role, the *Times* warned, would amount to a "Super-Yalta." Although it was critical of the "extremists," the *Times* cautioned against summit diplomacy. In an editorial, the *Times* stated that such conferences benefited only the Soviet Union. A final peace based upon the *status quo,* the *Times* averred, would "involve a Super-Yalta, before which the much criticized original Yalta would pale in significance." [21]

20. Harry S Truman, speech to the Federal Bar Association, Washington, D.C., April 24, 1950, Records of White House Official Reporter, Truman Papers, Truman Library. Transcript of press conference, March 30, 1950, Records of White House Official Reporter, Truman Papers, Truman Library.

21. *Newsweek,* 35 (April 10, 1950), 17; April 24, 1950, 36; 36 (August 28, 1950), 28–29; October 16, 1950, 22. *The New York Times,* February 16, 1950, 22; July 11, 1950, 30; August 15, 1950, 28; September 21, 1950, 30; October 4, 1950, 30; October 23, 1950, 22; November 5, 1950, 10E; December 22, 1950, 22. *The Nation,* 170 (April 8, 1950), 313–15; 171 (August 19, 1950), 157; September 2, 1950, 199–200; October 21, 1950, 362–64. *New Republic,* 122, 15

The outbreak of the Korean War focused attention on the Far East, provided the opportunity for a critical, partisan reappraisal of earlier policy decisions, and terminated any semblance of bipartisanship in foreign policy. Initially, even the "extremists" supported Truman's decision to commit U.S. ground troops to Korea. The outbreak of the war, however, enabled the "extremists," joined then by the "partisans" and "moderates," to condemn Yalta and the Administration's foreign policy more effectively. The "extremists'" consistent anticommunism, and their charges of betrayal and treason, added to their status. In 1950, their denunciations seemed more meaningful to a discouraged, confused public that was embittered about the nature of the Korean War and U.S. involvement in it. The Administration had failed to secure the peace, the threat of Soviet aggression appeared real, and the Cold War threatened to become a hot war.

The Republican National Committee and the Republican Senate and House Campaign committees formally adopted foreign policy as a campaign issue. Republican leaders never forthrightly attacked bipartisanship, but they did reinterpret this term. They took credit for the success of the containment policy in Europe and, at the same time, denied that the Far Eastern policy had ever been bipartisan.

By 1950, the *Chicago Tribune*, George Sokolsky, the congressional Republican leaders and the Republican National Committee had come to agreement. The "moderates" (Congressman John Davis Lodge, Senators H. Alexander Smith, and Irving Ives of New York), "extremists" (the *Chicago Tribune*, George Sokolsky, Senators William Jenner, Kenneth Wherry, Styles Bridges, Congressmen Carl Hinshaw of California, Lawrence Smith, Carl Curtis, and Ralph Gwinn) and "partisans" (Senators Homer Ferguson, William Knowland, and Congressman Walter Judd) concurred that Yalta had not been bipartisan and that the conference had at least contributed to Chiang Kai-shek's defeat. Far Eastern policy became the focus for these attacks on the Administration and for an altered political strategy on foreign policy. The "extremists" extolled the correctness of their earlier claim that bipartisanship was a "trap to ensnare" Republicans; accordingly, they demanded a critical examination of the Yalta agreements and other policy decisions. The "moderates" were

(April 10, 1950), 10–11; 17 (April 24, 1950), 5–6; 123, 9 (August 28, 1950), 5–6; 10 (September 4, 1950), 9, 17; 14 (October 2, 1950), 7–8; 15 (October 9, 1950), 10–20. U.S. *Congressional Record*, 81st Cong., 2d sess., 1950, XCVI, Parts 1, 7, 8, 14, 15, and 17, 639, 9234, 10171, A2158, A2908–9, A5973–74, A5984–85, A6394–95. Tom Connally, "Reviewing American Foreign Policy since 1945," *Department of State Bulletin*, XXIII, 588 (October 9, 1950), 563–78.

simply more temperate than the "extremists" and "partisans" when they denounced Yalta, the Far Eastern policy, and the secrecy of past policy. Indeed, the "moderate" H. Alexander Smith questioned:

> Was there something in the Yalta Pact or some other give-away program which brought American withdrawal from China and is continuing to exert its influence in respect to Formosa? Why does American policy seek to contain the aggressor in eastern Europe and pursue a diametrically opposite policy in Asia? What baleful influence has our State Department inherited which makes our foreign policy a contradictory mystery.[22]

Extending this view, the *Chicago Tribune*, Congressmen Lawrence Smith, Paul Shafer, Arthur Miller, Gordon Canfield (Republican, New Jersey), Walter Judd, Noah Mason, T. Millet Hand (Republican, New Jersey), Edward Jenison (Republican, Illinois), John Bennett, Senators James Kem, William Jenner, George Malone, Joseph McCarthy, Robert Taft, Edward Martin, *The Saturday Evening Post, U.S. News and World Report*, and Raymond Moley directly traced postwar problems and the Korean War to the Roosevelt and Truman administrations' decisions during crises and at Yalta and other conferences. After noting that the same "sell-out to Stalin" statesmen continued to formulate policy, they demanded new leaders to direct policy away from the Yalta spirit "of sympathetic acceptance of communism as a peace-loving philosophy which has made Russia a threat to the very existence of the world."[23]

Yalta continued to be blamed for the communization of Poland, but the emphasis and objectives of the declaimants of Yalta's injury to Poland had changed. In contrast to 1945, Polish-Americans were no longer the most outspoken Yalta critics. Rather, Republican Congressmen and Senators — John Davis Lodge, Antoni Sadlak (Connec-

---

22. *Chicago Tribune*, January 15, 1950, 18. *Chicago Herald-American*, January 9, 1950, 8. U.S. *Congressional Record*, 81st Cong., 2d sess., 1950, XCVI, Parts 1, 2, 5, 7, 13, 15, and 16, 80, 391, 395, 470–81, 487, 1754, 5771, 8979, A108, A160, A305, A677, A679, A705, A709, A796–97, A3434–36, A3459–60, A4547.

23. *Chicago Tribune*, June 25, 1950, 2; July 2, 1950, 20; July 3, 1950, 8; July 25, 1950, 12; July 29, 1950, 6; September 28, 1950, 16; October 10, 1950, 8. *U.S. News and World Report*, 29 (July 7, 1950), 11, 13. *Newsweek*, 36 (July 10, 1950), 92. *The Saturday Evening Post*, 223 (July 22, 1950), 10; September 2, 1950, 12. U.S. *Congressional Record*, 81st Cong., 2d sess., 1950, XCVI, Parts 7, 8, 16, 17, and 18, 9180, 9184–85, 9188, 9228, 9238–40, 9320, A4752, A4980, 1055–56, A4986, A5028, A5225, A5779, A5844, A5921, A6891. In contrast, the "moderates" Senators Alexander Wiley (Republican, Wisconsin) and Wayne Morse (Republican, Oregon) decried open partisanship. Although they were critical of past Administration mistakes, they urged concern for present, not past, developments. *Ibid.*, Part 7, 9161, 9231.

ticut), Kenneth Keating, Paul Shafer, Alexander Wiley, Homer Ferguson, Robert Hale, John Caleb Boggs (Delaware), and Robert Hendrickson (New Jersey) — had become the champions of Poland. Wiley appealed directly to Polish-Americans by referring to the "sellout of free, religious Poland at Yalta." Democratic Congressmen responded by denouncing Soviet violations of the Yalta agreements.[24]

Yalta received its most open and far-reaching assessment to date during the 1950 congressional campaign. The Republican National Committee, the Republican Senate Policy Committee, and Republican members of the Senate Foreign Relations Committee issued statements condemning Democratic foreign policy blunders, particularly Yalta. They emphasized Yalta's secrecy, denied that the conference had been bipartisan, and stressed the influence of Communists and Alger Hiss on past foreign policy decisions. They then renewed demands for a foreign policy that would redress the losses caused by those past mistakes. By impugning either the Administration's loyalty or its understanding of Soviet aims, they implied that these decisions helped only the Soviet Union. Indeed, one Republican campaign pamphlet asserted:

> While Communists and fellow travelers in strategic positions were manipulating American policies in the interest of Soviet Russia, Democrats were hampering and obstructing efforts, chiefly by Republicans, to expose and stop the Communist conspiracy. . . . The security of the American people depends upon the election of an Independent Republican Congress.[25]

In 1950, the Republicans urged independence from the Administration's foreign policy and surveillance of it. Some Republicans openly called the bipartisan foreign policy detrimental to national security. The Illinois Republican platform assailed Democratic "stupidity and bungling," cited the Yalta conferees' "betrayals" of Poland and China, pledged a vigorous "American" foreign policy, and openly opposed what they ironically called the "bipartisan" foreign policy.[26] The South Dakota Republican platform described the Republican

24. *Ibid.*, Parts 2, 6, 10, 13, and 17, 1610, 7727, 14102, 14141–50, A886, A889, A6776–77. Senator Paul Douglas, address to the Dinner Meeting of the Polish-American Congress, Chicago, Illinois, March 8, 1950, Polish-American Congress Library. *Chicago Tribune*, March 9, 1950, 9; March 14, 1950, 14.

25. Republican National Committee, *Red Herring and Whitewash: The Record of Communism in Government*, and *Background to Korea*; Republican Senate Policy Committee, *Supporting Material on Issue No. 2: The Democrat Administration's Fatal Compromise with Communism: The Administration's Compromise with Communism in the United States Army*. U.S. *Congressional Record*, 81st Cong., 2d sess., 1950, XCVI, Part 9, 12436, 12485.

26. *Chicago Tribune*, August 12, 1950, 6.

party as the party of peace. It charged that the Democrats, "since the turn of the century," had led the nation to war. From the time of the Yalta and Potsdam "betrayals," the New Deal and Fair Deal administrations, the platform further stated, had given "aid and comfort" to the spread of communism.[27] *Time* magazine reported that "all over the nation, G.O.P. orators" concentrated on the Administration's foreign policy, specifically Yalta, blaming it for the Korean War.[28] George Smith, former staff director of the Republican Senate Policy Committee, argued that the bipartisan foreign policy benefited the Democrats by enabling them to "dole out" information selectively. No Republican had attended Yalta, Teheran, or Potsdam. Nothing significant could be achieved with a bipartisan foreign policy, he argued, and the Republicans could have had greater force in making a more effective U.S. foreign policy if they had taken independent action.[29]

Senator Joseph McCarthy, the Republican most identified with denunciations of the Administration, used the 1950 campaign to develop more forcefully the theme of Democratic procommunism. If the public approved "Communist coddling" and wanted more Yalta "disasters," they should vote Democratic. He said that Dean Acheson had sent Alger Hiss to Yalta, "where Hiss, Gromyko and a third person drafted the Yalta Agreement."[30]

Generally, the "extremists" echoed McCarthy's charges. To them, the 1950 election was not merely another political campaign but a crusade wherein any method of dealing with the New Deal and Fair Deal was permissible. Foreign policy was the key issue in the campaign, and they enthusiastically welcomed the shift in Republican campaign tactics concerning bipartisanship in foreign policy. A heading on an editorial in the November 4 issue of *The Saturday Evening Post* captured this approach: "Has the G.O.P. Played Rough Enough to Win an Election?" Blaming Yalta for foreign policy problems, the "extremists" particularly criticized Roosevelt's dishonesty and disregard for the public. Indeed, the *Chicago Tribune* stated that "Roosevelt's treachery at Yalta" would replace Benedict Arnold's actions as the symbol of dishonor.[31]

27. U.S. *Congressional Record*, 81st Cong., 2d sess., 1950, XCVI, Part 16, A5484.
28. Time, 56 (August 28, 1950), 12; October 9, 1950, 23.
29. George Smith, "Bipartisan Foreign Policy in Partisan Politics," *American Perspective*, 4, 2 (Spring, 1950), 157–69.
30. U.S. *Congressional Record*, 81st Cong., 2d sess., 1950, XCVI, Part 18, A6900–6901.
31. Everett Dirksen's campaign for election to the U.S. Senate from Illinois

Reverting to the theme of secrecy of the Yalta Conference and the mistaken trust of the conferees, Republican Senators William Knowland, Karl Mundt, Kenneth Wherry, William Langer, Harry Cain (Washington), Eugene Millikin, Congressmen Joseph Martin, Lowell Stockman (Oregon), Gerald Ford (Michigan), Joseph O'Hara (Minnesota), Noah Mason, and Clare Hoffman defended the soundness, reasonableness, and legitimacy of criticisms of foreign policy. Their criticisms were not partisan in motivation; Yalta's secrecy and costly mistakes necessitated a more critical approach that provided a check against the repetition of past mistakes and the means of rectifying them. Langer specifically noted:

> So, Mr. President, because there were at the Democratic Convention a lot of weak men who wanted to win, who wanted to get a few more votes by nominating Roosevelt for President for a third time, they were willing to take this man and sell out the country. That is why a sick man went to Yalta, a man who, in the absence [sic] of the Secretary of State, and without even his knowledge, gave away the countries and advantages which I have already named [the Far East]. That is why we today have our boys fighting in Korea — and why our beloved country is facing ruin and destruction.[32]

Republican Senator Robert Taft, a candidate for re-election in 1950, concentrated on earlier foreign policy decisions. Never an avowed supporter of bipartisanship or internationalism, Taft adopted McCarthy's tone and tactics in 1950. He never wholeheartedly championed McCarthy; his embrace of McCarthyism corresponded with the shift in the Republican campaign position to an emphasis on national security. Taft reiterated his charges that the Administration's

---

followed the same approach. Dirksen raised these themes of Yalta's betrayal of Poland and China, Hiss's influence, and the responsibility for the Korean War. He supported repudiation. *Ibid.*, 7298–99. *The Saturday Evening Post*, 223 (November 4, 1950), 10. *Chicago Herald-American*, March 29, 1950, 32; April 24, 1950, 3; June 26, 1950, 11; September 4, 1950, 32; September 13, 1950, 32; September 21, 1950, 11; October 2, 1950, 3; October 17, 1950, p. 3; October 18, 1950, 3; October 25, 1950, 3; November 2, 1950, 3. *Chicago Tribune*, February 7, 1950, 4; April 19, 1950, 16; May 14, 1950, 3; May 17, 1950, 18; May 18, 1950, 1; May 21, 1950, 20; July 11, 1950, 13; August 11, 1950, 14; August 16, 1950, 1; August 17, 1950, 1; August 18, 1950, 7; October 14, 1950, 8; October 19, 1950, 16; October 21, 1950, 7; October 31, 1950, 14; November 6, 1950, 3.

32. Langer erred; Edward Stettinius, not James Byrnes, had been Secretary of State at the time of the Yalta Conference. Langer's charges were based on Byrnes's alleged ignorance of the Far Eastern agreements. U.S. *Congressional Record*, 81st Cong., 2d sess., 1950, XCVI, Parts 3, 4, 7, 8, 9, 11, 14, 15, and 17, 2893, 5152, 9526, 11326–27, 12521, 15642–43, A2641, A3877, A5670–71, A6718, A6720. *Detroit News*, October 24, 1950. "Washington News from Our Congressman," *Kendall County News*, March 1, 1950, 2.

domestic policy was "socialistic" and that Democratic foreign policy made possible World War III. He decried President Truman's allegation that McCarthy's criticisms of the Roosevelt and Truman administrations' past actions had harmed the bipartisan foreign policy. Truman was the one who had ruined the bipartisan foreign policy. "By our constant building up of Russia, by the pro-communist attitude of Wallace and Hopkins, culminating in the secret agreements of Yalta, confirmed at Potsdam, we have placed Russia in a position where it is a threat to the world." What the country needed, Taft concluded, was the elimination of "Communists" from the State Department, which was possible only with the election of a new President.[33]

The criticisms of the Yalta Conference and the demands for a reappraisal of the Yalta agreements and other foreign policy decisions made by the Roosevelt and Truman administrations continued after the campaign. For the "extremists," Yalta was an effective symbol that had brought them out of oblivion and made them respectable. By creating doubts about executive action, they sought to use Yalta as often as possible to curb as well the domestic and international procedures of the New Deal. The meeting of Truman and Attlee provided one such occasion. On December 18, Republican Senator James Kem introduced Senate Resolution 371 demanding publication of the results of Truman and Attlee's conference. Kem's resolution also demanded that any agreement concluded at this conference be embodied in a treaty and submitted to the Senate for approval. He said that the purpose of his resolution was to "prevent another Yalta or another Potsdam."[34] Senate Republicans tried to force a Senate vote on the resolution. They did not want it referred to the Foreign Relations Committee, where it could be killed. The Senate debate on whether the resolution should be referred to committee or immediately considered reflected the partisan aura of the foreign policy debate. The resolution to refer to committee passed 47–29; all 29 senators who voted "Nay" were Republicans.[35]

33. *New York Herald-Tribune*, May 16, 1950. *Chicago Tribune*, April 1, 1950, 5; May 17, 1950, 4. This militancy was echoed in the demands expressed by both major veterans organizations, the American Legion and the Veterans of Foreign Wars. The Legion demanded the repudiation of Yalta, while the V.F.W. asked that all government officials who had anything to do with the Yalta sellout be "found, removed from office and punished to the full extent of the law." *Ibid.*, August 27, 1950, 8; September 2, 1950, 5.

34. U.S. *Congressional Record*, 81st Cong., 2d sess., 1950, XCVI, Part 12, 16689.

35. *Ibid.*, 16691.

The arbitrariness with which the "extremists" and "partisans" appraised individual loyalty reflected the rigidity and intolerance of their position in the debates on foreign policy. They supported Douglas MacArthur and dismissed the patriotism and understanding of men like Alger Hiss, Dean Acheson, George Marshall, Harry Hopkins, and Franklin Roosevelt. The "extremists" and "partisans" portrayed MacArthur as a sage and used his statements on the Korean War to raise doubts about the loyalty of people within the Administration and about the conduct of foreign policy. Indeed, *The Saturday Evening Post*, Congressmen Noah Mason, Arthur Miller, and Senators George Malone and William Knowland blamed postwar crises on Yalta and criticized the Administration's failure to consult MacArthur about the Far Eastern situation before Yalta.[36]

The Administration's decision to limit the Korean War conflicted with MacArthur's position. These differences renewed the question of MacArthur's right to try to influence public opinion. In October, President Truman, seeking in part to curb MacArthur's political statements, met with him at Wake Island. Returning from Wake Island, President Truman described the conference as a beneficial effort to work out a united policy. He emphasized the military's role but added that both he and MacArthur recognized that the Korean War was more than a "military problem." Truman then stressed the equal importance of working for allied co-operation and understanding. Defending the Administration's vigilance in combating the Soviet threat, Truman blamed Soviet actions and policies for the problems confronting the United States. He asked for public support and understanding and expressed the hope that Wake Island might become the symbol of U.S. unity of purpose for world peace.[37]

Truman's efforts to promote understanding of his policies and to lessen partisanship were doomed. Foreign policy had already become enmeshed in partisan politics. The Administration's adoption of containment, its reliance on an anti-Communist rhetoric, the public's doubts and concerns about the Administration's priorities, and the outbreak of the Korean War had helped to create a new political climate and, thereby, a new political situation. This situation merged with a shift in the Republican campaign position on foreign policy

36. *Ibid.*, Parts 8, 10, 12, and 13, 10868, 13576, 16023–28, A588. *The Saturday Evening Post*, 222 (February 18, 1950), 12.

37. Harry S Truman, speech, San Francisco, California, October 17, 1950, Records of White House Official Reporter, Truman Papers, Truman Library.

and enabled the "extremists" to emerge as a major political force within the Republican party and the nation. By 1950, most people might ignore the "extremists'" anti-New Deal strictures, but they had come to consider the criticisms of Yalta and the Administration's security policies legitimate.

chapter 7

1951: disavowal of past commitments

In 1951, congressional debates on foreign policy continued to develop a decidedly partisan, anti-Yalta character. By this time, even the "moderates" had adopted the political tactic of concentrating on foreign policy decisions made in the past, more specifically on Yalta. Partly, this shift resulted from the altered perspective on foreign policy; partly, it was a product of developments during 1951 that raised doubts about the Administration's tactics and procedures: the dismissal of General MacArthur, the proposal of a peace treaty with Japan, and the proposed assignment of U.S. ground troops to Europe.

Congressional debates on these issues provided the forum for a partisan attack on the Administration's credibility. The critics focused on the relationship of current problems to past errors and to the Democrats' continuity in office. Such a focus suggested the need for the repudiation of the policies and policy makers associated with these past decisions and for new restraints on the use of executive authority. These developments, the containment rhetoric, and the changed Republican campaign tactics on foreign policy tended to increase the influence and respectability of the "extremists" in national politics.

Couching their criticisms of past decisions in tones of righteous anticommunism, the "extremists" demanded a vastly different approach to foreign policy. They wanted the United States to assume the initiative and repulse communism. They denounced limited war and containment and demanded reductions in economic and military foreign aid, U.S. withdrawal from overseas commitments, the renunciation of past policy decisions, and restrictions on the executive branch.

The Yalta Conference again provided a cover for attack; congressmen could cite it as the justification for their suspicions about the procedures of past policies and executive authority and for their advocacy of a re-examination of foreign commitments and executive powers. Indeed, demands for the proposed Bricker Amendment or for the Twenty-second Amendment's limiting the President to two terms were based on abuses of executive authority at Yalta. Senator Bricker argued that Yalta's results warranted restrictions on executive authority and an increased congressional role. The policy statements of the "extremists," "partisans," and "moderates" were similar, but the tone and emphasis of their criticisms remained different. They mainly emphasized the responsibility of Congress to provide constructive criticisms and an independent evaluation of earlier Administration policy decisions as the necessary prerequisites for a more realistic policy.[1]

In addition, these Republican critics stated that their actions were consistent with a truly bipartisan foreign policy. They denied that Yalta had been bipartisan and underlined the secrecy of the conference's proceedings. At the same time, they stressed the need for greater consultation and information about the Administration's foreign policy. As an example of the problem of secrecy that confronted the Congress and the public, Senator William Knowland cited his unsuccessful efforts to secure a copy of the telephone directory used by the Yalta delegation.[2] To justify their former silence over Yalta, some Republicans expressed their earlier ignorance about the extent of the Yalta commitments. In a different vein, Congressman Donald Jackson (Republican, California) noted that some Republicans had consistently opposed Yalta since 1945. More Republicans would have spoken out, Jackson averred, had they known the true nature and full results of the conference.[3]

The "extremists" attempted to exploit this heightened criticism of the Yalta agreements and other decisions to confirm the correctness of their earlier position on foreign policy. They invoked Yalta to discredit the Truman Administration's international commitments and thus to corroborate their demand for limits to such commitments. Congressmen Lawrence Smith, B. Carroll Reece, Senators Frank Carlson (Republican, Kansas), William Jenner, columnists West-

---

1. Thus, Senators Bricker and Morse averred, when supporting restrictions on executive authority, that Yalta would never have been ratified had it been submitted for Senate approval. Senators Taft and Lodge assailed past Administration "mistakes": Lodge condemned the Administration's mistaken appraisal of Soviet aims, and Taft added that the Administration had "secretly agreed" to Soviet zones of influence and thereby paved the way for Soviet domination of Eastern Europe and Manchuria. U.S. *Congressional Record*, 82d Cong., 1st sess., 1951, XCVII, Parts 1, 7, and 12, 147, 8449–50, A1827–28. *Time*, 57 (February 26, 1951), 27; January 15, 1951, 18–19. *Chicago Tribune*, September 19, 1951, 11. *Chicago Herald-American*, February 7, 1951, 18; July 14, 1951, 7.

2. U.S. *Congressional Record*, 82d Cong., 1st sess., 1951, XCVII, Parts 1, 6, 7, 10, 13, and 14, 381–82, 562, 959–60, 7591–92, 7595, 9122–23, 13665, A2875–76, A5586.

3. *Ibid.*, Part 6, 7752–54.

brook Pegler, George Sokolsky, and the *Chicago Tribune* demanded a more restricted policy course. They supported verbal militancy and internal security safeguards; their only positive proposal was to exclude the "men of Yalta," Truman or Acheson, from influence in the government. Summing up their idea of the main problem confronting the United States, Sokolsky stated that Stalin "organizes" strikes, "infiltrates universities," and "steals plans out of our laboratories."[4]

On February 14, 1951, 118 Republican congressmen, in a declaration on an alternative foreign policy, defended noninvolvement, demanded a retrenchment in U.S. international commitments, particularly those connected with the UN and NATO, and asserted that the Congress should direct foreign policy. During the debate on this declaration, Congressmen Lawrence Smith, Harry Towe (Republican, New Jersey), Joseph O'Hara, William Hill (Republican, Colorado), and Frank Fellows (Republican, Maine) referred to Yalta to justify retrenchment. Their main concern was the situation within the country. The Administration's foreign policy, Smith noted, had brought "war and more war, taxes, more regimentation and the imposition of militarism," while Administration domestic policies had done nothing but "rob, plunder, dispoil [*sic*] and eventually enslave Americans."[5]

This same negativism dominated Senate debate on the assignment of U.S. ground forces to Europe. In an effort to curb executive actions, Republican Senate leader Kenneth Wherry introduced a resolution prohibiting the assignment of U.S. troops to NATO without prior congressional approval. Wherry denied that the President had the constitutional right to send U.S. troops to Europe and argued further that the people in the United States wanted the Congress to regulate U.S. military commitments because they wished "no more Yaltas, Teherans, and Potsdams; no more back-room secret agreements sealing the fate of themselves and their children."[6]

4. *Time*, 57 (February 26, 1951), 27. *Chicago Herald-American*, February 3, 1951, 7; April 16, 1951, 15; January 27, 1951, 3; March 7, 1951, 23; June 26, 1951, 12, July 13, 1951, 12. *Milwaukee Sentinel*, January 14, 1951, 10. *Chicago Tribune*, July 20, 1951, 1, 4; July 21, 1951; July 22, 1951; September 7, 1951, 8; October 31, 1951, 20. U.S. *Congressional Record*, 82d Cong., 1st sess., 1951, XCVII, Parts 1, 5, 11, and 12, 291–92, 7189–90, A248–49, A1508–12.

5. *Ibid.*, Part 1, 1257–64. Democratic Congresswoman Reva Bosone replied that this declaration sought scapegoats, not solutions. She deemed the Republicans inconsistent for demanding a stronger policy while opposing a military build-up. On a final note, she defended the correctness of the Yalta Conference and blamed postwar developments on Soviet violations of the agreements. *Ibid.*, Part 2, 1699–1700.

6. *Ibid.*, Parts 1, 3, 320–25, 2907, 3015.

In the debate on Wherry's resolution, Senators James Kem, Robert Taft, Joseph McCarthy, John Bricker, John Butler (Republican, Maryland), and Francis Case (Republican, South Dakota) introduced the events at Yalta to show that congressional restrictions on executive direction of foreign policy were necessary. Unlike other Senate proponents of the resolution, McCarthy supported the assignment of U.S. ground troops to Europe, but he criticized the failure of the Administration to include West German and Spanish military forces in its planning. All of these senators, however, argued that Yalta occurred only because the Congress had not been consulted. Kem, Taft, and Bricker asserted that the Congress must regain its foreign affairs function. In addition, Taft ascribed the Soviet threat directly to the Roosevelt and Truman administrations' willingness to trust the Soviet Union at Yalta and Potsdam and to the Roosevelt Administration's naïve wartime characterization of the Soviet Union as a democracy. For Taft, the Communist threat was more internal than external. He pressed for a retrenchment in U.S. foreign commitments, advocated reliance on sea and air power, and at the same time, stressed the dangers of the proposed dispersal of U.S. ground troops.[7]

Although Congress did not implement Wherry's resolution, it did pass a modified version, Senate Resolution 99. This resolution required Senate approval for the assignment of U.S. troops to Europe, limited the commitment to four divisions, confirmed the Senate's responsibility to declare war, and required Senate approval for the assignment of additional U.S. troops. Wherry and eighteen other Republicans opposed Senate Resolution 99 because they thought it too weak. Democratic Senators J. William Fulbright (Arkansas) and Allen Ellender (Louisiana) also opposed the resolution; they objected to its restrictions on the executive branch.[8]

The "extremists" revealed their verbal militancy and their opposition to international involvement, even when such involvement was anti-Communist, in their votes on the Mutual Assistance Control Act

7. Republican Senator Edward Thye, arguing in support of the assignment of U.S. troops to Europe, also relied on the Yalta image of executive abuse of authority. He contended that U.S. troop commitments would promote increased legislative-executive consultations and would prevent "snap judgments or secret agreements such as those of Yalta and Potsdam." *Ibid.*, Parts 1, 2, and 3, 485–86, 1719–21, 2653, 2957–59, 3041, 3163–64, 3272–73.

8. *Ibid.*, Part 3, 3282. The nineteen Republicans were Wallace Bennett, John Bricker, Hugh Butler, Harry Cain, Francis Case, Guy Cordon, Everett Dirksen, Henry Dworshak, Zales Ecton, Homer Ferguson, William Jenner, James Kem, William Langer, George Malone, Karl Mundt, Andrew Schoeppel, Herman Welker, Kenneth Wherry, and John Williams.

of 1951, the Mutual Security Act of 1951, the Mutual Security Appropriations Act, and State Department appropriations for 1952. Among
those who opposed the Mutual Assistance Control Act of 1951 were
16 Republican senators.[9] The Mutual Security Act received negative
votes from 80 Republican and 18 Southern Democratic congressmen
and 20 Republican and 1 Southern Democratic senator.[10] Opposing
the Mutual Security Appropriations Act were 81 Republican and
18 Southern Democratic congressmen and 12 Republican and 1
Southern Democratic senator.[11] There were 112 Republican and 14
Southern Democratic congressmen and 25 Republican and 2 Southern Democratic senators who voted against the State Department
appropriations bill.[12]

The "extremists" also used Yalta to assail proposals for negotiations with the Soviet Union. Senator George Malone and Congressman Patrick Hillings (Republican, California) denounced the Administration's diplomacy during the Korean War. Hillings simply
attributed the war to Yalta's "appeasement" policy, while Malone
criticized the Kaesong peace negotiations as a "second Yalta." Malone
further charged that the scattered U.S. commitments and involvement in "impossible" situations in Europe and Asia invited Soviet aggression. As a corrective, he advocated controls on foreign imports.[13]

The Saturday Evening Post, Congressmen Ellis Berry (Republican, South Dakota), John Wood (Republican, Idaho), Lawrence
Smith, and Senators Robert Taft and George Malone interpreted
Yalta as a confirmation of the Roosevelt and Truman administrations'
false and harmful philosophy. The *Post* demanded that the Administration adopt a more forceful foreign policy that would entail
increasing U.S. military strength in Europe, using the previously
"untapped" military manpower of the "free Poles in exile," and demanding that the Soviet Union, in return for peace in Korea, cede
its economic "stranglehold" on Germany and Japan and fulfill the

9. *Ibid.*, Part 8, 10746. These sixteen included John Bricker, Styles Bridges,
Hugh Butler, John Butler, Homer Capehart, Everett Dirksen, Henry Dworshak,
Zales Ecton, James Kem, Karl Mundt, Andrew Schoeppel, Robert Taft, Arthur
Watkins, Kenneth Wherry, and John Williams.
10. *Ibid.*, Parts 9, 10, 12484, 12720.
11. *Ibid.*, Part 10, 13031–32, 13431–32. This same negativism characterized
Congressmen George Dondero's (Republican, Michigan) and Fred Crawford's
(Republican, Michigan) justifications for their opposition to the military budget
during the House debate on the Department of Defense Appropriations Bill for
1952. *Ibid.*, Part 7, 9734, 9746–47.
12. *Ibid.*, Part 10, 12990, 13083. Democratic Senator Fulbright's opposition
was based on his support for a larger appropriation.
13. *Ibid.*, Parts 6 and 7, 7761, 9304–6.

Yalta promises for free elections in Eastern Europe. Taft, however, repeatedly criticized the Truman Administration's "socialistic" domestic policies. The Soviet threat existed, he charged, because of such "weak and wrongheaded" policies as those followed at Yalta. He then charged that the Communist philosophy had been adopted at Yalta because Communists had succeeded in "planting" themselves among U.S. leaders. After Smith and Malone noted Hiss's and other pro-Communists' influence in the formulation of the Yalta agreements and other Administration policies, Smith denounced U.S. foreign aid and demanded that it be reduced. Berry, during the debate on universal military training, also noted Hiss's presence and said that the Administration's "fear, panic and hysteria" were the real reasons for the Yalta agreements, which had permitted millions of East Europeans and Asians to be enslaved. Although he wanted a firmer foreign policy, Berry opposed universal military training. He stated, "A vote for this 18½-year-old draft is a vote to ratify Yalta, Teheran, and Potsdam." According to him, the military leaders at Yalta had panicked, and because these leaders lacked any more free peoples to trade away, they were "grasping" for U.S. eighteen-year-olds.[14]

The official position of the Republican leaders did not coincide with these "extremist" attacks, but the leaders had made a definite commitment to use Yalta to impugn the Truman and Roosevelt administrations. One of their tactics was to propose to repudiate past mistakes by congressional resolution as a necessary preliminary to a bolder foreign policy. The principal resolutions introduced provided for either the formal repudiation of Yalta or U.S. moral encouragement or financial support for the liberation of the "satellite countries." Another tactic was to attack presidential appointments because of the individual's association with the Yalta decisions.

On January 8, 1951, Republican Congressman Robert Hale introduced House Joint Resolution 74, which was identical to his March 28, 1950, resolution. Both urged U.S. "withdrawal" from the Yalta agreements.[15] Hale's resolution was never reported out of committee, but it did secure a committee hearing. During the hearing, Hale emphasized Soviet violations of the Yalta agreements and the "unprincipled" sacrifice of the rights of the peoples of Poland and China. The obvious purpose of his resolution, he said, was to "encourage" the peoples of Poland and China. By accepting this resolution, he con-

14. *Ibid.*, Parts 1, 3, and 14, 677, 1033, 3440–41, A5286, A5458. *Chicago Tribune*, June 10, 1951, 1. *The Saturday Evening Post*, 223 (January 20, 1951), 10, 12; 224 (November 24, 1951), 12.
15. See Appendix E for text.

ceded, the Congress would recognize that the United States had made a mistake.[16] In 1951, in addition to emphasizing the "betrayal" of Poland, Hale stressed Yalta's injustice to China. Hale did not, however, make any exaggerated claims about liberation or about congressional authority to rectify "mistakes." In fact, when questioned by Congressman James Richards (Democrat, South Carolina) on Congress' right to renounce an executive agreement, he asserted that his resolution merely requested the president to take whatever action might "effectuate" U.S. withdrawal.[17]

Hale had also introduced two other resolutions — one expressing support for the creation of an Atlantic Union, the other attempting a definition of Soviet aggression — that he thought were more important than his Yalta resolution. He admitted, "To declare the Yalta agreement no longer binding may not be of particular high order of urgency but the quicker it can be done the better in my opinion."[18] Republican Congressman Walter Judd, a critic of Yalta, listed himself as cosponsor of Hale's resolutions about an Atlantic Union and an attempted definition of Soviet aggression, but he did not cosponsor the Yalta resolution.[19]

On May 14, Republican Congressman Lawrence Smith introduced House Concurrent Resolution 102. Smith's resolution, which was also never acted upon, was less temperate and conciliatory than Hale's resolution. Smith sought the "repudiation" of the Yalta agreements, not withdrawal from them. Repudiation, Smith argued, would warn the Soviet Union that the people of the United States opposed aggression and would provide the "enslaved" peoples with "hope." In addition to Soviet violations, he emphasized the Administration's complicity. Public confidence in the Administration's foreign policy would be restored when the "men and mentality of Yalta" were banished from conducting it. He demanded the repudiation of Potsdam as well as Yalta because both conferences had treated Eastern Europe and Asia "harshly" and had "dismembered" and "mutilated" Germany. A major topic of Smith's resolution was Yalta's and Potsdam's injustices to Germany.[20]

The Republican leaders' reaction to President Truman's nomination of Philip Jessup as U.S. Representative to the United Nations con-

16. U.S. House of Representatives, Committee on Foreign Affairs, *Preliminary Hearings on Various Bills Pending Before the Committee*, 82d Cong., 1st sess., 1951, 3.
17. *Ibid.*, 4–5.   18. *Ibid.*, 5.   19. *Ibid.*, 6.
20. See Appendix F for text. U.S. *Congressional Record*, 82d Cong., 1st sess., 1951, XCVII, Parts 4, 5, 13, and 14, 5279–80, 6279–80, A3409–10, A4170–71.

firmed anew their tactics. They tried to prevent Jessup's confirmation because he had defended Yalta, had helped formulate the postwar policy on China, and was on Senator McCarthy's list of security cases. Jessup, McCarthy had earlier charged, was a "serious" security risk who might "someday" be sent to Paris to negotiate with the Russians "even as Hiss in a less important capacity did the negotiating at Yalta."[21]

McCarthy's approach characterized the position adopted by other Republicans as diverse as Senators H. Alexander Smith, Owen Brewster, and Governor Harold Stassen during hearings on Jessup's confirmation that were conducted by a subcommittee of the Senate Foreign Relations Committee. These Republicans singled out Jessup's association with earlier Administration policy on China as grounds for his disqualification. McCarthy also accused the Truman Administration of playing politics with foreign policy by retaining Secretary of State Acheson. McCarthy averred that the record of the "administrative branch" of the Democratic party ("properly . . . labeled as the Communist Party") must be publicized if Acheson were ever to be ejected. Stassen, less confident and assertive, assailed past administrations' tragic mistakes in foreign policy, and thus Jessup's qualifications, but he refused to ascertain whether these errors were the result of "subversive treason" or "honest mistakes."[22]

During their testimony before the subcommittee, Jessup and UN Ambassador Warren Austin confronted this line of attack. Republican Senator Owen Brewster, when questioning both Jessup and Austin, emphatically gave his view on the Administration's and Yalta's responsibility for the "fall of China." In reply, Austin denied that the Administration had permitted Chiang's defeat and stressed the Generalissimo's partial responsibility.[23] Jessup also attributed Chiang's defeat to events subsequent to Yalta and simultaneously defended the conference. Postwar problems, Jessup asserted in his discussion of U.S. efforts to ensure free elections in Eastern Europe, were the consequences of the Soviet Union's failure to co-operate with the West.[24]

Jessup's nomination was never acted upon. In 1951, the subcommittee voted 3–2 against confirmation. The Senate later confirmed

21. *Ibid.*, Part 7, 9703–10.
22. U.S. Senate, Subcommittee of the Committee of Foreign Relations, *Hearings on the Nomination of Philip Jessup as United States Representative to the United Nations*, 82d Cong., 1st sess., 1951, 7, 733–39, 761.
23. *Ibid.*, 158–59, 177, 394, 396–99.
24. *Ibid.*, 547–48, 961.

nine of the ten Administration's proposed nominations for U.S. Representative to the UN; only Jessup's was postponed.[25] In 1952, after Republican congressional leaders had submitted a resolution opposing Jessup's nomination, the Administration quietly decided not to press the issue.[26]

Although criticisms of Yalta had become more partisan and more negative, Yalta's defenders in 1951 continued to apologize for the conference. They emphasized the advice of the military and dismissed criticisms as simply partisan or based upon hindsight. Indeed, President Truman's main concern was to diminish partisanship. In speeches that he made in June, September, October, and November, 1951, Truman attributed the past policy's failure to bring peace to the Soviet Union's refusal to honor its commitments and to cooperate. Stressing the need for domestic unity and for a view to the future, Truman extolled the bipartisan foreign policy and expressed his hope that foreign policy would not be a partisan issue in the 1952 campaign. Past policies, he averred, sought to secure the national interest, not partisan advantage. To document this statement, he cited his appointment of men to policy positions regardless of their party affiliation. Most Republicans, Truman argued, supported the Administration's foreign policy; only certain Republicans wanted to make foreign policy a political issue. Only in his speech in October did he mention or attempt to justify the Yalta Conference. He pledged to continue efforts to "secure" freedom for the Eastern European peoples and to pursue negotiations when agreements could be enforced, and he urged continued support for containment policies.[27]

In their apologetic defence of Yalta, Senators Herbert Lehman (Democrat, New York), Guy Gillette (Democrat, Iowa), and Brien McMahon, the *New Republic*, and W. Averell Harriman, Mutual Security Administration Director in the Truman Administration, tacitly shared this suspicion of the Soviet Union. Also, statements made by *The New York Times* about the Kaesong peace talks implied the

25. U.S. *Congressional Record*, 82d Cong., 1st sess., 1951, XCVII, Part 10, 13419, 13553.

26. *Ibid.*, 82d Cong., 2d sess., 1952, XCVIII, Part 3, 3441.

27. Harry S Truman, speech to the Woman's National Democratic Club, Washington, D.C., November 20, 1951, Records of the White House Official Reporter, Truman Papers, Truman Library. Harry S Truman, speech, Arnold Engineering Center, Tullahoma, Tennessee, June 25, 1951, Records of White House Official Reporter, Truman Papers, Truman Library. Transcript of press conference, September 20, 1951, Records of White House Official Reporter, Truman Papers, Truman Library. Harry S Truman, remarks to Delegation from the American Hungarian Federation, Washington, D.C., October 12, 1951, Records of White House Official Reporter, Truman Papers, Truman Library.

same distrust. None defended the Yalta spirit; all assumed that the Soviet Union was treacherous. Harriman traced postwar problems to Soviet violations of the Yalta agreements, while the *Times* maintained that the United States remained undeceived by the "seeming reasonableness" of the Communists at Kaesong. Commending the Administration's efforts to rearm the "free world," the *Times* stated, "It was the immediate and one-sided Western disarmament, in reckless disregard of both the proclaimed Communist ambitions and the absolute necessity for a balance of power in the world, rather than Yalta or any wartime agreement that encouraged Stalin to embark upon new conquests."[28]

House Concurrent Resolution 108, a resolution to repudiate Yalta that Congressman Thaddeus Machrowicz (Democrat, Michigan) introduced on May 17, exemplified this apologetic line. Soviet violations, Machrowicz argued, justified U.S. repudiation of Yalta, because Western adherence to the terms had been based on Soviet good faith. Since subsequent years had proven this trust unfounded, the United States no longer had any "legal or moral ground" for continuing to adhere to the terms of the Yalta agreements. Machrowicz' resolution was killed in committee, just as Hale's and Smith's had been.[29]

The demand made by Congressman Daniel Flood (Democrat, Pennsylvania) for the repudiation of Yalta more clearly indicated the bitter feelings of Polish-Americans. Flood described the agreements, which had been made without the knowledge or consent of the U.S. people, as "appeasement greater than Munich." Yalta, he charged, "shackled" the United Nations, "betrayed" Poland in the "most cynical" of the Yalta agreements, and "allowed, indeed forced" Communists into the postwar Polish government. According to Flood, these factors, the Soviet Union's violation of the agreements, and the need to renew the Polish people's faith in the good intentions of the United States made congressional repudiation of the conference imperative. By 1951, the repudiation of Yalta had become a major political objective of prominent Polish-American leaders and such organized Polish-American fraternal groups as the Polish National

28. Democratic Senator Brien McMahon specifically asserted that Soviet expansion could have been checked in 1945 had the U.S. public not demanded rapid demobilization at that time. U.S. *Congressional Record*, 82d Cong., 1st sess., 1951, XCVII, Parts 1, 5, 11, and 14, 242, 6275–76, A288–89, A4774, A5410–16. *The New York Times*, July 28, 1951, 10. *New Republic*, 125, 7 (August 13, 1951), 19–20; 9 (August 27, 1951), 5.

29. See Appendix G for text.

Alliance, the Polish Legion of American Veterans, the Polish-American Congress, and the Polish-American Association.[30]

Democratic congressmen tried to mitigate this Polish-American resentment, while Republican congressmen tried to profit from it. In an effort to acknowledge the attitude of Polish-Americans, both Democratic and Republican congressmen, particularly those with sizable Polish-American constituencies, had established February 7 as the anniversary of Yalta's treatment of Poland. A similar effort led to the establishment of a special House subcommittee to investigate the Katyn Forest massacre of Polish officers. In their statements on February 7 and during the Katyn Forest hearings and debate, the Democrats and Republicans differed in their assessment of the responsibility for postwar developments in Poland, but they shared a common aversion to those developments and the futility of the Yalta approach. Most Democrats simply admitted that Yalta had failed to produce world peace because of the Soviet Union's violations of trust. They denied that the Administration had acted incorrectly or immorally. The Republicans, however, stressed the Administration's responsibility and suggested that Yalta had caused the "fall of Poland." Some Republicans emphasized the stupidity of the Yalta conferees' failure to recognize Soviet perfidy; others stressed Communist influence at the conference. Assailing this appeasement policy, they urged Polish-Americans to repudiate Democratic leadership.[31]

Although he was more intemperate and partisan than his fellow Yalta critics, Congressman Timothy Sheehan (Republican, Illinois) summarized what had come to be standard Yalta mythology. He stated:

> Yesterday [February 7] marked the day that the Democratic Party, the Hisses, the New Deal, the Fair Deal — yes, even the "queer deal" — sold Poland into slavery and paved the way for the enslavement of eight more European nations and permitted the Soviet Union to become a great world force. . . . Because they [the Democratic party] will not admit their own blunders, and it will have to remain for the Republican Party

30. U.S. *Congressional Record*, 82d Cong., 1st sess., 1951, XCVII, Parts 11, 13, and 15, A880, A5945. Polish Legion of American Veterans, resolution to the President, August, 1951, Truman Papers, OF 463, Truman Library. Congress of Polish Sections and Clubs and Delaware Division of the Polish-American Congress, resolution, October 14, 1951, Truman Papers, OF 463, Truman Library.

31. U.S. *Congressional Record*, 82d Cong., 1st sess., 1951, XCVII, Parts 1, 4, 9, 11, and 13, 1082–87, 1108, 1131–41, 1212–13, 4825–37, 11549, A653, A1179–80, A3863. *Chicago Tribune*, February 11, 1951, 13; May 7, 1951, 10; November 12, 1951, 12; January 28, 1952, 16; February 3, 1952, 13; November 15, 1952, 2; November 17, 1952, 18; December 23, 1952, 9.

to restore decency and confidence in our foreign relations, and to restore Poland to its rightful place among the great nations of the world.[32]

Congressman Charles Kersten (Republican, Wisconsin) captured this reaction to earlier Administration foreign policy in various resolutions. Kersten's resolutions did not explicitly blame Yalta for the "enslavement" of the Russians, Rumanians, Bulgarians, Hungarians, Czechoslovakians, Poles, and the Chinese. Instead, the resolutions denounced Soviet military intervention and U.S. mistakes for this enslavement. Of his ten resolutions, only the resolutions on Hungary and Poland specifically referred to Yalta. The Hungarian resolution did not criticize the Yalta agreements but cited Soviet violations of past commitments. The Polish resolution deemed Yalta "partly" responsible for the "fall" of Poland and demanded the repudiation of only those Yalta, Teheran, and Potsdam agreements "concerning" Poland. His resolutions expressed U.S. "hope" for the liberation of the "captive nations," but they did not propose military support. The only positive Administration policy Kersten urged was the withdrawal of U.S. diplomatic recognition from these governments.[33]

Congress never acted upon any of these resolutions. On August 17, however, Kersten introduced an amendment to the Mutual Security Act of 1951 (House Resolution 5113), which proposed setting aside funds to establish special forces composed of exiles from the Soviet Union, Poland, Czechoslovakia, Hungary, Rumania, Bulgaria, Lithuania, Latvia, Estonia, and the Soviet zones of Germany and Austria and to incorporate these forces into NATO.[34] The amendment gave the President the final authority for establishing these military units if he was convinced that they were in the interest of the United States. Kersten said that his amendment provided the basis for the liberation of Eastern Europe, and he argued that, until the "satellite" countries were liberated, the entire world could look forward only to continued military preparations.[35] The amendment passed without protracted debate.

32. U.S. *Congressional Record*, 82d Cong., 1st sess., 1951, XCVII, Part 1, 1170. Republican National Committee Chairman Guy Gabrielson, in an address to the Ukrainian-American Congress Committee, similarly assailed the Yalta agreements and demanded their "denunciation." *Chicago Tribune*, November 12, 1951, 12.

33. U.S. *Congressional Record*, 82d Cong., 1st sess., 1951, XCVII, Parts 12, 13, and 14, A1765–67, A2629–31, A3739–44, A3746–47, A4083, A4086–87, A4444–46. See Appendix H for text of Polish resolution.

34. See Appendix I for the text of the amendment.

35. U.S. *Congressional Record*, 82d Cong., 1st sess., 1951, XCVII, Part 8, 10261–63.

The most critical and partisan debate involving Yalta occurred during the Senate's consideration of the Japanese peace treaty. Negotiations about the treaty had focused attention on those Yalta agreements that had ceded South Sakhalin and the Kurile Islands to the Soviet Union. Technically, the proposed treaty, in delineating Japan's territorial boundaries, could not refer to these areas as Japanese because the Soviet Union administered, occupied, and refused to renounce title to them. This territorial provision posed a problem for both the Administration and Senate Republicans. The issue was whether ratification of the Japanese peace treaty, which excluded South Sakhalin and the Kuriles, affirmed the Yalta agreements. The Senate debate verified that this issue was not confined to the territorial question but involved more substantive foreign policy issues raised by the Yalta mythology: secrecy in conduct of foreign policy, the extent of executive authority, and the question of the wisdom or patriotism of the Yalta conferees.

To bolster bipartisan co-operation and support for the peace treaty, President Truman had appointed John Foster Dulles chief U.S. negotiator during the Japanese peace talks. By so doing, Truman sought to preclude attacks on the treaty by people who were opposed to Secretary of State Acheson. Dulles' role in drafting and defending the treaty was intended to disarm Republican criticisms that the treaty would harm U.S. interests. Truman also hoped to avert possible Republican criticisms that the Administration's foreign policy was not bipartisan since Republicans were not asked to participate in formulating policies but were expected only to ratify those already established. Dulles immediately attempted to silence criticisms of the treaty. In April, 1951, before the San Francisco Conference convened, Dulles contended that ratification of Soviet title to South Sakhalin and the Kuriles should depend upon Soviet ratification of the Japanese peace treaty.[36]

The San Francisco treaty had not formally conferred the title to South Sakhalin and the Kuriles to the Soviet Union, but it had required Japan to renounce any claim to these territories. Accordingly, the "extremists" and certain "partisans" demanded specific assurances that ratification of the treaty would not be construed as confirmation of the Yalta agreements. During the Senate debate, Senators Watkins and Jenner introduced reservations specifying that

36. *Chicago Tribune*, April 1, 1951, 1; July 11, 1951, 5. *Time*, 57 (April 9, 1951), 25. John Foster Dulles, "Essentials of a Peace with Japan," *Department of State Bulletin*, XXIV, 614 (April 9, 1951), 577.

ratification in no way confirmed those agreements. Both Jenner and Watkins charged that the proposed treaty did "indirectly" uphold some of the agreements, and Jenner also emphasized the Senate's responsibility to review the treaty closely in order to guard against another Yalta.[37] Watkins' and Jenner's reservations set the tone for the subsequent debate on the treaty.

Administration leaders and the "moderates" tried to undercut reservationist sentiment because they were concerned about the effects of these reservations on ratification of the treaty. During the Senate Foreign Relations Committee's hearing and the Senate floor debate on the treaty, their strategy was to avoid issues that would involve either the Democrats' concern not to repudiate the Yalta agreements or the Republicans' commitment not to sanction them. Appearing before the Foreign Relations Committee, Secretary of State Dean Acheson reported that John Foster Dulles would conduct the Administration's defense of the treaty, and he emphasized Dulles' role in negotiating the treaty.[38] The emphasis on Dulles' role in drafting and defending the treaty was a conscious effort by the Administration to get Acheson out of the sights of Senate Republicans and to highlight the bipartisan character of the treaty.

Replying to Watkins' reservations and to similar questions posed by committee members, Dulles denied that the treaty confirmed Yalta. The Yalta conferees had only "contemplated" the cession of South Sakhalin and the Kuriles to the Soviet Union in a formal treaty of peace, and the proposed peace treaty did "not carry out the provision

---

37. Congressman Karl Stefan (Republican, Nebraska) echoed this protest when he argued that, before ratification, the Congress must first ascertain the whole truth about the treaty and be satisfied that it was not a "second Yalta." U.S. *Congressional Record*, 82d Cong., 1st sess., 1951, XCVII, Parts 4, 8, 9, and 15, 4477, 10524–26, 10811, 11945–46, A5940. In November, 1950, prior to the San Francisco Conference, the *Chicago Tribune* had expressed the same sentiments. It had denounced the draft treaty's territorial provisions as an attempt to "wriggle out of Roosevelt's idiotic commitments to Stalin at Yalta." Recognizing that the Soviet Union could not be dislodged except by recourse to arms, the *Tribune* instead had recommended the conclusion of a separate peace treaty with Japan that did not recognize Soviet title to these areas. *Chicago Tribune*, November 27, 1950, 14; January 25, 1952, 14. Earlier, on April 27, 1951, Jenner had introduced Senate Joint Resolution 67 prohibiting any U.S. official from signing any document "giving the force of law" to any of the Yalta agreements. See Appendix J for the text of the resolution. Senator William Knowland, during this debate, expressed these same criticisms of Yalta but never forthrightly supported the specific reservations. He simply affirmed that the Congress and a Republican President would never have ratified the Yalta agreements and criticized Roosevelt's unconstitutional actions at Yalta. U.S. *Congressional Record*, 82d Cong., 1st sess., 1951, XCVII, Part 8, 10811.

38. U.S. Senate, Committee on Foreign Relations, *Hearings on the Japanese Peace Treaty and Other Treaties Relating to Security in the Pacific*, 82d Cong., 2d sess., 1952, 4.

of the Yalta agreement." He added that the United States had no obligation to "give the Soviet Union title by this treaty to South Sakhalin and the Kuriles," since the Soviet Union had "flagrantly" violated other Yalta agreements in Europe and Asia. When Republican Senator Alexander Wiley pointedly asked Dulles whether ratification of the Japanese peace treaty would "in any way" constitute confirmation of Yalta, Dulles retorted, "This treaty is the first formal act which the United States will have taken which involves a clear abandonment of Yalta. . . . [The treaty] recognizes our total freedom from any obligations that stem from Yalta."[39]

General Omar Bradley's testimony also reduced objections that the treaty harmed U.S. interests. Replying by letter to Watkins' questions on military security, Bradley stated that, although the "present status" of South Sakhalin, the Kuriles, and the Habomai islands was undesirable militarily, their final disposition should be left until a later date. Existing tensions plus Soviet occupation of these islands necessitated postponing any action on this issue. He pointed out that reservations to the treaty denying title to the Soviets would have no effect on the status of the islands but would needlessly provoke tensions.[40]

The majority of the witnesses against the treaty alleged that it confirmed Yalta. These witnesses included Reverend William Johnson, a former missionary in China; Mrs. Frederick Griswold, a member of the conservative National Economic Council; William H. Evans, a former lieutenant in the Navy who had been relieved of his Far Eastern command; and Alfred Kohlberg, who was identified with the China lobby.

Describing the proposed treaty as "pro-Communist," Evans objected to the territorial provisions and to the stipulation that Japan join the United Nations. He feared that the Japanese treaty might create a precedent for a future treaty delineating Germany's eastern boundary on the Oder-Neisse. Raising the Yalta image, he described the UN's interests as a "dictated peace based on the principles of Teheran, Yalta, Potsdam and Alger Hiss," and he demanded the full rearmament and industrialization of Japan. Restoration of the balance of power that had been "deliberately" destroyed at Yalta depended upon Japan's strength. Kohlberg objected to the treaty's failure to provide for Japanese recognition of the Nationalist Government as the government of the Chinese mainland. Because

39. *Ibid.*, 18, 20, 22, 56–57.
40. *Ibid.*, 22–24.

of this failure, Kohlberg feared, "we" might not be able to "use Japanese bases for offensive war against the mainland."[41]

Recognizing the impact of these charges, members of the Foreign Relations Committee worked to neutralize possible allegations that the proposed treaty benefited the Soviet Union and harmed U.S. security. The draft treaty had been so worded that it did not formally ratify Soviet control of South Sakhalin and the Kuriles, but it did implicitly accept the situation. To avert a partisan Republican reaction to the treaty, the committee made at least a semantic concession to Watkins' demand. It appended a reservation to the treaty that preserved the form of Watkins' initial reservation but recognized the reality of Soviet occupation. Watkins' reservation stated, "The Senate advises and consents to the ratification of the treaty with the understanding that such ratification shall not constitute (1) any ratification, confirmation, or approval of any open or secret agreement entered into at the Yalta conference of 1945."[42] The Senate Foreign Relations Committee's reservation provided, "nothing in this treaty, or the advice and consent of the Senate thereof, implies recognition on the part of the United States of the provisions in favor of the Soviet Union contained in the so-called Yalta agreement regarding Japan of February 11, 1945."[43]

In presenting to the Senate the committee's report favoring ratification, Democratic Senator Tom Connally, chairman of the Senate Foreign Relations Committee, argued that the treaty did not give the Soviet Union title to South Sakhalin and the Kuriles. The treaty provisions applied only to allied powers, defined by Article 25 of the treaty as the signatories; thus, the provisions did not apply to the Soviet Union. Connally denied that the provisions of the treaty had anything to do with Yalta; he said that they were based solely on the Potsdam surrender terms.[44]

Republican Senators Edward Martin, Harry Cain, William Knowland, and H. Alexander Smith denied that the treaty in any way confirmed or ratified Yalta. Martin asserted that the treaty did "not recognize" the Yalta agreements, and Knowland stated that the treaty had "no remote connection or similarity" with them. Knowland contrasted the secrecy in which the Yalta discussions were conducted

41. *Ibid.*, 92–109, 117–26, 148–52, 165–67.
42. U.S. *Congressional Record*, 82d Cong., 2d sess., 1952, XCVIII, Part 2, 2584.
43. *Ibid.*, 2578.
44. *Ibid.*, 2322–29. See Appendix K for that part of the text of the treaty concerning South Sakhalin and the Kuriles.

with Dulles' openness in negotiating the Japanese peace treaty. Cain stated that the committee's reservations repudiated Yalta and that Senator John Sparkman (Democrat, Alabama) had admitted as much in committee. Wiley denied that the Soviet Union had any legal right to these territories but doubted that the Soviets could be excluded short of armed force. He contended that the Senate Foreign Relations Committee's reservation was sufficient evidence that Yalta was not confirmed by this treaty.[45]

The committee's and these Republicans' efforts to minimize partisanship by outflanking the "partisans" and "extremists" did not wholly succeed. Senators Arthur Watkins, Everett Dirksen, William Jenner, and Owen Brewster demanded the formal and explicit repudiation of Yalta. They maintained that the proposed treaty did not accomplish this result. Watkins and Jenner, in fact, asserted that, even with the committee's reservation, the treaty confirmed Yalta. Dirksen insisted upon further Senate consideration of the treaty.[46] Accordingly, Jenner reintroduced his four reservations to the treaty, the second of which corresponded to Watkins' original reservation. Defeated 27–54, this second reservation acquired primarily "extremist" and "partisan" support. It secured the votes of 23 Republicans and Democratic Senators James Eastland, Pat McCarran, John McClellan (Arkansas), and Russell Long (Louisiana).[47] The Japanese peace treaty as submitted by the Senate Foreign Relations Committee was ratified on March 10, 1952, by the vote of 66–10. The 10 opposed, all "extremists," were Senators Everett Dirksen, Henry Dworshak (Republican, Idaho), Zales Ecton (Republican, Montana), William Jenner, James Kem, George Malone, Joseph McCarthy, Herman Welker (Republican, Idaho), Milton Young (Republican, North Dakota), and Pat McCarran.[48]

Only the "extremists" demanded that the Japanese peace treaty explicitly repudiate Yalta. They and the "partisans" had supported Jenner's reservations, although the "partisans" finally supported the treaty without the reservations. Nonetheless, by 1952, the "partisans" and the "moderates" had adopted the "extremists'" rhetoric. *The New York Times*, Arthur Krock, *U.S. News and World Report*, and *Newsweek* described the reservation proposed by the committee and the unanimity of the committee's report as the first step toward repudia-

45. U.S. *Congressional Record*, 82d Cong., 2d sess., 1952, XCVIII, Parts 2 and 8, 2339–40, 2385, 2392, 2451–61, 2507, A1310–11.
46. *Ibid.*, Parts 1, 2, and 8, 1176–77, 1182, 2366, 2562–63, 2586, A994.
47. *Ibid.*, Part 2, 2567.
48. *Ibid.*, 2594.

tion of Yalta and toward Democratic acceptance of repudiation. Confirmation of the treaty, they contended, marked a return to realism and established a framework for future dealings with the Soviet Union. All argued that the confirmation had created a precedent for reconsidering and revising other Yalta agreements.[49]

President Truman's dramatic dismissal of General MacArthur on April 11, however, caused more controversy than the question of ratifying the peace treaty had. Defending his decision, Truman concentrated on the subordination of the military to civilian authority. He then said that official U.S. policy objectives were committed to limiting the Korean War, not to bombing Manchuria or assisting a Chinese Nationalist landing on the Chinese mainland. Because Mac-Arthur disagreed with this policy, Truman contended, "I have therefore considered it essential to relieve General MacArthur so that there would be no doubt or confusion as to the real purpose and aim of our policy."[50]

Truman's decision created an immediate furor. George Sokolsky, Congressmen Walter Judd, Henry Latham (Republican, New York), E. Ross Adair (Republican, Indiana), Senators Robert Taft, Everett Dirksen, Henry Dworshak, William Jenner, and William Knowland denounced Truman's action as a continuation of Yalta's "appeasement" policy. In fact, Sokolsky described the dismissal as perhaps "as great a military victory for Soviet Russia as Stalingrad and as great a diplomatic victory as Yalta." Taft, Dirksen, and Dworshak also raised the "Communists in Government" theme as the reason for the Yalta Far Eastern agreements and current Far Eastern difficulties. Dirksen and Dworshak, moreover, sarcastically described the Yalta Conference as bipartisan — Roosevelt had represented the Democratic party, "while Alger Hiss represented the Communist Party." In reply, Democratic Senator Brien McMahon challenged Taft to elucidate these charges. The alternatives for the United States, McMahon noted, were either to fight or to withdraw her troops. Emphasizing the amount of U.S. aid that Chiang had received during and since World War II, McMahon belittled the charge that the State Department had sought to undermine Chiang or to guarantee his defeat.[51]

49. *The New York Times*, February 7, 1952, 26; February 8, 1952, 22. *Newsweek*, 39 (February 18, 1952), 25. *U.S. News and World Report*, 32 (February 22, 1952), 22–23.

50. Harry S Truman, speech, radio broadcast, April 11, 1951, Records of White House Official Reporter, Truman Papers, Truman Library.

51. U.S. *Congressional Record*, 82d Cong., 1st sess., 1951, XCVII, Parts 3, 4, and 12, 3684, 3720–23, 4462–63, 4473, A1949, A2068–69. *Chicago Herald-American*, April 12, 1951, 10; May 1, 1951, 13.

These partisan denunciations of Yalta reached their peak during the Senate hearings on MacArthur's dismissal. Ostensibly convened to review President Truman's reasons for dismissing MacArthur, the hearings developed into a partisan reappraisal of the past Administration's foreign policy, particularly the policy followed at Yalta. The very witnesses called to testify — General Douglas MacArthur, Secretary of State Dean Acheson, Secretary of Defense George Marshall, General Omar Bradley, General Albert Wedemeyer, Admiral Oscar Badger, Patrick Hurley, and General David Barr — determined this result. The witnesses' official positions in the Administration or the military at the time of the Yalta Conference provided the grounds for such a review. During the hearings, the Republican senators used each witness' views about Yalta as an indice of his perception and astuteness. They questioned each witness about his general concept of the conference and specifically about the military necessity of the Far Eastern agreements. In concentrating on Yalta, these Republicans intended partly to divert public attention from the issue of civil-military relations, partly to discredit the proponents of MacArthur's dismissal, but most of all to center public attention on the past Administration's errors or treason.

Using the testimony of Generals MacArthur and Wedemeyer, Admirals Badger and King, Joint Chiefs of Staff Chairman Omar Bradley, former U.S. Ambassador to China Pat Hurley, Secretary of State Dean Acheson, and Secretary of Defense George Marshall, the Republican committee members tried to fulfill these intentions. In an attempt to degrade Bradley's defense of Truman's action, they repeatedly asked him to report the substance of his discussion with President Truman prior to the formal decision to drop MacArthur. Republican Senators William Knowland and Alexander Wiley argued that Bradley's grounds for refusal would prevent their getting information that they needed to understand such influences on past decisions as Alger Hiss's role at Yalta.[52] The Republican committee members especially wanted to point out the weakness of the Administration's policy, particularly its failure to understand Soviet objectives and to pursue a forceful anti-Communist course. Although these were most strongly developed by the "extremists," the "moderates" and "partisans" also adopted this approach.

The Yalta Far Eastern agreements, these Republicans argued, were harmful to Chiang Kai-shek and militarily unnecessary. Assail-

52. Bradley contended that his discussions with the President were privileged and that he was obligated to keep this confidence. Committee Chairman Richard Russell sustained Bradley on this point.

ing the secrecy of the conference and many of the agreements, they denounced the Administration's failure to invite Chiang to Yalta, where major decisions concerning China's future were decided. In addition, they contended, the success of the atomic bomb had been known before Yalta, and it obviated any military need for Soviet intervention. On a different tack, these Republicans used Acheson's and Marshall's continued defense of the Yalta agreements to discredit the anti-Communist credentials of these witnesses. MacArthur's opposition to the Yalta Conference and its results during the hearings, of course, made his credentials irreproachable.

Democratic Senators tried to substantiate the military and political soundness of the Yalta agreements. They emphasized the military necessity for the agreements, based on the contingencies of 1945 and the military advice of the Joint Chiefs of Staff. Since the atomic bomb had not been formally tested before Yalta, they argued, its success had not been definitely known. Seeking to buttress Acheson and Marshall and to discredit the critical judgments of Yalta developed by MacArthur, Wedemeyer, Barr, Hurley, and King, they queried the military critics about what their views on the necessity of Yalta had been in 1945. They wanted to highlight the partisanship of criticisms of Yalta and to show that the criticisms were not based upon the realities of 1945.[53]

The MacArthur hearings resolved nothing. The committee issued no formal report, although certain Republican members — Styles Bridges, Alexander Wiley, H. Alexander Smith, Bourke Hickenlooper, William Knowland, Owen Brewster, Harry Cain, and Ralph Flanders — independently summarized their views. Concentrating on the past Administration's foreign policy, these Republicans charged that the Administration lacked a positive plan for achieving a decisive victory. The Yalta agreements were the turning point of the Administration's Far Eastern policy because they abandoned fine principles and obligations and appeased the Soviet Union. Hurley's contradiction of Acheson's defense of Yalta and MacArthur's description of

53. U.S. Senate, Committee on Armed Services and Committee on Foreign Relations, *Hearings to Conduct an Inquiry into the Military Situation in the Far East and the Facts Surrounding the Relief of General of the Army MacArthur from His Assignment in That Area*, 82d Cong., 1st sess., 1951, 32, 128, 229, 392, 559–60, 562–65, 694–97, 852–54, 901, 912, 1781, 1801, 1839, 1845–46, 1869–72, 1875–76, 1878, 1881–83, 1885, 1893–94, 1907, 1917–18, 1923–24, 1984–85, 2034–35, 2059–61, 2069, 2071, 2085, 2113–14, 2127–28, 2130, 2172–73, 2186–87, 2228–29, 2281–82, 2389–90, 2392, 2416–17, 2431–32, 2457, 2493, 2499–2500, 2731–32, 2765, 2779, 2788, 2829, 2832, 2835–42, 2859–62, 2876, 2883–85, 2888, 2926, 2932–34, 2941–42, 2980, 2989, 3022, 3050–51, 3055–56, 3119–20, 3132, 3328–41.

Yalta as a great tragedy showed that Yalta's concessions were not militarily justifiable. The Roosevelt Administration had failed to use "able and competent" officers, such as MacArthur, "on the scene of action." The full extent of Yalta's commitments could not be determined. In the past, treaties had required the advice and consent of the Senate and were public documents. Fortunately, the MacArthur hearings had broken the Administration's secretive conduct of foreign policy. These Republicans further asserted:

> The true reason for Yalta remains an inscrutable mystery. The result of Yalta remains a triumph for Communist diplomacy . . . our diplomats gave away our victory in secret agreements, so that in the year 1951, our foreign policy in the Far East stands revealed as a complete failure.[54]

In a separate and less partisan statement on the MacArthur hearings, Senator Leverett Saltonstall (Republican, Massachusetts) emphasized the "unfortunate" method of MacArthur's dismissal. He conceded that serious and tragic mistakes had been made at Cairo, Teheran, and Yalta, but he concluded that the perspective for a policy debate should center on the future and not the past.[55]

Appraisals of the hearings varied depending on the reviewer's partisan commitment. At most, Yalta was only lamely defended. The media used the conference either to defend or to discredit the Truman Administration. Sympathetic reports by *Newsweek, The Nation,* and Ernest Lindley emphasized Republican partisanship during the conduct of the hearings and the Republican commitment to degrade the Truman Administration by critically reviewing the past Administration's policy at Yalta. Contrasting the comments made in 1951 by Yalta critics with what they had said in 1945, Lindley and the publications contended that contemporary criticisms ignored the realities of 1945 and were intended principally to achieve partisan advantage. *Newsweek* and *The Nation* also extolled the correctness of the Yalta agreements. *Newsweek* praised Acheson's admirable defense of the conference during the hearings, described Hurley as the "other Republican sponsored witness," and called the Republican senators' formal report on the hearings "in essence a campaign document."[56]

54. *Ibid.,* 3591–92, 3600, 3604.
55. *Ibid.,* 3560.
56. *Newsweek,* 37 (May 7, 1951), 22; May 14, 1951, 31; June 18, 1951, 19; June 25, 1951, 17; 38 (July 2, 1951), 16; August 27, 1951, 20, 22. *The Nation,* 172 (June 16, 1951), 553; June 30, 1951, 597; 173 (November 3, 1951), 378.

The New York Times and columnist Arthur Krock dismissed the statements of the more intemperate Yalta critics as prejudiced and distorted. The *Times* did advocate, however, a dispassionate reassessment of Yalta, one that considered the future and offered "temperate and constructive" criticism. At the same time, Krock charged that the Truman Administration's "bankrupt" and "blundering" post-Yalta policy on China had contributed to the "loss" of China and the Korean War. A better understanding of the future, Krock then asserted, required a reappraisal of past events. He recommended past Administration policies as the focus of the 1952 campaign.[57]

Raymond Moley and *Time* magazine demanded a re-evaluation of the Yalta agreements and other parts of the past Administration's policy because it would provide the background necessary for understanding the MacArthur dismissal. Were it not for Yalta, Moley charged, the Soviet "Manchurian" threat would not have existed. He emphasized the importance of "Acheson type" policies in shaping the decisions of a "sick and weary President" at Yalta. Similarly, *Time* belittled Acheson's defense of Yalta by comparing it with statements of the "piping peace-planning days of 1945" and blamed the Yalta agreements for Chiang Kai-shek's defeat. Discounting the military justification for the Far Eastern agreements, *Time* maintained that a report drafted in 1945 by a "high-powered team of fifty experts" — no one has yet found such a report in Defense Department files — emphatically warned General Marshall against Soviet involvement in Asia. Marshall, *Time* conceded, might never have seen this report. These experts and certain members of the Yalta delegation (a reference to Byrnes), *Time* further noted, were unaware of what had been "secretly given to Stalin at Yalta."[58]

The "extremists" most sharply attacked MacArthur's dismissal and the Yalta Conference. Congressmen Alvin Weichel (Republican, Ohio), Dewey Short, Senators William Jenner, Joseph McCarthy, the *Chicago Tribune*, *The Saturday Evening Post*, Fulton Lewis, Jr., and George Sokolsky blamed policy decisions of earlier administrations for contemporary Far Eastern problems. They noted the ways in which Chiang was "betrayed" and Stalin was "appeased" at Yalta and accordingly belittled Acheson's unconvincing defense of the Truman Administration's post-Yalta policy on China. Lewis and

57. *The New York Times*, May 11, 1951, 26; June 26, 1951, 28; August 20, 1951, 18.
58. *Time*, 57 (May 14, 1951), 20; May 21, 1951, 33; June 11, 1951, 21; June 18, 1951, 22–23; June 25, 1951, 19–20; 58 (July 2, 1951), 19–20. *Newsweek*, 37 (May 14, 1951), 112.

McCarthy traced postwar problems directly to a "pro-Communist" group in the State Department. Directing his attack at the "Acheson-Hiss group" and particularly at George Marshall, McCarthy explained why Marshall went to China in 1945: "Having, with the Yalta crowd, framed the China policy, he was intent on executing it down to its last dreadful clause and syllable. . . . The surrender at Yalta had to be concluded and perfected." Upon waking one morning, McCarthy feared, he might find that "in some secret chamber of the United Nations, the enemies of the United States, with Britain and India at their head, have made a secret deal — a new Yalta." [59]

Jenner's, Sokolsky's, the *Post's*, and the *Tribune's* criticisms were more clearly partisan. Jenner suggested that Truman had fired MacArthur in order to secure peace in Korea before the 1952 election by giving the Communists "everything they desire." For Sokolsky, the *Post*, and the *Tribune*, the hearings had initiated the task to be completed in 1952. Sokolsky also denounced the conference's cession of territory held by the Japanese to the Soviet Union. Before 1945, Sokolsky noted, no Asian nation had equalled Japan in dignity and strength, and he hoped that Japan would again become "the bulwark of civilization against Soviet Russia." After reiterating Hurley's charge of pro-Communist influence in the State Department, the *Tribune* denied that these State Department members had had to push Roosevelt very far. [60]

The "extremists" and "partisans," by again concentrating on the Administration's past foreign policy and raising the question of internal security, sought to discredit the New Deal and to prove that a conservative, anti-Communist approach was sound. Senators Joseph McCarthy, George Malone, William Knowland, Congressmen Paul Shafer, Charles Vursell, Leslie Arends (Republican, Illinois), Cliff Clevenger (Republican, Ohio), Arthur Miller, the *Chicago Tribune*, *The Saturday Evening Post*, and George Sokolsky argued that the real threat to U.S. security came from the existence of Communist or pro-Communist policy makers in the State Department. Reflecting their concept of U.S. omnipotence, they asserted that Roosevelt's

59. *Chicago Herald-American*, April 14, 1951, 35. *Milwaukee Sentinel*, October 15, 1951, 10. U.S. *Congressional Record*, 82d Cong., 1st sess., 1951, XCVII, Parts 4, 5, and 12, 5546–47, 5717–18, 6556–6602, A2694.
60. *Chicago Tribune*, June 7, 1951, 16; June 22, 1951, 20; June 29, 1951, 2; June 30, 1951, 10; August 22, 1951, 20. *The Saturday Evening Post*, 224 (July 7, 1951), 10. *Chicago Herald-American*, May 9, 1951, 21; May 15, 1951, 21; May 16, 1951, 45; May 17, 1951, 10; May 18, 1951, 17; June 8, 1951, 13; June 9, 1951, 12; June 13, 1951, 33; June 15, 1951, 15; June 22, 1951, 15; June 30, 1951, 7; July 17, 1951, 8; July 20, 1951, 13.

and Truman's "New Deal type" policies had made the Soviet Union a major world power through senseless concessions at Yalta. As a corrective, they demanded the rejection of such policies and the men who had formulated them. McCarthy's solution was to expose publicly the activities of these pro-Communists. To document the validity of this solution, he noted that Hiss, despite earlier F.B.I. investigations, had been able to influence the "dying" Roosevelt in drafting the Yalta agreement until Hiss's deeds had been publicly exposed. McCarthy remarked, "At the time [of Yalta] Hiss had not been exposed as a Communist agent. Although the State Department had been forewarned of Hiss, they nonetheless sent him to Yalta where he exercised Svengali-like influence over Secretary of State Stettinius." [61]

Developing these themes, Democratic Congressman John Rankin condemned the Yalta conferees' treatment of Germany. He charged that European communism was the product of a "racial minority" and stated, "The Yalta frame-up was to turn the world over to a racial minority in Europe to dominate them and destroy the white man's civilization." He compared the Germans' right to tell the Communists to leave their country with the South's right to exclude the carpetbaggers during and after Reconstruction. Rankin further condemned Roosevelt's lifting the embargo on U.S. exports in 1940 because it had enabled England and France to fight Germany and had led to U.S. involvement in World War II and the Yalta sellout. [62]

In 1951, Roosevelt's health became an important issue. Besides referring to his proclivity for communism, the "extremists" and "partisans" contended that Roosevelt's poor health had enabled Alger Hiss to influence him at Yalta. They were supported by Roosevelt's former Postmaster General James Farley. Republican Senate Minority Leader Kenneth Wherry inserted into the *Congressional Record* Farley's statement that a "gravely ill" Roosevelt, who lacked the stamina necessary for the job, had attended Yalta. Farley reiterated his 1940 opposition to the third term because of his fear that Roose-

61. U.S. *Congressional Record*, 82d Cong., 1st sess., 1951, XCVII, Parts 2, 6, 9, 13, and 14, 2389–90, 7111–12, 7743, 7804, 11479, A4062, A4797, A5035. *Chicago Tribune*, March 15, 1951, 16; June 3, 1951, 28; August 20, 1951, 18; September 13, 1951, 14; November 9, 1951, 16; November 27, 1951, 10, 11; December 7, 1951, 22. *The Saturday Evening Post*, 223 (May 5, 1951), 10; 224 (December 8, 1951), 12; December 15, 1951, 10. *Chicago Herald-American*, March 22, 1951, 11; April 2, 1951, 10.
62. U.S. *Congressional Record*, 82d Cong., 1st sess., 1951, XCVII, Part 7, 9047.

velt would listen to "courtiers and coattail riders." Farley regretted that his fears had come true.[63]

Vice-Admiral Ross T. McIntire, Roosevelt's personal physician, dismissed Farley's charges by pointing out that Farley had not seen Roosevelt for years. At Yalta, McIntire confirmed, Roosevelt was "as clear and as keen as ever." As evidence, he cited Roosevelt's good health during the strenuous 1944 campaign, the Quebec trips, and his continued good health thereafter.[64]

What bipartisanship remained after the 1950 foreign policy debate had been virtually discarded in 1951. Partisan considerations underlay both the Democratic and Republican appraisals of the Yalta Conference: The Republicans denounced Soviet perfidy and the Administration's complicity or stupidity, and the Democrats blamed the Soviet Union's bad faith. The "extremists'" charges of "Communists in Government," which had become a basic political issue in domestic politics, had helped to shift the political debate sharply to the right. The Truman Administration defended its purposes and policies as correctly anti-Communist; the "partisans," "moderates," and "extremists" suggested greater vigilance and a congressional review of executive actions. Domestic reform went by the board, and U.S. politics assumed an emotional aura.

63. *Ibid.*, Part 5, 6335.
64. *Ibid.*, Part 11, A1289. *U.S. News and World Report*, 30 (March 23, 1951), 22.

chapter 8
1952: yalta and the campaign

In 1952, the Republicans developed a new strategy and employed a new political rhetoric concerning the role of foreign policy and internal security in national politics. The watchwords for the Republican party's 1952 campaign, apart from communism and Korea, were "repudiate Yalta" and "liberate the satellite countries." Republican orators and political strategists developed Yalta's symbols of secret and personal diplomacy and Alger Hiss's presence at the conference into major political issues. They did not, however, propose positive alternatives; their commitment and outlook was obstructionist and negative. Republican congressmen used the symbols to support their opposition to policies that allegedly continued Yalta's appeasement or pro-Communist direction. The tone of this campaign, because of the anti-Communist stress, further strengthened the rising influence of the "extremists" and established them as a major political force.

Both the "extremists" and "partisans" blamed the secret diplomacy at Yalta for the Korean War. They singled out Alger Hiss's attendance and suggested that further secret agreements existed. They also tried to undermine approval of the United Nations, foreign aid, the Administration's pressure on South Korean President Syngman Rhee, and proposed liberalization of immigration policies by linking them with Yalta.[1]

During 1952, several congressmen introduced resolutions ostensibly for information purposes. On January 16, Senator James Kem urged a complete investigation of the State Department. He invoked the Republicans' experience with Teheran, Yalta, and Potsdam as justification for this proposal.[2] On January 21, Senator Pat McCarran introduced a resolution providing that executive agreements with foreign governments were without force until published in the *Federal Register*. His resolution further stipulated that these

1. U.S. *Congressional Record*, 82d Cong., 2d sess., 1952, XCVIII, Parts 2, 5, 7, 8, 10, and 11, 1952, 6816–17, 9451–52, A971–72, A1428, A2914, A4247, A4406. *Chicago Tribune*, January 27, 1952, 11; March 15, 1952, 8; March 28, 1952, 18; April 22, 1952, 20. *Milwaukee Sentinel*, April 1, 1952, 10; April 4, 1952, 16; April 10, 1952, 14.
2. U.S. *Congressional Record*, 82d Cong., 2d sess., 1952, XCVIII, Part 1, 226–27.

agreements expired six months after the end of the incumbent President's term, were subject to congressional approval, and, if secret, had to be submitted for Senate approval.[3] On February 4, Congressman Mathew Ellsworth (Republican, Oregon) sought to restrict the use of executive agreements,[4] and Congressmen Ernest Bramblett (Republican, California) and Joseph O'Hara introduced the same resolution on February 11 and February 14, respectively.[5] On February 20, in the same quest for information, the Senate Internal Security Subcommittee asked the State Department to deliver the handwritten notes taken by Alger Hiss at the Yalta Conference.[6]

None of these resolutions were acted upon, but they did show the attitude many congressmen brought to foreign policy discussions. When President Truman and British Prime Minister Churchill met secretly in January, 1952, to discuss foreign policy, resolutions were introduced in both the Senate and the House demanding that the Congress be fully informed on possible commitments and conclusions resulting from these talks. The House alone acted upon its resolution, which passed 189–143 in a predominantly partisan alignment. Only 1 of the 143 votes was cast by a Republican.[7]

Introduced later in January by Congressman John Rankin, the House resolution provided that any secret agreement made by President Truman and Prime Minister Churchill would not be effective until approved by both the House and the Senate. In discussion about the resolution, Rankin and fellow conservative Congressmen John Vorys, Charles Halleck, Charles Wolverton (Republican, New Jersey), Orland Armstrong, and Usher Burdick (Republican, North Dakota) criticized Yalta's secrecy and Roosevelt's personal diplomacy. They defended Congress' right to have access to information and its responsibility to prevent the recurrence of mistakes made at Yalta.[8] Rankin's resolution had no binding effect on the President, but it did reflect the commitment of the "extremists" and "partisans" to impugn the use of executive authority by dramatizing the abuses of it.

Senator John Bricker used the same imagery of Yalta in the constitutional amendment that he introduced on February 7. His amendment was endorsed by forty-four Republican and twelve Democratic

3. *Congressional Quarterly Weekly Report*, X, 4 (January 25, 1952), 59.
4. *Ibid.*, 6 (February 8, 1952), 101.
5. *Ibid.*, 7 (February 15, 1952), 119; 8 (February 22, 1952), 137.
6. *Ibid.*, 154.
7. U.S. *Congressional Record*, 82d Cong., 2d sess., 1952, XCVIII, Part 1, 1215–16.
8. *Ibid.*, Parts 1 and 8, 335, 1208, 1213–15, A1092–93.

senators. Among the forty-four Republicans were "moderates" Alexander Wiley, H. Alexander Smith, Henry Cabot Lodge, Irving Ives, (New York), George Aiken (Vermont), Ralph Flanders (Vermont), and Wayne Morse. In fact, the only Republican senators not listed among the original sponsors were Eugene Millikin and James Kem. Resolutions similar to Bricker's amendment were introduced in the House by Congressman Lawrence Smith on February 11 and by Congressmen Kenneth Keating and Felix Hébert (Democrat, Louisiana) on February 14.[9]

The Bricker Amendment simply required congressional ratification of any treaty or executive agreement affecting domestic policy. Bricker wanted to emphasize the interrelationship of foreign policy and domestic policy, of the ways in which executive actions in foreign policy could affect national security by posing the threat of what Bricker called socialism by treaty. Proponents of the amendment feared that treaties and executive agreements might be used to implement progressive socioeconomic reform. They cited a 1920 Supreme Court decision, *Missouri v. Holland*, in which the Court had upheld the constitutionality of a treaty restricting the state's rights to regulate migratory birds, even though the Congress could not constitutionally have legislated a similar restriction on state powers. Senators James Kem, Arthur Watkins, Henry Dworshak, William Knowland, and John Williams (Republican, Delaware), also supported the amendment because, according to them, it was a necessary constitutional safeguard against the repetition of executive abuse of authority, which had occurred at Yalta.[10]

A subcommittee of the Senate Committee on the Judiciary held hearings on the Bricker Amendment on May 21, 22, 27, 28, and June 9, 1952. During these hearings, Yalta was discussed only during the testimony of Dana Backus of the New York Bar and John Gunther of the Americans for Democratic Action. Both Backus and Gunther opposed the Bricker Amendment, and Senator Homer Ferguson and professional staff member Wayne Smithey referred to Yalta to question some of their criticisms.[11]

Otherwise, testimony centered on the domestic ramifications of treaties and executive agreements. In his presentation of the amend-

9. *Congressional Quarterly Weekly Report*, X, 6 (February 8, 1952), 108–9; 7 (February 15, 1952), 120; 8 (February 22, 1952), 138.

10. U.S. *Congressional Record*, 82d Cong., 2d sess., 1952, XCVIII, Parts 1, 8, and 10, 908–13, A1208–9, A2953–54.

11. U.S. Senate, Subcommittee of the Committee on the Judiciary, *Hearings on Senate Joint Resolution 130: Treaties and Executive Agreements*, 82d Cong., 2d sess., 1952, 81, 285–86.

ment, Senator Bricker emphasized this factor. He first stressed the important issue posed by the United Nations Covenant on Human Rights, which was "involved in the whole matter."[12] Bricker termed the Covenant only one of the issues that affected the Constitution and the sovereignty of the United States. The primary purpose of his amendment was "to prohibit the use of the treaty as an instrument of domestic legislation."[13] No formal action resulted from the hearings, however, because the presidential conventions and election were so near. Nonetheless, Republican political manipulation of Yalta and aspersions on the executive branch secured support for the amendment that it otherwise would not have received.

Senator Everett Dirksen had expressed the same concern about the effect of foreign policy on domestic developments during the Senate debate on ratifying the Japanese peace treaty. At that time, he had offered a reservation to the treaty that stated, "Nothing contained in this treaty shall be construed (a) to impose any limitation on the right of the United States as a sovereign power to exercise complete and unlimited control over its foreign policy, its Military Establishment, and its domestic concerns."[14] Although conservative Republicans and Southern Democrats shared a common commitment to preclude domestic reform by treaty, they split when the intent of a proposed action seemed to be primarily partisan. Dirksen's partisan reservation, with its implied curb on executive military authority, was defeated by a vote of 29–47. Of the 29 positive votes, 26 were cast by Republicans.[15]

Although they had different objectives, as diverse a group as Arthur Krock, *Newsweek*, *Time* magazine, George Sokolsky, and the *Chicago Tribune* emphasized the Yalta experience and supported congressional restrictions on use of executive authority in foreign policy. The Bricker Amendment debate, however, revealed the difference between the "moderates'" and "partisans'" concern about foreign policy and the "extremists'" wish to eliminate the policies of Roosevelt and the New Deal. Krock and *Newsweek* described the Bricker Amendment and the Japanese peace treaty as efforts to redress mistakes in foreign policy,[16] and *Time* interpreted the House vote on the meeting of Truman and Churchill as a "rare vote of no-

12. *Ibid.*, 2.

13. *Ibid.*, 21.

14. U.S. *Congressional Record*, 82d Cong., 2d sess., 1952, XCVIII, Part 2, 2574.

15. *Ibid.*, 2578.

16. *The New York Times*, February 8, 1952, 22. *Newsweek*, 39 (February 18, 1952), 25.

confidence" by Congress on executive procedures of nonconsultation or partial secrecy in foreign policy. The vote was not, *Time* asserted, a rejection of a particular policy or of the advisability of negotiations with the British; current congressional concern had been precipitated by the results of the secret "Churchill-Roosevelt agreements at Yalta." Since no precedent required the President to divulge his secret talks, *Time* doubted that Truman would comply with the resolution.[17]

To George Sokolsky and the *Chicago Tribune*, however, Yalta was symptomatic of an approach instituted by the New Deal. They wanted general, far-reaching changes restricting the use of executive authority. Sokolsky argued that the "startling" increase in presidential powers had upset the former balance of power among the executive, legislative, and judicial branches. Although Roosevelt's action at Yalta had been contrary to "normal constitutional methods," it had been accepted because the public had become "accustomed to a less restrained presidency, which would, in time, become an unrestrained presidency." The Constitution and the role of the President, Sokolsky maintained, should be an issue in the 1952 campaign.[18]

On February 7 and 11, the anniversaries of the conference communiqué and the Yalta agreements about Poland, both Democratic and Republican congressmen spoke about the Yalta Conference, particularly the Eastern European agreements and the fate of Poland. The views of Democratic congressmen about Yalta varied. None defended the spirit of the conference, and many of those congressmen who defended the conference denounced subsequent Soviet violations of Yalta and demanded its repudiation or rectification because of these violations.[19] Democrats who openly criticized Yalta — John Rooney (New York), Philip Philbin (Massachusetts), John F. Kennedy (Massachusetts), and Ray Madden (Indiana) — were from districts with large Polish-American populations. They concentrated on Yalta's treatment of Poland. (Kennedy, then a candidate for U.S. Senator from Massachusetts, inserted into the *Congressional Record* critical accounts by former Ambassador to Poland Arthur Bliss Lane and Polish General Bor-Komorowski.)[20]

The different stands of Michigan Congressmen John Lesinski, Sr., and his son John Lesinski, Jr., show the change in Democratic

17. *Time*, 59 (March 3, 1952), 18.
18. *Milwaukee Sentinel*, January 28, 1952, 8. *Chicago Tribune*, February 23, 1952, 8; February 29, 1952, 20.
19. U.S. *Congressional Record*, 82d Cong., 2d sess., 1952, XCVIII, Parts 1 and 8, 975–77, 1103, A710, A716, A942.
20. *Ibid.*, Parts 8, 9, and 10, A202–3, A856–57, A942, A2067, A2157–58, A2740–41.

thought about Yalta. In 1945 and 1946, Lesinski, Sr., had been one of the more outspoken Yalta critics. He had condemned the conference's injustices to Poland, but he had never denounced Roosevelt personally. Lesinski, Jr., who succeeded his father in 1950, argued in 1952 that, when considered in the context of the 1945 war situation, Yalta had "some merit." It reflected Western hopes of Allied co-operation, hopes that had been betrayed. He demanded the repudiation of Yalta to register U.S. "disapproval" of the Soviet Union's "illegal" subjugation of Poland.[21]

In contrast to this Democratic ambivalence, all the Republican speakers on these anniversaries described the conference as infamous, appeasement, or treacherous. They continued to attribute Poland's fate and world problems directly to the Yalta agreements and to demand a more principled, vigorous, and less secretive foreign policy.[22]

The heightened concern over Eastern Europe and Yalta shown in the anniversary speeches channeled support for liberation proposals that were introduced later in 1952. In May, during the debate on the Mutual Security Act, Congressman Charles Kersten urged the Republican party to renounce the "bankrupt Democratic policy of containment" and to adopt the more dynamic policy of liberation, "based on the Declaration of Independence." A liberation policy would hit at the "vital weakness" of the Soviet Union — its obsessive fear about Soviet refugees, a fear shown by Stalin's postwar demand for the repatriation of all Soviet refugees. A start toward this policy of liberation would be Congress' continuation of his amendment to the 1951 Mutual Security Act in the 1952 Mutual Security Act. His amendment provided $100,000,000 for subsidizing army units made up of refugees from Iron Curtain countries, and Kersten criticized the Administration's not using it. On March 29, 1952, Secretary of State Acheson had testified in committee hearings on the Mutual Security Act that not one dollar of the 1951 appropriation had been spent. Kersten demanded more dynamic leadership and cited Dulles' support for liberation.[23]

On June 20, Kersten demanded that liberation become the "keystone" of a "new and affirmative American" foreign policy. He maintained that his amendment proposing the formation of military units of exiles from Communist-controlled countries had provided the basis

21. *Ibid.*, Part 8, A708.
22. *Ibid.*, Parts 1, 8, and 10, 900, 938, 974, A733, A740–42, A752, A803, A822, A2675.
23. *Ibid.*, Part 5, 5898–5901.

for this new affirmative policy. In his June speech, Kersten for the first time sought the repudiation of the Yalta agreements, which "helped" dismember Poland, in order to remove every obstacle to freedom and independence for the "captive nations."[24]

In 1952, Republicans proposed either to repudiate past policies or to adopt a policy of victory, such as liberation. Proponents of both approaches demanded a more dynamic policy and urged that the United States assume the offensive. Repudiation of the Yalta agreements and liberation became standard Republican campaign demands in 1952. Republican spokesmen, Republican candidates, the Republican platform, and the Republican National Committee's campaign material mentioned Yalta as much as they could, but unlike those of 1948, Republican criticisms of Yalta in 1952 were nationwide.

Within the Republican party, however, a sharp difference existed about the best way to use Yalta and foreign policy in the 1952 campaign. The campaigns leading to the presidential preferential primaries most clearly showed the diverging views. Although Eisenhower and his principal supporters did not ignore Yalta and although they also denounced the past Administration's foreign policy, they did wage a distinctly less partisan and more temperate campaign than the Taft Republicans did. Eisenhower's candidacy, which had been initiated as a "stop Taft" movement, had not been intended to renounce the themes of foreign policy and internal security adopted by Taft and identified with McCarthy. The Eisenhower Republicans, the "moderates" primarily, were more liberal and internationalist; the Taft Republicans, the "extremists" and most of the "partisans," were more conservative and less committed to international involvement.

Taft's book *A Foreign Policy for Americans*, published in 1951, fairly well summarized his foreign and domestic views and his basic campaign strategy. He too deplored the indecisiveness, weakness, and lack of principle of the Administration's foreign policy at Yalta. Stressing Alger Hiss's major role at the conference, Taft called the Yalta concessions unnecessary. They had built the Soviet Union into a threat to U.S. security. The Administration had failed to appraise Soviet actions correctly, and, Taft stated, "Those who accept the principle of socialism, of government direction, and of government

24. *Ibid.*, Part 6, 7767–68. In his book, *Containment or Liberation?*, James Burnham similarly appraised the failures of Yalta and of the containment policy. As an alternative to the weakness, hesitancy, and failure inherent in the containment policy, Burnham proposed the policy of liberation as being less defensive and more responsive. James Burnham, *Containment or Liberation? An Inquiry into the Aims of United States Foreign Policy.*

bureaucracy have a hard time battling against the ideology of communism."[25]

He developed these themes in his well-financed campaign for the Republican presidential nomination. From the start of the campaign in September, 1951, Taft blamed Democratic foreign policy, and Yalta specifically, for the communization of China and Eastern Europe and for the outbreak of the Korean War. He sought to capitalize on the public reaction to the Korean War, by linking it to the communization of China and the communization of China to Yalta. How could the Administration have trusted Stalin's promises at Yalta since Stalin "had never kept a promise"? Implying that the Yalta decisions were so disastrous and inimical to U.S. interests that no U.S. statesman could have concluded them, Taft said that the U.S. position at Yalta had been caused by the "indirect influence of communism and Communists" on U.S. statesmen. These pro-Communist State Department policies confirmed McCarthy's demand for investigations of the State Department, and Taft would clean out the State Department. No bipartisan foreign policy had existed at Teheran, Yalta, and Potsdam because no Republican had been consulted about these conferences or had attended them. Moreover, Taft argued, President Truman had discarded the bipartisan foreign policy after 1948.

Taft pointedly stressed the right of Congress and the people of the United States to be consulted and fully informed. He pledged simultaneously to reduce military expenditures, to repudiate the secret and arbitrary diplomacy of Yalta and other conferences, and to initiate a campaign to "penetrate the iron curtain and free the Russian satellites." The repudiation of Yalta would mark the first step toward a more dynamic policy toward the Soviet Union. Although a meeting of the Big Three was a possibility, he doubted that it was propitious. He would not go to the Soviet Union but would insist that any such meeting be held in a "completely neutral" place. Such a place would not be close to the Soviet Union, but it would not necessarily be in the United States.

During his campaign, Taft also utilized Yalta to denounce Eisenhower's position on foreign policy. Eisenhower was evading criticisms of the Administration's disastrous foreign policy and attacking Republicans instead of concentrating on the Democrats in his addresses on foreign policy. Republicans should oppose "me-tooism"

25. Robert Taft, *A Foreign Policy for Americans*, 6–8, 18–22, 48–54, 56–60, 117.

and the "hypocrisy" of the bipartisan foreign policy, for they could win in 1952 only by a full-fledged attack on Yalta and other foreign policy decisions. The other Yalta conferees accepted Communists as peace loving democrats, and "Communists in the Administration" had converted the U.S. delegation at Yalta to this outlook. His more outspoken criticism of the New Deal and the Fair Deal, Taft asserted, made him a better candidate than Eisenhower.[26]

While not adopting Taft's wholesale denunciation of the Administration's foreign policy, Eisenhower's more moderate campaign strategy did not neglect Yalta. Eisenhower did not criticize Yalta openly until June, in the closing days of the primary campaign, and then he was not as vehement as Taft. Speaking in Abilene, Kansas, Eisenhower stated that mystery must be removed from foreign policy and promised, if he were elected President, to consult MacArthur. Though attributing the loss of China to Democratic administrations, Eisenhower did not specifically emphasize the Yalta conferees' responsibility. In a speech in Detroit on June 14, Eisenhower said that he disagreed with the "political decisions" of Teheran, Yalta, and Potsdam. He had not attended the Yalta or Teheran conferences, and he had not been consulted about the Yalta and Teheran decisions. He had learned of their results only through the press. He had attended Potsdam, but his military advice had been disregarded. Replying to criticisms of his failure to take Berlin in 1945, he maintained that the U.S. halt on the Elbe had been based on an earlier military decision.[27]

The Taft supporters' attacks on the General's anti-Communist credentials had forced him to renounce responsibility for Yalta, to defend the decision not to invade Berlin, and to criticize Yalta. The *Chicago Tribune* and George Sokolsky had consistently denounced Eisenhower as a New Dealer who was "implicated" in the execution of such "New Deal" policies as Yalta, Potsdam, and the Korean War. They particularly condemned Eisenhower's 1945 military decision to

26. *Chicago Tribune*, September 21, 1952, 4; October 24, 1951, 3; November 8, 1951, 4; November 10, 1951, 1, 3; December 4, 1951, 2; February 3, 1952, 1; February 13, 1952, 1, 6; February 14, 1952; March 7, 1952, 1; March 16, 1952, 1; April 5, 1952, 7; May 9, 1952, 3; June 2, 1952, 16, 17; June 25, 1952, 1, 2; June 28, 1952, 4. *The New York Times*, January 22, 1952, 15; February 16, 1952, 8; March 30, 1952, 49. *Milwaukee Journal*, March 30, 1952, 10. *Washington Post*, February 6, 1952. *Baltimore Sun*, October 16, 1951. *Washington Star*, February 17, 1952. Robert Taft, speech to the Women's National Republican Club, New York, January 26, 1952. Records of Publicity Division, Democratic National Committee, Truman Library. Taft Committee, *Why I Oppose Truman's Foreign Policy*, and *A Realistic Defense and Foreign Policy*.

27. *Congressional Quarterly Weekly Report*, X, 23 (June 6, 1952), iv, 565. *Chicago Tribune*, June 15, 1952, 8.

stop U.S. troops at the Elbe. The *Tribune* charged that Eisenhower
was Roosevelt's, Truman's, and Marshall's "man"; an associate of the
"Acheson team"; "another Willkie"; "The Perfect Candidate (Democratic)"; "Harriman's man"; and a "me-too Republican." It described
the Eisenhower organization as "Republicans for Truman."[28]

The contrast between Taft and Eisenhower reflected the rift
within the Republican party on the use of foreign policy in the campaign.[29] By 1952, the "extremists" had become a national political
force. Their objectives were to defeat the Democrats and to impugn
the Roosevelt and Truman administrations' internationalist and reformist policies. They suspected Eisenhower's moderation and his
tolerant view of the present foreign policy. They also feared that
Eisenhower might deny the nomination to Taft.

Despite their differences, the "extremists," "partisans," and "moderates" all used Yalta, a symbol of an earlier policy failure, as an
effective political issue. Their differences were in degree, not tactics.
Both Taft and Eisenhower supported John Foster Dulles for chairman of the committee that drafted the foreign policy plank of the
1952 Republican platform, and all three groups used Yalta both in
primary campaigns and on the floor of the Congress. Republican
Congressmen George Bender, Thomas Jenkins (Ohio), John Wood,
Fred Busbey (Illinois), Wesley D'Ewart (Montana), Senators
Everett Dirksen, Harry Cain, and Edward Martin attacked Yalta
and contended that only a Republican administration could institute
a vigorous new policy. The Democratic party, because of its involvement in the Yalta Conference and its commitment to Yalta, could
not make such a change. Bender denied that there had ever been a
bipartisan foreign policy: "Lest we forget, the issue must be restated
and restated through the months to come. Under the Democrats
we surrendered China to the Communists, . . . Is it not time for us
to start erasing from public life those who have written the record
upon our slate?" Martin echoed this view:

28. *Ibid.*, August 3, 1951, 12; August 8, 1951, 18; September 10, 1951, 5,
14; November 3, 1951, 10; January 3, 1952, 14; January 5, 1952, 1; January 8,
1952, 1, 16; January 9, 1952, 18; January 10, 1952, 20; January 11, 1952, 8;
January 12, 1952, 8; January 13, 1952, 22; January 18, 1952, 18; January 19,
1952, 8; January 25, 1952, 14; January 21, 1952, 1, 6; April 11, 1952, 1, 4;
April 19, 1952, 8; May 2, 1952, 6, 12; May 10, 1952, 8; May 29, 1952, 16;
May 30, 1952, 10; June 14, 1952, 7; July 6, 1952, 8; July 23, 1952, 20. *Milwaukee Sentinel*, June 28, 1952, 8.
29. The "extremists" resorted to the same tactics to discredit the "moderates'" defense of the bipartisan containment policy. Fulton Lewis, Jr., and the
Chicago Tribune specifically castigated Republican Senator Alexander Wiley
for this suggestion. *Milwaukee Sentinel*, June 2, 1952, 8. *Chicago Tribune*,
May 4, 1952, 20.

The cold, stark, ugly truth is that the party in power at Washington had no policy except that which grew out of the black-market deal at Yalta. My fellow Americans, the record of the last 20 years should convince everyone of us that we must clean house at Washington. The only way that we can get back on the road of real Americanism is to get rid of those responsible for this mess we are in and substitute bold, courageous intelligent leadership.[30]

The congressional Republicans' analysis of their foreign policy accomplishments during the Eighty-second Congress reflected this negativism. The analysis, drafted under the direction of Senator Styles Bridges, denounced the past Administration's foreign policy, particularly Yalta, and emphasized the ways in which Republicans "continued to expose the sins of Yalta." Through Watkins' reservation to the Japanese peace treaty, they had repudiated the agreement ceding Japanese territory to the Soviet Union. The analysis cited the secret classification of the Yalta telephone directory as evidence of the extent of the Administration's secretiveness about foreign policy. The U.S. public, it stated, still remained ignorant of many of the Administration's commitments and past decisions.[31]

The Democrats did not respond forcefully to any of these challenges. During the primaries and rest of the time preceding the convention, the Democratic National Committee and Democratic presidential candidates were relatively silent about the conference. A few Democrats made half-hearted efforts to counter Republican charges, but for the most part, Democratic spokesmen scrupulously avoided Yalta.

The main themes of the Democratic defense of Yalta were incorporated in *Fact Sheet RD-28*, published in April by the Research Division of the Democratic National Committee. *RD-28* dismissed the Republican charges that Yalta was responsible for Chiang's defeat as pure myths created to "smear the memory of President Roosevelt." Yalta was an act of real statesmanship; the Far Eastern agreements had been made in order to save the lives of U.S. soldiers and to help Chiang overcome the Chinese Communists. Yalta had promoted a Soviet-Nationalist Chinese alliance, not Soviet recognition of the Chinese Communists. "In spite of Yalta," the Nationalists

30. *Congressional Quarterly Weekly Report*, X, 2 (January 11, 1952), 22. U.S. *Congressional Record*, 82d Cong., 2d sess., 1952, XCVIII, Parts 5, 8, 9, and 11, 5675–77, 6736–39, A611–12, A783–84, A2139, A4058, A4522. *Chicago Tribune*, March 3, 1952, 2.
31. U.S. *Congressional Record*, 82d Cong., 2d sess., 1952, XCVIII, Part 11, A4805–9.

lost China because of their corruption and failure to institute reform. The Yalta terms, *RD-28* further observed, had restricted the amount of territory that Soviet troops could have taken, and it listed possible questions for Democratic speakers to use in reply to Yalta mythmakers. If Yalta were a sellout, why did the Soviet Union violate it? If Roosevelt should not have followed the advice of the Joint Chiefs of Staff, whose advice should he have followed? If China were sold out, why had Chinese Foreign Minister T. V. Soong granted more favorable terms to the Soviet Union in the later Sino-Soviet treaty? *RD-28* suggested that the best way to handle the Yalta "ranters" was to offer this final rejoinder: Had they read the text of the Yalta Far Eastern agreements?[32]

The Republican National Convention, which was held in July, changed the focus of the debate about Yalta. The tone and emphasis of the preconvention period reflected the "extremists'" dominance of the Republican National Committee and their commitment to Taft's nomination. Their emphasis was more critical than constructive. They called for a more resolute foreign policy in order to discredit the Administration's policy rather than to offer a workable alternative course.

The Taft forces' control of the Republican National Committee had permitted the continuity of this line by the main convention speakers — Douglas MacArthur, Herbert Hoover, Styles Bridges, Patrick Hurley, Katharine St. George, Walter Judd, and Joseph McCarthy.[33] Only Bridges did not explicitly criticize Yalta, and all of them made the familiar charge that the Democrats, because of the Democratic role at Yalta, had created current international problems. Democratic foreign policy was weak and vacillating; it appeased the Soviet Union. The United States needed more vigorous, resourceful leaders who were prepared to initiate bold, new policies and who were not committed to defending past policies. In contrast to

32. Democratic National Committee, *Fact Sheet RD-28.* In a July address to the Ukrainian-American Convention, Democratic National Committeewoman India Edwards dismissed Republican charges as simply electioneering that was intended to rewrite history in order to divert attention from the obstructionist record of the Republican party during the "past 20 years." Mrs. Edwards described the Democrats as the true friends of the peoples of Eastern Europe, recalling Wilson's 1919 diplomacy, which advocated self-determination for Eastern Europe, and identifying Roosevelt and Truman with that objective. Denying that Yalta was a sellout, she praised the Yalta Declaration on Liberated Europe and condemned Soviet violations of this agreement. India Edwards, speech to the Ukrainian-American Convention, New York, New York, July 4, 1952, Yalta Conference, Democratic National Committee Files, Truman Library.

33. *Official Report of the Proceedings of the Twenty-fifth Republican National Convention, 1952,* 68, 72–73, 83, 105, 137, 143–44, 147, 277, 327–29.

the 1948 Republican convention addresses, these 1952 speeches concentrated primarily on past Democratic policies. Their point was less that the Republicans were better qualified than that the decisions of past Democratic administrations had disqualified the Democrats. While not all of the speakers contended that Yalta was engineered by Communists in the State Department, as Hurley and McCarthy asserted and Bridges hinted, they did say that at Yalta the Democrats had "assigned" Eastern Europe and Asia to the Soviet Union.

Various nominating speeches — Senator John Bricker's on behalf of Robert Taft, Senator William Knowland's on behalf of Earl Warren, and Harlan Kelley's on behalf of Douglas MacArthur — also concentrated on Yalta. Dynamic leadership was needed, these speakers argued, to deal with the problems that Yalta had created. Kelley emphasized Yalta's secrecy and the Administration's refusal to inform the public; Knowland stressed the loss of U.S. "moral leadership" and Yalta's "enslavement" of millions of people; Bricker insisted on the need to prevent the reoccurrence of Yalta's "cynical betrayal." Those peoples who retained hope for their eventual liberation, Bricker observed, turned to the Republican party for their "redemption."[34]

For Republican orators, the 1952 campaign was a great moral and spiritual crusade. Messianic and apocalyptic in their approach, Republicans at the convention spoke of Yalta as the basis for all international problems, and Senator Joseph McCarthy maintained:

> Why, ladies and gentlemen, has the Administration deliberately built up Russia while tearing down the strength of America? I have been proving that it was because of abysmal stupidity and treason . . . whether it is because of treason or stupidity — if America and her sons are to live — then, that Yalta-Teheran-Potsdam crowd must go.[35]

Congressman Walter Judd argued that the objectives of the 1952 campaign were not "merely" to defeat the Democrats but to "save the United States."[36]

The 1952 Republican platform also denounced Yalta. The two planks relating to Yalta stipulated:

> Teheran, Yalta and Potsdam were the scenes of those tragic blunders with others to follow. The leaders of our Administration in power acted without the knowledge or consent of Congress or the American people. They traded our overwhelm-

34. *Ibid.*, 215, 249, 360.
35. *Ibid.*, 143.
36. *Ibid.*, 328–29.

ing victory for a new enemy and for new oppressions and new wars which were quick to come. . . . The Republican party is determined to wage war against secret covenants . . . will repudiate all commitments contained in secret understandings, such as those of Yalta, which aid Communist enslavements.[37]

This line of attack incorporated the "moderates'" and "partisans'" anti-Democratic and the "extremists'" anti-Roosevelt, anti-New Deal concerns. It was an impossible compromise that satisfied neither moderates nor conservatives.

The New York Times, Time magazine, and the Chicago Tribune praised this pledge to repudiate Yalta, but they differed on the meaning of the platform. Time magazine stated satisfaction with the plank for assigning the blame for the Korean War and the lost peace. The New York Times expressed fear that the platform's "persuasive points," its descriptions of Teheran, Yalta, and Potsdam as "major blunders," were weakened by its excesses in holding the Democratic party responsible. The Chicago Tribune, however, criticized the platform's praise of the United Nations and its ambiguous denunciation of Teheran, Yalta, and Potsdam. The platform was contradictory, ambiguous, and lacking in sense. The plank on foreign policy had one meaning for those who consistently protested the "rape of middle Europe and Asia" and opposed a "vindictive peace" toward Germany, but it meant nothing to "those who are manipulating delegates at the convention." The Tribune hoped that Taft would secure the nomination because he would give a clear interpretation of the plank. After Taft's defeat, the Tribune defended the Republican platform as "not quite as bad" as the Democratic, and the newspaper restricted itself to affirming the importance of sending "good men to Congress."[38]

The Democratic National Convention concentrated principally on domestic policy, as the title of the Democratic platform, "Twenty Years of Progress," indicated. Convention speakers minimized foreign policy, but they deemed past policies resolute and correct. They again defended Yalta by ascribing existing problems to Soviet viola

37. Republican National Committee, The 1952 Republican Platform: Point Up the Highlights.
38. Time, 60 (July 21, 1952), 14. The New York Times, July 11, 1952, 16. Chicago Tribune, July 4, 1952, 1; July 11, 1952, 20; July 23, 1952, 20; July 26, 1952, 12. In a different vein, The Nation argued that this Republican plank on foreign policy reflected the "Asia-first, allies-be-damned views of General MacArthur." It noted that, although the Republicans had pledged to repudiate Yalta, they did not specify in the platform how this repudiation was to be effected. The Nation, 175 (July 19, 1952), 42–43.

tions of the agreements. In his keynote address, Governor Paul Dever of Massachusetts asserted that foreign and domestic policy could not be separated. To check communism abroad, the United States had to maintain and then expand prosperity at home. Soviet actions had frustrated the Administration's efforts to attain a permanent peace after World War II. He further contended that the Soviet Union had been checked only through the Administration's resoluteness.[39]

Thaddeus Machrowicz, a congressman from a Polish-American district in Michigan and a supporter of a resolution to repudiate Yalta, was the only convention speaker who directly alluded to Yalta. Referring to Republican criticisms of the administrations' roles at Yalta and Potsdam, Machrowicz called the Republicans' failure to criticize the Soviet Union surprising. He remarked that one might have thought that the United States, and not the Soviet Union, had violated the terms of these "treaties."[40]

The Democratic party, the Democratic platform asserted, had worked to secure peace with honor and had provided leadership in ending isolation and countering the spread of communism. The platform stated that the administrations' foreign policy, specifically Yalta, was basic to international peace and national security, and it further pledged, "We will not abandon the once-free peoples of Central and Eastern Europe who suffer now under the Kremlin's tyranny in violation of the Soviet Union's most solemn pledges at Teheran, Yalta and Potsdam." Another section of the platform expressed the Democratic hope that someday the peoples of Eastern and Central Europe would be liberated from Soviet domination.[41]

The Republican and Democratic conventions and platforms previewed the treatment of Yalta in the national campaign. The Republicans assailed Democratic weakness or betrayal; the Democrats attributed postwar problems to Soviet bad faith. Although his primary campaign had been more moderate than Taft's, Eisenhower's national campaign had to continue Taft's basic themes because of Taft's influence in the Republican party. The tone of Taft's campaign in the primaries had thus set limits to the Republican national campaign. The congressional anti-Communist record of vice-presidential candidate Nixon, a former member of the House Committee on Un-American Activities who had played a primary

39. *Official Report of the Proceedings of the Democratic National Convention, 1952,* 46–47.
40. *Ibid.,* 132.
41. *Ibid.,* 254–58. The convention itself went on record as fully supporting the foreign policy decisions and leadership of Franklin Roosevelt and Harry Truman. *Ibid.,* 404, 536.

role in convicting Alger Hiss, ensured the continuity of Taft's line. Also, the Republican platform's plank on foreign policy and the congressional Republicans' consistent charges during 1951 and 1952 made Yalta a symbol and an issue in the campaign. Remaining silent or asking the Republican National Committee not to attack Democratic foreign policy so violently would have cost Eisenhower an effective campaign issue, alienated the already frustrated Taft Republicans, and enabled the Democrats to question the basis for earlier Republican charges.

Eisenhower's compromise, adopting the "extremists'" rhetoric on foreign policy, became obvious during discussion of liberation, an attractive campaign issue alluded to in both the Democratic and Republican platforms. Early in the campaign, the Republican candidates formally supported "liberation of the satellite countries," and on August 12, John Foster Dulles invited Congressman Charles Kersten, author of the so-called liberation amendment to the 1951 and the 1952 Mutual Security acts and the chief congressional spokesman for liberation, to meet Eisenhower the next day in Denver. Dulles had invited Kersten to Denver purposely; he feared that the Democrats might adopt liberation and "beat the Republicans to the punch."[42]

Immediately after their meeting on August 13, Eisenhower and Kersten held a press conference. Eisenhower pledged to initiate a foreign policy that offered hope "of obtaining by peaceful means freedom for the people now behind the Iron Curtain in both Europe and Asia." Kersten, however, charged that any negotiated peace that left half the world enslaved was "immoral, unethical and un-American." The Truman Administration's foreign policy was negative; U.S. foreign policy should aim at the "ultimate" freedom for the "captive nations." The United States should establish army units composed of refugees from the "satellite" countries. Kersten did not establish a timetable for effecting liberation or claim that liberation could be achieved without bloodshed. He merely asserted that a U.S. commitment to liberation would increase the "captive" peoples' resistance to Stalin and shake "Stalin's hold" on the "enslaved" nations. At the end of the conference, James Hagerty, Eisenhower's press secretary, made it clear to the press that Eisenhower's statement was "in no way" an "endorsement" of Kersten's views.[43]

In an address to the American Legion on August 25, Eisenhower reiterated his belief that the United States needed to use its "influ-

---

42. Congressman Charles Kersten, interview, August 3, 1962.
43. *The New York Times*, August 14, 1952, 1.

ence and power" to "help" the Communist-controlled nations of Eastern Europe and Asia throw off the "yoke of Russian tyranny." The strengthening of U.S. military power was imperative. The United States should inform the Soviet Union that the United States would "never" recognize the "permanence" of the Soviet position in Eastern Europe and Asia and that U.S. "aid" to the "enslaved" peoples would not stop until their countries were free. He concluded by saying that the United States must once again become the symbol of man's hopes and goals.[44]

The Republican National Committee's Nationalities Division underscored the party's commitment to liberation. It reprinted and released Taft's interview that had originally appeared in *The New York Times* on June 2, 1952. The interview was entitled "Republican Policy of Liberation or Democratic Policy of Containment?" In it, Taft noted that millions of heroic anti-Communists who were presently enslaved still desired freedom and independence. They had been "delivered" to the Soviet Union at Yalta. He demanded the formal discarding of the Yalta agreements by congressional resolution as the first step toward an "American" foreign policy.[45]

The proposal of a policy of liberation constituted only one part of the Republican effort. Although they varied in their use of Yalta, the Republican National Committee, the Republican Congressional Policy Committee, the Republican Senate Policy Committee, and the Citizens for Eisenhower-Nixon all criticized Democratic foreign policy and maintained that bold Republican leadership would rectify international problems. The United States had been strong at the conclusion of World War II, but Democratic policies at such conferences as Yalta had diminished that strength. The Yalta agreements had come from the Administration's stupidity, its policy of appeasement, or Communist influence. Roosevelt and the Democratic administrations had failed to recognize the "true aims" of communism when they proposed U.S. recognition of the Soviet Union in 1933 and the policies of lend-lease, Teheran, Yalta, and Potsdam. Democratic foreign policy had not been bipartisan; no Republican had attended Yalta. The Republican National Committee's speech kit included a statement about Yalta for Republican speakers to use in the 1952 campaign:

The Republican Party did not know of these agreements. Republicans were never told or consulted about them. Not one

44. *Ibid.*, August 26, 1952, 1, 12.
45. Republican National Committee, *Republican Policy of Liberation or Democratic Policy of Containment.*

Republican leader was ever invited to the conferences at Teheran, Yalta, and at Potsdam where these under-cover agreements were made. The Republican Party, therefore, has no responsibility for their disastrous results.

The Republicans then contrasted the Democrats' opposition to repudiation with the Republicans' partial repudiation of Yalta in the Japanese peace treaty and with their 1952 platform pledge to repudiate Yalta and other secret agreements.[46]

Republicans also stressed the theme of "Communists in Government." Charging that Yalta had benefited the Soviet Union, Republican spokesmen linked Alger Hiss's attendance at Yalta and his conviction for perjury in 1950. In addition, Republican campaign pamphlets specifically questioned the anticommunism of Adlai Stevenson, the Democratic presidential candidate. Reviewing Stevenson's past record and statements, one such pamphlet maintained that he had disparaged the subversion issue in the past, criticized McCarthy, vetoed as governor of Illinois the "antisubversive" Broyles bills, given a deposition attesting to Alger Hiss's good character, stressed the need for friendly relations with the Soviet Union in 1943, and defended coexistence and Administration foreign policy by attributing international problems to Soviet violations.[47]

Republicans did not forget the Polish-Americans' interest in Yalta. Congressmen Charles Kersten, Alvin O'Konski, Alvin Bentley (Republican, Michigan), Senator Joseph McCarthy, and former Ambassador to Poland Arthur Bliss Lane denounced the Democrats' betrayal at Yalta. Moreover, the Nationalities Division of the Re-

46. Republican National Committee, *Statement of Republican Principles and Objectives*. Republican National Committee, *Republican Speakers: Here Is Your Ammunition on Taxes, Labor, Agriculture, Foreign Policy*. Republican National Committee, *Republican Speakers: Waste, Corruption, Communism: The Sorry Record of Twenty Years of Red Influence In and On Two Democratic Administrations*. Republican National Committee, *The Republican Party: Its History in Brief*. Republican National Committee, *Fighting Men Won the War!!! Floundering Politicians Lost the Peace*. National Republican Congressional Committee, *Speech Kit*. Republican Senate Policy Committee, *Secrecy in Government: The Growth of Federal Censorship, Concealment and Deception under 20 Years of Democratic Administration 1933–1952*. Citizens for Eisenhower-Nixon, "The Man Who Can Bring Us Durable Peace." Republican Senate Policy Committee, *Major Issues of 1952*. Republican State Central Committee, Lansing, Michigan, *Do You Want War . . . Or a Sound Foreign Policy?*

47. Republican National Committee, *Adlai Stevenson on the Red Menace: The Communist Issue, Alger Hiss, Russia and Communism Abroad*. Republican National Committee, *Republican Speakers: Waste, Corruption, Communism: The Sorry Record of Twenty Years of Red Influence In and On Two Democratic Administrations*. National Committee of the Jefferson Party, "Crime, Corruption and Communism."

publican National Committee published a special pamphlet assailing the Democratic betrayal of Eastern Europe at Yalta. The pamphlet, reprinted in Polish, emphasized Alger Hiss's influence at Yalta and the secrecy of the conference and contended that, had the Democratic Administration taken a strong stand, all of Eastern Europe could have been saved.[48]

In Pulaski Day addresses, both Dwight Eisenhower and Richard Nixon criticized the Yalta Conference. Nixon traced Poland's "enslavement" directly to the Yalta agreements and demanded their repudiation, but Eisenhower did not forthrightly denounce Yalta and only indirectly cited the Administration's responsibility. Eisenhower noted the Republican platform's pledge to repudiate secret commitments and stated that he supported it because "through the violation of the Atlantic Charter and through its unilateral violation by the Soviet government, [Yalta] has resulted in the enslavement of Poland."[49]

Many Polish-American leaders were impressed by the Republican campaign. On August 28, various Polish-American leaders in New York announced their support for Eisenhower. The chairman of the New York division of the Polish-American Congress singled out Eisenhower's liberation statements as the basis for his support. On August 30, the chairman of the National Committee of Americans of Polish Descent reported his reactions to messages from both presidential candidates. He contrasted Eisenhower's open endorsement of Polish freedom with Stevenson's evasive comments and stated, "Stevenson ratifies the Yalta and Potsdam agreements and intends to follow the policies of Roosevelt and Truman." In October, a group of Polish-Americans in Chicago expressed support for Re-

48. Congressman Charles Kersten, interview, August 3, 1962. Congressman Alvin O'Konski, interview, July 10, 1962. Congressman John Lesinski, Jr., interview, July 11, 1962. Congressman Alvin Bentley, letter, February 1, 1963. Bentley also exploited Yalta's images of secret, executive diplomacy when appealing to conservative voters in his congressional district. He pointed to Yalta as posing the need for more public information and for restrictions on executive authority. Congressman Clement Zablocki, interview, July 24, 1962. Democratic National Committee, Publicity Division, Files on McCarthy, Marquis Childs, October 7, 1952, Truman Library. In addresses before the Ukrainian-American and Slovak League of America, Republican Senator Everett Dirksen developed these themes of Yalta's betrayal of Eastern Europe and responsibility for the loss of freedom of the peoples of these areas. Dirksen urged these ethnic groups to support the repudiation of Yalta and the leaders who made these blunders. *Chicago Tribune*, August 25, 1952, 6; October 13, 1952, 4. Republican National Committee, *Betrayal! Over 100,000,000 Eastern Europeans by the Democratic Administration.*
49. *The New York Times*, October 6, 1952, 1. *Washington Post*, October 12, 1952.

publican candidates because of the Democrats' betrayal of Poland at Yalta and the Republicans' pledge to repudiate Yalta.[50]

The 1952 election results showed the impact of Republican demands for repudiation of Yalta and for a policy of liberation. The Republican ticket polled very well in Polish-American districts of Chicago; it carried Cook County by a vote of 1,188,973 to 1,172,454. Louis Harris' analysis of the 1952 election results disclosed the national impact. According to Harris, the Democrats, who usually received more than 70 per cent of the Polish vote, had lost much of it in this election because many Polish-Americans believed that Poland had been betrayed at Yalta and in succeeding years. Those voters of Polish descent who expressed a preference for Eisenhower increased from 20 per cent in September to 50 per cent in November. Preparatory to the 1956 campaign, Abe Herman, then director of the Republican National Committee's Nationalities Division, reported that many Polish-Americans and other Eastern European groups had voted Republican in 1952 because of Yalta. He recommended further Republican efforts to retain the support and participation of these nationality groups in the Republican party.[51]

The Democratic National Committee's strategy in 1952 did attempt to rebut these Republican attacks on Yalta, but the focus of the Democratic campaign was on domestic policy and the future. With the exception of Truman, the Democrats avoided the Republicans' moralistic aura of crusading and ran a low-key campaign in which they tried to appeal to reason, tolerance, and understanding.

When the committee did discuss foreign policy, its approach was decidedly defensive. In its information kit to Democratic speakers and other campaign material, the Democratic National Committee described Yalta as a great U.S. diplomatic success that reflected the high principles of U.S. diplomacy. The committee did not defend the spirit of the conference; it emphasized the military and political limits to U.S. diplomacy in 1945 that influenced the Eastern European and Far Eastern agreements made at Yalta. It noted that the Sino-Soviet treaty of August, 1945, was more favorable to the Soviet Union than any Yalta agreement had been, that Chiang lost China "in spite of Yalta," and that Alger Hiss did not dominate the conference. Denying that Yalta was a sellout to the Soviet Union or ap-

---

50. *Chicago Tribune*, October 31, 1952, 3. Republican Campaign Headquarters, *News Bulletin, Every Hour on the Hour*.

51. Republican National Committee, "Nationality Groups: 'Margin of Victory in Marginal Districts,'" *Straight from the Shoulder*. Louis Harris, *Is There a Republican Majority? Political Trends, 1952–1956*, 100–101.

peasement of that country, the committee argued that the Cold War resulted from Soviet violations of the Yalta terms precisely because the Yalta ideals ran counter to Soviet aims. According to the committee, the world would have been far different had the Soviet Union adhered to its Yalta pledges.[52]

President Truman complicated Democratic campaign strategy. In a sense, there were two Democratic presidential candidates, Adlai Stevenson and Harry Truman. Ostensibly stumping the country for Stevenson, Truman really was defending his own Administration. He dismissed Republican criticisms as partisan and irresponsible. His Administration's foreign policy was realistic and resolute; the Soviets had violated international agreements. Administration policies were fighting "communism at home and abroad," and these policies of confrontation had been adopted gradually because of differing post-war estimates of Soviet actions. In 1945, while Stevenson and Harriman had warned "us to be on our guard," others like Eisenhower had "said we had nothing to fear from the Russians." Liberation was "cheap politics" and a play on the "needs and fears" of the "captive" peoples. Truman, however, never directly referred to Yalta.[53]

Adlai Stevenson's campaign was more reasoned and less openly partisan. He seemed to give a series of lectures rather than stump speeches. The problems facing the United States were complex, and there were no easy solutions to the Cold War. New Deal and Fair Deal policies had been attempts to achieve peace, and the Republicans' congressional record on foreign policy and their campaign charges were more negative than positive. In a Pulaski Day speech in Milwaukee, Wisconsin, and an address in predominantly Polish-American Hamtramck, Michigan, on September 1, he condemned Republican campaign demands for repudiation of Yalta and a policy of liberation as false campaign issues. The boldness of Republican words conflicted with the paucity of their actions: The Republicans had tried to reduce military expenditures and had opposed the Administration's Cold War policies. The United States should build Europe's strength so that "eventually" the Soviet Union "must keep its Yalta promises and release the peoples of central and eastern

52. Democratic National Committee, *The Truth About Yalta.* Democratic National Committee, *How to Win in '52: The Facts About the Democratic Road to Prosperity, Peace and Freedom.*

53. Harry S Truman, speeches: Oakland, California, October 4, 1952; Jersey City, New Jersey, October 21, 1952; Radio and TV broadcast, November 3, 1952; Parkersburg, West Virginia, September 2, 1952, Records of White House Official Reporter, Truman Papers, Truman Library.

Europe from communist bondage." Replying to Eisenhower's references to liberation, he argued, "It will be the strength of a united and powerful Europe which will make Soviet rulers respect the promises they made to us at Yalta." Debating the past should not be the means for ignoring present and future problems; foreign and domestic policies could not be separated. In an address at Providence, Rhode Island, on October 27, Stevenson charged, "Our problems are not, however, beyond our borders. There are many to be resolved here at home. We must not allow the over-riding urgency of foreign policy to distract us from domestic concerns."[54]

Despite Yalta's prominence in the 1952 campaign, fundamental differences remained between the "moderates" and "extremists" in their criticisms of the conference and Democratic foreign policy. The "moderates" only assailed such past policy decisions as those made at Yalta; the "extremists" concentrated on Yalta, Alger Hiss, the secrecy of past administrations' foreign policy, and identified domestic communism as *the* issue in the 1952 campaign. Thus, *The New York Times* endorsed the repudiation of Yalta because that repudiation would undermine the "legal" arguments of the Soviet Union and also stir the "hopes of the captive peoples." It added that no agreement was binding if it was violated by one of the parties, and noted that part of the Yalta agreements had already been repudiated with Senate ratification of the Japanese peace treaty.[55] However, the *Chicago Tribune*, George Sokolsky, *U.S. News and World Report*, Senators Everett Dirksen and Robert Taft, Edward Hayes (former national commander of the American Legion), General Albert Wedemeyer (former chairman of Republicans for Taft) and Caleb Holder (state chairman of the Indiana Republican party) pointed to Hiss's attendance at the conference as confirmation of Communist influence in the Administration and to the Yalta agreements as the embodiment of "New Deal" foreign policy. They blamed this policy for making the Soviet threat possible. The *Tribune* further suggested that the

54. Adlai Stevenson, speeches: Hamtramck, Michigan, September 1, 1952; Milwaukee, Wisconsin, October 9, 1952, Records of Publicity Division, Democratic National Committee, Truman Library. Text of Remarks by Adlai Stevenson at Providence, Rhode Island, Press Release of Publicity Division, Democratic National Committee, Library of Congress. Adlai Stevenson, *Major Campaign Speeches of Adlai E. Stevenson, 1952.* Stevenson's running mate, Alabama Senator John Sparkman, did not openly defend Yalta in his campaign addresses. Sparkman concentrated on domestic policy, but he dismissed Republican charges as partisan and defended in general terms the past administrations' foreign policy. Senator John Sparkman, interview, July 19, 1962.

55. *The New York Times*, October 1, 1952, 32; October 4, 1952, 16; October 19, 1952, 10E.

Democratic party had been "reconstituted by the New Dealers" and had become a "fellow traveler or defender of communism."[56]

In spite of its obvious importance as an issue, Yalta's individual significance in the 1952 campaign cannot be ascertained. By that time, Yalta was a symbol that epitomized the foreign policy against which the Republicans campaigned, and the way they used it contributed to Eisenhower's victory. Although few expected Eisenhower's election to lead to radical political changes, his success was indirectly welcomed by even the "extremist" *Chicago Tribune* and George Sokolsky. To the *Tribune*, the election results marked the repudiation of Roosevelt, Truman, and the New Deal Democratic party. Sokolsky and the *Tribune* were not positively enthusiastic about the victory, but they fully expected the implementation of the 1952 Republican platform planks, particularly the repudiation of Yalta and the elimination of "Yalta-men" from policy-making roles. They emphasized the need for extensive congressional investigations of Roosevelt's "secret diplomacy" at Yalta, Teheran, and Pearl Harbor and of Alger Hiss's role at the Yalta Conference. The *Tribune* commented, "The time has come to bring out the whole sordid story of fraud, thievery, conniving and betrayal."[57]

Similarly, the Republican National Precinct Workers in 1953 published a pamphlet, *Mission Accomplished*, outlining their views about the election results. The pamphlet referred to the coining of the term "egghead" to describe a "double-domed, confused, muddle-thinking individual of spurious intellectual pretensions" who "sold America down the river" at Yalta and Potsdam. Eisenhower's victory, the pamphlet concluded, had ended the reign of these eggheads, who for twenty years had been the "most powerful" influence in Washington.[58]

The 1952 foreign policy debate had developed a frenzied, crusadelike aura. Since 1950, the "extremists" and "partisans" in fact had dominated Republican political strategy, but during 1952, their domination was especially visible. Their influence was reflected in the Republican leaders' adoption of a position supporting the repudia-

56. *Chicago Daily News*, October 30, 1952, 12. *U.S. News and World Report*, 33 (September 26, 1952), 18; October 31, 1952, 86–87. *Milwaukee Sentinel*, October 16, 1952, 24. *Chicago Tribune*, August 20, 1952, 14; September 9, 1952, 20; September 11, 1952, 18; September 12, 1952, 14; September 16, 1952, 1, 4; October 6, 1952, 16; October 20, 1952, 11; November 3, 1952, 8, 12.
57. *Ibid.*, November 6, 1952, 16; November 8, 1952, 10; November 9, 1952, 26; November 18, 1952, 4; December 2, 1952, 20; December 3, 1952, 18; December 4, 1952, 20; December 6, 1952, 10. *Milwaukee Sentinel*, December 13, 1952, 10.
58. Republican National Precinct Workers, *Mission Accomplished*.

tion of Yalta, the liberation of the "satellite countries," the removal
of "Yalta-men" from the Federal Government, and the passage of
the Bricker Amendment. Thus, the one notable development during
the year was the "moderates'" successful "stop Taft" movement. Although the "moderates" had based their campaign strategy on denunciations of Yalta and the past Administration's foreign policy,
they had tried to distinguish their position from the simple negativism
of the "extremists" and the blunt partisanship of the "partisans." In
spite of the stabilizing effect brought by the "moderates'" success,
the influence and strategy of the "extremists" and "partisans" posed
one of the political problems that Eisenhower faced when he formulated his Administration's foreign policy.

chapter 9
1953–1954: renunciation of the campaign, part one

althrough John Foster Dulles had helped draft the 1952 Republican
foreign policy plank, which pledged to repudiate Yalta, and during
the 1952 campaign Dwight Eisenhower had urged the repudiation
of Yalta as one basis for a bold new foreign policy, in 1953 neither
Dulles nor Eisenhower acted on this Republican campaign promise.
The Eisenhower Administration did not disavow secret agreements
or try to liberate the "satellite countries." Its declaratory policy was
bold, but its operative policy continued the containment policies of
the Truman Administration. The oratory of the 1952 campaign and
the denunciations by congressional Republicans in 1950, 1951, and
1952 had made demands that did not correspond with the needs
and responsibilities of an administration in power.

These Republican charges limited the actions that the new Administration could take. The Republican party had publicly supported the repudiation of past agreements, thorough investigations
of people in the Federal Government, and the cleaning out of State
Department. As a Republican Administration, the Eisenhower Administration could not summarily renounce these Republican promises. Because it was in power, it could not simply make promises; it
had to pursue policies that could be effected and that also agreed
with the objectives of its NATO allies. Moreover, the Eisenhower
Administration had to allay the public's doubts and suspicions about
the use of executive authority and the conduct of foreign policy that
Senators Joseph McCarthy, John Bricker, Karl Mundt, Richard Nixon,
Robert Taft, and many other congressional Republicans had exploited from 1950 through 1952. Eisenhower and Dulles had tacitly
supported these Republicans' attacks, but in 1953 and 1954, the
Eisenhower Administration renounced them one by one. Some of
the renunciations were open, others were indirect, but all posed the
prospect of conflict with the "extremists" and the "partisans."

As early as January, 1953, the "extremists" attempted to capitalize
on the 1952 Republican victory and enforce the party's campaign
pledges. They relied on Yalta's images of secrecy and betrayal and

the fact of Alger Hiss's attendance at the conference. The Internal Security Subcommittee of the Senate Committee on the Judiciary sought to secure the notes that Alger Hiss had made at the Yalta Conference in order to document Hiss's influence. According to Senator Homer Ferguson, a member of the subcommittee, ascertaining Hiss's role at Yalta and his influence on the direction of the Roosevelt Administration's foreign policy was especially important. Blaming the Cold War and a possible third world war on Yalta's and Potsdam's secret agreements, he stated that the new Senate intended to pursue a more open, aggressive, and definite foreign policy.[1]

The most pressing demand faced by the Eisenhower Administration, however, dealt with the Yalta agreements directly. Criticisms of the Yalta conferees' betrayal of U.S. principles and ideals were basic to the charges that Republicans had made in the past. They had used Yalta to denounce the Administration's foreign policy at times for its secrecy, at times for its appeasement, and at times for its affinity for communism. The Republican party had pledged not to repeat these mistakes, and it had promised to initiate a bolder, more dynamic foreign policy. The repudiation of Yalta would be the springboard for this new course. From 1950 to 1952, and especially in the 1952 campaign, prominent Republicans had said that repudiation would restore the United States' moral position in the world, renew the "captive" peoples' faith in the United States, and warn the Soviet Union that the United States did not consider itself bound by the past and would not tolerate weakness or appeasement. Repudiation would wipe the slate clean and set the tone for a victorious U.S. foreign policy. Some Republicans contended that repudiation would absolve past "defeats" and restore "freedom" to Eastern Europe and Asia.

On January 3, Republican Congressmen Robert Hale and Lawrence Smith introduced resolutions to repudiate Yalta. Hale, the first congressman to have introduced a formal anti-Yalta resolution, reintroduced his original resolution, which requested the United States' withdrawal from Yalta because of Soviet violations.[2] Smith's resolution, first introduced in 1951, sought the repudiation of Yalta and Postdam. It stated that Yalta had sanctioned Soviet domination of Eastern Europe and Asia and had treated Germany unjustly.[3]

1. *Newsweek*, 41 (January 5, 1953), 18. *U.S. News and World Report*, 34 (January 9, 1953), 24. *The Saturday Evening Post*, 225 (January 10, 1953), 10. U.S. *Congressional Record*, 83d Cong., 1st sess., 1953, XCIX, Part 9, A4508.
2. For text see Appendix E.
3. For text see Appendix F. Congressman Albert Bosch (Republican, New York) introduced a resolution that differed from Smith's only in its concluding

On January 9, Democratic Congressman Thaddeus Machrowicz introduced House Joint Resolution 111, which was identical to Hale's resolution. In 1951, Machrowicz had submitted a resolution to repudiate Yalta. This earlier resolution had indirectly commended Yalta; it had emphasized Soviet violations of Yalta's spirit and had justified repudiation on the grounds that U.S. adherence had been based on Soviet good faith. Machrowicz' 1953 resolution was less apologetic and did not imply that the Yalta agreements would have been sound if the Soviet Union had complied with their terms.[4]

The Administration's official position on the repudiation of Yalta was first expressed in January, during hearings conducted by the Senate Foreign Relations Committee on John Foster Dulles' confirmation as Secretary of State. Senators Alexander Wiley, Homer Ferguson, and Hubert Humphrey (Democrat, Minnesota) had pressed Dulles on his foreign policy views and his 1952 campaign statements. The Republican platform, Dulles replied, was not "just campaign oratory but an accurate statement of the facts." However, he had used more extravagant words in the campaign than he would have used in a period of judicial contemplation. He would continue some, if not all, of Truman's and Acheson's programs. The main change in the new Administration's foreign policy would be one of "spirit." Dulles then affirmed the need to have a more forward policy and to sustain the hope of liberation.[5]

Yalta was also a topic in the Senate debate on the confirmation of Winthrop Aldrich as U.S. Ambassador to Great Britain. During this debate in January, Republican Senators Alexander Wiley, William Knowland, and Wayne Morse denounced the Far Eastern agreements. Knowland said that the recent election indicated the U.S. public's demand for no more Yaltas or Munichs and no more "handing over" other peoples' freedoms. He stated:

> Those who hold to the old ideas of Yalta and Munich, the idea that one can barter away the freedom of human beings, may have gotten some satisfaction under past administrations,

---

recommendation. Instead of repudiation, Bosch's resolution, House Concurrent Resolution 22, demanded the publication and re-examination of the Yalta agreements. For text see Appendix L. On January 20, Congressman Charles Kersten and on February 18, Congressman Alvin Bentley also introduced resolutions to repudiate Yalta. Condemning Yalta's secret diplomacy, both resolutions blamed postwar developments on Yalta agreements and deemed repudiation a necessary first step toward a policy of liberation. For the text of Kersten's resolution, see Appendix M. For the text of Bentley's, see Appendix N.

4. To contrast the texts, see Appendixes E and G.

5. U.S. Senate, Foreign Relations Committee, *Hearings on the Nomination of John Foster Dulles as Secretary of State-Designate*, 83d Cong., 1st sess., 1953, 4–6, 24–26.

but I do not believe such persons will get any satisfaction under the administration of President Eisenhower.[6]

Knowland's description of the Eisenhower Administration's foreign policy seemed to be an accurate one. On that same day, February 2, 1953, President Eisenhower, in his State of the Union address, boldly proclaimed a new course. The Administration could deter aggression and eventually secure peace by applying U.S. influence with fortitude and foresight. The agonizing and frustrating nature of post-1945 U.S. foreign policy would be terminated. Because the free world's remaining in a position of paralyzed tension gave the initiative to the enemy, the United States should have a "new, positive foreign policy" that would be truly bipartisan and would provide for executive-legislative co-operation. Alluding to Yalta, Eisenhower contended that the United States must not break faith with its friends or

. . . acquiesce in the enslavement of any people in order to purchase fancied gain for ourselves. I shall ask the Congress at a later date to join in an appropriate resolution making clear that this Government recognizes no kind of commitment contained in secret understandings of the past with foreign governments which permit this kind of enslavement.[7]

Eisenhower's speech was positive and assertive in tone. He sharply criticized the past administrations' failures to consult or co-operate with the Congress and with the Republican party, but he did not propose definite ways to implement this new course in foreign policy. He hinted that Yalta should be repudiated, espoused liberation, and tacitly supported the demand that the United States take the offensive in relations with the Soviet Union.

In contrast to the sharply critical resolutions and the tone of his own State of the Union address, President Eisenhower, in a press conference on February 17, stressed that "by no means" did he assume it "feasible or desirable that the United States Government should take any action saying that everything that was agreed to at such and such a place or time was repudiated." The Administration must clearly show that it had "never agreed to the enslavement" of any people. When asked if he had discovered any secret agreements other than Yalta or Potsdam, Eisenhower stated that he had not, and he defended the military necessity for the secrecy of those agreements.[8]

6. U.S. *Congressional Record*, 83d Cong., 1st sess., 1953, XCIX, Part 1, 735–37.
7. *Ibid.*, 748.
8. U.S. Senate, Foreign Relations Committee, *World War II International Agreements and Understandings*, 83d Cong., 1st sess., 1953, 75.

On February 18, Secretary of State Dulles first told the press of the Administration's proposed Yalta resolution. The resolution was intended to "reject dramatically" Soviet violations and also to "register dramatically" U.S. "hopes" that "enslaved peoples be liberated." It was a foreign policy, not domestic political pronouncement, and it did not involve "any actual repudiation." He added, "We believe that the enslavement of these captive peoples is due to abuse and violation of the understandings."[9]

On February 23, Republican Congressman John Vorys, chairman of the House Foreign Affairs Committee, introduced the Administration's resolution on Yalta, House Joint Resolution 200. The resolution did not propose the repudiation of Yalta but instead criticized the Soviet Union for violating the "clear intent" of the Yalta agreements and thereby "subjugating" whole nations. The United States, the resolution declared, rejected "interpretations" of Yalta that "have been perverted to bring about the subjugation of free peoples." It "hoped" that these peoples would "again enjoy the right of self-determination."[10]

In preparation for hearings on the resolution and congressional debate about it, the House Foreign Affairs Committee, under Vorys' direction, summarized the results of the various wartime secret conferences. This committee study emphasized Soviet "violations" or "perverted interpretations" of these conferences' agreements. Soviet violation of the Yalta Conference's Declaration on Liberated Europe and the Far Eastern agreements were cited.[11]

On February 26, the House Foreign Affairs Committee conducted formal hearings on House Joint Resolution 200. The Administration tried to promote the resolution and to avoid a partisan imbroglio. Dulles' testimony before the committee reflected the Administration's strategy: He said that the resolution was correct in its present form, but he avoided condoning or condemning the conference. Necessarily, Dulles was evasive; he directed his testimony against possible criticisms raised by the "extremists." He described the resolution as a "declaration of our purposes to the millions of enslaved peoples in Europe and Asia." It thereby ended the "captive nations'" uncertainty about the United States' resolve to aid them. The United States had a moral obligation to affirm for-

9. *Ibid.*, 76.
10. For text see Appendix O.
11. U.S. House of Representatives, Committee on Foreign Affairs, *World War II International Agreements and Understandings: Entered into During Secret Conferences Concerning Other People*, 83d Cong., 1st sess., 1953, v, vi, 39–40, 43, 46.

mally that it did "not acquiesce and never" had in the Soviet assault on freedom. Directed at the Soviet leaders "who have contrived this enslavement," it looked to the future, not the past. At the same time, Dulles contended, the resolution did not limit the Administration from future action because it did not violate any agreement or give up any rights, "if we chose to assert them."[12]

During the committee's questioning, Dulles stressed his and the President's satisfaction with the "present form" of the resolution. He defended the absence of specific criticisms of Yalta and added that the peoples of Poland and China had been looking for this kind of resolution for years. When questioned about whether the United States should admit failures, Dulles replied that a resolution to the world was not the "place" to repent for past actions. Although the resolution would not result in a Soviet change of heart, it would, in "due course," release the "forces, aspirations and hopes" of the captive peoples and make the "perpetuation" of Soviet rule impossible. It would also force the Soviet Union to realize that the United States was "not quiescent, submissive, in the face of violations," and thus it "might" induce the Soviet Union to adhere "more seriously" to future commitments. The United States should not repudiate "all" the Yalta agreements; it would be best to wait and at a later date press the Soviet Union about certain Yalta provisions. By pursuing this course, the Administration retained the freedom either to treat the agreements as void or to attempt to enforce them. "In no way," Dulles concluded, was ratification of the proposed resolution an expression concerning the validity of any of the various interpretations of Yalta.[13]

The contrast between Eisenhower's earlier words and his proposed resolution was not lost upon the Congress or the press. The Democrats were especially quick to point it out. At the same time, the resolution made many Republicans do considerable soul searching, and new political lines emerged during the debate. The "extremists" predictably denounced this betrayal, now by a Republi-

12. U.S. House of Representatives, Committee on Foreign Affairs, *Hearings on House Joint Resolution 200: Joining with the President of the United States in a Declaration Regarding the Subjugation of Free Peoples by the Soviet Union*, 83d Cong., 1st sess., 1953, 3–5.

13. *Ibid.*, 5–22. These themes became basic to the Administration's position. A July, 1953, article in the *State Department Bulletin* highlighted this revised stance concerning Yalta. The article denied that Yalta, or other wartime conferences, had "compromise[d] our interests" and affirmed, "In spite of controversy, the threat to America insofar as Yalta and Potsdam were concerned arises not so much out of agreements made there but out of the Soviet Union's violations of those agreements." Francis Stevens, "U.S. Foreign Policy and the Soviet Union," *Department of State Bulletin*, XXIX, 735 (July 27, 1953), 109–14.

can administration. The "moderates" and most of the "partisans" fell in line, rationalizing and defending this renunciation of a 1952 Republican campaign pledge.

House Joint Resolution 200, unanimously approved by the House Foreign Affairs Committee, never came to a vote in the Senate. Because its proposed form implied approval of the Yalta Conference and thereby abrogated a 1952 Republican campaign pledge, the resolution amounted to a rejection of the political course charted by the "partisans" and "extremists." Yet, the "partisans" and "extremists" could not simply urge the defeat of the resolution. That action would reveal their partisanship. Inaction, however, would indicate acquiescence. Faced with this dilemma, Senators Robert Taft and Bourke Hickenlooper (Republican, Iowa) proposed a reservation to the resolution during its consideration by the Senate Foreign Relations Committee. The reservation stated, "The adoption of this resolution does not constitute any determination by the Congress as to the validity or invalidity of any of the provisions of the said agreements or understandings."

The Democratic members of the committee refused to support the reservation. They argued that it was partisan and unnecessary, and according to Lyndon Johnson (Democrat, Texas), it violated the President's nonpartisan measure. Both Johnson and Hubert Humphrey doubted that the United States could criticize the Soviet Union for violating a nonvalid agreement.

While the Senate Foreign Relations Committee was still deliberating, the Democratic Senate Policy Committee met and formally endorsed House Joint Resolution 200. The Democratic committee's statement, to which every member subscribed, hailed Eisenhower's original resolution on Yalta and opposed any change in it. By so acting, the Democrats put the Republicans on the defensive and forced the "extremists" and "partisans" to decide whether to fight the issue on the floor of Congress. These Republicans faced a dilemma: Doing nothing and allowing the resolution to pass unamended would imply acceptance of the nonrepudiation of Yalta; amending the resolution would contrast their partisanship with the Eisenhower Administration's straightforward concern for the nation. Realizing the harm of either result, Taft had the resolution killed in committee on March 10, 1953.[14]

14. *Chicago Tribune*, March 1, 1953, 2; March 4, 1953, 12. George Reedy (Administrative Assistant to Lyndon Johnson and head of the Democratic Senate Policy Committee in 1953), interview, July 13, 1962.

House Joint Resolution 200 had given the Democrats and their supporters a chance to assume the offensive. Senator Guy Gillette, Congressman Wayne Aspinall (Democrat, Colorado), the Democratic National Committee, the *New Republic*, *The Nation*, *Newsweek*, and the *Chicago Sun-Times* forthrightly assailed the partisan motives of Republicans who had criticized Yalta. They noted that the resolution conflicted with former Republican statements because it upheld Yalta by implication rather than repudiating the conference or the agreements. The resolution rightfully assessed Stalin's blame for postwar problems. The National Committee, the *Sun-Times*, the *New Republic*, and *The Nation* welcomed the Republicans' return to reason and their rejection of campaign rhetoric and political propaganda.[15]

The reaction to statements by Congressman Thaddeus Machrowicz also showed the change. During the House committee's hearings, he had demanded a stronger resolution expressing U.S. hopes and expectations that Yalta would be forthrightly repudiated. When he charged that the resolution disappointed popular expectations based on "previous [Administration] statements," Congressmen Walter Judd (Republican, Minnesota) and Jacob Javits (Republican, New York) immediately replied. The resolution was good in its present form, and Javits especially emphasized the tremendous force of the mere expression of hope. Congressman Alvin Bentley (Republican, Michigan) denied that the supporters of the resolution intended to use it to fulfill campaign promises or for other political purposes. It gave the Administration leverage for psychological warfare. At the same time, Bentley contended, "it must be recognized" that the United States was not bound by any of the Yalta commitments.[16]

Congressmen Robert Hale, Alvin O'Konski, Albert Bosch (Republican, New York), and James Fulton (Republican, Pennsylvania), however, believed that the resolution should go further and that its language should be more vigorous. Bosch did call the resolution a "good beginning," and O'Konski noted that the resolution, which was

15. U.S. *Congressional Record*, 83d Cong., 1st sess., 1953, XCIX, Part 9, A1057, A1101. *Newsweek*, 41 (March 9, 1953), 21; March 16, 1953, 36–37; March 30, 1953, 24–25; April 6, 1953, 15. *The Nation*, 176 (February 21, 1953), 159–60; February 28, 1953, 177; March 7, 1953, 204; March 21, 1953, 239–40. *Chicago Sun-Times*, February 28, 1953. *New Republic*, 128, 7 (February 16, 1953), 10–11; 9 (March 2, 1953), 3; 12 (March 23, 1953), 6. "Government by Renege: Onward and Backward with the GOP," *Democratic Digest*, November, 1953, 30.

16. *Hearings on House Joint Resolution 200*, 83d Cong., 1st sess., 1953, 25–35.

better than nothing, needed strengthening. He demanded the outright repudiation of Yalta. The National Republican Committee of Americans of Polish Descent criticized the resolution only because it had not listed the "follies of Yalta."[17]

The "extremists" Congressmen Charles Kersten and Lawrence Smith found House Joint Resolution 200 completely unacceptable. They demanded the formal repudiation of Yalta. Kersten charged that the resolution, by implying that Yalta would have been a successful conference had its terms been implemented, implicitly ratified those terms. Smith argued that Eisenhower had renounced his campaign promises by submitting this resolution.[18]

This political dilemma had been accentuated by the rapidity with which congressional Republicans, and conservative Democrats, had enthusiastically acclaimed Eisenhower's State of the Union address. They thought that he had given his commitment to repudiate Yalta when he had alluded to secret agreements that enslaved peoples. Congressmen Charles Kersten, John Heselton (Republican, Massachusetts), Edmund Radwan (Republican, New York), Lawrence Smith, Daniel Reed, and Thomas Abernethy (Democrat, Mississippi) had made that interpretation and then had contrasted Eisenhower's expressed shift with Roosevelt's secret, personal diplomacy. Repudiation, they conceded, would not "free" the "enslaved" nations, but it would raise hopes and show these peoples and the Soviet Union that the United States would initiate a more forceful foreign policy. Indeed, Kersten had proclaimed, "By reversing the process of the Yalta agreement and permitting the forces of freedom of Poland and China to be reborn, we will seize the initiative from the Communists and win the cold war."[19] At the same time, Republican Senator Styles Bridges had confidently predicted that Yalta would be repudiated in the next four years.[20]

Since House Joint Resolution 200 did not proffer the repudiation of Yalta, congressional Republicans had to make a quick shift. The different statements made by The New York Times typified this about-face. On February 3, the Times had described Eisenhower's State of the Union address as "reasonable and sound" in recognizing that the containment policy was no longer adequate and that Yalta must be repudiated. The Times called Eisenhower's request for the

17. *Ibid.*, 24, 36–37, 44, 46–48, 51–56.
18. *Ibid.*, 38–46, 48–50.
19. U.S. *Congressional Record*, 83d Cong., 1st sess., 1953, XCIX, Parts 1 and 9, 754, 937, A528, A553–55, A736.
20. *Ibid.*, Part 9, A1227–28.

repudiation of such secret agreements as Yalta one of the "more important declarations" of his address, "no more than a fulfillment of the Republican campaign slate," and a preliminary step that would "restore our moral position" and open the way for a "new policy."[21]

After the introduction of House Joint Resolution 200, however, the *Times* reversed its position. On February 22, February 25, and March 5, the *Times* argued that the resolution removed some obstacles "both here and abroad" because it did not mention repudiation. To have maximum "effect" on the captive peoples, the *Times* then asserted, an anti-Yalta resolution would have moral authority only if it received "virtually unanimous support." Such a resolution would not have this support because some Democrats would consider it an adverse reflection on Roosevelt. Besides, formal repudiation was not imperative; in "actual practice," the agreements were a "dead letter anyway." Commending House Joint Resolution 200, the *Times* argued:

> By reaffirming the Atlantic Charter, we [in House Joint Resolution 200] repudiate any territorial gains made without the free will of the people concerned. For the present, the draft resolution can only express the hopes of captive peoples for freedom. It does set a new tone and pledges our support with all peaceful means at our disposal.[22]

Although *Time* magazine on February 9 and *U.S. News and World Report* on February 13 had interpreted Eisenhower's State of the Union remarks as a request for congressional repudiation of Yalta, these magazines also switched after the introduction of House Joint Resolution 200. *U.S. News* was surprisingly silent, but *Time* quickly defended the resolution in its issues of March 2, 16, and 30. It maintained that the Administration carefully avoided condemning Yalta in order to "please the Democrats and State Department professionals." At the same time, the Yalta conferees and the Democrats were still responsible for the sellout of China and Poland. Republicans were understandably chagrined about the resolution because they had condemned Yalta's infamy ever since the war's end. The Administration had been "none too clear in its advance thinking," but it was already considering more effective ways to weaken Communist enslavement than issuing resolutions. *Time* added:

21. *The New York Times*, February 3, 1953, 24; February 4, 1953, 26.
22. *Ibid.*, February 22, 1953, 8E; February 25, 1953, 26; March 5, 1953, 26. The *Times* columnist Arthur Krock, in contrast, defended Taft's action, noting that the Administration, by making concessions to the Democrats, had backtracked on its campaign promises. *Ibid.*, March 5, 1953, 26.

But both the White House and State know that repudiation, for the U.S., was not now feasible. Even in today's jungle of diplomacy, the U.S. cannot offhandedly cancel its formal agreements. . . . By declining to tax the Democrats anew for the faults of Yalta and Potsdam, the resolution shot over the heads of domestic politics to the captive peoples for whom it is intended.[23]

George Sokolsky similarly reappraised his position about repudiation. On February 7, Sokolsky had praised Eisenhower's State of the Union address because it marked a commitment to repudiate Yalta. As such, it was a reversal of Roosevelt's and Truman's appeasement policy that had enabled Stalin to assume the initiative in international affairs. Repudiation would institute a new foreign policy by offering the "hope of liberation" and clearing the air of "uncertainty." After House Joint Resolution 200 appeared, Sokolsky reiterated his bitter criticisms of Yalta's betrayal and Communist influence, but he demanded only the publication of the Yalta papers. Sokolsky then concluded, "If those agreements are now canceled, their harm cannot be undone. The only value in their cancellation would be publication of all documents relating to them. It would educate the world to the evils of secret diplomacy. It would fix responsibility precisely."[24]

The *Chicago Tribune*, however, consistently demanded the repudiation of Roosevelt's outlook and of Yalta's pro-Soviet course. In early February, the *Tribune* praised Eisenhower's State of the Union address for supporting the repudiation of Yalta and for stressing the "harm" that Roosevelt and Truman had caused the United States. Roosevelt's action at Yalta had been unconstitutional and immoral. Had "Roosevelt never sat in the White House," much of Yalta's "tale of woe" would never have happened. Repudiation would not rectify Yalta's damage, but it would "untarnish national morals." The *Tribune* bitterly condemned House Joint Resolution 200 because it was inconsistent with the State of the Union address and because it seemed to be "absolving" Roosevelt and Truman from responsibility for post-

23. *Time*, 61 (February 9, 1953), 15; March 2, 1953, 11; March 16, 1953, 26; March 30, 1953, 13. *U.S. News and World Report*, 34 (February 13, 1953), 22–24. *The Saturday Evening Post*, although never referring specifically to the State of the Union address or House Joint Resolution 200, had argued that the Eisenhower Administration intended to liquidate past errors and adopt a new policy course different from the weakness and vacillation of the Democratic Administrations. *The Saturday Evening Post*, 225 (February 28, 1953), 10.

24. *Milwaukee Sentinel*, February 7, 1953, 8; February 24, 1953, 10; February 25, 1953, 14; February 26, 1953, 14.

war problems. Roosevelt's intentions were not subsequently perverted; Roosevelt had been fully aware of Soviet deceit and treachery. He had known "precisely" what would result and had concluded the Yalta agreements anyway. Congress should reconsider House Joint Resolution 200 and support instead the repudiation of the secret Yalta agreements. An effective resolution should frankly admit that "New Deal diplomacy brought shame, humiliation and danger upon this country as well as the captive nations." The Congress, the *Tribune* added, must recognize Roosevelt's "high crimes" or at the least ratify the Bricker Amendment in order to protect the country from the "viciousness" of the executive branch and the "stupidity" of the Congress.[25]

Some Republican congressmen continued to denounce Yalta even after the controversy about House Joint Resolution 200 had died down. Senator Alexander Wiley and Congressmen Edward Bonin (Republican, Pennsylvania) and Lawrence Smith still demanded the repudiation of Yalta, but only Smith referred to House Joint Resolution 200. He called the repudiation of Yalta a necessary moral gesture and said that House Joint Resolution 200 had renounced the Republicans' 1952 campaign promises. It could just as well have been written by the Truman Administration. Taft was correct in blocking the resolution; had it passed, the Administration would have gone on record as endorsing the Yalta Conference by implication. Smith denied that Yalta was simply a part of the past and asserted that the renewal of the "Yalta spirit is always with us."[26]

During the time of the controversy about House Joint Resolution 200, the Administration challenged another demand and tactic of the "extremists" and "partisans." On February 27, President Eisenhower submitted for Senate confirmation the nomination of Charles Bohlen as Ambassador to the Soviet Union. Because Bohlen had served as an interpreter at Yalta, his nomination directly conflicted with a 1952 Republican campaign pledge and with the "partisans'" and "extremists'" demand that all "men of Yalta" be removed from positions of influence. House Joint Resolution 200 had posed an

25. *Chicago Tribune*, February 3, 1953, 1, 12; February 6, 1953, 18; February 17, 1953, 4; February 22, 1953, 20; February 24, 1953, 3, 14; February 25, 1953, 20; March 5, 1953, 14; March 12, 1953, 16; July 20, 1953, 22.
26. U.S. *Congressional Record*, 83d Cong., 1st sess., 1953, XCIX, Parts 9 and 11, A795, A1024, A1157, A3937–38. Former Yalta critic Senator Homer Ferguson, sharply reversing his earlier appraisal of the conference, condemned Soviet domination of Rumania as a violation of the Yalta "free election" agreement. *Ibid.*, Part 2, 1676.

indirect change from the "partisans'" and "extremists'" approach to foreign policy, but the Bohlen nomination was a blatant reversal.

The Eisenhower Administration intended to ignore past politics and to restore national unity and confidence, but it had to face the public's distrust of the State Department and executive conduct of foreign policy that had been fostered in the early 1950's by Styles Bridges, Robert Taft, William Knowland, Joseph McCarthy, John Bricker, and many other "extremists" and "partisans." Their attacks had increased congressional restraints on the implementation and formulation of foreign policy. Reflective of this influence, R. W. Scott McLeod, former legislative assistant to Styles Bridges, had been appointed chief security officer of the State Department in January, 1953. McLeod's appointment had been a concession to the "extremists," who wanted an effective purge of undesirable elements.

One issue in the debates about the Bohlen nomination and House Joint Resolution 200 was whether the Administration could free itself from its campaign rhetoric and the restrictions of the "extremists" and "partisans." Another issue in the debate about Bohlen was whether the Administration had the right and responsibility to appoint qualified men to positions that involved foreign policy, regardless of their past association with the Yalta agreements or other controversial foreign policy decisions. The Administration had to assure foreign service officers of its confidence and support. It also had to diminish McCarthy's baneful influence on the State Department and to correct an imbalance between congressional surveillance and executive authority that had been created in the early 1950's. In 1953, the Eisenhower Administration attempted to minimize the "extremists'" influence and thus to restore a semblance of normality to the State Department. To do so, it undercut what had been an effective campaign issue.

Many Republicans found the Bohlen nomination difficult enough to accept, and Bohlen's praise of Yalta during testimony before the Senate Foreign Relations Committee increased this difficulty. Queried endlessly about the conference and the specific agreements, Bohlen defended the correctness and soundness of the Yalta agreements. He denied that they violated U.S. interests or sacrificed Poland, Eastern Europe, or China. President Roosevelt had not exceeded his authority; he had merely delineated the U.S. position at a future peace conference. The series of Yalta concessions was an executive agreement, not a formal treaty. Because it was not, neither Poland nor China was bound by the terms of the agreements. The Soviet army had physically occupied Eastern Europe, and to have done nothing would have been worse. Postwar problems had developed because the Soviets had violated the agreements, not because the agreements were immoral or vague. In fact, Soviet violations confirmed the soundness of the agreements. Even without Yalta, the map of the world would have been very much the same. Yalta resulted from certain world realities that could not have been changed by wishing that they were not there. While he defended the conference, Bohlen minimized his role. He was only an interpreter, not a man in a "policy determinate" position. He added that as ambassador he would accept the policy defined by the President and Secretary of State. An ambassador, Bohlen noted, made only recommendations and suggestions; he did not make decisions. If he disagreed with the Administration's policy, he had the right to resign.[27]

The hearings inevitably became a review of the nature and necessity of the Yalta agreements rather than an investigation of Bohlen's qualifications for the ambassadorial post. Republican committee members Homer Ferguson, William Knowland, and H. Alexander Smith asked about Alger Hiss's influence at the conference. In response, Bohlen denied that Hiss had played a major role at Yalta, that Hiss had attended the sessions in which the Far Eastern agreements had been discussed, and that Hiss had had anything to do with drafting them. Hiss's activities had been confined to issues concerning the United Nations. Besides, Hiss had attended the conference as Stettinius' adviser, not Roosevelt's. While conceding that Hiss might have influenced Stettinius, Bohlen denied that Hiss's advice was contrary to the already prepared U.S. position.[28]

Secretary of State Dulles, in testimony before the Senate Foreign Relations Committee, tried to direct the committee's attention to Bohlen's record as a career officer. He noted that Bohlen had been "just" an interpreter at Yalta. Dulles especially emphasized the continuity and loyalty of the nonpartisan foreign service and stated that the Administration recommended confirmation because of Bohlen's background, his qualifications, and his record of loyalty and understanding. At the same time, Dulles said that the Administration's appreciation of continuity did not imply its acceptance of all foreign policy decisions made in the past. He confirmed his own opposition

27. U.S. Senate, Foreign Relations Committee, *Hearings on the Nomination of Charles Bohlen as Ambassador to the Soviet Union*, 83d Cong., 1st sess., 1953, 1–8, 13, 17–19, 21–34, 44–48, 50–73, 88–100, 112–24, 126.
    28. *Ibid.*, 19–20, 37–43, 49.

to some of the former administrations' policies and to some of Bohlen's decisions and proposals.[29]

Bohlen's defense of Yalta during the March 2 hearings, which coincided with the controversy over House Joint Resolution 200, caught Republican committee members by surprise. The committee postponed its decision on Bohlen's nomination, despite Dulles' plea that Stalin's death necessitated a quick decision on a U.S. Ambassador to the Soviet Union. Meeting secretly on March 10, the committee approved six of the seven pending diplomatic appointments, but it again postponed action on Bohlen's confirmation. Following the meeting, Senator Homer Ferguson told reporters that he had requested the postponement after learning about certain papers pertaining to Yalta that had not yet arrived from the State Department.[30]

On March 13, Senator Styles Bridges informed the press that important officials in the Administration had been asked to contact Eisenhower and request that he withdraw the nomination. Also on March 13, Joseph McCarthy and Robert Taft took positions on the nomination. McCarthy stated that he would oppose Bohlen's confirmation. Taft expressed disapproval of Bohlen's selection but said he would support the Administration because the issue was not of "sufficient importance to have a battle about." Taft further argued, "Our Russian Ambassador can't do anything, all he can do is observe and report. He will not influence policy materially."[31]

Because Bridges and McCarthy had raised the question of Bohlen's security clearance, the Senate Foreign Relations Committee met on March 18 to review this issue. Secretary of State Dulles appeared before the committee and emphasized that a report prepared by the F.B.I. confirmed Bohlen's loyalty. Dulles summarized and appraised that report in order to dispel any doubts or rumors about Bohlen's loyalty and his security clearance. He stated, "There is no derogatory material whatsoever which questions the loyalty of Mr. Bohlen to the United States or which suggests that he is not a good security risk." Responding to Bourke Hickenlooper's question about the appointment's involving "any" security risk, Dulles said he doubted that he could affirm that about anybody. When Hickenlooper asked if Bohlen was a "good security and loyalty risk," Dulles said he was.[32]

After Dulles' testimony, the committee unanimously recom-

29. *Ibid.*, 102–12.
30. James Rosenau, *The Nomination of "Chip" Bohlen*, 7.
31. *Ibid.*, 7–8.
32. *Ibid.*, 9–10.

mended confirmation of Bohlen's nomination, but the opponents of the nomination were not satisfied. McCarthy said that he continued to oppose Dulles' attempt to shove the appointment through the Senate. The appointment was one "which looks bad on its face," and Dulles should advise Eisenhower to look at the whole Bohlen file. If Eisenhower did look at the file, McCarthy said, "I feel reasonably certain that he will withdraw the appointment." He was not alone in his doubts. Styles Bridges contended:

> On the basis of the information I have now, I am still opposed to Bohlen. The Foreign Relations Committee, of course, has had the opportunity to go over such evidence as was presented to it. I think, however, the committee should have the benefit of the full F.B.I. report of Bohlen and not an evaluation of that report by the man [Dulles] who made the appointment.[33]

Both McCarthy and Bridges were prepared to use the same tactics that had helped to defeat the Democrats in the 1952 campaign. They alluded to still-secret information and hoped, by making vague threats and veiled criticisms, to force Eisenhower's and Dulles' hand. They were ready for a showdown.

They got help from "extremist" Senator Pat McCarran, who addressed the Senate on March 20. McCarran contended that the 1952 election was a mandate for purging the State Department and said he regretted that the job was not being done. Hinting that the Bohlen nomination had not been originated by Eisenhower but by the State Department, McCarran charged that a clique within the State Department protected loyalty and security risks. The appointment of Scott McLeod to head the State Department's security organization was "outstanding." When McLeod had received the F.B.I. report on its investigation of Bohlen, "the first such," he concluded that he could not clear Bohlen. Dulles was wrong for not telling the Senate Foreign Relations Committee that his own security chief did not clear Bohlen. McCarran then demanded that McLeod be called to testify before the committee and recommended that the Senate refuse to pass upon the nomination "until there is made available, for the inspection of any Senator who desires to see it, the full and complete F.B.I. report on the nominee."[34]

The battle over the Bohlen nomination had just begun. Dulles called a press conference the afternoon of March 20 and denied that McLeod had made any recommendation to him. McLeod had re-

33. *Ibid.*, 10.
34. U.S. *Congressional Record*, 83d Cong., 1st sess., 1953, XCIX, Part 2, 2155–57.

ferred to certain information about Bohlen, but he had not suggested that Bohlen be rejected. Besides, the decision to recommend Bohlen was his province and responsibility. Dulles said that he had no intention of withdrawing the nomination.[35]

Later in the day, McCarthy counterattacked by accusing Dulles of "falsification" and proposing that the Secretary of State testify under oath before the Senate Foreign Relations Committee. On March 21, McCarthy attempted to subpoena McLeod to testify before his own Senate Permanent Investigation Subcommittee, but neither McLeod nor Dulles could be contacted. McCarthy told reporters that he intended to press the case in the Senate but that he did not think he would be successful.[36]

This clash provided the setting for formal Senate debate on confirmation. On March 23, Republican Senator Alexander Wiley, chairman of the Foreign Relations Committee, presented to the Senate the committee's report recommending confirmation. Wiley contended that the two most controversial issues concerning Bohlen's confirmation were Bohlen's service as interpreter at Yalta and Potsdam and the charge that the F.B.I. report on Bohlen had not been properly evaluated. Bohlen had been thoroughly investigated by the F.B.I., and Dulles, after reading the F.B.I. report, had recommended Bohlen. Bohlen had been a consistently loyal and capable foreign service officer under Presidents Roosevelt and Truman, and he would contribute the same loyal, dutiful service to President Eisenhower. Loyalty was all that could be expected of a foreign service officer. Further, Joseph Grew, Norman Armour, and Hugh Gibson — eminent former diplomats whose recommendations would be respected by conservatives and those informed about foreign relations — had unanimously agreed that Bohlen was uniquely qualified for the Moscow assignment. At Yalta and Potsdam, Bohlen had been merely an interpreter and not a policy maker. As Ambassador to the Soviet Union, Bohlen would not be making policy; he would simply carry out the President's and the Secretary of State's instructions. Were Bohlen's role at Yalta an important issue, Wiley finally averred, it should have been contested in 1951 when his nomination as counselor to the State Department had been unanimously approved.[37]

Nonetheless, McCarthy insisted on investigating Bohlen's background further and on subpoenaing McLeod to testify before his

35. James Rosenau, *The Nomination of "Chip" Bohlen*, 11–12.
36. *Ibid.*, 12–13.
37. U.S. *Congressional Record*, 83d Cong., 1st sess., 1953, XCIX, Part 2, 2188–90. In a later Senate statement, Wiley sought to rebut the charges that

subcommittee. McLeod, McCarthy affirmed, had not agreed upon Bohlen's clearance and had, contrary to Dulles' testimony, felt so strongly about the security risk that he had gone over Dulles' head to the White House. If information in Bohlen's file was correct, McCarthy hinted, "Moscow would be the last place in the world to which he should be sent." He commended Dulles' record "on the whole," but he reaffirmed the Senate's responsibility to examine the files and discover the facts.[38]

McCarthy's assault on the Administration, in this guise of exercising congressional responsibility, isolated him from some of his former associates. Senator William Knowland opposed allowing even the senators on the Foreign Relations Committee to examine the F.B.I. files. The effective operation of any government required confidence in its Administration. Knowland argued that Congress should trust Eisenhower and Dulles rather than rumors.[39]

After Senator Russell Long suggested that one senator from each party be appointed to review the F.B.I. files and to report their findings to the Senate, Senator Robert Taft entered the debate. Taft opposed forcing McLeod and Dulles to testify. He also opposed opening the F.B.I. files to senators because such an act would be detrimental to national security. At the same time, Taft stated that the Senate must accept the judgment of others and that he had confidence in Dulles. Taft then seconded Long's recommendation that the Senate appoint two members "whose judgment other Senators would respect" to read the whole F.B.I. file on Bohlen.[40]

On March 24, the Senate Foreign Relations Committee accepted Taft's suggestion and asked Secretary of State Dulles to permit two of its members to examine the F.B.I. files. Dulles agreed on the con-

---

Bohlen had been disloyal. As chairman of the Foreign Relations Committee, Wiley had sent letters to "certain" Senators asking them for evidence, not charges. No evidence had been produced. While he had not seen Bohlen's file, Dulles had, and he was willing to trust Dulles. *Ibid.*, 2200. *The New York Times*, *Newsweek*, columnist Ernest Lindley, and the *New Republic* commended the nomination as a "first class choice" and denied that opposition could be justified simply because Bohlen had attended Yalta and still defended it. The *Times*, moreover, added that Bohlen's views about Yalta were not grounds for disapproval since he had not been appointed to a policy-making position. Had he been appointed to such a post as Under Secretary of State, the *Times* conceded, his views about Yalta would have been just grounds for rejecting the appointment. *The New York Times*, March 16, 1953, 18; March 19, 1953, 30. *Newsweek*, 41 (March 23, 1953), 21, 23–24; March 30, 1953, 26, 32; April 6, 1953, 21–23. *New Republic*, 128, 12 (March 23, 1953), 6; 14 (April 6, 1953), 5–6.

   38. U.S. *Congressional Record*, 83d Cong., 1st sess., 1953, XCIX, Part 2, 2191–92, 2194–95.
   39. *Ibid.*, 2199.
   40. *Ibid.*, 2201–2.

dition that the senators would not reveal the contents of the files and that they would not think that his permission established a precedent. Thereupon the committee appointed Robert Taft and John Sparkman to examine the files.[41] On March 25, Taft reported to the Senate. He first admitted that he and Sparkman had examined only the summary. They had done it because McLeod and Dulles had read only that document and because J. Edgar Hoover had assured them that the summary contained everything of importance. Taft said he would have demanded more information had he found the summary incomplete. The derogatory information on Bohlen concerned "political" differences about Bohlen's friends or his association with Yalta. He found no evidence to raise a prima facie case that would make Bohlen a security risk. In conclusion, Taft described Bohlen as a good security risk.[42]

Taft's statement made Bohlen's confirmation a certainty, but many Republicans who supported confirmation again confessed to soul searching. They could not justify opposition, but they were especially uneasy about appearing to accept Bohlen. They insisted that their vote indicated support for the Administration, not approval of Bohlen. Taft, Edward Thye, and Homer Capehart tried to avoid the issue by saying that Bohlen had been a functionary at Yalta and that, as ambassador, he would be a functionary in Moscow. Homer Ferguson, Arthur Watkins, and Robert Hendrickson announced that their votes for Bohlen's confirmation did not show that they supported Bohlen's views on Yalta. They approved his confirmation only because he would have nothing to do with policy making. More pointedly, Senator John Butler argued:

> My vote for Mr. Bohlen . . . is not a vote for him personally. It is a vote to uphold what I deem to be the best possible system for selecting our public servants, and I am a firm believer in the orderly process and feel that a vote in opposition would be a vote to weaken the fundamentals of our Government and the principles of justice.[43]

The "extremists" continued to harass the Administration. Styles Bridges charged that Senator Wiley had misinformed the Senate

41. James Rosenau, *The Nomination of "Chip" Bohlen,* 17–18.
42. U.S. *Congressional Record,* 83d Cong., 1st sess., 1953, XCIX, Part 2, 2277–78.
43. *Ibid.,* 2279, 2381–84, 2387–88, 2391–92. Reiterating this argument, *Time* magazine and *U.S. News and World Report* criticized the Bohlen nomination but accepted Senate confirmation because it terminated a possibly costly intraparty fight. Stressing the legitimacy of Republican doubts about Bohlen, they noted that Republicans concurred in the nomination simply "because the Administration wanted him." Summing up these sentiments, *Time* ob-

when he had declared that Hugh Gibson, Norman Armour, and Joseph Grew had unanimously concurred on the Bohlen nomination. Bridges stated that he had contacted Gibson's lawyer — Gibson himself was sick — who had reported that Gibson, Armour, and Grew had not been asked about Bohlen and that they had not approved him. Wiley belittled this charge by noting that his source of information was the Secretary of State, while Bridges quoted a man who said he spoke to a man who reportedly was sick. Later in the day, Senator Everett Dirksen stated that he personally had called Gibson to determine his position on the Bohlen nomination. Gibson had admitted knowing Bohlen superficially, but he had denied that he, Grew, or Armour had been asked to approve Bohlen. Dirksen contended that Grew and Armour must be contacted in order to ascertain beyond a doubt their position.

Senator William Knowland immediately countered Dirksen's allegation. Knowland first denied that Wiley had knowingly misled the Senate. In an effort to find out the facts, Knowland stated, he had just contacted Dulles, who had checked his files and produced a letter recommending a long list of men for various diplomatic posts. Gibson, Grew, and Armour had signed that letter. Attached to it was a memorandum listing Bohlen's name opposite the space for Ambassador to the Soviet Union. Regretting the subsequent misunderstanding that the attached memorandum had caused, Knowland again denied that Wiley had intentionally deceived the Senate.[44]

The next day, March 26, in his weekly press conference, President Eisenhower attempted to allay any further doubts. Eisenhower admitted knowing Bohlen for years. He had even played golf with him. No "left-wing holdovers" in the State Department from Truman's Administration had "slipped Bohlen over on him." He had nominated Bohlen for the post because he considered him the best qualified man for the position. He was sorry about the dissension among Republicans, but he intended to push for Bohlen's confirmation. The President, in reply to Bridges' charge that Bohlen was associated with Democratic policies rejected by the new Republican Administration, stated that a foreign service officer must be loyal to his superiors.[45]

---

served, "The serious question buried in the Bohlen case was whether a man who defends the Yalta-Potsdam record, as Bohlen does, is the right man to send to Moscow in a period when the old policies are supposed to be changed." Time, 61 (March 23, 1953), 24; March 30, 1953, 14; April 6, 1953, 27. U.S. News and World Report, 34 (March 27, 1953), 58; April 3, 1953, 18.

44. U.S. Congressional Record, 83d Cong., 1st sess., 1953, XCIX, Part 2, 2287, 2295–96.

45. James Rosenau, The Nomination of "Chip" Bohlen, 23–24.

March 27 was the final day of Senate debate, the day for the formal vote on confirmation. Having lost all hope of postponing the vote or defeating the nomination, the "extremists" concentrated on the real issue posed by the Bohlen nomination — Bohlen's participation at Yalta and his continued defense of the agreements. Whether Bohlen was a good security risk or whether Wiley had intentionally misled the Senate were incidental to the more basic political question of whether to repudiate Yalta and the "men of Yalta." Confirmation of Bohlen by a Republican Congress and Administration, coupled with the introduction of House Joint Resolution 200, would kill Yalta as a national political issue and seriously hurt McCarthyism. On that day, the "extremists" emphasized their principal concern about principles and tactics. Senators Everett Dirksen, Bourke Hickenlooper, Joseph McCarthy, Styles Bridges, Andrew Schoeppel (Republican, Kansas), Herman Welker, and Karl Mundt formally stated that they opposed the Bohlen nomination because Bohlen had attended Yalta. As Dirksen expressed it, "I reject Yalta, so I reject Yalta men." They also argued that in 1952 the U.S. public had voted to repudiate Yalta and the "men of Yalta" and that the nomination of Bohlen amounted to a renunciation of the whole Republican campaign. A bolder foreign policy required repudiating the past. Their central concern, however, was the implicit elimination of an effective campaign issue that they might have been able to use again. Summing up these themes, Welker argued:

> But I must say that I came to the United States Senate well-nigh solely because I had campaigned strenuously against the foreign policy of the prior administration. I campaigned against Dean Acheson, against the Yalta agreements, and all other agreements that have caused us the headaches we now suffer. I could not return to my home state and say that I voted to confirm the nomination of a man who still justifies and defends Yalta.[46]

When the Bohlen nomination finally came to a vote, it passed

46. U.S. *Congressional Record*, 83d Cong., 1st sess., 1953, XCIX, Part 2, 2285–86, 2289–94, 2376–78, 2385–90. The *Chicago Tribune*, George Sokolsky, David Lawrence, and *The Saturday Evening Post* denounced the mere nomination of Bohlen as an unwise and unnecessary concession to Democratic sensitivities. They further condemned this action as a repudiation of the campaign promises and election results of 1952, and they were most concerned about this obvious failure to assail the New Deal. *Ibid.*, Part 10, A1801, A1740. *Chicago Tribune*, March 6, 1953, 20; March 31, 1953, 18. *Milwaukee Sentinel*, March 27, 1953, 14; March 30, 1953, 10. *The Saturday Evening Post*, 225 (April 25, 1953), 10; May 2, 1953, 12. *U.S. News and World Report*, 34 (April 3, 1953), 92.

by a resounding vote of 74–13. The eleven Republicans and two
Democrats who opposed it were John Bricker, Styles Bridges, Everett
Dirksen, Henry Dworshak, Barry Goldwater (Republican, Arizona),
Bourke Hickenlooper, Edwin Johnson (Democrat, Colorado), George
Malone, Pat McCarran, Joseph McCarthy, Karl Mundt, Andrew
Schoeppel, and Herman Welker.[47] U.S. politics had begun to return
to a state of normality.

The "extremists'" and "partisans'" influence had waned, but
they did not stop trying to redirect the Administration's foreign
policy by capitalizing on Cold War fears and suspicions. They continued to use Yalta as a symbol that might discredit policies resem-
bling those of the New Deal. *Time* magazine, the *Chicago Tribune*,
Republican Senator Robert Taft, and *The Saturday Evening Post*
at various times during 1953 sought to raise the issues of Alger Hiss's
attendance at Yalta or the policy of concessions and understanding
that were Roosevelt's basic political tactics at Yalta. *Time* stated that
the Roosevelt Administration's concessions to the Soviet Union had
allowed that country to gain strength. Taft, the *Post*, and the *Tribune*
indirectly criticized the New Deal, and the *Tribune* tried to discredit
the United Nations as well. It described Roosevelt as Stalin's "most
serviceable friend," argued that he made it easy for Communist spies
to operate in the United States, and further suggested that he might
have started W.P.A. as a step toward communism.

Taft extended the political context for these charges by saying
that the 1952 election represented the desire of people in the
United States to change the New Deal and Fair Deal philosophies
of government. To win in 1954, the Republicans must carry out their
1952 domestic and foreign policy promises as well as develop and
publicize certain themes about the Democrats. Republicans should
point out that the Cold War was "inherited from Yalta's 'mistakes',"
that the Democratic Administration had been excessively partial toward the Soviet Union, and that domestic Communists had significantly influenced New Deal policies. In the campaign, the Republicans should constantly develop and expose the mistakes of Yalta
and other Administration policies. He recommended that a Senate
committee ensure that there would be no lack of factual material to
support these arguments.[48]

47. U.S. *Congressional Record*, 83d Cong., 1st sess., 1953, XCIX, Part 2,
2392.
48. *Chicago Tribune*, March 7, 1953, 8; March 29, 1953, 20; April 7, 1953,

The "extremists" also invoked Yalta to neutralize or discredit a more conciliatory approach toward the Soviet Union. In 1953, they were especially concerned about responses that the Eisenhower Administration had made in April to Soviet peace feelers. Committed to a policy of confrontation, they raised the historical calamity of Yalta as a warning against trusting the Soviet Union too much. They expressed their fears that the "Acheson line" still persisted in the State Department and their hopes that the Administration would guard against the repetition of the Yalta experience.[49] In May, when the British proposed a summit conference to discuss possible Korean peace terms, the "extremists" again invoked Yalta. They denounced first Churchill's suggestion and then the subsequent meeting of Eisenhower and Churchill in Bermuda.

The "extremists" were not the only ones opposed to conferences with the Soviet Union. The "moderates" and most of the U.S. public were also skeptical about the worth of conferences between the United States and the Soviet Union. They openly expressed serious reservations and sought guarantees that would enforce any agreements concluded. George Sokolsky, the *Chicago Tribune, The Saturday Evening Post, U.S. News and World Report*, Congressmen Lawrence Smith, Walter Judd, Timothy Sheehan, George Long (Democrat, Louisiana), and Senator Edwin Johnson urged the Administration to stand firm. Raising the Yalta images of secrecy and concession, they rebuked Eisenhower for being willing to bow to foreign pressure and seek accommodation. The Soviet Union understood only force and had to be confronted by it. The *Tribune* then advocated, on the basis of the secrecy at Yalta and Bermuda, ratification of the Bricker Amendment. *U.S. News and World Report* praised Dulles' shift to a less conciliatory stance and noted, "The Dulles plan for an approach to Russia falls short of the Churchill plan. Deals, Yalta style, are not to be made. But the men in the Kremlin, if they so desire, are given an opportunity to meet the Western condition for an over-all peace settlement — freedom for Germany."[50]

5; April 25, 1953, 10; May 9, 1953, 10. *Look*, April 21, 1953, 44. *The Saturday Evening Post*, 225 (April 4, 1953), 10. *Time*, 61 (March 16, 1953), 42.

49. *Milwaukee Sentinel*, April 10, 1953, 14; April 18, 1953, 10; April 25, 1953, 10. *Chicago Tribune*, April 18, 1953, 8; February 24, 1953, 2; March 14, 1953, 8; April 19, 1953, 24; October 21, 1953, 16. In sharp contrast, *The Nation* praised Eisenhower for reaffirming the New Deal-Fair Deal concept of world affairs. It further argued that the bold 1952 campaign promises, including the pledge to repudiate Yalta, had been abandoned by the Eisenhower Administration. *The Nation*, 176 (May 2, 1953), 359–61.

50. *U.S. Congressional Record*, 83d Cong., 1st sess., 1953, XCIX, Parts 5,

Even *Newsweek* and *The New York Times* expressed misgivings about the proposed conference with the Soviet Union. The value of a summit conference would be little until the Soviet Union gave definite assurances of good faith. According to *Newsweek*, such a conference might only enhance Soviet Prime Minister Malenkov's position at home and in the "satellites," and the Administration should not give the Soviets a breathing spell but sustain the initiative. The *Times* attributed Churchill's support for a conference to pressure from the British Labor Party and said that he had asked for one "despite serious misgivings of his own and most Western Foreign Offices, which remember Tehran, Yalta and Potsdam."[51]

Cold War suspicions and the rigidity and intolerance of postwar thinking about U.S. foreign policy were by no means dead. The inevitable theme of "Communists in Government" was resurrected by Senator Joseph McCarthy, *U.S. News and World Report*, the *Chicago Tribune*, and George Sokolsky. They were abetted by Attorney General Herbert Brownell. In November, 1953, Brownell described former White House aide Harry Dexter White as a security risk and asserted that Truman had kept White in his Administration in spite of an adverse F.B.I. report on him. McCarthy, the *Tribune*, and Sokolsky confirmed White's influence in previous Democratic — the *Tribune* and Sokolsky substituted New Deal — administrations. They argued that between 1945 and 1952 White and his associates had "handed over" millions of people to Communist "enslavement" and that White's presence reflected the extent of Communist infiltration of the Administration. *U.S. News and World Report* echoed this assertion that U.S. Communists had infiltrated the Roosevelt Administration. The 1940's were the Communists' pay-off for years of infiltration and hard work; they had secured "key" advisory roles at Yalta and Potsdam. This baneful influence still dominated the State Department despite Eisenhower's victory. Noting State Department opposition to the publication of the Yalta papers, *U.S. News and World Report* argued:

On Yalta alone there is still much unpublished material, which

---

8, 11, and 12, 6114–15, 6853–54, 10950, A3260, A4409. *Milwaukee Sentinel*, May 16, 1953, 10; May 19, 1953, 8; May 30, 1953, 8; October 14, 1953, 16; September 18, 1953, 16; December 12, 1953, 10. *Chicago Tribune*, May 14, 1953, 16; May 15, 1953, 14; June 24, 1953, 16; October 6, 1953, 16. *The Saturday Evening Post*, 226 (November 21, 1953), 10. *U.S. News and World Report*, 34 (June 19, 1953), 115, 119; 35 (July 24, 1953), 26–27.

51. *The New York Times*, October 29, 1953, 30. *Newsweek*, 42 (October 26, 1953), 46.

will not do the Democrats any good when published. What
we wonder is whether the top command of the Department
of State will permit publication of a good deal of material on
Yalta and other conferences. . . . There is a whole era of
secret negotiations that is being kept from the American
people. [52]

The "extremists" again chose to stress Yalta's secrecy and to
claim the existence of additional undisclosed Yalta agreements. In
October, 1953, the *Chicago Tribune* uncovered another Yalta secret
agreement. A well-known scientist formerly employed by the government had testified that at Yalta Roosevelt had promised Stalin a
cruiser equipped with the latest secret electronic equipment. Whether
this promise had been fulfilled was not known. In a postscript, the
Tribune noted that the cruiser promise had never before been included in the list of the "dying" Roosevelt's vast concessions and
gifts to Stalin at Yalta.[53]

Except the "extremists" and certain "partisans," Republican
spokesmen had lessened their use of Yalta, partly because of the
Democrats' political responses during 1953. Congressman Sam Rayburn (Democrat, Texas) and Senator Mike Monroney (Democrat,
Oklahoma) contrasted past Republican charges and promises concerning Yalta with their actions in 1953. Rayburn observed that,
despite much earlier talk, the Republicans ha.' failed to initiate a
new foreign policy. Monroney defended the past twenty years as
years of progress. In the 1952 campaign, the Democrats had talked
sense and had dealt in facts, not vain promises. He stated, "We told
them [the U.S. public during the 1952 campaign] that Yalta, Potsdam, and Teheran were necessary steps to set up the United Nations,
to insure certain victory over Japan without pyramiding American
casualties and to guarantee our position in Berlin and Vienna as out-
posts of western civilization."[54]

Although Yalta had become less central, both Democrats and
Republicans still implicitly rejected its principles and spirit. The
Democrats, because they were not in power, had assumed the of-
fensive, but they only criticized the Republicans' 1952 campaign

52. *New Republic*, 129, 16 (November 16, 1953), 2; 19 (December 7,
1953), 7–8. *Chicago Tribune*, November 22, 1953, 1, 4. *Milwaukee Sentinel*,
November 23, 1953, 18. *U.S. News and World Report*, 35 (November 27, 1953),
22, 25; December 18, 1953, 22.
53. *Chicago Tribune*, October 28, 1953, 6.
54. Senator Mike Monroney, "We Told the Facts," *Democratic Digest*
(August, 1953), 48. Representative Sam Rayburn, "Three Members Look at
the 83rd Congress," *Democratic Digest* (October, 1953), 36.

pledges and pointed out the Eisenhower Administration's subsequent renunciation of those pledges. The Eisenhower Administration successfully confronted the "extremists" on political grounds because it did not have the legacy of Truman's association with the Roosevelt Administration or his partisan defense of Yalta. The Eisenhower Administration's rejection of the "extremists," however, only changed the partisan context of the foreign policy debate.

chapter 10
1953–1954: renunciation of the campaign, part two

although the Bohlen nomination and House Joint Resolution 200 dominated congressional and Republican politics in early 1953, another former campaign issue also emerged during this period. On January 7, Senator John Bricker introduced an amendment to the U.S. Constitution that sought to limit the use of executive authority in foreign policy by requiring congressional ratification of all executive agreements and treaties affecting domestic politics. Bricker had originally introduced his amendment in May, 1952, and the Republicans had tacitly adopted it as a 1952 campaign issue. The "moderates," "partisans," and "extremists" had then shared a common commitment to discredit the Democrats, but they differed in their concepts of proper legislative restrictions on the executive branch. In 1953, this difference became obvious. In 1952, such "moderates" as Senator Alexander Wiley, Senator H. Alexander Smith, and John Foster Dulles had supported the amendment as a campaign issue; in 1953, they charged that it would inevitably cripple the use of executive authority in foreign policy. What had been a good political issue became, after 1953, a liability for the Republican leaders who were responsible for foreign policy.

Hearings on the Bricker Amendment, Senate Joint Resolution 1, were held from February 18 through April 10, 1953. During the hearings, both proponents and opponents discussed the possibility of the amendment's enabling Congress to prevent future Yaltas. Alfred Schweppe, a member of the American Bar Association, and George Williams, an attorney from Baltimore, Maryland, agreed with Senators Arthur Watkins and Everett Dirksen that the Bricker Amendment would prevent future Yaltas by providing for congressional ratification of executive agreements. Watkins, moreover, described this prevention as the principal objective of the amendment.[1]

1. U.S. Senate, Subcommittee of the Committee on the Judiciary, *Hearings on Senate Joint Resolution 1 and Senate Joint Resolution 43: Treaties and Executive Agreements*, 83d Cong., 1st sess., 1953, 67–68, 225–26, 409–10, 797–98, 802–4, 885, 968, 974.

Opponents of the Bricker Amendment — Carl Rix of the American Bar Association's Committee on Peace and Law Through the United Nations, Theodore Pearson of the New York Bar Association, Mrs. Louelle Berg of the American Association of University Women, and Professor Covey Oliver of the University of California — denied that the amendment could prevent future Yaltas or that Congress could repudiate such executive agreements as those concluded at Yalta. Mrs. Berg also blamed Soviet violations of the Yalta agreements for the lack of peace after the war. She denied that even a treaty could have prevented this development.[2]

The same breakdown occurred in the majority and minority reports of the Special Subcommittee of the Committee on the Judiciary. The subcommittee's majority report emphasized the necessity of congressional control of executive agreements for the proper functioning of government. The Yalta agreements substantiated this retriction. Those agreements, valid or not, were a *fait accompli*. The Bricker Amendment would have prevented them. The majority report specifically stated that the Senate would not have consented to "any agreement so repugnant to the ideals of this Nation and to the principles enunciated in the Atlantic Charter."[3] In their minority report, Senators Estes Kefauver (Democrat, Tennessee), Harley Kilgore (Democrat, West Virginia), Thomas Hennings (Democrat, Missouri), and Alexander Wiley doubted that the Bricker Amendment would have been proposed if Yalta and Potsdam had not occurred. They stressed the differing interpretations of Yalta and Potsdam and concluded that the issue under consideration concerned, not the wisdom of these agreements, but the advisability of reducing presidential powers.[4]

Although Yalta was not the key impetus to the Bricker Amendment or the basis for it, Yalta was a valuable symbol for those who supported the amendment. They had periodically criticized Yalta in order to capitalize on the controversy about the conference. According to congressional and newspaper proponents, the secrecy of Yalta and Roosevelt's independent concessions justified the amendment's restrictions on the use of executive authority. These conservatives who were intent upon stringently limiting the power of the executive branch were primarily concerned about more contemporary issues.

2. *Ibid.*, 78, 225, 604, 689.
3. U.S. Senate, Subcommittee of the Committee on the Judiciary, *Majority Report, Minority Report on Treaties and Executive Agreements*, 83d Cong., 1st sess., 1953, 26, 31.
4. *Ibid.*, 51.

As such, they worked in common with Southern leaders and the American Medical Association. The Southerners were afraid that U.S. involvement in the United Nations would affect segregation; the A.M.A. thought that such involvement would effect socialized medicine.

Although political issues postponed congressional consideration of the Bricker Amendment until 1954, the "extremists" Senator Bricker, former President of the American Bar Association Frank Holman, Illinois State Senator Lottie O'Neill, the *Chicago Tribune*, and *The Saturday Evening Post* had kept the amendment before the public by using the still-dominant concern about Yalta. Their principal objective was to limit the future use of executive authority, so they criticized Roosevelt's abuse of executive authority at Yalta. Their main charge, which was implicitly anti-New Deal and anti-internationalist, stated that law by treaty threatened U.S. sovereignty and posed the potential danger of executive usurpation of legislative authority. Support for the amendment, they said, came largely from a public that resented Yalta and demanded the repudiation of such agreements. The amendment would prevent "Yaltas." The *Post* reflected the underlying anti-Roosevelt bias when it contended that the amendment "would restrain some future Roosevelt who might be tempted to indulge in another spree at Yalta or propose a human rights covenant which would obligate this country to accept sociological reforms or changes which it could never accept of its own accord."[5]

The congressional debate on the Bricker Amendment, which took place in January and February, 1954, also emphasized Yalta and law by treaty. The same rift that had separated the "moderates" from the "partisans" and "extremists" during the reports and hearings in 1953 reappeared in discussion about the Bricker Amendment's usefulness in preventing future Yaltas and the amendment's potential impact on the executive branch. According to Senators John Bricker, Everett Dirksen, Pat McCarran, William Jenner, and Congressmen Wint Smith (Republican, Kansas) and Clare Hoffman, the amendment would prevent future Yaltas. These "extremists" demanded the restoration of a balance between the executive and legislative branches and the repudiation of Roosevelt's style of presidential leadership. They persistently stated that Yalta justified their

5. *Congressional Quarterly Weekly Report*, XII, 3 (January 15, 1954), 47. *Chicago Tribune*, April 12, 1953, 7; June, 1953; December 3, 1953, 2. *The Saturday Evening Post*, 225 (May 16, 1953), 10; 226 (November 21, 1953), 10, 12.

fears and made the enactment of the proposed amendment imperative. Jenner summed up this view when he described the United
Nations as a grave threat to U.S. interests and concluded, "I hope
President Eisenhower's administration will go down in history as
the moment when the revolutionary cabals, which perverted our
treaties and executive agreements in foreign affairs, in order to con-
vert us into a one-party state, are defeated at last, and the defenders
of our Constitution gain their final victory."[6]

According to *The New York Times*, Congressman Jacob Javits,
and Senators H. Alexander Smith, Alexander Wiley, and Leverett
Saltonstall, the amendment would not prevent future Yaltas. Future
Presidents could still conclude secret agreements despite the amendment's proposed limitations on the executive branch, and past abuses
of executive authority did not warrant the amendment's undue
restrictions on the effective conduct of foreign policy. Smith, in fact,
asserted that the amendment could not prevent "another Yalta" if
"our Chief Executive were insensible to what he should have recognized were the implied constitutional limitations on executive
powers." The *Times* charged that the amendment would not prevent future abuses but would complicate the making of any treaty.
Wiley and Javits denied that restrictions on the executive were
needed since effective safeguards already existed either in the form
of public control through the electoral process or through congressional appropriation and general legislative authority. "No new
amendment is necessary to avoid Yaltas or Potsdams," Wiley maintained. "We have ample safeguards now — if we will but use them."[7]

Democrats differed about the amendment less on its relationship
to Yalta than on domestic policy lines. Southern Democrats supported the amendment because they feared that executive agreements
or treaties might affect their segregation policies. They were particularly concerned about the United Nations Covenant on Human
Rights. Senators Russell Long and Walter George (Democrat, Georgia) announced their intention not to discuss Yalta, Teheran, or
Potsdam. Long demanded that the executive branch provide greater
publicity and information to the Congress about decisions and agreements concluded at international conferences. George, who had introduced an amendment to the Bricker Amendment, expressed

6. U.S. *Congressional Record*, 83d Cong., 2d sess., 1954, C, Parts 1 and 2,
484–86, 945, 1062–66, 1178, 1307, 1918, 1866–67, 1873–74, 2121–26, 2354.
7. *Ibid.*, 398–99, 671, 857, 927–28, 1070–71, 1206, 1246, 1302, 2059.
The New York Times, January 17, 1954, 8E; January 18, 1954, 22; January 24,
1954, 10E.

concern only about executive agreements that "might have the effect of domestic law." Noting that the President and Secretary of State could conclude secret agreements with foreign nations, "violating Federal and State constitutional rights and annulling State laws passed by State legislatures," Senator Burnet Maybank (Democrat, South Carolina) and Congressman Elijah Forrester (Democrat, Georgia) stressed the Congress' responsibility to limit that use of executive authority. Maybank blamed Yalta for the Korean War, and both he and Forrester denounced Yalta's secret, executive agreements that had not been submitted for Senate approval. They said that future abuses by either the President or the Supreme Court must be prevented.[8]

Other Democrats disagreed. Senators Harley Kilgore, Estes Kefauver, Hubert Humphrey, Mike Mansfield (Democrat, Montana), and Thomas Hennings forthrightly defended Yalta's correctness, denied that Roosevelt had exceeded his authority at Yalta, and emphasized their trust in both President Eisenhower and Secretary of State Dulles. Postwar problems, Kefauver specified, resulted from Soviet violations of the Yalta agreements, and he added that on the whole the record of past Presidents had been good. Kilgore, Kefauver, Humphrey, Mansfield, and Hennings stated that safeguards sufficient to prevent abuses of executive authority already existed. Underlining the importance and value of executive agreements, they contended that the efficient and effective conduct of foreign policy necessitated broad executive power.[9] The Democratic National Committee unequivocally opposed the amendment. The issue posed by the amendment, an article in the *Democratic Digest* stated, was whether Congress had confidence in the President and in the people who elect him. The supporters of the Bricker Amendment who claimed that Yalta exemplified the evil that supposedly resulted from executive agreements were partisan. The Constitution should not be made the "sounding board for partisan arguments."[10]

The amendment originally proposed by Senator Bricker was never voted upon by the Senate. Instead, on February 26, the Senate voted on Senator George's amendment to the Bricker Amendment. George's amendment did not attempt to limit the use of executive authority in foreign policy per se; it simply provided that the Con-

9. *Ibid.*, Parts 1 and 2, 1017, 1222, 1230–34, 1406–7, 1893, 2241.
8. U.S. *Congressional Record*, 83d Cong., 2d sess., 1954, C, Part 2, 1667, 2154–58.
10. "The ABC's of the Bricker Amendment: It Ties the President's Hands," *Democratic Digest* (February, 1954), 93.

gress must approve all executive agreements and treaties affecting domestic law. George's amendment failed to secure the necessary two-thirds majority by one vote: 60–31. The main supporters of his amendment were 21 Southern Democrats and 32 conservative Republicans.[11]

The defeat of the Bricker Amendment increased the bitterness of the "extremists" who had cited Yalta in order to develop broader support for restrictions upon the executive branch's use of authority. What they really wanted was to repudiate Roosevelt's leadership and the New Deal. *U.S. News and World Report*, David Lawrence, *The Saturday Evening Post*, George Sokolsky, Congressman Lawrence Smith, and the *Chicago Tribune* had consistently demanded action to avert future Yaltas and to repudiate Roosevelt's style of presidential leadership. According to them, more senators had begun to support the amendment because the public opposed a repetition of the Yalta experience, and Eisenhower's opposition to the amendment contravened the platform and pledges that had led to his election. The *Tribune*, alienated by the defeat of the amendment and Eisenhower's firing of presidential assistant Clarence Manion, concluded that a new national political party had to be organized "since the New Dealers have captured the Democratic and Republican parties."[12]

The Bricker Amendment had been only one of several Republican efforts during early 1954 to degrade Roosevelt and limit presidential powers. On February 1, Senator William Knowland had introduced Senate Resolution 209 authorizing the Senate Foreign Relations Committee to study executive agreements with foreign governments or international organizations in order to ascertain the

11. U.S. *Congressional Record*, 83d Cong., 2d sess., 1954, C, Part 2, 2374–75.

12. *U.S. News and World Report*, 36 (January 22, 1954), 37–39; January 29, 1954, 73, 116. *The Saturday Evening Post*, 226 (January 23, 1954), 12; March 6, 1954, 10, 12. *Milwaukee Sentinel*, January 16, 1954, 8; January 28, 1954, 22. U.S. *Congressional Record*, 83d Cong., 2d sess., 1954, C, Part 10, 13849. *Chicago Tribune*, January 18, 1954, 14; January 27, 1954, 14; January 28, 1954, 12; February 3, 1954, 1; February 4, 1954, 1; February 10, 1954, 1; February 16, 1954, 16; February 28, 1954, 20; March 3, 1954, 3; May 14, 1954, 16. The *Tribune's* reference to Manion and to the need for the formation of a new party were related. On February 18, Manion had been dismissed as chairman of the President's Commission on Intergovernmental Relations ostensibly because of his frequent absence on speech-making tours. Manion contended that his conservatism and support for the Bricker Amendment were the real reasons for the dismissal. Subsequently, on May 8, 1954, Manion accepted the co-chairmanship of the For America party, an organization designed to fight intervention, internationalism, and communism within both major parties. *The New York Times*, February 18, 1954, 1; February 22, 1954, 22; May 8, 1954, 6.

number and nature of these agreements operating as "internal law" in the United States. On February 3, Senators Homer Ferguson and William Knowland introduced Senate Resolution 3067 requiring that all U.S. international agreements except treaties be submitted to the Senate thirty days after their execution.

The Bricker Amendment's defeat did not end this use of the Yalta image. On March 2, Senators Homer Ferguson, William Knowland, Eugene Millikin, and Leverett Saltonstall introduced Senate Joint Resolution 217 authorizing the Senate Foreign Relations Committee to study executive agreements, "especially since 1938," made between the United States and foreign governments or international organizations. On March 9, Senator Alexander Wiley introduced Senate Joint Resolution 138 providing for the establishment of a commission on international agreements.[13] The purpose of these resolutions, which were never implemented or seriously considered in committee, was primarily political. Republican orators referred to them in order to emphasize their personal opposition to secret agreements, such as those made at Yalta, and personal diplomacy. These resolutions, however, did not explicitly impose restrictions on the executive branch and proposed only to collect information and conduct studies, which obviously could provide future campaign material.

The tone of these resolutions reflected the change in Republican strategy involving discussion of Yalta. This change had been caused by the defeat of measures taken to redeem former Republican pledges: to restrict the use of executive authority (the Bricker Amendment); to repudiate Yalta (House Joint Resolution 200); and to oust the "men of Yalta" (the Bohlen nomination). The "extremists" and "partisans" continued to attack Yalta and Roosevelt's leadership, but the Republican National Committee and spokesmen for the Eisenhower Administration ceased to exploit Yalta's symbolism as a national campaign issue. Such an altered approach showed that the Administration's real intention was to restore bipartisan harmony and public confidence in executive direction of diplomacy. Republican accomplishments were the important considerations; the Democrats were misguided, not treasonous. A supercilious tone dominated Republican pronouncements.

The standard 1952 Republican campaign themes of the need to repudiate Yalta, "Communists in Government," Alger Hiss's influence

13. *Congressional Quarterly Weekly Report*, XII, 6 (February 5, 1954), A23; 10 (March 5, 1954), A45; 11 (March 12, 1954), A51.

on policy making, secrecy in foreign policy, weakness, and betrayal reappeared in the Republican National Committee's material for the 1954 campaign, but they were used more discreetly. The committee no longer demanded the repudiation of Yalta; it contrasted Eisenhower's firmness, strength, and openness in conducting foreign policy with Roosevelt's and Truman's "capitulation and appeasement of the Communists in the *secret* agreements of Yalta and Potsdam." The Republican Administration had seized the initiative in the struggle for world-wide peace, had taken the people into its confidence, had pursued a truly bipartisan foreign policy, had brought new dignity and confidence to U.S. international negotiations, and had eliminated security risks. The Republican Administration had removed 2,400 security risks from the Federal Government and had passed a law, which was "aimed directly at Alger Hiss, who was jailed as the result of Republican efforts to break up a Communist conspiracy in the State Department," denying pensions or retirement benefits to employees convicted of felony.[14]

The "partisan" Vice-President Richard Nixon continued to denounce past Democratic administrations for treason and betrayal, but he never mentioned Yalta. Under Truman and Acheson, Nixon charged when stumping the country in 1954, the Democrats had "lost" to the Soviet Union six hundred million people in Europe and Asia. The problems in Korea and Indochina had also been caused by past Democratic policies. Secretary of State Dulles, in contrast, was not taken in by the Soviet Union and had stood up to it. Communism remained an important campaign issue, despite Republican removal of 2,400 "subversives" from the Administration. Nixon further contended that Red China would profit if the Republicans were defeated in 1954.[15]

Because Polish-Americans were still interested in Yalta, Democrats and Republicans continued to refer to the conference. Their statements about Yalta, however, had changed considerably since 1953. There was no standard Republican or Democratic position; criticisms once again cut across party lines. Because of the Eisenhower Administration's opposition to repudiation, some Republicans continued to change their appraisals of Yalta. Congressmen Antoni

14. Republican National Committee, "New Foreign Policy Firmness Achieves Diplomatic Triumph at Berlin, Caracas Meetings," *Straight From the Shoulder*. Republican National Committee, *How a GREAT TEAM Worked for YOU! The Record of IKE and the Republican 83rd Congress*, 5–7.

15. *Chicago Tribune*, October 3, 1954, 6; October 6, 1954, 8; October 26, 1954, 6. *New Republic*, 130, 12 (March 22, 1954), 3; 131, 2 (July 12, 1954), 3.

Sadlak and Edward Bonin, speaking on the anniversary of the War-
saw uprising, contended only that the United States was "partly
responsible" for Poland's "enslavement." Congressman Timothy Sheehan, who had formerly denounced Yalta, now attacked the Soviet
Union. In his speeches, he condemned the Soviet Union's forced
repatriation policies toward Ukrainia. He also urged the withdrawal
of U.S. diplomatic recognition of Poland because of Soviet "violations" of the Yalta agreement to have free elections in Poland. He
demanded a congressional investigation to determine who was responsible for implementing the Yalta agreement requiring Germany
to pay reparations. Sheehan argued that this "forced reparation"
agreement had subsequently been "abused" by the Soviet Union.
That country's means of implementing this agreement, Sheehan
charged, went "far above and beyond the original intention" of
Yalta.[16]

The "extremists" and some "partisans," however, did not stop
reviling Yalta. At various times in 1954, the *Chicago Tribune*, colum-
nists Westbrook Pegler and George Sokolsky, *Time* magazine, *U.S.
News and World Report, The Saturday Evening Post*, Congressmen
James VanZandt (Republican, Pennsylvania), Noah Mason, Lawrence Smith, Alvin Bentley, Congresswoman Katharine St. George
(Republican, New York), and Senators William Langer, Arthur
Watkins, and Joseph McCarthy blamed Yalta particularly and past
Democratic foreign policy generally for postwar developments in
Eastern Europe, Germany, Korea, China, and Indochina. They
resurrected the image of Yalta's betrayal of U.S. and Allied interests
and of Alger Hiss's influence at the conference. They said that the
conferees' willingness to trust the Soviet Union, Roosevelt's recognition of the Soviet Union, and his enactment of lend-lease and
unconditional surrender were policies that benefited only the Soviet
Union. According to McCarthy, the Democrats had been guilty of
"20 years of treason and betrayal." VanZandt voiced the underlying
domestic theme when he asserted that the "New Deal-Fair Deal"
group, which was repudiated in the 1952 elections, "would have us
forget Alger Hiss, Judith Coplon, Gerhart Eisler, and ignore the
sellout of the American people at Yalta, Teheran and Potsdam."[17]

16. U.S. *Congressional Record*, 83d Cong., 2d sess., 1954, C, Parts 7, 9,
and 10, 9703–4, 12479–80, 12850, 13189–90.
17. *Ibid.*, Parts 7, 9, 10, and 11, 8675–76, 12626–27, 12709, 13053,
A3148–50, A3228. *Congressional Quarterly Weekly Report*, XII, 13 (March 26,
1954), 384. *Chicago Tribune*, February 7, 1954, 20; August 2, 1954, 18; August 31, 1954, 22; October 1, 1954, 9; October 29, 1954, 16; December 27,

Some Democrats implicitly criticized the Yalta Conference by pointedly attacking Soviet actions in Poland. On February 16, 1954, Senator Paul Douglas (Democrat, Illinois) introduced Senate Joint Resolution 62 calling for the condemnation of Soviet violations of international agreements and the nonrecognition of the Soviet "conquest of free peoples" and authorizing an investigation of the "illegal seizure of certain countries and the destruction of freedom in areas controlled by communism." During his 1954 campaign for re-election, Douglas neither openly defended Yalta — as he had in 1950 — nor did he criticize it. He did recommend the withdrawal of U.S. diplomatic recognition of Poland and the resort to economic pressures on the Soviet Union as the means to free the "enslaved" Poles. On July 22, Congressman Thaddeus Machrowicz introduced House Joint Resolution 663 expressing the "American people's opposition to Communist enslavement of Poland and other captive nations."[18]

By 1954, the Democrats' more aggressive campaign position also indicated the changed political context. At this time, the Democrats responded positively to both the restrained criticisms of the "moderates" and the more intemperate attacks of the "extremists." On March 6, Adlai Stevenson forthrightly denounced the Republican National Committee's partisan and irresponsible conduct during the 1952 and 1954 campaigns, in which it had referred to "Twenty Years of Treason" and attacked the Democrats as "traitors, Communists and murderers of our sons." Stevenson contrasted earlier Republican demands for the repudiation of Yalta and for liberation with what the Republicans had done after they were elected, and he then called for greater honesty and candor from Republican spokesmen. In his discussion of Republican attitudes toward Senator McCarthy, Stevenson stated that Eisenhower had to choose between uniting his party or uniting the nation. According to Republican policy, Stevenson noted, McCarthy was "a scoundrel if he attacks Republicans, but a patriot when he attacks ordinary people or calls men like Franklin Roosevelt and Harry Truman the patrons of traitors. In short, politics first and principles second."[19] The *Democratic Digest* sarcastically

---

1954, 7. *Milwaukee Sentinel*, April 26, 1954, 12; July 8, 1954, 14; October 29, 1954, 22; November 29, 1954, 14. *Time*, 64 (December 20, 1954), 21. *The Saturday Evening Post*, 227 (December 18, 1954), 10, 12. *U.S. News and World Report*, 36 (January 1, 1954), 32, 41.

18. On July 23, Republican Congressman Pat Radwan introduced the identical resolution to Machrowicz'. *Congressional Quarterly Weekly Report*, XII, 8 (February 19, 1954), A34; 31 (July 30, 1954), A167. *Chicago Tribune*, June 17, 1954, 14.

19. *New Republic*, 130, 11 (March 15, 1954), 17; 15 (April 13, 1954), 6.

belittled Herbert Hoover's attempt to blame the Depression and Communist expansion on the Democrats and his charge that Democratic Presidents at Yalta, Teheran, and Potsdam "actually signed treaties with Russia involving 'appeasement and surrender'." After asking if Hoover had ever read the texts of these "treaties," the *Digest* stated that postwar problems resulted from Soviet "violations" of these agreements.[20]

Democratic Congressman Sam Rayburn more pronouncedly contrasted past Republican charges with their lack of action on their campaign pledges. Rayburn, the House minority leader, dismissed the Republicans' 1952 campaign criticisms of Yalta as political oratory. "Since coming into power," he charged, "I presume somebody [Republican] in the State Department read the provisions of those [Yalta] agreements and understood them. I have heard nothing about them since — not even a suggestion of a change in them." Rayburn then asserted that the Eisenhower Administration had followed the "Truman-Acheson foreign policy" and had administered this policy in a "very sorry fashion."[21]

In July, Senator Mike Mansfield assailed Indochinese developments as a "disastrous" U.S. diplomatic defeat. The Geneva Conference, he contended, had enhanced the prestige of the Chinese Communists, and he stated, "Even Yalta, which for so long had served as a substitute for facing living realities, cannot be stretched and pulled far enough out of the dim past to conceal the impact of Geneva." Mansfield made this slighting reference to the Republicans' inability to invoke Yalta in order to counter Postmaster General Arthur Summerfield's explanations about Far Eastern developments. Summerfield had blamed the colonial war in Indochina on the conferences at Yalta, Teheran, and Potsdam and had added that the Eisenhower Administration had simply inherited another disastrous Democratic legacy. Extending his reply, Mansfield also contrasted the actions of Republicans when they were in power with the pledges to repudiate Yalta that they had made in 1952. The Administration's 1953 resolution did not attempt to repudiate the Yalta agreements but condemned Soviet "violations" of them. After noting that nothing had resulted from this resolution, Mansfield stated, "Unless the administration has changed its position, unless it now proposes to seek

20. "Herbert Hoover's Hindsight Is No Clearer than His Foresight," *Democratic Digest* (October, 1954), 86–87.

21. Sam Rayburn, "The House Report," *ibid.*, 92. U.S. *Congressional Record*, 83d Cong., 2d sess., 1954, C, Part 3, 3020.

repudiation of these agreements, I cannot see any value in beginning a reappraisal with them."[22]

The Democratic 1954 congressional victory emboldened the "extremists." The *Chicago Tribune* said that the Democratic victory would increase the difficulty of learning about "our wavering foreign policy." It repeated its 1948 warnings and denounced the Republican leaders' failure to stress past Democratic decisions in foreign policy during the campaign. The Eisenhower Administration had been wrong not to initiate intensive investigations of past Democratic policies. Singling out the Administration's decision to withhold publication of the Yalta papers until after the election, the *Tribune* charged, "The Republicans had an issue to blow up the Democrats but chose not to because internationalism is sacred to them."[23]

Publication of the Yalta papers had been a principal Republican concern for many years. Both before and after the 1952 election, the Republican National Committee and many leading Republicans had pledged to end secrecy in the conduct of foreign policy, to review past Democratic foreign policy decisions, and to publicize past Democratic policy secrets. Charges of past secrecy had been the basis for Republican pledges in 1952 to repudiate Yalta, to clean out the "Yalta-men," and to implement the Bricker Amendment. Underlying these allegations was the one Republican pledge that had not been renounced, the pledge to publish the Yalta papers.

As early as 1953, certain congressional Republicans had tried to get the Yalta papers published. In May, 1953, a subcommittee of the Senate Committee on Appropriations had recommended allocating the State Department enough money to publish the Foreign Relations volumes. Testifying before the subcommittee, Assistant Secretary of State Carl McCardle agreed that the department would give priority to the publication of the Foreign Relations volumes about events from 1941 through 1950.[24] In May, the House approved the appropriations, and in June, the Senate gave its approval.[25]

In 1954, however, these appropriations became involved in partisan and budgetary politics. A subcommittee of the House Committee on Appropriations voted to abolish the entire Foreign Rela-

22. *Ibid.*, Part 8, 9997–99. The *New Republic* and *The Nation* reiterated this contention of Republican partisanship and irresponsibility. *The Nation*, 179 (August 21, 1954), 142–44. *New Republic*, 131, 15, Part 2-A Supplement (October 11, 1954), 14–16; 22 (November 29, 1954), 2.

23. *Chicago Tribune*, November 10, 1954, 14; November 28, 1954, 20.

24. U.S. *Congressional Record*, 83d Cong., 2d sess., 1954, C, Part 4, 5346.

25. *Ibid.*, 83d Cong., 1st sess., 1953, XCIX, Part 5, 4543, 6080.

tions publication program, a move sharply criticized by Republican Senators Alexander Wiley and John Bricker.[26] The House's fiscal restriction was rejected by the Senate. Eventually, a compromise was worked out in conference between members of the House and Senate committees and $200,000 was restored to State Department appropriations. This restoration made publication of the Foreign Relations series possible.[27]

In October, 1954, the State Department announced its intention to publish the Yalta papers sometime after the November elections. It attributed this delay to an unanticipated failure to secure clearance from other United States governmental departments and from the British.[28] The delay and the Administration's failure to publish the Yalta papers earlier in 1953 or 1954 concerned the "extremists" and the more intransigent "partisans," who demanded that the Administration use Yalta as a campaign issue. Their main desire, which was reflected in their appraisal of the papers when they finally were published, was to discredit Roosevelt and the New Deal, and they lamented the Eisenhower Administration's failure to share this commitment.

In March, 1954, *U.S. News and World Report* had stated doubts about the U.S. public's ever fully learning about "events that preceded the loss of China," "New Deal secret diplomacy" during World War II, and the conferences at Yalta, Teheran, and Potsdam. It had cited the Republicans' 1952 campaign pledge to disclose "New Deal secret diplomacy" and hinted that the refusal of the House to provide the necessary publication funds might be an effort to hide something. The State Department had erred when it failed to secure permission from the Defense Department to review the Yalta military documents. An understanding of the military justification for the Yalta Far Eastern agreements required a review of those documents. Unfortunately, the Yalta papers might not be published before 1955, when it would be "too late for 1954 and too early for 1956."[29] In October, this magazine reported that the Yalta papers would not be published until after the November elections, and "by then the United States will

26. *Ibid.*, 83d Cong., 2d sess., 1954, C, Parts 3 and 4, 3937, 5347. Bricker had argued that elimination of publication funds was intended to protect the reputations of "particular individuals." He noted the Republican 1952 campaign pledge to have a "policy of candor in dealing with the American people" and added that the "documentary facts [must be released by the Republicans] while we still have the opportunity."

27. *Ibid.*, Part 7, 9331, 9256.

28. *Washington Post and Times Herald*, October 11, 1954.

29. *U.S. News and World Report*, 36 (March 26, 1954), 48, 50, 52.

have elected a new Congress — without benefit of the official story of Yalta." In November and December, *U.S. News* expressed doubts that the papers would be published in full or in the near future. Nonetheless, when they were published, the papers would reveal how important Hiss had been at the conference, how these secret deals were made, how Hiss and Roosevelt tried to please Stalin, and how these concessions contributed to Russia's rise to postwar power and the Communist take-over of China. Recalling Yalta's secrecy, *U.S. News* noted, "even some of the [Yalta] delegates" did not know all the results. It agreed with the post-election appraisal of certain Republican leaders who were "familiar" with the details of the conference and who thought that the Republicans might have won in 1954 if the Yalta papers had been published before the election.[30]

In November, coincidental to this debate, Alger Hiss was released from prison. The *Chicago Tribune*, at that time, reported the rumors that Hiss would be called to testify before two congressional committees and concurred with the contention of Congressman Kit Clardy (Republican, Michigan) that Hiss ought to be questioned about his "alleged introduction" of Communists and Communist sympathizers into the State Department and about his role at Yalta and San Francisco.[31] According to *Newsweek*, Hiss undoubtedly would be investigated by the House Committee on Un-American Activities. Hiss "probably" knew more about Communist infiltration of the State Department than any other U.S. citizen. He could also answer questions about whether he had been in "direct contact" with the Soviets at Yalta. The controversy engulfing Hiss and the prejudices against him were reflected in *Newsweek*'s concept of Hiss's "patriotic duty." Hiss, *Newsweek* asserted, could either "truthfully" answer questions about his participation in the Communist party and whether he

30. *Ibid.*, 37 (October 8, 1954), 4; November 19, 1954, 44–46; December 24, 1954, 24–25. The *Chicago Tribune* compared nonpublication with the Eisenhower Administration's nonfulfillment of campaign pledges on the Bricker Amendment and repudiation of Yalta. Distinctly anti-Roosevelt, the *Tribune* regretted that the Administration preferred "unrestricted power for the President" over "powerful ammunition to defeat the Democrats." It assailed the Administration's criticisms of McCarthy as depriving the Republicans "of the issue of New Deal communist coddling." *Chicago Tribune*, October 1, 1954, 2; October 4, 1954, 22; October 12, 1954, 24; November 10, 1954, 14; November 28, 1954, 20; December 3, 1954, 18. *Newsweek*, while not concurring with these anti-Roosevelt, anti-Yalta strictures, did agree that nonpublication removed an effective partisan issue. It concluded that publication would have been embarrassing to the Democrats and would have confirmed Alger Hiss's influence on "top-level" Roosevelt Administration decisions. *Newsweek*, 44 (August 9, 1954), 9; November 1, 1954, 42–43.

31. *Chicago Tribune*, November 18, 1954, 1.

"colonized" the State Department or he could "again perjure himself" and "cover up" for his friends by "explaining" these questions away.[32]

These appraisals of Hiss's influence demonstrated the continued conservatism of U.S. politics, a product of the impact of the Cold War. Yet, during 1954, the rhetoric and priorities of national politics had changed perceptibly. By the end of 1954, the rift that had formerly separated the "moderates" and "extremists" re-emerged. Faced with the responsibilities of power, the Eisenhower Administration hesitantly renounced the "extremists'" tactics concerning foreign policy. In helping to defeat the Bricker Amendment and in persistently blaming the Soviet Union for current problems, the Eisenhower Administration had followed the same guidelines that President Truman had developed. This tack served to undermine uncritical anticommunism and to neutralize efforts to discredit Roosevelt and the New Deal by simply questioning earlier foreign policy and internal security decisions.

32. *Newsweek*, 44 (November 22, 1954), 31.

chapter 11
1955: the waning of yalta

The Eisenhower Administration's policies in 1953 and 1954 had altered the Republicans' ability to exploit the symbolism of Yalta. Nonetheless, in 1955, the "extremists" and the "partisans" did not ignore the conference; in fact, their denunciations of Yalta exceeded those of previous years. Their attacks in 1955, however, were decidedly different in form. They could no longer charge that undisclosed, far-reaching agreements remained. The publication of the Yalta papers in March, 1955, disarmed this charge and would finally eliminate Yalta as an effective national political issue. The Yalta papers showed that no new secret agreements existed, that Alger Hiss's role at the conference had been a minor one, and that the U.S. delegation had been fully briefed and prepared. Further, the "extremists" and "partisans" could not then effectively accuse the Eisenhower Administration of whitewash, because it was an anti-Communist Republican Administration that had no commitment to protect Roosevelt's reputation or to aid the Communists.

Yalta remained a symbol of appeasement and naïveté, but only the "extremists" persisted in denouncing the conference during and after publication of the papers. They then charged that important sections of the Yalta papers had been deleted, sections that documented Hiss's importance at the conference. They also renewed the theme of Yalta's injustice to Poland and their inevitable demands for the repudiation of Yalta. The opponents of any détente with the Soviet Union resurrected Yalta to justify guardedness, if not total distrust, toward the proposed conference with the Soviet Union at Geneva.

In 1955, however, these old charges had far different results than they had had from 1950 to 1952. The charges were stale. Since the Eisenhower Administration and the Republican-controlled Eighty-third Congress had done nothing to repudiate old policies or to initiate new ones, the charges became less credible. In addition, the Senate had censured McCarthy, and the Yalta papers were published. In 1955, a Republican Administration sat down at the conference table with the Soviet Union, entered into negotiations, and apparently believed that the Soviet Union could be trusted to adhere

to its pledges and agreements. For the "extremists," 1953 through
1955 were frustrating years.

Consideration of resolutions to repudiate Yalta amply reflected
the changed tone of most Republicans. On January 5, 1955, Democratic Congressman Thaddeus Machrowicz introduced House Joint
Resolution 63 urging Yalta's repudiation. Identical to the resolutions made by Republican Congressman Robert Hale in 1950, 1951,
and 1953, and to the resolution he had introduced in 1953,[1] Machrowicz' resolution was never seriously considered by the House
Committee on Foreign Affairs. Machrowicz did not even attempt to
debate his resolution on the floor of Congress. In 1955, Hale did not
reintroduce his resolution, nor did any other Republicans except
such "extremists" as Congressman Lawrence Smith and Senator Joseph McCarthy.

On January 25, Smith introduced House Concurrent Resolution
56, which mirrored his 1951 and 1953 resolutions to repudiate Yalta.[2]
When he introduced Senate Resolution 75 on March 11, McCarthy
did not demand Yalta's repudiation because of Soviet violations or
the harm the agreements caused. Rather, McCarthy concentrated
on domestic political considerations, emphasizing the Administration's failure to implement "as yet" the 1952 Republican platform
pledge or to fulfill Eisenhower's 1953 State of the Union remarks.[3]

By 1955, however, most Republicans rejected the "extremists'"
tactics and the Republican charges that had been made from 1950
through 1952. On March 19, *The New York Times* reported the
Voice of America's assertion that the Yalta agreements "might have"
resulted in a peaceful and prosperous postwar world had the Soviet
Union adhered to its pledges, and the *Times* expressed regret that
the Yalta agreements could not be "enforced."[4] Also in March, Vice-
President Richard Nixon denied that Yalta was a "deliberate" attempt by the Roosevelt Administration to sell out to the Communists.
Yalta's fault was "not of the heart but of the head." The Roosevelt
Administration had failed to understand the "true nature" of communism. At Yalta, however, it had been forced by the need for Soviet
military support in the Japanese war to make concessions to the
Soviets. Nixon did reiterate his earlier contentions that the concessions made at Yalta had harmed the interests of the United States

1. For text see Appendix E.
2. For text see Appendix F.
3. For text see Appendix P.
4. *The New York Times*, March 19, 1955, 3.

and the "free world" and that these concessions had caused the "fall" of China and the Korean and Indochinese wars.[5]

Senator William Knowland's estimate of Yalta had changed by 1955. In late March, Knowland blamed Yalta only for "contributing" to Chiang Kai-shek's defeat. The Yalta concessions had been necessary, but the conferees had given up too much. When asked by a *Newsweek* reporter whether Yalta should be repudiated, he replied:

> Careful study should be given by the executive and legislative branches of our government as to whether or not it is in the national interest or in the interest of the free world to permit the Soviet Union to violate numerous sections of the Yalta agreement and then to claim the benefits under the other sections. Whatever can be done to rectify the mistakes of Yalta should be done at the earliest possible time. At this late date we can never fully atone for all the damage done.[6]

The comments made by Republican and Democratic congressmen on February 7, one of the informal anniversaries of the Yalta Conference, best exemplified Yalta's altered role in congressional debates. In 1950, this date had become the occasion for many vitriolic anti-Yalta speeches that stressed Yalta's effect on Poland. From 1950 to 1954, Republican speakers had emphasized the "cynical" Yalta agreements that made the Roosevelt Administration partially responsible for postwar developments in Poland, and they had demanded the repudiation of Yalta. In 1955, however, only the "extremists" demanded such repudiation. The "moderates" and "partisans," then, simply denounced the Soviets' injustice to Poland while contending that Yalta had had a disastrous effect on Poland.[7] Republican Congressman John Vorys' lame defense of the Republicans' failure to pass House Joint Resolution 200 was consistent with this reversal. The resolution's involvement in "partisan debate" had defeated it; however, Vorys claimed, the Republican-controlled Eighty-third Congress had subsequently passed a resolution expressing hope for the unification of Germany and for the freedom of the peoples of Eastern Europe. This latter resolution, he stated, represented "a formal concurrent expression of the House and Senate on the results of Yalta."[8]

The Democratic National Committee and Democratic congress-

5. *Baltimore Sun*, March 18, 1955.
6. *Newsweek*, 45 (March 28, 1955), 26.
7. U.S. *Congressional Record*, 84th Cong., 1st sess., 1955, CI, Parts 1 and 2, 805, 1221–23, 1225, 1231, 1236, 1240, 1261–62, 1349, 1524–25, 1798.
8. *Ibid.*, Part 1, 1348–49.

men assumed the offensive. Congressmen Peter Rodino (Democrat, New Jersey) and Henry Reuss (Democrat, Wisconsin) defended the correctness of Roosevelt's diplomacy at Yalta and denounced Soviet violations of the agreements. The national committee and Polish-American Congressmen Clement Zablocki (Democrat, Wisconsin) and Thaddeus Machrowicz accused Republicans who had formerly criticized Yalta of bad faith. The *Democratic Digest* maintained that Eisenhower, after reading the Yalta agreements, had backed down and abandoned the Republicans' campaign myths when he asked the Congress to "reaffirm" Yalta. Zablocki, who supported "negating" Yalta because of Soviet violations, argued that "Yalta's extremist critics" had founded their former condemnations on political expediency. Machrowicz reaffirmed his continued commitment to the repudiation of Yalta and charged:

> The present Secretary of State decided that such an act of renouncement [the various resolutions to repudiate Yalta introduced since 1952] would be unwise and uncalled for. As a matter of fact, administration spokesmen did a complete turnabout, defending the Yalta agreement in principle, and denounced only its violation by the Soviets [House Joint Resolution 200]. That was the exact position of those who had defended the Yalta agreement previously, a position bitterly criticized before by Republican spokesmen. . . . Ten years ago there may have been some justification in not realizing the complete untrustworthiness of the Soviet leaders. Today there can be no such excuse.[9]

By 1955, some Democratic congressmen demanded action to repudiate Yalta and criticized Republican appeasement. They directly appealed to Polish-Americans, emphasizing Republican bad faith and partisanship. If the Republicans had tried to invoke Yalta later, Zablocki's and Machrowicz' Polish backgrounds and their arguments after 1953 would have made the gambit difficult.

Senator McCarthy, other "extremists," and the Polish-American organizations remained consistent critics of Yalta diplomacy. In 1955, McCarthy accused the Eisenhower Administration of discouraging Republican support in 1953 for a resolution to repudiate Yalta. The influence of "bureaucrats, holdovers from the Roosevelt-Truman days" on the Eisenhower Administration had brought this change, and Milton Eisenhower was "typical of the palace guard of New

9. *Ibid.*, Parts 1 and 2, 1223–24, 1349, 1352, 1642–43. "Backdown Government: The Eisenhower Record at Mid-Term," *Democratic Digest* (March, 1955), 11.

Dealers which leads Ike around without his ever knowing exactly where they are taking him." McCarthy warned that, unless the 1952 pledges to repudiate Yalta were implemented, Republicans would have little chance of success in 1956.[10]

The "extremists" and Polish-American organizations echoed this demand for Yalta's repudiation. The Polish-American Congress and the For America Committee demanded repudiation of the Yalta agreements. President of the Polish-American Congress Charles Rozmarek, exiles from Eastern Europe who were attending the Assembly of Captive European Nations, the *Chicago Tribune*, and Senator William Knowland charged that Yalta was the foundation for current international problems. According to the Assembly of Captive European Nations, Yalta had shown that "enslavement of some nations does not assure freedom, peace and security to other nations." It warned against any new concessions to the Soviet Union and affirmed that humanity could be saved only through the liberation of "all captive nations." Rozmarek agreed that peaceful collaboration with the Soviet Union was fruitless. He called Yalta a warning and symbol of past blunders that required rectification. Knowland, who did not support liberation, reaffirmed the public's opposition to concessions to the Soviet Union. He criticized the Eisenhower Administration's Far Eastern policy by comparing it to Yalta and stating that the U.S. public would "never again pay the price of another Yalta or another Geneva [the 1954 conference terminating the war in Indochina] in order to buy a temporary respite from the insatiable appetite of the international Communists to destroy human freedom."[11]

Far more important than these sporadic demands for Yalta's repudiation was pressure from conservatives, who were led by the *Chicago Tribune* and Senators William Knowland and Joseph McCarthy, for the publication of the Yalta papers. The original publication dates of October and then December, 1954, had not been met. In 1955, these conservatives made heightened efforts to get immediate publication. In January, after blaming current Far Eastern problems on secret concessions made at Yalta, Knowland demanded greater public information about Roosevelt's and Truman's foreign policy. The *Tribune* stated that publication of the Yalta papers was neces-

10. U.S. *Congressional Record*, 84th Cong., 1st sess., 1955, CI, Part 3, 3031–33.

11. Charles Rozmarek to the editor, *Chicago Sun-Times*, February 9, 1955. *Chicago Tribune*, February 12, 1955, 2, 3; March 20, 1955, 9; March 26, 1955, 5. *The New York Times*, February 12, 1955, 4. *U.S. News and World Report*, 38 (February 25, 1955), 110–12.

sary in order to fix responsibility and to end the cover-up of Yalta's disastrous results. The *Tribune* doubted that the Congress, now controlled by Democrats, would permit publication for fear of the adverse reflection on Roosevelt. On January 20, Republican Congressman Albert Bosch introduced House Concurrent Resolution 44, which was identical to his 1953 resolution, demanding the "full disclosure" and "examination" of the proceedings of the secret Yalta and Potsdam conferences. He expressed concern about the State Department's failure to publish the Yalta papers by 1955 and noted that the State Department reputedly favored publication of these papers and intended to do so. He also recommended that the Administration, in addition to publishing past decisions and proceedings, repudiate the Yalta agreements.[12]

Publication of the Yalta papers, which this pressure helped to bring about, changed only the form of this controversy. The Administration's actions abetted the continued controversy, but there were reasons for its seeming reluctance either to publish or to refrain from publishing the Yalta papers. The Administration could not simply publish the papers; it had to exercise restraint before releasing them for publication. It could not afford to alienate the Democrats; it had to depend upon Democratic congressional support for its policies. It also had to consult Great Britain and to preserve good relations with that country. On the other hand, the Eisenhower Administration could not simply refuse to publish the Yalta papers. It was a Republican Administration eager for good relations with the more partisan and conservative Republicans.

Faced with this dilemma, the Administration tried to get at least tacit acquiescence from Democratic leaders and from the British. On March 8, while awaiting final British approval for publication, the Administration offered to make the Yalta papers available to all members of the House and Senate appropriation and foreign policy committees.[13] On March 15, refusal to accept the Yalta papers came from Congressmen James Richards, chairman of the House Foreign Affairs Committee; Carl Vinson (Democrat, Georgia), chairman of the House Armed Services Committee; and Senator Walter George, chairman of the Senate Foreign Relations Committee. They argued that the State Department should either keep the papers or make them public. Releasing the papers to the committees was tanta-

12. For text of House Concurrent Resolution 44, see Appendix L. U.S. *Congressional Record*, 84th Cong., 1st sess., 1955, CI, Part 1, 471–72, 493. *Chicago Tribune*, February 8, 1955, 20.
13. *Ibid.*, March 9, 1955, 7.

mount to publication, because of the probability of a leak. If such a leak occurred, the papers would be published without the Administration's having to take the responsibility for releasing them. Congressman Clarence Cannon (Democrat, Missouri), chairman of the House Appropriations Committee, did express his willingness to accept the papers for information purposes, and Senator Styles Bridges also welcomed this decision to make the Yalta record available at least to certain congressmen.[14] However, Richards', Vinson's, and George's refusal to accept the Yalta papers created an impasse, and the papers were not delivered to the congressional committees on March 15. In a press conference on that day, Secretary of State John Foster Dulles asserted that the State Department "still" intended to publish the Yalta papers. Contending that he could not state when the papers would be published, he asked the press not to question him about the reasons for the delay.[15]

On March 16, the day after the Administration's hesitant attempt to allow selected congressional committees to review the Yalta papers, it finally released the papers for publication. The Yalta papers could have been published immediately, because Assistant Secretary of State Carl McCardle had given *The New York Times* an advance copy of the full text of the Yalta papers. *New York Times* reporter James Reston had suggested that the Administration would certainly want the papers to be published in full, and he had assured McCardle of the *Times's* intention to publish the complete text of the papers if the Administration gave sufficient time to set them in type.

The *Chicago Tribune* learned of McCardle's action from certain undisclosed congressmen and protested this "favoritism." It asked Illinois Senator Everett Dirksen to use his influence to help the *Tribune* secure a copy. Dirksen contacted Senators William Knowland, Styles Bridges, Joseph McCarthy, and John Bricker, Illinois Congressmen Leslie Arends, Robert Chiperfield, Charles Vursell, and Congresswoman Marguerite Church, who protested to Secretary of State Dulles. Dulles first denied that a leak existed, but later in the day, White House Press Secretary James Hagerty released the text of the Yalta papers to the *Tribune*. The next day, March 17, both *The New York Times* and the *Chicago Tribune* published the complete text of the Yalta papers.[16]

14. *Ibid.*, March 15, 1955, 1, 6.
15. *Ibid.*, March 16, 1955, 2.
16. *Washington Evening Star*, April 7, 1955. *Chicago Tribune*, March 17,

On March 18, Secretary of State Dulles stated that publication was natural and in accordance with traditional Administration procedure of releasing information for the public record. He also stressed that the Yalta agreements were not binding on the United States because they were merely executive agreements and not formal treaties. He warned that no one should think that this publication foreshadowed any "denunciation" of Yalta.[17]

President Eisenhower first professed ignorance and unconcern. On March 17, he denied even knowing about the decision leading to the publication. It was a State Department matter. He had never read the papers.[18] In a press conference on March 23, he defended publication of the Yalta papers as well as those of any other secret conference. Such publication was justified, however, only if the intent was to learn from past mistakes and not to damage reputations or to try to discredit individuals. The Yalta participants had acted in good faith. When people appraised the past, they generally tended to forget the spirit of the time. He hoped that publication would not inhibit future international negotiations and that Yalta would not become a political issue.[19]

Despite the Administration's stated intent, publication of the Yalta papers created a political storm. Instead of ending, the controversy over Yalta assumed a different form. The Democrats said that the mode of release confirmed the Republicans' partisan motivation. The "extremists" and "partisans" rejected the Administration's plea that the Yalta papers not be used for partisan purposes. In addition, the "extremists" denied that all the Yalta papers had been published.

Debate on the mode and meaning of publication dominated congressional sessions during March and April. This debate ignored the basis for the conference and its nature. There was an almost total absence of communication between the orators; each speaker operated in a vacuum, virtually ignoring the charges of opposing speakers.

In this debate about Yalta, the Democrats assumed the offensive. They said that the mode of publication was designed to serve partisan purposes and that it was harmful to the national interest. Publi-

1955, 1. *Washington Post*, April 20, 1955. *U.S. News and World Report*, 38 (May 6, 1955), 132–34.

17. *The New York Times*, March 19, 1955, 1.

18. *Miami Herald*, March 18, 1955, 1.

19. *The New York Times*, March 24, 1955, 1. *Washington Star*, March 24, 1955. *Chicago Tribune*, March 24, 1955, 2.

cation, they affirmed, was a diversionary tactic intended to offset the Republican Administration's failure to resolve foreign and domestic problems. Eisenhower's and Dulles' stated ignorance of the decision leading to publication posed a serious threat to internal security. The Democrats wanted to lessen the political impact and to question the effect of publication on the future conduct of foreign relations. Some Democratic spokesmen even forthrightly defended the agreements and the spirit of the conference as justifiable efforts to solve the problems of 1945 and attributed the lamentable lack of success to subsequent Soviet bad faith. Others stressed the recommendations of the Joint Chiefs of Staff that supported Soviet intervention in the Far Eastern war. Republican criticisms of Yalta, these Democratic spokesmen suggested, were products of hindsight or were simply efforts to "unelect Roosevelt."[20]

The Republican congressional leaders were forced on the defensive. Republican spokesmen first denied that publication was partisan in motivation. Instead, they championed the public's traditional right to information, a right that had been recently abrogated. Besides, publication would not harm U.S. foreign relations, and it would prevent future Yaltas. Then, taking the offensive, they assailed Roosevelt's deceitful March 1, 1945, report to the Congress, the secrecy of the conference proceedings, Hiss's importance at the conference, and the lack of military necessity for the Far Eastern agreements. Democratic criticisms of publication were an effort to divert public attention from Yalta's disastrous results. Publication served a useful purpose by documenting the untrustworthiness of the Communists and the senselessness of discussions and agreements with the Soviet Union.[21] Senator McCarthy, even before he had read the papers,

20. U.S. *Congressional Record*, 84th Cong., 1st sess., 1955, CI, Parts 3, 4, and 6, 3138, 3190, 3336–37, 3351–52, 3375–88, 3450–51, 3476, 3595–96, 3726, 3917, 4258–59, 4276, 4631–32, 5144–46, 8376. *Newsweek*, columnist Ernest Lindley, *The Nation*, and the *New Republic* similarly argued that partisan considerations underlay the decision to publish the Yalta papers. *Newsweek* again criticized the conference. The others, however, praised it as a realistic effort to promote peace, an effort subsequently frustrated by Soviet bad faith. *Newsweek*, 45 (March 28, 1955), 15, 19, 25–28, 31; April 4, 1955, 17, 20. *The Nation*, 180 (March 26, 1955), 253. *New Republic*, 132, 14 (April 4, 1955), 2; 15 (April 11, 1955), 2; 13 (March 28, 1955), 2.

21. U.S. *Congressional Record*, 84th Cong., 1st sess., 1955, CI, Parts 3 and 4, 3137–38, 3332–36, 3352, 3373–88, 3765, 3915–16, 3919–20, 4175–76, 4572. *Time* magazine emphasized these themes, noting that publication formally disclosed Yalta's decade-old secrets, Roosevelt's underhanded dealings with the Germans and the French, his shocking Polish concessions, the senselessness of the Far Eastern agreements, and the mood and manner of Yalta's vivisection of the world. Admitting that no new secrets had been uncovered, *Time* maintained that publication did reveal the spirit of Yalta, "a stubborn refusal to face political reality." *Time*, 65 (March 28, 1955), 15, 27–29, 32–34.

asserted that they did not disclose the "whole picture." Much of what had transpired at Yalta, McCarthy charged, had been censored from this published account.[22]

During Senate debate about publication, Styles Bridges asserted that General MacArthur had advised the Administration of Japan's imminent collapse before the Yalta Conference had convened. Herbert Lehman, however, maintained that MacArthur had in fact sought Soviet involvement in the Far Eastern war. During this debate, William Knowland joined Bridges and affirmed that MacArthur had advised against Soviet involvement in the Far Eastern war. They admitted that MacArthur might have requested Soviet aid in 1944, but they stated that he had deemed Soviet aid superfluous in 1945. Had MacArthur been consulted prior to Yalta, Knowland argued, he might have supported Soviet military aid, but he would not have countenanced political concessions. Lehman answered by quoting from MacArthur's statement to the Joint Chiefs in 1945 and from MacArthur's remarks that were published in Stimson's and Forrestal's diaries. The quote from Forrestal's diary urged a Soviet campaign in Manchuria because it would commit Japanese forces and help the U.S. offensive.[23]

Following Lehman's speech, General MacArthur attempted to rebut this assessment of his 1945 position. He denied that he had been consulted prior to the conference or that he was aware of the Yalta agreements. Had he been aware of the Far Eastern agreements, he would have opposed Soviet intervention at that late date. Before Yalta, he had advised the Administration on the imminence of the Japanese collapse. MacArthur admitted, however, recommending Soviet involvement in 1941 and 1942. In April, 1955, when it was rumored that post-Yalta studies on implementing the Yalta decisions and the plans for doing so might be released, MacArthur demanded the release of the pre-Yalta discussions as well. He reiterated his earlier charges that he had not been consulted prior to Yalta and that in 1945 he deemed Soviet military aid unnecessary. Courtney Whitney, MacArthur's aide, dismissed the quote from Forrestal's diary to which Lehman had referred by saying that it reported "what Forrestal told MacArthur, not what MacArthur told Forrestal."[24]

22. U.S. *Congressional Record*, 84th Cong., 1st sess., 1955, CI, Part 3, 3031.
23. *Ibid.*, 3374–76.
24. *Chicago Tribune*, March 24, 1955, 1, 2; April 5, 1955, 16. *Time*, 65 (April 4, 1955), 14–15. *Newsweek*, 45 (April 11, 1955), 34. *U.S. News and World Report*, 38 (April 15, 1955), 61–63. *The New York Times*, March 24 1955, 1. *New York Herald-Tribune*, April 4, 1955.

In October, 1955, the Defense Department released documents on what had been the Far Eastern military situation and on Soviet entry into the Japanese war. These documents, MacArthur asserted, confirmed that he had not been consulted about the Yalta Conference. He further explained:

> However once such decisions [the Yalta Far Eastern agreements] had been taken and communicated to me following Yalta, they became binding upon me as upon any other theatre commander. All future discussions thereon with the War Department representatives necessarily became limited to consideration of their ultimate application to the conduct of the war. The attempt to interpret any statement I made in the course of such post-Yalta discussions as reflecting my previous Yalta views and convictions is wholly unwarranted.[25]

Despite MacArthur's absolute denial that he was not consulted about the Yalta decisions and his repeated assertion that he would have opposed political concessions in return for Soviet military intervention, the documents confirmed the opposite. A February 13, 1945, memorandum from Colonel Paul Freeman to General George Marshall reported an earlier conversation with MacArthur. Freeman wrote that MacArthur "understands Russia's aims, that they would want all of Manchuria, Korea and possibly part of North China. This seizure of territory was inevitable; but the United States must insist that Russia pay her way by invading Manchuria at the earliest possible date after the defeat of Germany." A March 8, 1945, memorandum from Brigadier General George Lincoln to General Marshall on their conversation of February 25, 1945, disclosed, "As to Russia, General MacArthur pointed out that politically they want a warm water port, which would be Port Arthur." These memoranda showed MacArthur's understanding that Soviet military intervention would require political concessions and that Soviet intervention was both desirable and inevitable. A memorandum from MacArthur to the Joint Chiefs of Staff, which was sent sometime between the Yalta and Potsdam conferences, buttressed this view. The memorandum was read at a meeting of the Joint Chiefs with President Truman on June 18, 1945. At the time, the State and War departments were reassessing U.S. support for the Yalta Far Eastern agreements. MacArthur argued that the "hazard and loss" of the proposed invasion of the Japanese mainland would be "greatly lessened if an attack is

25. *The New York Times*, October 21, 1955, 10.

launched from Siberia sufficiently ahead of our target to commit the enemy to major combat." [26]

The published Yalta papers had provided the opportunity for such "partisans" and "extremists" as McCarthy, Bridges, Mundt, Dirksen, and Capehart to use Yalta to attack past Democratic foreign policy. They expressly affirmed, despite Eisenhower's admonition that the Yalta papers should not become a partisan issue, their intention to discuss Yalta in subsequent campaigns. McCarthy stressed treason in government, Mundt assailed Hiss's influence and active espionage at Yalta, Dirksen cried censorship and charged that "interesting footnotes" on the Yalta agreements were "still buried in the State Department archives," but they all concurred that the lesson of Yalta must be brought to the U.S. public. Republican National Chairman Leonard Hall and Senator Homer Capehart asserted that Yalta was "as big a campaign issue for the Republicans as the 1929 depression was for the Democrats." [27]

In March, 1955, the Republican Senate Policy Committee, under the direction of Styles Bridges, drafted a fifty-two-page report on the Yalta papers. Bridges highlighted the partisan objective of this study on March 20, when he announced that the policy committee had been directed to secure information for Republican speakers to use in subsequent campaigns.[28] The report, entitled *Highlights of the Yalta Papers and Related Data,* emphasized the secrecy of the conference, some of its results, Roosevelt's bad health, Hiss's influence at the conference, the unjust treatment of Germany, the injustices to Poland and other Eastern European countries, the lack of military necessity for the Far Eastern concessions, and Roosevelt's deceitful, overconfident, and casual handling of crucial problems. This Republican study stressed particularly Roosevelt's disparaging remarks about the Poles, the English, and the Jews. Roosevelt, who was principally concerned about the Polish-American vote, "wanted at least 'a gesture' to take back to six million Americans of Polish extraction." Publication had not harmed U.S. foreign policy; it fulfilled the public's right to be informed. Much was already known about Yalta, but publication would add to public knowledge by disclosing "how and by what processes of thought decisions at Yalta were reached and what principles of law and moral standards were

26. *Ibid.*
27. *Chicago Tribune,* March 27, 1955, 12; March 28, 1955, 14. *Chicago Daily News,* March 17, 1955. *Louisville Times,* March 19, 1955.
28. *Washington Star,* March 21, 1955.

used." The committee ended the report by asserting that not all of the Yalta papers had been published but that the present publication confirmed the need for more astuteness in negotiations with the Soviet Union and for recognition that the Soviet Union could not be trusted.[29]

The Democratic National Committee replied to these Republican allegations not by defending Yalta so much as by belittling the report. In April, Democratic National Chairman Paul Butler stated that publication of the Yalta papers had had minimal political impact. He first charged that the papers revealed nothing not already known for ten years, and he doubted that any U.S. citizen would believe that Roosevelt deliberately betrayed the United States.[30] In March, 1955, the Democratic National Committee published for Democratic speakers fact sheets denying that Yalta resulted in the enslavement of Eastern Europe or the loss of China and that Hiss had played an influential role at Yalta. In June and August, 1955, the committee repeated these denials in articles in the *Democratic Digest*. Publication of the Yalta papers was politically motivated. It was an attempt by the Eisenhower Administration to appease the anti-Eisenhower faction in the Republican party and to divert public attention from the Administration's problems with domestic and foreign policy. Eisenhower had disavowed any political use of Yalta, and the Republican Senate Policy Committee's report showed his lack of leadership. Moreover, publication was a campaign strategy comparable to the Republicans' 1952 campaign charges concerning Yalta, charges subsequently ignored when the Eisenhower Administration attained power. The Democratic National Committee charged that publication, although it had a minimal effect on domestic politics, damaged U.S. foreign relations, particularly with Great Britain.[31]

Publication occasioned only a momentary political flurry. As a source for effective campaign issues, the Yalta papers had failed. Publishing them did stop the productive use of Yalta in national political campaigns. Although the way in which the papers were released had raised justifiable doubts about the possible effect on

29. Republican Senate Policy Committee, *Highlights of the Yalta Papers and Related Data*.

30. *Chicago Tribune*, April 23, 1955, 9.

31. Democratic National Committee, *Fact Sheet RD-55-7. Special Memorandum on the Yalta Agreements*. Democratic National Committee, *Fact Sheet RD-55-9. Reactions and Effects of the Release of the Yalta Papers*. "Would the Administration Keep on Doing Things Eisenhower Doesn't Like . . . If Ike Were President?" *Democratic Digest* (June, 1955), 25, 29. "Is It Explanation Enough that the President Didn't Know?" *ibid*. (August, 1955), 27.

the conduct of foreign relations, the papers had disclosed nothing new or startling. Further, President Eisenhower's denial that partisanship had dictated publication and his demand for unity dramatized the narrow commitment of the Bridges-Knowland Republicans to malign Roosevelt and the Democrats in the guise of fighting communism.

The Democratic National Committee's change in strategy further reflected the issue's lack of political impact. On April 1, 1955, Professor Walter Johnson of the University of Chicago, who was concerned about the reaction that publication might elicit, wrote to Democratic National Chairman Paul Butler, offering to compile a memorandum on the Yalta papers and on the manner by which they had been released. Johnson contended that the memorandum could be used by Democratic speakers to rebut Republican charges. Butler answered Johnson's letter on April 5. He termed Johnson's ideas on the memorandum "wonderful" and "timely" and added that Phillip Stern, director of research of the Democratic National Committee, agreed. Butler suggested that Johnson contact Stern.[32]

In a letter to Stern on April 28, Johnson reaffirmed his willingness to draft a memorandum rebutting Republican charges. Stern replied on May 2 that he opposed issuing a fact sheet. "Most" Republicans were not emphasizing the Yalta issue, and "the whole Yalta thing seems to have been something of a dud." By concentrating on Yalta, the Democrats might be forced on the defensive. Stern recommended, instead, that the Democrats develop those issues in which they could put the Republicans on the defensive. Johnson's reply on May 9 concurred that politically the Yalta papers had proven to be a "dud."[33]

The real problem posed by the publication of the Yalta papers was the Eisenhower Administration's refusal to follow the course indicated by the "extremists." The results of this refusal were the formal and complete rift between the "moderates" and the "extremists" and the effective isolation of the "extremists" in national politics. The conflicting interpretations of the rationale and justification for publication offered by the news media showed the nature of this rift. *The New York Times* supported the Administration, but the *Chicago Tribune, The Saturday Evening Post*, columnists David Lawrence, George Sokolsky, and Westbrook Pegler denounced this tacit renunciation of an anti-New Deal posture.

32. Walter Johnson, letter to Paul Butler, April 1, 1955. Paul Butler, letter to Walter Johnson, April 5, 1955.
33. Walter Johnson, letters to Phillip Stern, April 28, 1955, May 9, 1955. Phillip Stern, letter to Walter Johnson, May 2, 1955.

Before the Administration's decision to publish the Yalta papers, *The New York Times* had disagreed with those Republicans who demanded publication of the papers. Publication, the *Times* stated, would hurt U.S. relations with Great Britain and the Soviet Union. It would not contribute to an understanding of the Administration's policy or reveal anything not already known about the conference. It would, the *Times* asserted, precipitate a bitter partisan debate, and it might be construed as a commitment to repudiate Yalta.[34]

After the papers were published, the *Times* supported the Administration's action. The papers revealed no new secrets, but they did quash the myths that Roosevelt had given in to Stalin and that Alger Hiss had been an important conferee. Many of the criticisms of Yalta were based on hindsight, and Yalta ought to be judged in the context of 1945, not 1955. With the exception of the provisions on Germany and China, the world would have been "better today if [the] Yalta [agreements] had been carried out in good faith" by the Soviet Union. The lesson of Yalta was that words without guarantees were no longer acceptable to the United States. The *Times* denounced Soviet violations, but it did not recommend repudiation. Instead of repeating the charge it had made during the 1952 presidential campaign that Yalta had legalized Soviet postwar gains, the *Times* stated, "But in point of fact, by flagrantly breaking all their wartime agreements, including Yalta, the Soviets have released the Western Powers from any commitments, without releasing themselves from the moral and legal obligations to honor their own promises."[35]

The *Chicago Tribune, The Saturday Evening Post, U.S. News and World Report*, Westbrook Pegler, George Sokolsky, and David Lawrence, however, did not change their views. They used the published papers to develop those themes they had emphasized since 1945 and refined since 1949: the amorality and wrongness of the New Deal, Roosevelt's abuse of executive authority, Roosevelt's willingness to aid Soviet interests, Hiss's influence at the conference, the lack of necessity for the Far Eastern agreements, the immorality and harmfulness of the Yalta concessions, Yalta's contribution to world problems, and the sinister secrecy of the conference. The published record dispelled the distorted Roosevelt image at home and abroad by revealing that he "talked out of both sides of his mouth," had

34. *The New York Times*, March 14, 1955, 1; March 15, 1955, 1, 9.
35. *Ibid.*, March 17, 1955, 1, 27, 44; March 18, 1955, 26; March 20, 1955, 10E.

"feet of clay," was unprincipled, and was willing to betray U.S. interests and those of its allies, France and Great Britain. Yalta confirmed the disastrous results of secret, personal diplomacy and of any
policy based upon trust or compromise with the Soviet Union. As
David Lawrence noted, "The full story of Yalta illustrates graphi-
cally the dangers, as well as the possible values, of such talks; the
need of adequate prior preparations and the importance of a clear
definition of principles which will not be sacrificed to secure agreement." Sokolsky added that Yalta documented the need for the
Bricker Amendment as a safeguard "from tired, sick, cynical or
whimsical presidents."[36]

According to Pegler, *U.S. News*, and the *Tribune*, the published
papers had been heavily censored. Pegler stated only that the agreement about the access route to Berlin had been deleted, but the
protests of the *U.S. News* and the *Tribune* were more sweeping.
Deleted portions of the Yalta record would have confirmed Hiss's
"real importance" and revealed the full story of the Polish and Far
Eastern negotiations. They would have given Roosevelt's slighting
remarks about Jews and Poles and the reasons that some of the
Yalta decisions favored Soviet interests. The *Tribune* commended
those Republicans who intended to use the Yalta papers politically in
order to prevent the "catastrophe of future Yaltas."[37]

36. *U.S. News and World Report*, 38 (March 18, 1955), 6; March 25,
1955, 6, 42–46, 48, 50, 53; April 1, 1955, 132; April 8, 1955, 12, 55, 58, 64;
April 15, 1955, 8, 26; April 22, 1955, 127, 130–31. *The Saturday Evening Post*,
227 (April 16, 1955), 10. *Milwaukee Sentinel*, March 24, 1955, 12; March 25,
1955, 18; March 29, 1955, 29; March 31, 1955, 24; April 4, 1955, 16; April 7,
1955, 22; April 20, 1955, 16. *Chicago Tribune*, March 9, 1955, 22; March 16,
1955, 14; March 17, 1955, 1, 6, 10, 12, 20; March 18, 1955, 1, 2, 4, 5, 7, 12;
March 21, 1955, 10, 11; April 3, 1955, 20; April 4, 1955, 24; April 5, 1955, 20.
Independent of the publication controversy, in 1955 the "extremists" sought to
use Yalta to assail the Trade Agreements Act, S.E.A.T.O. and U.S. German
policy. They also condemned Roosevelt's injustices toward Poland and his aid
to Britain or stressed that he had been a "dying man" at Yalta. They again attributed the Yalta agreements to the New Deal's "blind pro-Soviet psychosis."
U.S. *Congressional Record*, 84th Cong., 1st sess., 1955, CI, Parts 1, 3, 4, and 8,
1058, 1218–20, 4280, 5352, 5396–97, 5503–20, 9932–36, 10257–60. *Chicago
Tribune*, April 4, 1955, 24. *U.S. News and World Report*, 38 (February 4, 1955),
121–22; April 8, 1955, 132 *Newsweek*, 45 (March 7, 1955), 96. *Milwaukee
Sentinel*, January 3, 1955, 12; February 17, 1955, 20; April 4, 1955, 16; April 6,
1955, 12.
37. *Milwaukee Sentinel*, March 31, 1955, 24; April 20, 1955, 16. *U.S. News
and World Report*, 38 (March 18, 1955), 6; March 25, 1955, 6, 42–46, 48,
50, 53; April 8, 1955, 12, 55, 58; April 15, 1955, 8, 26; April 22, 1955, 127,
130–31. *Chicago Tribune*, March 17, 1955, 1, 6, 20; March 18, 1955, 2, 7;
March 19, 1955, 5; March 22, 1955, 12; March 25, 1955, 16; March 26, 1955, 5;
March 27, 1955, 9, 20; April 23, 1955, 12.

The *Tribune* did not abandon the censorship charge after general interest over the Yalta papers had abated. In October, 1955, it reported Donald Dozer's "authoritative" claim that he had been fired from the State Department for objecting to the suppression of important documents from the published Yalta papers. Dozer and Bryton Barron, another former State Department official who allegedly resigned over this issue of censorship, contended that the published papers presented only a partial and distorted picture of the conference. "Truman holdovers" in the department, particularly G. Bernard Noble, the director of State's historical division, had consistently opposed publication because they feared that the complete record might embarrass people who had been important members of the Democratic administrations. Dozer testified that he and Barron were dismissed because they had attempted to ensure that the complete Yalta papers would be published at an early date.[38]

Senator Styles Bridges conducted an investigation of Dozer's charges. Dozer, Bridges subsequently concluded, had been hindered by Noble and other State Department officials who opposed "being frank with the public." Bridges then listed the Yalta deletions: two "original" Soviet documents indicating that Alger Hiss had been an important participant at the conference, certain papers concerning the Berlin corridor, fifty completed galleys of the Yalta proceedings, and the papers of Harriman, Stettinius, Byrnes, and Morgenthau, Roosevelt's Secretary of the Treasury.[39]

On December 29, 1955, G. Bernard Noble addressed a session of the American Historical Association. *The New York Times* of December 30 reported Noble's affirmation that the published papers had not been intentionally censored. The State Department had tried to secure access to the private papers of Harriman, Morgenthau, Stettinius, and Byrnes. In the AHA address, Noble also announced the publication of the Yalta papers in book form. This book included a number of documents not released with the original March, 1955, publication. A State Department aide confided to the *Times* that the

38. *Ibid.*, October 20, 1955, 1. *Chicago Sun-Times*, October 23, 1955, 22. Barron renewed these censorship charges in his study of the State Department. Barron claimed that undesirable holdovers from the Roosevelt-Truman administrations had suppressed certain compromising documents from the published record. These efforts, he added, had succeeded because of the Eisenhower Administration's hesitancy to institute sweeping changes in the State Department. Bryton Barron, *Inside the State Department: A Candid Appraisal of the Bureaucracy.* Bryton Barron, telephone interview, July 24, 1962.

39. *Chicago Tribune*, October 21, 1955, 2. *Boston Sunday Post*, November 13, 1955.

new documents had been uncovered as "a result of scraping of the
barrel" at the Roosevelt Library.

The national campaigns in 1956 and 1960 further substantiated
Yalta's lack of effectiveness as a future campaign issue. In 1956, the
Republican platform and campaign material avoided any specific
reference to Yalta, but the Democratic National Committee's 1956
fact book stressed the partisan basis for Republican references to
Yalta in past campaigns. The committee contrasted the Republicans'
1952 campaign remarks about Yalta and their pledge to repudiate
the agreements with the Eisenhower Administration's reaffirmation
of Yalta. The committee blamed "G.O.P. partisans in Congress" for
pigeonholing the Administration's resolution on Yalta. It also criticized the partisan publication of the Yalta papers.[40]

Secretary of State Dulles virtually echoed the Democratic National Committee's description when he testified before the House
Foreign Affairs Committee in January, 1958. He said that the trouble
with the Yalta agreements came from the Soviet Union's failure to
adhere to them.[41]

Senator Styles Bridges' subsequent appraisal of Yalta marked
the most surprising Republican reversal on the question. He had
persistently denounced the Yalta Conference from 1945 to 1955, but
in 1960, Bridges described it as an "honest" effort to reach an understanding with the Soviet Union. By 1960, Stalin had become Bridges'
villain. Not that Bridges changed completely; he ascribed the Soviet
refusal to participate in the May, 1960, summit conference to the
discovery that "they [the Soviet Union] would not be able to get
all kinds of concessions as they did at Yalta and Potsdam."[42] However, a 1960 Republican National Committee summary of U.S. foreign policy between 1945 and 1960, compiled under Bridges' direction, noted that the Yalta Conference dealt with a changing war
situation. This summary maintained that the Soviet Union, apart
from "some indirect aid to the Chinese Communists in Manchuria,"
did not play a "controlling" part in developments in China. The
summary further stated:

> While the Soviet Union strongly worked for its own interests
> in these arrangements [Teheran, Yalta, Cairo, and Potsdam],

40. Democratic National Committee, *The 1956 Democratic Fact Book: The
Issues and the Record, 1952–1956*, 8, 90.

41. *Washington Post*, January 11, 1958. *Democratic Digest* (February,
1958).

42. Republican National Committee, *The Republican Record* (*1953–1960*),
68.

it also gave reasonable indication that it was prepared to co-operate fully in liberating conquered territories, establish-ing free, democratic, and independent governments, rectify-ing boundaries with consideration for justice and future peace, and joining in the establishment of a United Nations for international peace, security, and cooperation.

The summary attributed the status of the Eastern European states to Soviet military occupation, and it charged that this latter situation resulted from World War II military developments.[43]

One issue in this debate about the Yalta papers was the nature of U.S. policy toward the Soviet Union. By 1955, the "moderates" shared the unthinking, emotional distrust of the Soviet Union that had been unique to the "extremists" in 1945. Although the "moder-ates" were skeptical and cautious, they did support the proposed summit conference in Geneva. The "partisans" and the "extremists" differed about the desirability of summit diplomacy but concurred on Yalta's lessons for negotiating with the Soviets. *The Saturday Evening Post*, the *Chicago Tribune*, George Sokolsky, and Senator William Knowland expressed reservations about the value of in-ternational conferences and urged the Administration to be cautious. After citing the danger to internal security that Alger Hiss's atten-dance at Yalta had caused, Knowland demanded safeguards to pre-clude the repetition of this experience.[44]

Congressman Robert Hale, *Time* magazine, *Newsweek*, and *The New York Times* expressed guarded support for international con-ferences and counseled against disunity among the NATO allies and unrealistic expectations. They especially advocated iron-clad guar-antees that would enable the conferees to enforce any agreements concluded. Expressing these suspicions and basic distrust of inter-national conferences with the Soviet Union, the *Times* charged, "The Yalta record must raise new doubts as to the value of any agreement with the Communists. But a new attempt may be worth-while when the West can lead from strength instead of weakness and can nego-tiate without the necessity of agreement at any cost, dictated by the pressures of war."[45]

43. Republican Senate Policy Committee, *ABC's of U.S. Foreign Policy, 1945–1960: A Factual Survey by the Republican Policy Committee Staff under the Direction of U.S. Senator Styles Bridges*, 14–16, 20, 44.
44. *The Saturday Evening Post*, 227 (January 8, 1955), 10; June 18, 1955, 10. U.S. *Congressional Record*, 84th Cong., 1st sess., 1955, CI, Parts 2, 3, and 4, 1887–89, 3627, 3634, 4603–4. *Milwaukee Sentinel*, April 2, 1955, 12. *Chicago Tribune*, April 24, 1955, 20.
45. *The New York Times*, January 27, 1955, 22; March 19, 1955, 14;

This spirit of distrust pervaded congressional debate on the pending conference in Geneva, and the "extremists" used the deep anti-Soviet bias to assail summit diplomacy. Some "extremists" and "partisans" — Senators William Jenner, Joseph McCarthy, Styles Bridges, George Bender, William Langer, Arthur Watkins, William Knowland, Frank Barrett (Republican, Wyoming), and Charles Potter (Republican, Michigan) — expressed their deep skepticism about negotiations with the Soviet Union and their commitment to pressure the Administration to proceed carefully. Besides wanting to avert the Yalta experience, they also were anxious to perpetuate the symbolism of Yalta, which would fade if the Administration altered its policy of doubt and distrust.

Accordingly, they cited Yalta to justify their suspicions of conferences with the Soviet Union and to support their demand that the Administration take an open, firm stance at the proposed conference. Bridges developed this theme by stating that he did not oppose international conferences per se but feared only their results. Teheran, Yalta, and Potsdam had given "legal cover" for postwar Soviet conquests. The Administration should act prudently at Geneva because Yalta had helped to "expedite and accelerate" the "fall" of China and Eastern Europe. (Earlier, Bridges had said that Yalta had caused these situations.) The published Yalta papers proved that Roosevelt should have stood firm at Yalta. Had he been more firm, the Eisenhower Administration would have had a better bargaining position at Geneva. Bridges added, "History will not forget that surrender [Yalta], regardless of the apologetics of New Deal campaign speechmakers."

Knowland raised the problem of threats to internal security when he recalled that Alger Hiss had had full information about Yalta, while the Congress had been denied access to the Yalta papers until 1955. He also recalled that Generals Eisenhower and MacArthur had not been invited to the conference. He received support from Bridges and from Bender and Potter, who stated that Congress had the responsibility to avoid a repetition of the Yalta experience.[46]

The "moderates" and "partisans" were forced to support the Eisenhower Administration's decision to attend Geneva, and their

March 22, 1955, 30; March 25, 1955, 22. *Time*, 65 (May 23, 1955), 21–22. *Newsweek*, 45 (May 23, 1955), 30–31; May 30, 1955, 19–21. U.S. *Congressional Record*, 84th Cong., 1st sess., 1955, CI, Part 4, 5157.
    46. *Ibid.*, Part 5, 6074–84.

support led to their conflict with "extremist" Senators William Jenner and Joseph McCarthy, who never changed their earlier anti-Soviet position. At this time, they tried to cast doubts about the wisdom of attending Geneva and questioned the loyalties of any official who counseled trust and understanding of the Soviet Union.

Their assault on the Administration started with a congressional resolution alluding to Yalta. On April 28, Jenner introduced a resolution providing that no U.S. official could conclude any agreement or make any commitment that would lead to the transfer of another state's territory to the Communists. After arguing that his resolution would prevent the reoccurrence of Yalta's policy of surrender and appeasement, Jenner stated:

> Any American official who attempts to negotiate another Yalta agreement will be on notice that he cannot commit the United States. Any nation that attempts to inveigle our officials into another Yalta agreement will be on notice that it can gain nothing. . . . I want a rule of policy so simple and clear that there can be no more Yaltas.[47]

Jenner's resolution was never acted upon by the Senate, but McCarthy extended Jenner's attack by introducing a resolution of his own in June, 1955. In the course of Senate debate on the Geneva Conference, both Jenner and McCarthy formally denounced any negotiations with the Soviet Union. On June 16, McCarthy spoke for the resolution that he introduced, Senate Resolution 116. He criticized the Eisenhower Administration's "complaisant and lethal" outlook on foreign policy, particularly the Administration's willingess to attend the Geneva Conference without securing definite concessions from the Soviet Union. At Geneva, President Eisenhower would be negotiating "with a deck stacked against us," since areas under Communist control would not be discussed. Unless these areas were discussed, the conference would be another "thumping Communist victory." Citing past Soviet violations of international agreements, McCarthy further contended that negotiations with the Soviet Union were worthless.[48]

McCarthy's charges were challenged by his former Senate cohort, William Knowland. Although he, too, observed that Geneva might become another Yalta, Knowland emphasized his full confidence in President Eisenhower and Secretary of State Dulles. Eisenhower and Dulles were "fully alive to the grave consequences which

47. *Ibid.*, Part 4, 5220–21.
48. *Ibid.*, Part 7, 8422–24.

accrued from other meetings." Eisenhower, however, did not intend to solve the problems of the world in "one setting — which was the grave fault of Yalta, Teheran and Potsdam." In addition, Knowland predicted that the problems of the "satellite countries" eventually would be discussed. Republican Senators Edward Thye and George Bender also expressed their trust of the Eisenhower Administration.[49]

On June 21, in hearings before the Senate Foreign Relations Committee on his Senate Resolution 116, McCarthy again charged that, since only those areas under "Western or free world control" would be discussed at Geneva, negotiations would concentrate only on "what we can give away." The United States could at best break even and would probably negotiate "another giveaway" that would turn the conference into "another Yalta." Congress had a great responsibility to make recommendations on foreign policy, and he would have acted the "very same" way at the time of Yalta if he had been a senator then.[50]

Again, Knowland disagreed with McCarthy. Knowland denied that Congress should limit presidential action and maintained that Eisenhower would act responsibly. Even Senator Homer Capehart, who supported McCarthy's right to introduce his resolution, questioned the advisability of the resolution. He and Mundt expressed their complete confidence in the President and in the Secretary of State, and Mundt denied that Geneva would be another Yalta. Further, Democratic Senator Alben Barkley characterized McCarthy's resolution as a serious reflection on President Eisenhower.[51]

By 1955, the tone of congressional debates about Yalta had changed markedly. When Republicans of Mundt's, Knowland's, and Capehart's political views would sharply rebuke McCarthy and affirm their confidence in secret negotiations with the Soviet Union conducted by the executive branch alone, Yalta could hardly be resuscitated as a political issue. It still was a symbol of Cold War distrust and rigidity, and as such, it was used most frequently to criticize the Soviet Union, not the Roosevelt Administration. Only the "extremists" and "partisans" continued to revile Yalta. The "extremists" pointed to the Yalta experience with the hopes of discour-

49. *Ibid.*, 8425–30.
50. U.S. Senate, Committee on Foreign Relations, *Hearings on Senate Resolution 116 Favoring the Discussion at the Coming Geneva Conference of the Status of Nations Under Communist Control*, 84th Cong., 1st sess., 1955, 4–22.
51. *Ibid.*, 22–25. *Newsweek*, 45 (June 27, 1955), 17.

aging negotiations with the Soviet Union and, by charging appeasement or treason, of discrediting the New Deal. The "partisans,"
committed to the continuance of the Cold War, discouraged negotiations with the Soviet Union. Their effectiveness in U.S. politics was
predicated on the continuance of the insecurities and fears basic
to the Cold War.

conclusion

An analysis of the reaction to Yalta provides a framework for assessing the domestic context in which postwar U.S. foreign policy was formulated and discussed. Ostensibly, nonpartisanship was the keynote of the bipartisan foreign policy, but in fact, partisan considerations limited the responses of both Democratic and Republican administrations to Soviet offers to negotiate and other international events. Inevitably *ad hoc*, these responses were determined by the complexity of international politics, considerations of national security, and appraisals based on political feasibility. The primary underlying concern was to avoid the stigma of being soft toward communism.

By the 1950's, many people in the United States considered foreign policy something removed and burdensome as well as potentially threatening. Forced to accept the responsibilities of world leadership in a remarkably short period of time, these people did not understand the limitations to U.S. influence or feel a commitment to fulfill the costs attendant to international involvement. President Truman's failure to provide imaginative, articulate leadership indirectly aided the "extremists," who seemingly offered simplistic but bold solutions to the frustrating problems of the Cold War. The Truman Administration's indecisiveness and partisanship and the "extremists'" irresponsible attacks increased the public's frustration, and the postwar debate about Yalta reflected it.

Also, by 1950, many people had made the emotional appraisal that Yalta had created the problems of the postwar period. They had come to believe that the conference agreements had contributed to Soviet power and influence and thus had thwarted the attainment of a desirable peace, one in which U.S. interests would have been dominant. The change in popular concepts about Yalta after 1947 mirrored the changed idea of what constituted correct relations between the United States and the Soviet Union — the renunciation of negotiations based on good faith and understanding for negotiations from a position of strength. Conversely, the postwar shift in the Truman Administration's policy toward the Soviet Union from one of trust to one of distrust altered the concept of the wisdom of Yalta. As the

Administration reversed its views on the reasonableness and desirability of trusting the Soviet Union, Yalta became a conference that it had never been.

The spirit of Yalta was one of guarded co-operation and trust. Its basic assumption was that peace and understanding were dependent upon a willingness to negotiate and to compromise. Roosevelt recognized the risks inherent in an international policy based on détente and felt they should be welcomed; he understood that a perfect world would not immediately ensue but could be expedited by discussion, compromise, and a willingness to respect the special interests of other nations. As time passed and the Cold War emerged, his views were rejected or ignored. The shift in the Truman Administration's policy methods, the failure to achieve the millennium instantly, and the failure of the postwar world to correspond to U.S. hopes intensified popular frustration and intolerance.

Yalta's spirit of tolerance for diversity was not a characteristic of the Cold War period. International developments and Administration policies were then judged in simplistic, monolithic terms of black and white. The United States and the so-called free world possessed a monopoly on virtue and morality. A rigidity in thought, an intolerance toward ideas and dissent, a paralysis in accepting innovation, and a belief in the omnipotence and altruism of U.S. power evolved. The United States should rely on military strength and an approach based on confrontation.

In reality, World War II had revolutionized the political and military situation in Eastern Europe and Asia. The prewar world could not have been restored — radical economic and political changes were inevitable. Roosevelt understood this situation, and at Yalta, he attempted to deal with it realistically. Truman, unfortunately, did not.

Roosevelt's death had forced Truman to assume leadership of U.S. foreign policy and thereby to influence the course of the postwar world. Truman's inadequate understanding of the complexities of international politics and of the limitations on U.S. policy responses made him unsuitable for these important responsibilities. This lack colored his appraisal of Soviet responses and also minimized his effectiveness in promoting public support for complex but controversial Administration decisions in foreign policy. Thus, while Truman did secure support of the Truman Doctrine, the Marshall Plan, and NATO, he did not effectively explain to the public the limits to these policies or the world responsibilities facing

the United States. Besides adversely reflecting on the wisdom of
Yalta, his own suspicions of the Soviet Union increased the public's
anxieties and the prejudice against any negotiated settlement with
that country.

Further, Truman did not clearly articulate the Administration's
objectives. It was his responsibility to convince the U.S. public that
particular policy decisions were justified and that the criticisms of
the "extremists" and the "partisans" were groundless or irresponsible.
Instead of confronting his opposition by discussing the issues, Truman brought to the Presidency the tactics and responses of a capable
but partisan politician. A feisty, hard-hitting, loyal Democrat, Truman unintentially diverted public attention from principles and realistic objectives to partisan strategy and objectives. At a time when
the U.S. public required a forceful presentation of the responsibilities
of foreign policy and the limitations on it, Truman's partisanship
and inarticulateness abetted the insecurity engendered by the Cold
War, the insecurity that the McCarthyites would exploit.

Congressional Democrats also failed to provide the necessary
leadership. Their defenses of Yalta, for example, were partisan rather
than principled. Operating on the assumption that the Soviet Union
was completely untrustworthy, they did not, and could not, defend
Yalta's spirit of co-operation. By criticizing Soviet violations of
the Yalta agreements, however, they did obliquely try to defend
Roosevelt's reputation and to avert the possible loss of votes.

The nature of the postwar political debate can be understood
not only as the result of this failure of leadership but also as the
product of the very policies espoused by the President. With the
adoption of the containment policy, the Truman Administration had
tacitly rejected Yalta's spirit of tolerance and the joint co-operation
intended to prevent the resurgence of a German, or any other, threat
to the peace. In essence, the containment policy formally admitted
that a policy based on the Soviet Union's good faith was inadequate,
if not hazardous. Containment assumed that peace could be secured
only through firmness and military preparedness. The welcoming of
West German rearmament as one means to contain Soviet expansion
was a dramatic example of this reversal. The Truman Administration, limited by its desire to assure the U.S. public of its vigilant
anticommunism, also had to be temperate and conservative when
reviewing alternatives to U.S. foreign policy. For political reasons,
Truman could not consider a summit conference with the Soviet

Union. Only after the election of Eisenhower, and then only in 1955, could the United States explore this possibility.

The Truman Administration and the "moderates," despite their references to victory, recognized the complexities of world power. Thus, they seemed only to offer either lame apologies for the failure of past policies to achieve victory or temporizing proposals for dealing with the Soviet threat. Lame apologies and temporizing proposals were no political match for the boldness and confidence of the "extremists'" rhetoric.

McCarthyism did not emerge from a vacuum; it captured the fears and insecurities inherent in the public's support for the containment policy. The McCarthyites' bold solutions to complex problems were credible because they avoided the frustration and extended commitments of containment. Also, their anti-Communist posture was attuned to the suspicions, distrust, and reliance on power politics that characterized the Cold War.

In a sense, a domestic cold war paralleled the international Cold War. The mutual suspicions engendered and perpetuated by the international Cold War had reduced the dialogue essential for an open society. Radical ideas and principles were viewed with suspicion or were summarily rejected; disruptive changes in Europe and the underdeveloped countries were assessed not as political movements but as military events. Revolutionary sentiments were interpreted not as indigenous, native radicalism, but as the product of Soviet manipulation and influence. Accordingly, a narrow view of international change emerged. In the United States, anticommunism had become almost a religious ideology, and proposals and interpretations were tested by this standard. Anticommunism became the principal rationale for foreign and domestic policies. Proposals to curb reform movements or limit civil liberties, which might otherwise have been summarily rejected — the Truman Doctrine, the Federal Employee Loyalty Program, the Bricker Amendment, the McCarran Internal Security Act — acquired support when couched in anti-Communist terms.

This process served to increase the political influence and respectability of political conservatism and permitted negativist attacks. The actions instituted and supported by the "extremists" were investigations of the ideas and associations of former members of the New Deal and Fair Deal administrations. The "extremists" did not offer realistic solutions to international problems, nor were they primarily concerned about international developments.

Instead, they focused on internal security. They were sincerely and politically committed to the continuance of the Cold War, and they consistently opposed any policy that might lead to détente with the Soviet Union. Ironically, these most vociferous declaimants of the Administration's containment policy had initially condemned this same policy as too aggressive. They also consistently opposed any policy that would necessitate economic and military commitments to other countries, but such commitments seemingly were essential for the implementation of the dynamic, resolute foreign policy of victory and liberation that they espoused.

The extent of the "extremists'" alternative to Administration policy was simply a *verbally* resolute anticommunism, a policy basically of bluff and brinkmanship. The inconsistency between their rhetoric and response came from their primary obsession with domestic political and economic issues: They sought to protect U.S. society by discrediting the New Deal and its reformist ideas. To them, the real Communist danger to the United States was the acceptance of federal controls and welfare legislation. Foreign policy, for the "extremists," could be used as a cover to discredit the New Deal and Fair Deal. At the same time, they decried international commitments because these commitments could increase the stature of the Presidency and add to federal spending.

After 1948, the "extremists'" tactics were adopted in modified form by the Republican congressional and national leaders. This shift was the result of post-1947 international and domestic developments that altered the political setting in the United States. The principal catalysts were the Czechoslovakian coup, the Berlin crisis, the Soviet explosion of an atomic bomb, Chiang Kai-shek's defeat, and the Korean War. These events indicated that the Cold War might escalate into a hot war, that the Soviet threat was military and not simply political. Many people in the United States considered the Soviet explosion of an atomic bomb threatening. It canceled the secure belief that the U.S. atomic monopoly could deter war and added a more complex, confusing dimension to national security. These factors, plus the fear that Communist subversion had led to the Russians' development of an atomic bomb and to the formulation of a seemingly indecisive foreign policy, created the fears and insecurity that led to McCarthyism.

The Alger Hiss perjury trial and the various loyalty and security cases of the late 1940's and early 1950's further intensified popular anxieties about internal security by seeming to confirm charges about the disloyalty of some federal employees. In Congress and during the 1952 national campaign, the Republicans responded by making national security their dominant issue. Foreign policy, when related to subversion, became one means for political success, because the Cold War and the emphasis on national security had created a cover and a new political rhetoric that sanctioned conservatism without emphasizing antireformism. A rhetoric extolling confrontation, stressing U.S. omnipotence, and exaggerating the Communist threat had legitimated a self-centered, parochial domestic smugness.

The Cold War had not only contributed to the emergence of McCarthyism but also complicated the internal rift within the Republican party about national strategy. By denouncing Democratic foreign policy and internal security after 1949, the "moderates" averted an intraparty fight and were able to prevail over the "extremists" at the 1952 Republican National Convention. Criticisms of the Democrats had provided common ground for uniting the Republican party. Eisenhower's candidacy temporarily enabled the "moderates" to curb the party's more conservative congressional wing, but by avoiding a showdown with the "extremists," the "moderates" won only a temporary victory in 1952. Subsequently, when the Eisenhower Administration was forced to reverse Republican campaign proposals, the "moderates" never denounced the principles but only the intemperance of the "extremists'" and "partisans'" methods. Despite their victory in nominating Eisenhower, the "moderates" had not wrested control of the state machinery from the conservatives. Their adoption of the "extremists'" tactics with foreign policy placed them at a competitive disadvantage in the long run, as Barry Goldwater's nomination in 1964 and Richard Nixon's in 1968 attest.

In conclusion, an important lesson of Yalta is the need for a searching but responsible foreign policy debate. The postwar Yalta debate and its partisan impact on the formulation and execution of foreign policy also clearly show the need for a critical examination of heretofore unquestioned assumptions about Cold War policy.

appendixes

APPENDIX A: House Concurrent Resolution 31

Introduced by Congressman Barry on February 26, 1945.

Resolved by the House of Representatives (the Senate concurring), That the Congress hereby expresses its disapproval of the decision made at the Crimean Conference held at Yalta, contained in a statement on the results of such conference, dated February 11, 1945, made by the Prime Minister of Great Britain, the President of the United States of America, and the Chairman of the Council of People's Commissars of the Union of Soviet Socialist Republics, that the eastern frontier of Poland should follow the Curzon line with minor digression, thus giving to Russia all Polish lands east of such line.

It is the sense of Congress that the frontiers of Poland should be established at the boundary lines which were in effect at the outbreak of the present war.

APPENDIX B: Memorandum of Secretary of State Stettinius to Secretary of War Stimson of May 12, 1945

In order to determine the policy of the United States Government in the Far East in connection with the political effects of the expected Soviet entry into the Pacific war and the relationship of the Yalta Agreement on this subject, I would appreciate receiving from you the views of the War Department on the following questions:

1. Is the entry of the Soviet Union into the Pacific war at the earliest possible moment of such vital interest to the United States as to preclude any attempt by the United States Government to obtain Soviet agreement to certain desirable political objectives in the Far East prior to such entry?
2. Should the Yalta decision in regard to Soviet political desires in the Far East be reconsidered or carried into effect in whole or in part?
3. Should a Soviet demand, if made, for participation in the military occupation of the Japanese home islands be granted or would such occupation adversely affect our long term policy for the future treatment of Japan?

In the opinion of the Department of State it would be desirable politically to obtain from the Soviet Government the following commitments and clarifications regarding the Far East prior to any implementation on our part of the Yalta Agreement:

1. The Soviet Government should agree to use its influence with the Chinese Communists to assist this Government in its en-

deavors to bring about the unification of China under the National Government headed by Chiang Kai Shek. The achievement of Chinese unity on the basis considered most desirable by the United States Government should be agreed to by the Soviet Union before the United States should make any approach to the Chinese Government on the basis of the Yalta Agreement. The difficulties in regard to Sinkiang should be settled by amicable agreement between the Soviet and Chinese Governments.

2. Unequivocal adherence of the Soviet Government to the Cairo Declaration regarding the return of Manchuria to Chinese sovereignty and the future status of Korea.

3. Definite agreement of the Soviet Government that immediately Korea is liberated, whether before final capitulation of Japan or after, it is placed under the trusteeship of the United States, Great Britain, China, and the Soviet Union. This agreement should make clear that the four trustees are to be the sole authority for the selection of a temporary Korean Government.

4. Before giving final approval to the annexation by the Soviet Union of the Kurile Islands it might be desirable to receive from the Soviet Government emergency landing rights for commercial planes on certain of these islands.

APPENDIX C: Selected Written Questions on the Greek and Turkish Aid Bill

Question 11: Does the United States Government have any undisclosed commitments to foreign nations as a result of promises made at previous conferences by the late President Roosevelt or by President Truman or former Secretaries of State Hull, Stettinius, and Byrnes?

Answer: All tripartite agreements among the United States, the Union of Soviet Socialist Republics and the United Kingdom have now been made public with the publication on March 24 of the texts of the Teheran, Yalta and Potsdam agreements.[1]

Question 89: Was any agreement or understanding reached at Yalta or Potsdam, or any other meeting between the United States, Great Britain, and Russia under which Greece and Turkey were recognized as being within the British 'sphere of influence'? Were any other 'spheres of influence' established by the Big Three?

Answer: The United States is not and has not been a party to any spheres of influence agreement.[2]

Question 105: Was there any agreement at Teheran or Yalta which placed Turkey and Greece, or either of them, in the sphere of influence of the United States or Great Britain? Is there anything in either of those agreements, which placed China, Korea, Poland, Hungary, or the Balkan States, or any of them, in the Russian sphere of influence, and would the statement by the President apply to those countries?

1. U.S. House of Representatives, Committee on Foreign Affairs, *Hearings on H.R. 2616: A Bill to Provide Assistance to Greece and Turkey*, 80th Cong., 1st sess., 1947, 347.

2. *Ibid.*, 376.

Answer: The complete text of the agreements made at Teheran and at Yalta were published in Washington on March 24, 1947. Neither in these documents nor in any others has the United States been a party to the creation of spheres of influence in any part of the world.[3]

APPENDIX D: 1948 Republican Foreign Policy Plank

We shall erect our foreign policy on the basis of friendly firmness which welcomes cooperation but spurns appeasement. . . . We shall protect the future against the errors of the Democratic Administration, which has too often lacked clarity, competence or consistency in our vital international relationships and has too often abandoned justice. . . . We pledge that under a Republican Administration all foreign commitments shall be made public and subject to constitutional ratification. . . . We are proud of the part that Republicans have taken in those areas of foreign policy in which they have been permitted to participate. We shall invite the Minority Party to join under the next Republican Administration in stopping partisan politics at the water's edge. We faithfully dedicate ourselves to peace with justice.

APPENDIX E: House Joint Resolution 444, House Joint Resolution 74, House Joint Resolution 36, House Joint Resolution 111, House Joint Resolution 63

First introduced by Congressman Hale on March 28, 1950.

Whereas the agreement signed at Yalta, Union of Soviet Socialist Republics, on February 12, 1945, by representatives of the United States, the United Kingdom of Great Britain and North Ireland, and the Union of Soviet Socialist Republics committed all three governments to the principle that the people of the nations liberated from nazism and fascism should have the right to choose the form of government under which they will live; and

Whereas despite the fact that the Provisional Government of Poland was pledged to the holding of free elections as soon as possible on the basis of universal suffrage and secret ballot, the Soviet Government conspired with such provisional government to delay election for twenty-three months until the machinery of the police state was organized; and

Whereas the Soviet Government declined to act in conjunction with the Governments of the United States and Great Britain in condemning the fraudulent character of the elections held in Poland on January 19, 1947; and

Whereas the Soviet Government has also forcibly interfered in the internal affairs of Albania, Bulgaria, Czechoslovakia, Hungary, Rumania, and Yugoslavia, thus making it impossible for the respective people of such nations to held free elections to form governments of their own choice; and

3. *Ibid.*, 383.

Whereas the withdrawal of the United States from the Yalta Agreement for the above reasons will re-emphasize to the people of the world the adherence of the United States to the principles of the Atlantic Charter and will serve to give hope to the subjugated peoples of Europe through knowledge that the United States is mindful of their desire to achieve independence and self-government: Therefore be it

Resolved by the Senate and House of Representatives of the United States of America in Congress assembled, That in view of the repeated violations by the Soviet Government of the agreement between the Governments of the United States, the United Kingdom of Great Britain and North Ireland, and the Union of Soviet Socialist Republics signed at Yalta, Union of Soviet Socialist Republics, on February 12, 1945, such agreement is hereby declared to be no longer binding on the United States, and the President is requested to take such action as may be necessary to effectuate the withdrawal of the United States from such agreement.

APPENDIX F: House Concurrent Resolution 102, House Concurrent Resolution 13, House Concurrent Resolution 56

First introduced by Congressman Lawrence Smith on May 14, 1951.

Whereas the private agreements concluded in 1945 at Yalta and Potsdam were based on a complete disregard for the strategic interests of the United States and the free world, and represent a denial of the free and democratic ideals, as expressed in the North Atlantic Charter, which have always been cherished by the American people and for which millions fought World War II; and

Whereas, specifically, the Yalta agreement sanctioned Soviet domination of Eastern Europe and East Asia, the betrayal of Poland and the mutilation of its natural boundaries, the transfer of the allegiance of millions of persons without plebiscite or other recognition of their rights to self-determination, and the uprooting of other millions of persons; and

Whereas, specifically, the Potsdam agreement sanctioned the betrayal of China, granting the Soviets a preferred position in Manchuria, the richest and most industrialized area of China, a position which was promptly used as the assembly point and main military base for the Communist conquest of China; and

Whereas the Potsdam agreement, in addition to promising the Soviet Government other vast and invaluable territorial concessions, authorized the dismemberment of Germany and the use of Germans as slave labor by the Soviets, and promised the Soviet Government that the United States would return Soviet political and other refugees for repatriation; that is, for concentration camps or death; and

Whereas the Potsdam agreement provided for the expulsion or transfer of millions of Germans of German ethnic origin from Eastern Europe, Central Europe, and the Balkans to Germany where they have deterred economic and political recovery in Western Germany and have thereby endangered the peace of all Europe; and

Whereas the Soviet Government has consistently disregarded the provisions of the Yalta and Potsdam agreements which it has found inconvenient to honor, including the provisions for free and unfettered elections in Poland and the provisions for treating Germany as an economic unit and for encouraging political parties in Germany; and

Whereas, although the Yalta and Potsdam agreements are the closest approach to a peace settlement for World War II existing today, and although these two agreements, by their inexpedient provisions, have cost the United States untold billions for defense, occupation costs, and foreign economic support, and have led the free world to the brink of another global war, these agreements were made in secrecy and without congressional participation, approval, or ratification: Now, therefore, be it

Resolved by the House of Representatives (the Senate concurring), That it is the sense of the Congress of the United States that the private agreements concluded in 1945 at Yalta and Potsdam should be forthwith repudiated by the United States.

APPENDIX G: House Concurrent Resolution 108

Introduced by Congressman Machrowicz on May 17, 1951.

Whereas the agreements concluded in 1945 at Yalta and Teheran were entered into by the representatives of the United States based on the good faith of Soviet Russia; and

Whereas the Government of Soviet Russia has consistently and flagrantly violated the spirit and word of these agreements; and

Whereas the Government of Soviet Russia has failed to provide for free and unfettered elections in Poland and has abused the terms of these agreements in order to dominate Eastern Europe and Eastern Asia; and

Whereas there no longer exists any legal or moral grounds for the United States to continue to be bound by the terms of such agreements: Now therefore be it

Resolved by the House of Representatives (the Senate concurring), That it is the sense of the Congress of the United States that the agreements concluded in 1945 at Yalta and Teheran should be forthwith repudiated by the United States.

APPENDIX H: House Concurrent Resolution 120

Introduced by Congressman Kersten on June 7, 1951.

Whereas the American people have long adopted the basic principles set forth in the American Declaration of Independence . . .

Whereas the American people believe these principles are universal and apply to all men, everywhere, at all times; and . . .

Whereas communism, after thus treacherously and forcefully seizing power in Poland, . . .

Whereas past tragic mistakes in the policies of certain of the free nations, including that of the United States toward Poland, based on the assumption that collaboration with the Communists was possible, particularly in entering into the agreements of Teheran, Yalta, and Potsdam, and a failure to fully understand the true nature, extent, and the enormity of of communism's aggressive designs, placing the Communist conspiracy where it now is a clear and present danger to world peace and the free progress of mankind compelling the United States and other free nations again to undertake a vast program of rearmament; and . . .

Resolved by the House of Representatives (the Senate concurring), . . .
Sec. 3. To give meaning to their historic friendship for the Polish people, the Congress of the United States hereby expresses the strong hope of the American people for the liberation of the Polish people from their Communist enslavement. To assist in bringing about that liberation at the earliest possible date, the President of the United States is hereby requested —

(1) To formulate a new and stronger foreign policy which, among other things, recognizes the essentially evil nature of the international Communist regime, bent on the destruction of the United States and of the free world, and distinguishes between this regime and the people enslaved by it, repudiates the Yalta, Teheran and Potsdam agreements concerning Poland, and excludes all further agreements, commitments and recognition of the present Communist regime in Poland; . . .

APPENDIX I: Amendment to the Mutual Security Act of 1951, House Resolution 5113

Introduced by Congressman Kersten on August 17, 1951.

After "United States" line 8, page 3, strike period and add: "and for any selected persons who are residing in or escapees from the Soviet Union, Poland, Czechoslovakia, Hungary, Rumania, Bulgaria, Albania, Lithuania, Latvia, and Estonia or the Communist-dominated areas of Germany and Austria, and any other countries absorbed by the Soviet Union, either to form such persons into national elements of the military forces of the North Atlantic Treaty Organization or for other purposes, when it is similarly determined by the President that such assistance is important in the defense of the North Atlantic area and of the security of the United States."[1]

APPENDIX J: Senate Joint Resolution 67

Introduced by Senator Jenner on April 27, 1951.

To prohibit the signing by any officer or representative of the United States of any document giving the force of law to any provision of the Yalta agreement,

Resolved by the Senate and House of Representatives of the United States of America in Congress assembled, That no officer of the United States or representative of the United States to the United Nations or to any other international organization, conference, or meeting shall sign any treaty, agreement, or other document which in any way validates or gives

1. U.S. *Congressional Record,* 82d Cong., 1st sess., 1951, XCVII, Part 8, 10261.

the force and effect of law to, or otherwise binds the United States to observe, any clause or provision of the Yalta agreement.

APPENDIX K: Text of the Japanese Peace Treaty Concerning the Kurile Islands and South Sakhalin

Article 2, c. Japan renounced all right, title and claim to the Kurile Islands and to that portion of Sakhalin and the islands adjacent to it over which Japan acquired sovereignty as a consequence of the Treaty of Portsmouth of September 5, 1905.

❖ ❖ ❖ ❖ ❖ ❖ ❖ ❖ ❖ ❖

Article 25. . . . the present Treaty shall not confer any rights, titles or benefits on any State which is not an Allied Power as herein defined; nor shall any right, title or interest of Japan be deemed to be diminished or prejudiced by any of the Treaty in favor of a State which is not an Allied Power as so defined.

APPENDIX L: House Concurrent Resolution 22, House Concurrent Resolution 44

First introduced by Congressman Bosch on January 16, 1953.

Whereas the private agreements concluded in 1945 at Yalta and Potsdam were based on a complete disregard for the strategic interests of the United States and the free world, and represent a denial of the free and democratic ideals, as expressed in the North Atlantic Charter, which have always been cherished by the American people and for which millions fought World War II; and

Whereas, specifically, the Yalta agreement sanctioned Soviet domination of Eastern Europe and of East Asia, the betrayal of Poland and the mutilation of its natural boundaries, the transfer of the national allegiance of millions of persons without plebiscite or other recognition of their rights to self-determination, and the uprooting of other millions of persons; and

Whereas, specifically, the Potsdam agreement sanctioned the betrayal of China, granting the Soviets a preferred position in Manchuria, the richest and most industrialized area of China, a position which was promptly used as the assembly point and main military base for the Communist conquest of China; and

Whereas the Potsdam agreement provided for the expulsion and transfer of millions of Germans of German ethnic origin from Eastern Europe, Central Europe, and the Balkans to Germany where they have deterred economic and political recovery in Western Germany and have thereby endangered the peace of all Europe; and

Whereas the Soviet Government has consistently disregarded the provisions of the Yalta and Potsdam agreements which it has found inconvenient to honor, including the provision for free and unfettered elections in Poland and the provisions for treating Germany as an economic unit for encouraging free political parties in Germany; and

Whereas, although the Yalta and Potsdam agreements are the closest approach to a peace settlement for World War II existing today, and although these two agreements, by their inexpedient provisions, have cost the United States untold billions for defense, occupation costs, and foreign economic support, and have led the free world to the brink of another global war, these agreements were made in secrecy and without congressional participation, approval, or ratification: Now, therefore, be it

Resolved by the House of Representatives (the Senate concurring), That it is the sense of the Congress of the United States that the text of the agreements, private or otherwise, concluded in 1945 at Yalta and Potsdam should be forthwith made public and re-examined to the end that a basis shall be found to accomplish the universal desire of all the people of the United States, to wit, a just and equitable peace.

APPENDIX M: House Joint Resolution 162

Introduced by Congressman Kersten on February 2, 1953.

Whereas the private agreement, signed at Yalta, Union of Soviet Socialist Republics, on February 11, 1945, by J. Stalin, Franklin D. Roosevelt, and Winston S. Churchill, represents a denial of the principles of national freedom and self-government, as expressed in the North Atlantic Charter and our Declaration of Independence, which principles have always been cherished by the American people and for which millions fought in World War II; and

Whereas the Yalta agreement was not legal or binding on the United States since it was signed by Mr. Franklin D. Roosevelt as an individual and was not signed by him in his official capacity as President of the United States; nor was the agreement approved by the Senate of the United States as is required of any political agreement under section 2 of article II of the United States Constitution; and

Whereas, under the Yalta agreement, Mr. Roosevelt attempted to commit the United States to an infringement of the sovereign rights of Poland and the Republic of China by attempting to make concessions to the Soviets at their expense, in violation of treaties and of the natural law itself; and

Whereas, specifically, the Yalta agreement attempted to sanction Soviet domination of Eastern Europe and of East Asia, the betrayal of Poland and the mutilation of its natural boundaries, the transfer of the national allegiance of millions of persons without plebiscite or other recognition of their rights to self-determination, and the uprooting of other millions of persons; and

Whereas the Yalta agreement violated the national sovereign rights of the Republic of China by attempting to grant territorial concessions to the Soviets and a preferred position in Manchuria, the richest and most industrialized area of China, in violation of the Nine-Power Treaty of February 6, 1922, and the Sino-Soviet Treaty of 1924; and

Whereas, under the Yalta agreement, Mr. Roosevelt agreed to take measures on the advice of Marshal Stalin, a foreign despot, to obtain the concurrence in the agreement of Generalissimo Chiang Kai-shek, an obligation beyond his power or right as President of the United States or as a private individual to perform; and

Whereas J. Stalin, a party to the Yalta agreement, has consistently disregarded the provisions of the agreement which he has found inconvenient to honor, including the provision for free and unfettered elections in Poland and the provisions for treating Germany as an economic unit and for encouraging free political parties in Germany; and

Whereas the Soviets, under the direction of J. Stalin, have also forcibly interfered in the internal affairs of Albania, Bulgaria, Czechoslovakia, Hungary, Rumania, and Yugoslavia, thus making it impossible for the respective peoples of such nations to hold free elections to form governments of their own choice; and

Whereas the denial by the United States of the validity of the Yalta agreement for the above reasons will re-emphasize to the people of the world the adherence of the United States to the principles of the Atlantic Charter and our own Declaration of Independence, and will serve to give hope to the subjugated peoples of the world through the knowledge that the United States is mindful of their desire to achieve independence and self-government: Therefore be it

Resolved by the Senate and the House of Representatives of the United States of America in Congress assembled, That the private agreement signed at Yalta, Union of Soviet Socialist Republics, in February, 1945, is hereby declared to be null and void and of no binding force whatsoever on the United States.

APPENDIX N: House Concurrent Resolution 68

Introduced by Congressman Bentley on February 18, 1953.

Resolved by the House of Representatives (the Senate concurring), That the Congress finds the Government of the Soviet Union and its satellites have followed a course of systematic enslavement of peoples in flagrant violations of their agreements with the United States and other free nations.

Sec. 2. (a) The Soviet pattern of subjugation has included numerous violations of pledges contained in the Protocol of the Proceedings of the Crimean Conference of February, 1945 (referred to in this resolution as the "Yalta agreement"). Examples of such violations are given in the subsequent subsections of this section.

(b) (1) The Yalta agreement provided that the Governments of the United States, the United Kingdom, and the Soviet Union would work together "in assisting the peoples liberated from domination of Nazi Germany and the peoples of the former Axis satellite states of Europe to solve by democratic means their pressing political and economic problems." It declared that European reconstruction "must be achieved by processes which will enable the liberated peoples to destroy the last vestiges of nazism and fascism and to create democratic institutions of their own choice." It provided that the three Governments would "jointly assist the people in any European liberated state or former Axis satellite state in Europe where in their judgement conditions require . . . to form interim governmental authorities broadly representative of all democratic elements in the population and pledged to the earliest possible establishment through free elections of governments responsive to the will of the people . . ."

(2) Despite the pledges quoted in paragraph (1), the Government of the Soviet Union has consistently refused to cooperate with the Governments of the United States and the United Kingdom in creating democratic institutions in liberated Europe, but instead, through local Communist parties and through its own agents and armed forces, has subverted the will of the people to totalitarianism, in negation of fundamental freedoms, in Albania, Bulgaria, Czechoslovakia, Estonia, Hungary, Latvia, Lithuania, Poland, and Rumania. In 1945 Soviet authorities demanded and obtained the replacement of the secretary general of Bulgaria's largest political party; in 1947 Soviet troops arrested the former secretary general of the Smallholders Party in Hungary; and in the election of 1946 in Rumania, Soviet troops broke up meetings of the opposition. These are only three of the innumerable examples of Soviet interference with democratic processes in liberated Europe.

(3) Despite the pledges quoted in paragraph (1), the Government of the Soviet Union consistently refused to cooperate with the Governments of the United States and the United Kingdom to assist in solving the pressing economic problems of liberated Europe. While refusing United States' proposals for tripartite examination of the economic problems of Hungary and Rumania, the Soviet Government has forced discriminatory economic agreements upon Hungary, and has preclusively exploited the Rumanian economy. There are many similar examples of economic exploitation by the Soviet Government in these and other countries of liberated Europe.

(c) The Yalta agreement provided that the Polish Government "shall be pledged to the holding of free and unfettered elections as soon as possible on the basis of universal suffrage and secret ballot. In these elections all democratic and anti-Nazi parties shall have the right to take part and put forward candidates." Despite this pledge, when it became apparent that the Polish Government was ruthlessly suppressing democratic opposition in the 1947 elections, the Soviet Government refused to join the Governments of the United States and the United Kingdom in calling for a strict fulfillment of Poland's obligations.

(d) The Yalta agreement provided that "the final delimitation of the Western frontier of Poland should . . . await the Peace Conference." Despite this provision, the Government of the Soviet Union has repeatedly maintained that the Oder-Neisse line constitutes the definitive German-Polish frontier; in 1950 the Soviet controlled Government of Poland and Eastern Germany signed an agreement to that effect.

Sec. 3. Repeated violations of the Yalta agreement have confirmed the hope of the negotiators that the Soviet Government would fulfill its obligations under the agreement were groundless. In return for worthless promises by the Soviet Government, certain concessions were made in the Yalta agreement which have facilitated the enslavement of peoples by the Soviet Union and its satellites.

Sec. 4. It is, therefore, the sense of Congress that (1) the United States should recognize no commitment contained in the Yalta agreement which purports to confer upon the Soviet Union any right, title, or interest in or to any territory formerly belonging to any other nation of Europe; and (2) in reaffirmation of the position taken by the United States Senate in giving its advice and consent to the peace treaty with Japan on March 20, 1952, the United States should recognize no commitment contained in the Yalta agreement which purports to confer upon the Soviet Union any right, title or interest in or to South Sakhalin Islands, the Island of Shikotan, or any other territory, rights, or interests possessed by Japan on December 7, 1941.

Sec. 5. The Congress joins with the President in declaring, as he did in his address to the Congress on February 2, 1953, that the United States will "never acquiesce in the enslavement of any people in order to purchase fancied gain for ourselves," and that "this Government recognizes no kind of commitment contained in secret understandings of the past with foreign governments which permit this kind of enslavement."

APPENDIX O: House Joint Resolution 200

Introduced by Congressman Vorys on February 23, 1953.

Joining with the President of the United States in a declaration regarding the subjugation of free peoples by the Soviet Union.

Whereas during World War II, representatives of the United States, during the course of secret conferences, entered into various international agreements or understandings concerning other peoples; and

Whereas the leaders of the Soviet Communist Party, who now control Russia, have, in violation of the clear intent of these agreements or understandings, subjected the peoples concerned, including whole nations, to the domination of a totalitarian imperialism; and

Whereas such forcible absorption of free peoples into an aggressive despotism increases the threat against the security of all remaining free peoples including our own; and

Whereas the people of the United States, true to their tradition and heritage of freedom, are never acquiescent in such enslavement of any peoples; and

Whereas it is appropriate that the Congress join with the President in giving expression to the desires and hopes of the people of the United States: Therefore be it

Resolved by the Senate and House of Representatives of the United States of America in Congress assembled, That the Congress join with the President in declaring that the United States rejects any interpretations or application of any international agreement or understandings, made during the course of World War II, which have been perverted to bring about the subjugation of free peoples; and be it further

Resolved, That Congress join with the President of the United States in proclaiming the hope that the peoples who have been subjugated to the captivity of Soviet despotism shall again enjoy the right of self-determination within a framework which will maintain the peace; that they shall again have the right to choose a form of government under which they will live, and that sovereign rights of self-government shall be restored to them all in accordance with the pledges of the Atlantic Charter.

APPENDIX P: Senate Resolution 75

Introduced by Senator McCarthy on March 11, 1955.

Whereas the 1952 Republican platform, adopted July 10, 1952, declared that "the Government of the United States, under Republican leadership, will repudiate all commitments contained in secret understandings such as those of Yalta which aid Communist enslavements"; and

Whereas the President in his address to Congress on February 2, 1953, declared that the United States will never "acquiesce in the enslavement of any people in order to purchase fancied gain for ourselves," and that "this Government recognizes no kind of commitment contained in secret understandings of the past with foreign governments which permit this kind of enslavement"; and

Whereas the Yalta agreement has not as yet been repudiated: Therefore be it:

Resolved, that it is the sense of the Senate that the President should, and he is hereby requested to, take such action as may be necessary to repudiate the Yalta agreement and to relieve the United States of all commitments undertaken by it in such agreement.

APPENDIX Q: Prominent Congressional Critics of Yalta

Identifying senatorial or congressional districts as specifically isolationist or ethnic presents real methodological problems. Many factors influence the voting behavior of the electorate and the voting record of the politician. A politician's seeking to curry the favor of groups with special interests does not necessarily confirm the power of those groups; he may be trying to play it safe. Moreover, a politician can affect the interests of his constituency as much as they can affect him. His domestic conservatism might help to establish his foreign policy arguments, and although ethnic minorities might respond to intended ethnic appeals, their real concerns might be domestic issues: Civil rights and open occupancy, not the liberation of Poland, might be the central concern of a Polish-American constituency.

Recently, scholars have recognized the complexity of public opinion and have tried to avoid sweeping generalizations. Three recently-published books[1] offer methodological techniques to assess the postwar foreign policy debate. While the approaches of the authors, the nature of their scholarship, and their conclusions vary, their books offer valuable insights for identifying the influences that explain the position on foreign policy taken by certain groups in the nation.

In this appendix, I shall use three criteria to list those senators and congressmen who became prominent critics of Yalta. The first list presents those Republican senators elected in 1946; the second, those senators and congressmen who represented areas in which there were strong beliefs in ruralism, isolationism, and conservatism; the third, those congressmen who represented areas in which there was a population concentration of Polish-Americans. These criteria do not lead to mutually exclusive lists, and the lists are intended only to identify political phenomena that significantly influenced the Yalta debate.

Those congressmen and senators who represented Polish-American or rural-isolationist-conservative districts and those Republican senators who were elected in 1946 provided distinctive sources for opposition to

1. Michael P. Rogin, *The Intellectuals and McCarthy*; Leroy N. Rieselbach, *The Roots of Isolationism: Congressional Voting and Presidential Leadership in Foreign Policy*; and Norman Graebner, *The New Isolationism*.

Yalta. Representing a predominantly Polish-American constituency sharp-
ened the office-holder's focus on Yalta, and representing a rural, isolationist
district increased the office-holder's opposition to Roosevelt's methods at
Yalta. Nonetheless, the position adopted by individuals elected from these
districts varied, and neither the ethnic nor the rural-isolationist conservatism of the district can be pinpointed as the office-holder's principal motivation for opposing Yalta. Unless they acted diametrically opposite to
their constituents' views, conservatives elected from safe districts (as would
be true of all individuals elected from safe districts) would have greater
leeway on foreign policy matters. One such conservative was Alvin Bentley,
a Republican congressman from Michigan. Bentley had resigned the foreign service to enter politics, and he represented a distinctly conservative
constituency. He was not an expert, but he used his seeming expertise to
influence the foreign policy views of his constituents. Also, his solid conservatism and his reputation as a prominent businessman added weight
to his foreign service experience and enabled him to act independently
on foreign policy matters. Conversely, Southern Democrats had great leeway in supporting the Administration's foreign policy — as Tom Conally,
James Richards, and John Kee did — or opposing it — as John Rankin did.
Bentley's and Rankin's examples illustrate the methodological problems of
using the rhetoric or voting record of a politician to try to identify the
views of the politician's constituents. Moreover, the internationalism of
Southern Democrats was not abstract. Indeed, Southern Democrats bitterly
opposed the United Nations Covenant on Human Rights, a form of internationalism, and cited States' rights to support the Bricker Amendment.

Further, diverse economic interest groups affected the position adopted
by a representative. A Southern Democrat's or a New England Republican's position on foreign trade reflected, not internationalism, but concern
over the cotton trade or foreign commerce — much as the protectionism
of a Nevada congressman reflected, not isolationism, but concern over
copper imports.

Lastly, and perhaps less obviously, those Republican senators elected
in the Republican landslide of 1946, because of the peculiarities of that
election, did not necessarily represent their constituents' dominant views
of foreign policy. Their positions and that of their constituencies would
converge as the Cold War evolved and intensified. Their election in 1946
resulted from their domestic conservatism and from public disaffection
with the leadership of President Truman and the continuance of wartime
controls. Foreign policy questions were less central in 1946 than they
would be in 1950.

With these disclaimers, I shall use these three criteria to identify congressmen and senators who became prominent critics of Yalta.
These Republicans were elected to the Senate in 1946.

Arthur Watkins (Utah)	William Knowland (California)
Harry Cain (Washington)	John Bricker (Ohio)
William Jenner (Indiana)	James Kem (Missouri)
Zales Ecton (Montana)	George Malone (Nevada)
Joseph McCarthy (Wisconsin)	Edward Martin (Pennsylvania)

Isolationism and domestic conservatism were especially important in the
rural areas of New York, Ohio, Indiana, Illinois, Wisconsin, Missouri, Michigan, Nebraska, Kansas, the Dakotas, Utah, and Idaho.

Congressmen:	Senators:
Fred Busbey (Illinois)	George Malone (Nevada)

Thomas Jenkins (Ohio)
Lawrence Smith (Wisconsin)
William Cole (Missouri)
Daniel Reed (New York)
Paul Shafer (Michigan)
Clare Hoffman (Michigan)
Roy Woodruff (Michigan)
Dewey Short (Missouri)
Robert Grant (Indiana)
Frederick Smith (Ohio)
Ralph Church (Illinois)
Howard Buffett (Nebraska)
Alvin Bentley (Michigan)
Leslie Arends (Illinois)
Gerald Ford (Michigan)
Carl Curtis (Nebraska)
Charles Vursell (Illinois)
Clarence Brown (Ohio)
William Lemke (North Dakota)
Charles Halleck (Indiana)
Noah Mason (Illinois)
John Sanborn (Idaho)
George Dondero (Michigan)
Arthur Miller (Nebraska)
John Wood (Idaho)
E. Ross Adair (Indiana)

Hugh Butler (Nebraska)
Robert Taft (Ohio)
Styles Bridges (New Hampshire)
Henry Dworshak (Idaho)
William Langer (North Dakota)
C. Wayland Brooks (Illinois)
Kenneth Wherry (Nebraska)
Patrick McCarran (Nevada)
Homer Ferguson (Michigan)
Arthur Watkins (Utah)
Homer Capehart (Indiana)
William Jenner (Indiana)
John Bricker (Ohio)
Francis Case (South Dakota)*
Andrew Schoeppel (Kansas)
George Bender (Ohio)*
Karl Mundt (South Dakota)*
Charles Potter (Michigan)*
Everett Dirksen (Illinois)*
* denotes a former congressman

The Polish-American vote had particular impact in New York City, Chicago, Cleveland, Detroit, Milwaukee, Gary, Buffalo, upstate Wisconsin, and the industrial areas of Connecticut, New Jersey, and Pennsylvania.

John Lesinski, Jr. (16th, Michigan)
John Lesinski, Sr. (16th, Michigan)
Thaddeus Machrowicz (1st, Michigan)
Alvin O'Konski (10th, Wisconsin)
Harold Donohue (4th, Massachusetts)
Daniel Flood (11th, Pennsylvania)
Alfred Sieminski (13th, New Jersey)
John Kluczynski (5th, Illinois)
John Butler (44th, New York)
Edmund Radwan (43rd, New York)
Thaddeus Wasielewski (4th, Wisconsin)
Antoni Sadlak (at Large, Connecticut)
Augustine Kelley (27th, Pennsylvania)

John Dingell (15th, Michigan)
Philip Philbin (3rd, Massachusetts)
Edward Garmatz (3rd, Maryland)
Michael Feighan (20th, Ohio)
Joseph Ryter [at Large, Connecticut)
Clement Zablocki (4th, Wisconsin)
Thomas Lane (7th, Massachusetts)
Ray Madden (1st, Indiana)
Martin Gorski (5th, Illinois)
Chester Gorski (44th, New York)
Louis Rabaut (14th, Michigan)
George Sadowski (1st, Michigan)
John Rooney (12th, New York)
Thomas Gordon (8th, Illinois)
Charles Kersten (5th, Wisconsin)

APPENDIX R: Congressional and Presidential Vote, Polish-American Districts (or Counties), 1945–1954; Cook County Vote, 1948–1954 (Congressmen)

The diversity of electoral districts and the nature of available voting statistics makes it extremely difficult to identify a specifically Polish-American vote and thus assess the potential impact of Yalta on Polish-American voting behavior. Not that Polish-Americans are geographically dispersed. They usually live in the major urban, industrial centers, and they constitute a significant voting bloc. These centers include New York City; Buffalo, New York; Jersey City, New Jersey; the industrial towns of Connecticut; Boston; Detroit; Chicago; Milwaukee; Gary, Indiana; northwestern Wisconsin; Cleveland; Pittsburgh; and Philadelphia. This concentration has led to the election of Polish-American congressmen or of congressmen who actively court the Polish vote by ethnic appeals.

An analysis of the impact of Yalta within these congressional districts, identified in Appendix Q, poses certain methodological problems.

The first problem involves identifying the Polish-American precincts of an identifiable Polish-dominated district. A precinct-by-precinct breakdown is not readily available, and votes cast within the larger congressional district blur the specifically Polish vote. Further, it is more difficult to isolate the ethnic character of this vote from other considerations — the personality of the candidate, the efficiency of the campaign apparatus, the general tide of national politics, and the greater concern over domestic issues.

Available statistics, however, do confirm the impact of Yalta in the 1946 and 1952 elections. Although it was important in the 1946 congressional contests, Yalta benefited the Republicans primarily in national campaigns, particularly the campaign in 1952. After 1945, the Polish-Americans' allegiance to the Democratic party did break, undoubtedly for both economic and foreign policy reasons. The real impact of that shift affected the results of the national election.[1] Again, certain problems of documentation arise. Before 1952, presidential voting statistics were compiled by county, not by congressional district. Thus, in the accompanying chart, the presidential elections of 1944 and 1948 offer little comparison with either that of 1952 or the corresponding congressional vote.

I have compiled two charts to confirm the potential impact of Yalta on the traditionally Democratic Polish-American vote. The first chart consists of voting results for the congressional and presidential contests for the period 1944 through 1954. I have broken down these results, as noted, by congressional district where possible; where I found it impossible, I have enumerated the county vote. Because the 1952 and 1954 district lines in New York and Pennsylvania were based on 1950 census returns that resulted in the realignment of districts, I have so listed the old and new numbers of the revised districts. In the second chart, I have compiled a congressional vote profile of Cook County (Chicago) for the 1948 through 1954 elections. In this chart, I have identified first the total Democratic and Republican vote, then the vote by precincts that can be identified as Polish American.

---

1. Louis Gerson in a recent book, *The Hyphenate in Recent American Politics and Diplomacy*, offers an explanation of the role of ethnic appeals involving foreign policy. Gerson's account, in part because it is overdrawn and methodologically uncritical, fails to distinguish between special groups or individuals and the general constituency. Because it does not discuss the general context of the politics of this period and the conservatism of some of these congressmen or commentators, his account is of limited value. It is, however, the only comprehensive treatment of the Polish-American vote and the postwar debate about Yalta.

Congressional and Presidential Vote, Polish-American Districts (or Counties), 1944–1954

| | 1944 | | | | 1946 | |
| | Congressional | | Presidential | | Congressional | |
	Dem.	Rep.	Dem.	Rep.	Dem.	Rep.
Illinois, 5th	38,370	11,929	1,275,367[1]	924,659[1]	34,904	13,859
Illinois, 8th	39,866	10,474			38,317	11,266
Indiana, 1st	75,635	46,968	75,066	48,147	51,809	46,677
Maryland, 3rd	39,032	14,046	163,493[2]	112,817[2]	24,347	13,761
Massachusetts, 3rd	78,848	49,300	795,891[3]	663,959[3]	69,038	42,033
Massachusetts, 4th	76,097	60,967			59,847	58,663
Massachusetts, 7th	78,008	36,877			59,871	37,250
Michigan, 1st	103,782	24,542	554,670[4]	316,270[4]	57,753	29,293
Michigan, 14th	98,988	76,358			60,808	69,968
Michigan, 15th	100,879	57,070			59,111	54,296
Michigan, 16th	95,483	59,456			57,773	52,376
New Jersey, 13th	89,736	38,336	191,354[5]	117,087[5]	69,440	36,270
New York, 12th [14th, 1952]	51,411	42,007	758,270[6]	393,926[6]	36,399	31,052
New York, 43rd [41st, 1952]	71,216	74,366	195,905[7]	185,975[7]	38,108	71,758
New York, 44th [42nd, 1952]	72,164	72,402			49,798	67,495
Ohio, 20th	75,218	23,945	330,659[8]	217,824[8]	49,670	24,476
Pennsylvania, 11th	71,843	65,922	496,367[9]	346,380[9]	56,570	58,413
Pennsylvania, 27th [21st, 1952]	61,203	41,289	350,690[10]	261,218[10]	46,137	41,030
Wisconsin, 4th	103,583	55,375	205,282[11]	142,448[11]	44,938	49,144
Wisconsin, 5th	88,606	78,834			59,764	76,364
Wisconsin, 10th	29,773	54,731	53,224	47,027	32,238	40,263
Connecticut, at Large	424,146	397,725	435,146	390,527	277,872	377,972
Total Vote	1,963,887	1,392,919	5,881,384	4,168,264	1,334,512	1,303,679

1. Cook County
2. Baltimore County
3. Essex, Hampden, Hampshire, Middlesex, Suffolk, and Worchester Counties
4. Wayne County
5. Hudson County
6. Kings County
7. Erie County
8. Cuyahoga County
9. Philadelphia County
10. Allegheny County
11. Milwaukee County

Congressional and Presidential Vote, Polish-American Districts (or Counties), 1944–1954

	1948 Congressional		1948 Presidential		1950 Congressional	
	Dem.	Rep.	Dem.	Rep.	Dem.	Rep.
Illinois, 5th	43,610	14,660	1,216,636[1]	1,015,800[1]	91,589	48,052
Illinois, 8th	101,098	54,316			77,736	53,305
Indiana, 1st	78,898	50,194	77,025	51,413	62,666	56,063
Maryland, 3rd	32,138	13,131	134,615[2]	110,879[2]	27,646	14,430
Massachusetts, 3rd	104,601	36,855			93,591	37,258
Massachusetts, 4th	89,064	61,448	892,311[3]	637,171[3]	76,881	57,483
Massachusetts, 7th	100,333	26,339			91,854	24,307
Michigan, 1st	101,954	19,609			75,478	14,619
Michigan, 14th	99,227	74,474	489,654[4]	321,773[4]	76,938	72,137
Michigan, 15th	92,579	49,286			73,238	40,865
Michigan, 16th	97,826	57,730			80,229	50,873
New Jersey, 13th	84,487	39,661	182,879[5]	111,113[5]	55,008	43,851
New York, 12th [14th, 1952]	55,021	29,061	579,922[6]	330,494[6]	42,396	22,796
New York, 43rd [41st, 1952]	77,388	66,729	197,618[7]	175,118[7]	58,327	61,781
New York, 44th [42nd, 1952]	79,795	71,275			66,541	69,260
Ohio, 20th	64,241	. . . . .	257,958[8]	214,889[8]	60,565	21,044
Pennsylvania, 11th	68,628	63,797	432,699[9]	425,962[9]	77,466	65,015
Pennsylvania, 27th [21st, 1952]	64,943	39,517	326,303[10]	253,272[10]	53,229	40,037
Wisconsin, 4th	89,391	63,161	187,637[11]	138,672[11]	83,564	53,702
Wisconsin, 5th	91,072	72,782			71,203	75,955
Wisconsin, 10th	39,523	52,124	56,621	41,773	35,281	46,722
Connecticut, at Large	429,348	433,311	423,297	437,754	426,485	433,912
Total Vote	2,085,165	1,389,460	5,455,175	4,266,083	1,857,764	1,403,467

1. Cook County
2. Baltimore County
3. Essex, Hampden, Hampshire, Middlesex, Suffolk, and Worchester Counties
4. Wayne County
5. Hudson County
6. Kings County
7. Erie County
8. Cuyahoga County
9. Philadelphia County
10. Allegheny County
11. Milwaukee County

Congressional and Presidential Vote, Polish-American Districts (or Counties), 1944–1954

	1952 Congressional		1952 Presidential		1954 Congressional	
	Dem.	Rep.	Dem.	Rep.	Dem.	Rep.
Illinois, 5th	104,900	57,775	99,141	62,277	92,780	33,987
Illinois, 8th	87,871	61,048	88,605	63,951	74,837	34,535
Indiana, 1st	93,187	71,617	90,721	74,073	81,217	50,439
Maryland, 3rd	60,659	24,879	57,614	35,677	45,531	.....
Massachusetts, 3rd	108,743	52,348	38,346	80,658	110,013	.....
Massachusetts, 4th	93,530	77,536	74,890	100,331	83,053	62,318
Massachusetts, 7th	105,662	34,663	85,019	60,534	102,659	.....
Michigan, 1st	118,695	21,442	117,151	27,689	91,435	11,731
Michigan, 14th	117,027	103,366	109,925	114,471	97,297	69,503
Michigan, 15th	109,109	54,236	105,198	62,536	85,100	31,815
Michigan, 16th	133,215	84,998	126,181	96,445	121,557	56,815
New Jersey, 13th	72,987	54,581	73,436	59,570	60,108	26,638
New York, 12th [14th, 1952]	91,952	45,004	80,347	58,626	61,879	21,598
New York, 43rd [41st, 1952]	75,552	95,755	79,405	96,773	45,144	77,259
New York, 44th [42nd, 1952]	81,201	100,434	80,593	106,154	60,880	82,707
Ohio, 20th	109,211	58,271	96,705	86,762	81,304	38,865
Pennsylvania, 11th	79,722	80,310	72,579	88,967	70,254	67,682
Pennsylvania, 27th [21st, 1952]	73,223	65,252	80,068	58,923	70,224	44,789
Wisconsin, 4th	131,098	72,869	106,200	99,096	100,120	40,723
Wisconsin, 5th	105,013	112,048	98,274	120,381	77,208	70,565
Wisconsin, 10th	35,597	73,527	47,665	65,449	33,219	49,325
Connecticut, at Large	489,645	601,238	481,649	611,012	455,887	474,585
Total Vote	2,477,799	2,003,197	2,289,712	2,230,355	2,101,706	1,345,879

Cook County Vote, 1948–1954 (Congressmen)

	1948		1950	
	Dem.	Rep.	Dem.	Rep.
Total Vote	1,187,323	850,271	929,286	853,749
Polish-Dominated Vote	608,059	405,063	474,632	395,957
% Total Vote	58%	41%	52%	47%
% Polish-Dominated Vote	50%	42%	51%	46%
% Polish-Dominated Vote Constituted of Total Vote	29%	19%	26%	22%

	1952		1954	
	Dem.	Rep.	Dem.	Rep.
Total Vote	1,116,239	1,024,570	968,536	645,137
Polish-Dominated Vote	566,675	515,065	498,693	326,550
% Total Vote	52%	47%	59%	40%
% Polish-Dominated Vote	50%	50%	51%	50%
% Polish-Dominated Vote Constituted of Total Vote	26%	24%	30%	20%

bibliography

Public Documents

U.S. *Congressional Record*. Vols. XCI–CI.
U.S. Department of State. *The Conferences at Malta and Yalta, 1945* in the *Foreign Relations of the United States Diplomatic Papers*. Washington: U.S. Government Printing Office, 1955.
———. *The Department of State Bulletin*. Vols. XXIII–XXXII.
U.S. House of Representatives. *Report on the Yalta Conference*. Document No. 106. 79th Cong., 1st sess., 1945.
———. *Tenth Interim Report of Hearings Before the Select Committee on Communist Aggression*. 83d Cong., 2d sess., 1954.
———, Committee on Foreign Affairs. *Hearings on H.R. 2616: A Bill to Provide Assistance to Greece and Turkey*. 80th Cong., 1st sess., 1947.
———. *Report of Subcommittee on National and International Movements on the Strategy and Tactics of World Communism: Supplement II Official Protests of the United States Government Against Communist Policies or Action, and Related Correspondence*. 80th Cong., 2d sess., 1948.
———. *Preliminary Hearings on Various Bills Pending Before the Committee*. 82d Cong., 1st sess., 1951.
———. *Hearings on House Joint Resolution 200: Joining with the President of the United States in a Declaration Regarding the Subjugation of Free Peoples by the Soviet Union*. 83d Cong., 1st sess., 1953.
———. *World War II International Agreements and Understandings: Entered into During Secret Conferences Concerning Other People*. 83d Cong., 1st sess., 1953.
———, Special Subcommittee on House Concurrent Resolution 58. *Hearings on Favoring Extension of Diplomatic Relations with the Republics of Ukraine and Byelorussia*. 83d Cong., 1st sess., 1953.
———, Committee on Un-American Activities. *Hearings Regarding Communist Espionage in the United States Government*. 80th Cong., 2d sess., 1948.
U.S. Senate. *The Crimean Conference*. Document No. 8. 79th Cong., 1st sess., 1945.
———. *State Department Loyalty Investigation*. Report No. 2108. 81st Cong., 2d sess., 1950.
———. *Individual Views of Certain Members of the Joint Committee on Armed Services and Foreign Relations of the United States Senate Relating to Hearings on the Dismissal of General MacArthur and the Military Situation in the Far East*. Document No. 69. 82d Cong., 1st sess., 1951.
———. *Review of Bipartisan Foreign Policy Consultation Since World War II*. Document No. 87. 82d Cong., 2d sess., 1952.
———, Committee on Armed Services and Committee on Foreign Relations. *Hearings to Conduct an Inquiry into the Military Situation in the Far East and the Facts Surrounding the Relief of General of the*

Army MacArthur from His Assignment in That Area. 82d Cong., 1st sess., 1951.

————, Committee on Foreign Relations. *Hearings on the Investigation of Far Eastern Policy.* 79th Cong., 1st sess., 1945.

————. *Hearings on the Nomination of Dean G. Acheson to be Secretary of State.* 81st Cong., 1st sess., 1949.

————. *Hearings on the Japanese Peace Treaty and Other Treaties Relating to Security in the Pacific.* 82d Cong., 2d sess., 1952.

————. *Hearings on the Nomination of Charles Bohlen as Ambassador to the Soviet Union.* 83d Cong., 1st sess., 1953.

————. *Hearings on the Nomination of John Foster Dulles as Secretary of State-Designate.* 83d Cong., 1st sess., 1953.

————. *World War II International Agreements and Understandings.* 83d Cong., 1st sess., 1953.

————. *Hearings on Senate Resolution 116 Favoring Discussion at the Coming Geneva Conference of the Status of Nations Under Communist Control.* 84th Cong., 1st sess., 1955.

————. *Hearings on Senate Resolution 75.* 84th Cong., 2d sess., 1956.

————, Subcommittee of the Committee on Foreign Relations. *Hearings on the Nomination of Philip Jessup as United States Representative to the United Nations.* 82d Cong., 1st sess., 1951.

————, Subcommittee of the Committee on the Judiciary. *Hearings on Senate Joint Resolution 130: Treaties and Executive Agreements.* 82d Cong., 2d sess., 1952.

————. *Hearings on Senate Joint Resolution 1 and Senate Joint Resolution 43: Treaties and Executive Agreements.* 83d Cong., 1st sess., 1953.

————. *Majority Report, Minority Report on Treaties and Executive Agreements.* Report No. 412. 83d Cong., 1st sess., 1953.

Addresses and Press Conferences

Douglas, Paul. Address, Dinner Meeting of the Polish-American Congress (Chicago, Illinois), March 8, 1950. Polish-American Congress Library.

Edwards, India. Speech, Ukrainian-American Convention (New York, New York), July 4, 1952. Yalta Conference, Democratic National Committee Files, Truman Library.

Stevenson, Adlai. Speeches, 1952 Campaign. Records of the Publicity Division, Democratic National Committee, Truman Library.

Taft, Robert. Speech, Women's National Republican Club, January 26, 1952. Records of the Publicity Division, Democratic National Committee, Truman Library.

Truman, Harry S. Speeches, April, 1945, to January, 1953. Truman Papers, Truman Library.

————. Press conferences, transcripts of, April 17, 1945, to January 15, 1953. Records of the White House Official Reporter, Truman Papers, Truman Library.

————. Press conferences, transcripts of, May 15, 1945, to August 31, 1950. Records of the White House Official Reporter, Ross Papers, Truman Library.

————. Press conferences, transcripts of, December 18, 1950, to September 12, 1952. Records of the White House Official Reporter, Short Papers, Truman Library.

Campaign Material

DEMOCRATIC:

Democratic National Committee. *Campaign Issues . . . 1946: A Handbook for Candidates, Speakers and Workers of the Democratic Party.* 1946.
———. *Capital Comment.* May 3, 1947–July 29, 1950.
———. *Democratic Digest.* May, 1946–August, 1955.
———. *Fact Sheet No. 9. Foreign Policy.* 1948.
———. *Fact Sheet No. 10.* August 17, 1948.
———. *Fact Sheet No. 11. Communism and Loyalty.* 1948.
———. *Fact Sheet RD-28.* April 29, 1952.
———. *Fact Sheet RD-53-6.* February 20, 1953.
———. *Fact Sheet RD-53-38. The Democratic Record Against Communism in America.* December 9, 1953.
———. *Fact Sheet RD-55-7. Special Memorandum on the Yalta Agreement.* March 17, 1955.
———. *Fact Sheet RD-55-9. Reactions and Effects of the Release of the Yalta Papers.* March 26, 1955.
———. *The 1956 Democratic Fact Book: The Issues and the Record, 1952–1956.* 1956.
———. *How to Win in '52: The Facts About the Democratic Road to Prosperity, Peace and Freedom.* 1952.
———. *The Truth About Yalta.* n.d.
———, Research Division. Files, 1945–1952.
———, Library Files. Thomas Dewey, 1948 Campaign, 1951–1954.
———, Library Files. Robert Taft, 1950–1952.
Truman for President Club of Minnesota. Resolution Endorsing Truman, 1948.
Official Report of the Democratic National Convention, 1948.
Official Report of the Proceedings of the Democratic National Convention, 1952.

REPUBLICAN:

Republican National Committee. *Background to Korea.* 1950.
———. *Betrayal! Over 100,000,000 Eastern Europeans by the Democratic Administration.* 1952.
———. *Republican Speakers: Waste, Corruption, Communism: The Sorry Record of Twenty Years of Red Influence In and On Two Democratic Administrations.* 1952.
———. *Dewey in '48: He Gets Things Done.* 1948.
———. *The 80th Congress Delivers!* 1948.
———. *Fighting Men Won the War!!! Floundering Politicians Lost the Peace.* 1952.
———. *How a GREAT TEAM Worked for YOU! The Record of IKE and the 83rd Congress.* 1954.
———. *Red Herring and Whitewash: The Record of Communism in Government.* 1950.
———. *Republican Accomplishments in the Eighty-second Congress.* 1952.
———. *The Republican News.* 1945–1950.
———. *The Republican Party: Its History in Brief.* 1952.

————. *Republican Policy of Liberation or Democratic Policy of Containment.* 1952.

————. *The Republican Record (1953–1960).* 1960.

————. *Republican Speakers: Here Is Your Ammunition on Taxes, Labor, Foreign Policy.* 1952.

————. *Statement of Republican Principles and Objectives.* 1952.

————. *Adlai Stevenson on the Red Menace: The Communist Issue, Alger Hiss, Russia and Communism Abroad.* October, 1952.

————. *Straight from the Shoulder.* 1954–1955.

————. *The Veterans Case Against the Democrat-New Deal.* 1948.

————. *Veterans the Peace for which You Fought.* 1948.

————. *Veterans . . . Look! Before You Vote.* 1948.

————. News Releases, 1948 and 1952 Campaigns.

————, Research Division. Files, 1945–1955.

Republican Senate Policy Committee. *ABC's of U.S. Foreign Policy, 1945–1960: A Factual Survey by the Republican Policy Committee Staff under the Direction of U.S. Senator Styles Bridges.* May, 1960.

————. *Chronology of Secret Agreements at Yalta.* February 1, 1946.

————. *Highlights of the Yalta Papers and Related Data.* March, 1955.

————. *Major Issues of 1952.* August, 1952.

————. *Secrecy in Government: The Growth of Federal Censorship, Concealment and Deception under 20 Years of Democratic Administration 1933–1952.* September 18, 1952.

————. *Supporting Material on Issue No. 2: The Democratic Administration's Fatal Compromise with Communism: The Administration's Compromise with Communism in the United States Army.* September, 1950.

Citizens for Eisenhower-Nixon. "The Man Who Can Bring Us Durable Peace." 1952.

National Committee of the Jefferson Party. "Crime, Corruption and Communism." 1952.

National Republican Congressional Committee. Speech Kit, 1952.

Republican National Finance Committee. *Republican Fact Book.* Autumn, 1948.

Republican National Precinct Workers. *Mission Accomplished.* 1953.

Republican State Central Committee, Lansing, Michigan. *Do You Want War . . . Or a Sound Foreign Policy?* 1952.

Taft Committee. *A Realistic Defense and Foreign Policy.* 1952.

————. *Why I Oppose Truman's Foreign Policy.* 1952.

Official Report of the Proceedings of the Twenty-fourth Republican National Convention, 1948.

Official Report of the Proceedings of the Twenty-fifth Republican National Convention, 1952.

Interviews and Correspondence

Acheson, Dean (Secretary of State, 1949–1953). Interview, July 17, 1962.

————. Letter, April 25, 1963.

Bailey, James (Administrative Assistant to Senator Alexander Wiley). Interview, July 20, 1962.

Baarslag, Carl (Staff of the Republican Senate Policy Committee). Interview, July 25, 1962.

Barron, Bryton (State Department official who resigned in 1955 over alleged censorship of the Yalta papers). Telephone interview, July 24, 1962.

Bentley, Alvin (Congressman, 1953–1961). Letter, February 1, 1963.

Butler, Paul (Chairman, Democratic National Committee). Letter to Walter Johnson, April 5, 1955.

Crawford, Boyd (Staff Administrator, House Foreign Affairs Committee, 1939 to the present). Interview, July 10, 1962.

Dirksen, Everett (Congressman, 1933–1949, and Senator, 1951–1969). Interview, July 18, 1962.

Fellers, Bonner (Brigadier General [Ret.], former Military Secretary to General MacArthur, head of the Citizens Foreign Aid Committee of the For America party). Interview, July 19, 1962.

Hale, Robert (Congressman, 1943–1959). Interview, July 16, 1962.

Johnson, Walter (Professor of History, University of Chicago). Letter to Paul Butler, April 1, 1955.

———. Letter to Karl Mundt, January 25, 1950.

———. Letters to Philip Stern, April 28, 1955, and May 9, 1955.

Kania, Joseph (President, Polish Roman Catholic Union of America). Telegram to the President, April 17, 1947. Truman Papers, OF 463, Truman Library.

Kersten, Charles (Congressman, 1947–1949, and 1951–1955). Interview, August 3, 1962.

Lesinski, John, Jr. (Congressman, 1951–1965). Interview, July 11, 1962.

Mason, Noah (Congressman, 1937–1963). Interview, July 11, 1962.

Miscellaneous authors. Letters to the President on Foreign Policy, April, 1945, to December, 1952. Truman Papers, OF 386, Truman Library.

———. Letters to the President on the 1952 Campaign. Truman Papers, OF 2004N, Truman Library.

———. Letters to the President on Poland, April, 1945, to December, 1952. Truman Papers, OF 463, Truman Library.

———. Letters to the President on U.S.-U.S.S.R. Relations, April, 1945, to December, 1952. Truman Papers, OF 220, Truman Library.

———. Mail Reports. Recap of Mail Received by the White House, March 11, 1949, to December, 1951. Truman Library.

———. Telegram Reports. Recap of the Telegrams Received by the White House, July 22, 1949, to December, 1951. Truman Library.

Mundt, Karl (Congressman, 1939–1948, and Senator, 1949 to the present). Interview, July 23, 1962.

———. Letter to Walter Johnson, February 2, 1950.

O'Konski, Alvin (Congressman, 1943 to the present). Interview, July 10, 1962.

Rankin, William H. Memorandum to the President on Radio Broadcast of H. V. Kaltenborn, April 2, 1947. Truman Papers, OF 386, Truman Library.

Reedy, George (Head, Democratic Senate Policy Committee, 1953–1960, and assistant to Lyndon Johnson). Interview, July 13, 1962.

Rourke, William (Administrative Assistant to Congressman Harold Donohue). Interview, July 9, 1962.

Shaw, Jack (Assistant to Senator Homer Capehart). Interview, July 16, 1962.

Sparkman, John (Congressman, 1937–1946, Democratic vice-presidential nominee in 1952, and Senator, 1946 to the present). Interview, July 19, 1962.

Stern, Philip (Research Director, Democratic National Committee). Letter to Walter Johnson, May 2, 1955.

Truman, Harry S. (Senator, 1934–1945, and President of the United States, 1945–1953). Interview, June 28, 1963.

Vorys, John (Congressman, 1939–1959). Letter, September 12, 1962.

Webb, Charles (Legislative Assistant to Senator John Bricker). Interview, July 24, 1962.

Watkins, Arthur (Senator, 1946–1959). Interview, July 21, 1962.

Wiewiura, Joseph (Public Relations Director, Polish-American Congress). Interview, June 20, 1963.

Zablocki, Clement (Congressman, 1949 to the present). Interview, July 24, 1962.

Books

Agar, Herbert. *The Price of Power: America Since 1945*. Chicago: The University of Chicago Press, 1957.

Allen, Robert S., and William V. Shannon. *The Truman Merry-Go-Round*. New York: The Vanguard Press, Inc., 1950.

Almond, Gabriel A. *The American People and Foreign Policy*. New York: Harcourt, Brace and Company, 1950.

Alperovitz, Gar. *Atomic Diplomacy: Hiroshima and Potsdam*. New York: Simon & Schuster, Inc., 1965.

Baldwin, Hanson W. *Great Mistakes of the War*. New York: Harper and Brothers, 1949.

Barron, Bryton. *Inside the State Department: A Candid Appraisal of the Bureaucracy*. New York: Comet Press, 1956.

Beaty, John. *The Iron Curtain Over America*. Dallas: Wilkinson Publishing Company, 1951.

Bell, Daniel, ed. *The Radical Right*. Garden City: Doubleday & Company, Inc., 1964.

Bernstein, Barton, and Allen Matusow, eds. *The Truman Administration: A Documentary History*. New York: Harper & Row, Publishers, 1966.

Blumberg, Nathan B. *One-Party Press? Coverage of the 1952 Presidential Campaign in 35 Daily Newspapers*. Lincoln: University of Nebraska Press, 1954.

Bontecou, Eleanor. *The Federal Loyalty-Security Program*. Ithaca: Cornell University Press, 1953.

Boswell, A. Bruce. *Eastern Poland: Its Historical, Etnographic [sic], Economic, Political and Cultural Background*. Chicago: Polish National Alliance Educational Department, n.d.

Brown, Ralph S., Jr. *Loyalty and Security*. New Haven: Yale University Press, 1958.

Brown, Stuart Gerry. *Conscience in Politics: Adlai E. Stevenson*. Syracuse: Syracuse University Press, 1961.

Burnham, James. *Containment or Liberation? An Inquiry into the Aims of United States Foreign Policy*. New York: The John Day Company, Inc., 1952.

Byrnes, James F. *Speaking Frankly*. New York: Harper and Brothers, 1947.
———. *All in One Lifetime*. New York: Harper & Row, Publishers, 1958.

Carr, Albert Z. *Truman, Stalin, and Peace*. Garden City: Doubleday & Company, Inc., 1950.

Carr, Robert K. *The House Committee on Un-American Activities, 1945–1950.* Ithaca: Cornell University Press, 1952.

Ciechanowski, Jan. *Defeat in Victory.* New York: Doubleday & Company, Inc., 1947.

Cohen, Bernard C. *The Political Process and Foreign Policy.* Princeton: Princeton University Press, 1957.

Cook, Thomas, and Malcolm Moos. *Power Through Purpose: The Realism of Idealism as a Basis for Foreign Policy.* Baltimore: The Johns Hopkins Press, 1954.

Cooke, Alistair. *A Generation on Trial: U.S.A. v. Alger Hiss.* New York: Alfred A. Knopf, Inc., 1950.

Crocker, George N. *Roosevelt's Road to Russia.* Chicago: Henry Regnery Company, 1959.

Daniels, Jonathan. *The Man of Independence.* New York: J. B. Lippincott Company, 1950.

Davies, Richard C. *Housing Reform During the Truman Administration.* Columbia: University of Missouri Press, 1966.

Dean, Vera. *The Four Cornerstones of Peace.* New York: McGraw-Hill, Inc., 1946.

Deane, John R. *The Strange Alliance: The Story of Our Efforts at Wartime Co-operation with Russia.* New York: The Viking Press, Inc., 1947.

DeConde, Alexander. *Isolation and Security.* Durham: Duke University Press, 1957.

Dulles, John Foster. *War Or Peace.* New York: The MacMillan Company, 1950.

———. *A Peace Treaty in the Making.* Washington: U.S. Government Printing Office, 1951.

Dunn, Frederick S. *Peace-Making and the Settlement with Japan.* Princeton: Princeton University Press, 1963.

East, John Leonard. *Republican Precinct Workers Handbook.* Chicago: National Precinct Workers, Inc., 1946.

Eisenhower, Dwight. *The White House Years: Mandate for Change, 1953–1956.* Garden City: Doubleday & Company, Inc., 1963.

Epstein, Julius. *The Mysteries of the Van Vliet Report: A Case History.* Chicago: Polish-American Congress, 1951.

Feis, Herbert. *The China Tangle: The American Effort in China from Pearl Harbor to the Marshall Mission.* Princeton: Princeton University Press, 1953.

Ferguson, LeRoy, and Ralph Smuckler. *Politics in the Press: An Analysis of Press Content in 1952 Senatorial Campaigns.* East Lansing: Governmental Research Bureau of Michigan State College, 1954.

Fisher, Harold H. *America and Russia in the World Community.* Claremont: Claremont College, 1946.

Gerson, Louis. *The Hyphenate in Recent American Politics and Diplomacy.* Lawrence: The University of Kansas Press, 1964.

Goldman, Eric F. *The Crucial Decade: America, 1945–1955.* New York: Alfred A. Knopf, Inc., 1956.

Goodman, Walter. *The Committee.* New York: Farrar, Straus and Giroux, 1968.

Graebner, Norman. *The New Isolationism.* New York: The Ronald Press Company, 1956.

Harris, Louis. *Is There a Republican Majority? Political Trends, 1952–1956.* New York: Harper and Brothers, 1954.

Higgins, Trumbull. *Korea and the Fall of MacArthur*. New York: Oxford University Press, Inc., 1960.

Hiss, Alger. *In the Court of Public Opinion*. New York: Alfred A. Knopf, Inc., 1957.

Hoover, Herbert. *Addresses Upon the American Road, 1948–1950*. Stanford: Stanford University Press, 1951.

————. *Addresses Upon the American Road, 1950–1955*. Stanford: Stanford University Press, 1955.

Jackson, J. Hampden. *The World in the Postwar Decade 1945–1955*. Cambridge: Riverside Press, 1955.

Javits, Benjamin. *How the Republican Party Can Win in 1952*. New York: Henry Holt and Company, Inc., 1952.

Johnson, Walter. *1600 Pennsylvania Avenue: Presidents and the People, 1929–1959*. Boston: Little, Brown and Company, 1960.

Jowitt, Earl. *The Strange Case of Alger Hiss*. New York: Doubleday & Company, Inc., 1953.

Kecskemeti, Paul. *Strategic Surrender: The Politics of Victory and Defeat*. Stanford: Stanford University Press, 1958.

Kirkendall, Richard, ed. *The Truman Period as a Research Field*. Columbia: University of Missouri Press, 1967.

Kolko, Gabriel. *The Politics of War*. New York: Random House, Inc., 1969.

Kornitzer, Bela. *The Real Nixon: An Intimate Biography*. New York: Rand McNally & Company, 1960.

LaFeber, Walter. *America, Russia, and The Cold War*. New York: John Wiley & Sons, Inc., 1967.

Lane, Arthur Bliss. *I Saw Poland Betrayed: An American Ambassador Reports to the American People*. New York: The Bobbs-Merrill Company, Inc., 1948.

Latham, Earl. *The Communist Controversy in Washington*. Cambridge: Harvard University Press, 1966.

Leahy, William D. *I Was There: The Personal Story of the Chief of Staff to Presidents Roosevelt and Truman Based on His Notes and Diaries Made at the Time*. New York: Whittlesby House, 1950.

Lednicki, Waclaw. *Russian-Polish Relations: Their Historical, Cultural and Political Background*. Chicago: Polish National Alliance Educational Department, n.d.

Littleton, Robert. *An Era of Infamy*. Cleveland: 1952.

Lohbeck, Don. *Patrick J. Hurley*. Chicago: Henry Regnery Company, 1956.

Lubell, Samuel. *The Revolt of the Moderates*. New York: Harper & Row, Publishers, 1956.

Martin, Joe. *My Fifty Years in Politics as Told to Robert J. Donovan*. New York: McGraw-Hill, Inc., 1960.

Matusow, Allen J. *Farm Politics and Policies of the Truman Years*. Cambridge: Harvard University Press, 1967.

McCarthy, Joe. *McCarthyism: The Fight for America*. New York: The Devin-Adair Company, 1952.

Melton, Harve. *New Deal vs. Old Deal: Keynote for the 1948 Campaign*. Oklahoma City: Harve Melton, 1948.

Mikolajczyk, Stanislaw. *The Rape of Poland: Pattern of Soviet Aggression*. New York: McGraw-Hill, Inc., 1948.

Morray, J. P. *From Yalta to Disarmament*. New York: Monthly Review Press, 1952.

Neumann, William L. *Making the Peace, 1941–1945*. Washington: Foundation for Foreign Affairs, 1950.

Neustadt, Richard. *Presidential Power: The Politics of Leadership*. New York: John Wiley & Sons, Inc., 1960.

Nixon, Richard. *Six Crises*. New York: Doubleday & Company, Inc., 1962.

O'Conor, John F. *Cold War and Liberation: A Challenge of Aid to the Subject Peoples*. New York: Vantage Press, Inc., 1961.

Oxnam, G. Bromley. *I Protest*. New York: Harper and Brothers, 1954.

Phillips, Cabell. *The Truman Presidency*. New York: The MacMillan Company, 1966.

Rieselbach, Leroy N. *The Roots of Isolationism: Congressional Voting and Presidential Leadership in Foreign Policy*. Indianapolis: The Bobbs-Merrill Company, Inc., 1966.

Rogin, Michael P. *The Intellectuals and McCarthy*. Cambridge: The M.I.T. Press, 1967.

Rosenau, James. *The Nomination of "Chip" Bohlen*. Eagleton Institute Cases in Practical Politics. Rutgers: McGraw-Hill, Inc., 1960.

Rovere, Richard H. *Senator Joe McCarthy*. New York: Harcourt, Brace & World, Inc., 1959.

Rowse, Arthur E. *Slanted News: A Case Study of the Nixon and Stevenson Fund Stories*. Boston: Beacon Press, 1957.

Schlesinger, Arthur, Jr. *The Vital Center*. Boston: Houghton Mifflin Company, 1949.

Schmidt, Karl M. *Henry A. Wallace: Quixotic Crusade 1948*. Syracuse: Syracuse University Press, 1960.

Smith, Walter Bedell. *My Three Years in Moscow*. Philadelphia: J. B. Lippincott Company, 1950.

Snell, John, ed. *The Meaning of Yalta: Big Three Diplomacy and the New Balance of Power*. Baton Rouge: Louisiana State University Press, 1955.

Spanier, John. *The Truman-MacArthur Controversy and the Korean War*. Cambridge: Belknap Press, 1959.

Stettinius, Edward. *Roosevelt and the Russians: The Yalta Conference*. Edited by Walter Johnson. Garden City: Doubleday & Company, Inc., 1949.

Stevenson, Adlai. *Major Campaign Speeches of Adlai E. Stevenson, 1952*. New York: Random House, Inc., 1953.

Stone, I. F. *The Truman Era*. New York: Monthly Review Press, 1953.

Taft, Robert A. *A Foreign Policy for Americans*. New York: Doubleday & Company, Inc., 1951.

Tang T'sou. *America's Failure in China*. Chicago: The University of Chicago Press, 1963.

Truman, Harry S. *Memoirs*. Garden City: Doubleday & Company, Inc., 1955, 1956. 2 vols.

Vandenberg, Arthur. *The Private Papers of Senator Vandenberg*. Edited by Arthur Vandenberg, Jr. Boston: Houghton Mifflin Company, 1952.

Wechsler, James A. *The Age of Suspicion*. New York: Random House, Inc., 1953.

Wedemeyer, Albert C. *Wedemeyer Reports!* New York: Henry Holt and Company, Inc., 1958.

Welles, Sumner. *Seven Decisions that Shaped History*. New York: Harper and Brothers, 1950.

Westerfield, H. Bradford. *Foreign Policy and Party Politics: Pearl Harbor to Korea*. New Haven: Yale University Press, 1955.

Whitney, Courtney. *MacArthur: His Rendezvous With History*. New York: Alfred A. Knopf, Inc., 1956.

Wick, James L. *How Not to Run for President: A Handbook for Republicans.* New York: Vantage Press, Inc., 1952.

Williams, William A. *American-Russian Relations, 1781–1947.* New York: Holt, Rinehart & Winston, Inc., 1952.

Wittmer, Felix. *The Yalta Betrayal: Data on the Decline and Fall of Franklin Delano Roosevelt.* Caldwell: The Caxton Printers, Ltd., 1953.

Ziff, William B. *Two Worlds: A Realistic Approach to the Problems of Keeping the Peace.* New York: Harper and Brothers, 1946.

Articles and Pamphlets

Alperovitz, Gar. "How Did the Cold War Begin?," *New York Review of Books* (March 23, 1967), 6, 8, 9, 11, 12.

Bernstein, Barton. "America in War and Peace: The Test of Liberalism," in Bernstein, ed., *Towards a New Past*, 289–321. New York: Random House, Inc., 1968.

Bullitt, William C. "How We Won the War and Lost the Peace, Part One," *Life*, 25, No. 9 (August 30, 1948), 82–97.

———. "How We Won the War and Lost the Peace, Part Two," *Life*, 25, No. 10 (September 6, 1948), 86–103.

"Check List of Errors," *Life*, 29, No. 4 (July 24, 1950), 26.

Commanger, Henry Steele. "Concession to Reality," *The New York Times Magazine* (August 3, 1952), 7.

In Defense of Poland's Western Boundary: An Economic Study. Chicago: Polish-American Congress, n.d.

Foreign Policy of the United States: Memorandum of the Polish-American Congress to Cordell Hull. Washington: Polish-American Congress, 1944.

Hamby, Alonzo. "Henry A. Wallace, the Liberals, and Soviet-American Relations," *Review of Politics* (April, 1968), 153–69.

Jenner, William E. *What Has Happened to Our Country? A Summing Up.* Washington: U.S. Government Printing Office, 1958.

Judd, Walter H. *The Mistakes that Led to Korea*, reprint from an *American Affairs* pamphlet entitled *Autopsy on our Blunders in Asia.*

———. *The War of Ideas in Europe and Asia.* Washington: U.S. Government Printing Office, 1948.

Krock, Arthur. Syndicated column in *The New York Times.* January, 1945–May, 1955.

Lasch, Christopher. "The Cold War Revisited and Re-visioned," *The New York Times Magazine* (January 14, 1968), 26–27, 44–51, 54, 59.

Lawrence, David. Syndicated column in *U.S. News and World Report.* January, 1945–May, 1955.

Millis, Walter. "From 'Argonaut' to 'Yalta'," *Saturday Review* (April 16, 1955), 24–25.

Moley, Raymond. Syndicated column in *Newsweek.* January, 1945–May, 1955.

Paterson, Thomas G. "The Abortive American Loan to Russia," *Journal of American History* (June, 1969), 70–92.

Pegler, Westbrook. Syndicated column in *Chicago Herald-American.* January, 1945–February, 1951. Also in *Milwaukee Sentinel.* January 1951–May, 1955.

Polish-American Congress. *Memorandum on Poland to Honorable George C. Marshall.* Chicago: Polish-American Congress, 1947.

————. *A Memorandum to the Senate of the United States on the Crimea Decisions Concerning Poland.* Chicago: Polish-American Congress, March, 1945.

Polsby, Nelson W. "Towards an Explanation of McCarthyism," *Political Studies* (1960), 250–71.

Schlesinger, Arthur, Jr. "Origins of the Cold War," *Foreign Affairs* (October, 1967), 22–52.

Smith, George. "Bipartisan Foreign Policy in Partisan Politics," *American Perspective,* 4, No. 2 (Spring, 1950), 157–69.

Sokolsky, George. Syndicated column in *Chicago Herald-American.* January, 1945–February, 1951. Also in *Milwaukee Sentinel.* January, 1951–May, 1955.

Trow, Martin. "Small Businessmen, Political Tolerance and Support for McCarthy," *American Journal of Sociology* (November, 1958), 270–81.

Warner, Geoffrey. "From Teheran to Yalta: Reflections on F.D.R.'s Foreign Policy," *International Affairs* (July, 1967), 530–36.

"Washington News from Our Congressman N. M. Mason," column in *Kendall Co. News, Leland Times, DeKalb Chronicle, Ottowa Rep. Times, Earlville Leader, Mendota Reporter, Belvidere Republican, Morris Herald,* and *Genoa Republican.* 1945–1955.

Williams, William A. "The Cold War Revisionists," *The Nation* (November 13, 1967), 492–95.

Wilmot, Chester. "A Sacrifice of Principles," *The New York Times Magazine* (August 3, 1952), 7.

Winnacker, Rudolph. "Yalta — Another Munich?" *The Virginia Quarterly Review* (Autumn, 1948), 521–37.

Zacharias, Ellis M. "The Inside Story of Yalta," *United Nations World* (January, 1949), 12–17.

Periodicals and Newspapers

Chicago Tribune. January, 1945–May, 1955.
Congressional Quarterly Weekly Reports. January, 1945–May, 1955.
The Nation. January, 1945–May, 1955.
New Republic. January, 1945–May, 1955.
Newsweek. January, 1945–May, 1955.
The New York Times. January, 1945–May, 1955.
Polish-American Congress Bulletin. 1945–1955.
The Saturday Evening Post. January, 1945–May, 1955.
Time. January, 1945–May, 1955.
U.S. News and World Report (formerly *U.S. News*). January, 1945–May, 1955.

index

Acheson, Dean, 41, 78, 79, 100, 117, 123, 156, 176; attacks on, 78, 93, 103, 112, 124, 126, 174, 187; testimony of, 58, 78, 118, 124

Aldrich, Winthrop, 156

Anticommunism: impact of, 2, 3, 67–68, 87, 90, 103, 129; uses of, 60–61, 64, 67, 105, 127–28, 220–21

Atlantic Charter, 24, 29, 35, 90–91, 148, 163

Austin, Warren, 24; defense of Jessup, 112

Ball, Joseph, 48

Barkley, Alben, 24, 26, 216

Barry, William: and Yalta resolution, 28, 225

Bender, George, 5n3, 59, 61, 139, 214, 216

Bennett, John, 59, 98

Bentley, Alvin, 5n3, 147, 148n48, 161, 188; and Yalta resolution, 156n3, 233–35

Bipartisan foreign policy, 87, 91, 96–97, 99, 100–101, 106, 113, 117, 129, 137, 146–47, 186, 218; criticism of, 81, 83, 87, 97, 99–100; support for, 71–72, 78, 81, 89–90

Bohlen, Charles, 13, 44, 165; debate on ambassadorial nomination, 166, 168, 169, 170–71, 172–73, 174; defense of Yalta, 166–67, 168; role at Yalta, 13, 167, 170, 172; issue of loyalty, 168–72. See also Bohlen nomination

Bohlen nomination, 8, 9, 165–66, 180, 186; debate on, 166, 168, 169, 170–71, 172–73, 174; vote on, 175; hearings on, 166–68. See also Bohlen, Charles

Bosch, Albert, 161; and resolution on Yalta, 155n3, 200, 231–32

Bradley, Omar: defense of Japanese peace treaty, 119; testimony during MacArthur dismissal hearings, 123, 123n52

Brewster, Owen, 93, 112, 121, 124

Bricker, John, 5n2, 108n8, 109n9, 142, 154, 166, 175, 192, 201; and use of Yalta to justify restrictions on executive authority, 108, 131, 182. See also Bricker Amendment

Bricker Amendment, 8, 9, 105, 131–33, 153, 165, 180, 182–85, 186, 194, 201; hearings on, 132, 180–81; debate on, 182–85; George amendment to, 184; vote on, 185. See also Bricker, John; Southern Democrats

Bridges, Styles, 5n2, 34, 37–38, 42, 54, 78, 87, 91, 93, 97, 109n9, 124, 140, 141, 166, 168, 169, 172–73, 174, 175, 204, 212, 214; and Yalta papers, 201, 206, 211

Buffett, Howard, 5n2, 50, 59, 60, 61

Bullitt, William, 21, 66–67

Butler, Hugh, 59, 108n8, 109n9

Butler, John, 108, 109n9, 172

Butterworth, W. Walton, 79; nomination of, 78

Byrnes, James, 12, 67, 92, 211; and Far Eastern agreements, 19–20, 36, 37–38, 41–44; role at Yalta, 13, 20, 101n32, 126

Cain, Harry, 100, 108n8, 120–21, 124, 139

Campaign of 1948, 62–69; Truman's strategy in, 67–68; Republican focus in, 62–63, 63–66; "extremists'" position on, 7–8, 52, 63, 66; impact of, 7, 8

Campaign of 1952, 136–49, 155, 156, 160, 165, 169, 175, 178–79, 180, 185, 192, 196, 223; Taft's primary campaign in, 136–38; Eisenhower's primary campaign in, 138; references to Yalta in, 130, 136, 137, 138, 139, 140, 141, 142, 143, 144, 146, 147, 148, 149–52, 154, 165, 174, 191, 199, 207; impact of, 7, 8, 149, 151–53

Capehart, Homer, 5n3, 84, 91, 94, 109n9, 172, 206, 216
Chambers, Whittaker: testimony of, 73, 75, 76, 77
Chiang Kai-shek, 70; impact of defeat by Chinese Communists, 8, 21–22, 71, 222; response of supporters of, 32, 46, 79, 80–82, 97–98, 119, 122, 123–24, 126, 197
Chicago Tribune, 4n1, 5n2, 50, 53, 80, 97, 107, 126–27, 176, 199, 213; criticisms of Roosevelt and New Deal, 29, 36, 45, 55, 60, 66, 79, 85, 91, 98, 100, 127–28, 133–34, 175, 177, 178, 188; demand that Republicans focus on foreign policy, 52, 63, 97, 191, 193n30; and loyalty issue, 38, 60, 78, 79, 127, 151–52, 177, 193; charges about secret agreements, 35, 46, 178; and Truman Doctrine, 59–60; and Marshall Plan, 61; and campaign of 1948, 63, 66; and campaign of 1952, 138–39, 143, 151–53; and House Joint Resolution 200, 164–65; and Bohlen nomination, 174n46; and Bricker Amendment, 182, 185; and publication of the Yalta papers, 199–200, 201, 208, 209–11; criticisms of German policy, 35, 46–47, 55, 84, 95, 143, 188
China policy, 44–45, 46, 94, 122, 126–27, 140–41, 149; alleged responsibility for Chiang Kai-shek's defeat, 8, 21–22, 71, 79, 80–82, 97–98, 119–20, 123–25, 126, 137, 139, 196–97; and White Paper, 80–81
Churchill, Winston, 10–11, 176, 177; Fulton (Mo.) speech, 50; and meeting with Truman, 131, 133–34. *See also* Great Britain
Cold War: impact of, 1, 3, 4–5, 7, 69, 72, 87–88, 90, 97, 175–77, 216–17, 218, 219, 221, 222–23
"Communists in Government," 20, 22, 61, 64, 67, 70, 71, 73–75, 76, 86, 88, 90, 91, 92, 98, 99, 100, 107, 122, 130, 138, 146, 147, 177, 186–87; "in the Department of State," 8, 20, 37–38, 71, 77–78, 80, 81, 87, 93, 127–28, 137, 142, 187, 193–94; allegations of influence of, 1, 22, 60, 66, 67, 73, 79, 83, 85, 89, 93–94, 102, 109–10, 136–37, 141, 169, 175, 214–15
Congressional campaigns, 51–53, 99–100, 101–2, 187, 189–90
Congressional debates: about appropriation for Foreign Relations volumes, 191–92; on Yalta anniversaries, 115, 134, 197; about presidential nominees, 78–79, 111–13, 156, 165–75; about publication of Yalta papers, 199–204, 211. *See also* U.S. House of Representatives; U.S. Senate
Connally, Tom, 24, 49, 78–79, 82, 96, 120
Containment policy, 39, 70, 83n25, 83, 90, 105, 154, 218, 221; impact on Yalta, 4, 220; impact on postwar debate, 3, 103
Curtis, Carl, 5n2, 38, 90, 97
Curzon line agreement, 18, 28, 52, 85, 225. *See also* Yalta Conference

Democratic National Committee, 68, 197, 208; publications, 140, 149, 184, 189–90, 198, 207; criticisms of Republican partisanship, 141n32, 161, 198, 207, 208; defense of Yalta, 54, 140–41, 149–50
Dewey, Thomas, 5n4, 25, 89; and campaign of 1948, 7–8, 65n20, 65–66, 71–72
Dirksen, Everett, 5n2, 34–35, 50, 108n8, 109n9, 121, 122, 139, 148n48, 151, 173, 174, 175, 180, 182, 201; and reservation to Japanese peace treaty, 133
Dondero, George, 5n2, 90, 109n11
Dulles, John Foster, 5n4, 54–55, 71–72, 84, 89, 135, 139, 145, 156, 176, 212, 215; and debate on Bohlen nomination, 167, 168–72, 173; role in drafting Japanese peace treaty, 117, 118–19, 121; and Bricker Amendment, 180; and publication of Yalta papers, 201–2, 203; and repudiation of Yalta, 154, 158–59, 198
Dworshak, Henry, 48, 108n8, 109n9, 121, 122, 132, 175

Eastern European agreements, 14–15, 21, 28–29, 51, 52–54, 59, 109–10, 112, 113, 114, 149, 150, 197–98, 206–7; and alleged responsibility for communization, 1, 21, 84, 110–11, 114–16, 134–36, 145–49, 100, 209–10, 214. *See also* Yalta Conference
Eastland, James, 57, 90, 91, 121
Eisenhower, Dwight, 5n4, 189, 203, 216; and campaign of 1952, 136, 137–39, 144–46, 148, 152, 154; Administration of, 155, 176, 177, 183, 187, 190; and break with "extremists," 8, 154, 166, 179, 185, 193, 194, 195, 198–99, 208, 211, 215, 223; criticisms of Yalta, 138, 148, 154;

and resolution on Yalta, 155, 156–60, 162–65; and Bohlen nomination, 165–73; and Bricker Amendment, 8, 180, 184, 185; and publication of Yalta papers, 195, 200–202, 206–8; and Geneva Conference of 1955, 8, 214–16, 221

European Recovery Program, 81–82

Executive authority: resolutions on and suspicions about use of, 99, 101, 102, 106, 107, 108, 118n37, 131–32, 133, 154, 157, 165, 175, 180, 181, 185, 186, 198–99, 213, 230–31

"Extremists": definition of, 5–6, 5n2; criticisms of Yalta by, 6, 7, 19, 22, 23, 27–29, 30, 35, 40, 46–47, 53, 55, 59, 60, 61, 78, 90, 109, 121, 126–27, 130, 178, 182, 185, 188; position on foreign policy, 6, 7, 30–31, 32, 50, 56, 57, 59, 61, 85, 97, 100, 105, 106–7, 109, 143, 176, 180, 213, 222; position on New Deal, 6, 29, 30, 32–33, 36, 39, 40, 45, 51–53, 56, 57, 60, 61, 66, 70, 79, 80, 81, 87, 90, 94, 100, 134, 185, 198–99, 206, 209–10; use of loyalty issue, 6, 7, 20, 38, 60, 70, 71–73, 77, 80, 81, 87, 91–94, 106–7, 127–28, 151; rift with "moderates," 6, 7, 8, 9, 55, 56, 63, 71–72, 83–84, 154, 165–66, 173, 174, 180, 185, 192, 194, 197, 208, 213; influence of, 8, 21, 22, 31, 38, 46, 52, 63–64, 69, 71, 86, 88, 97–98, 104, 110, 121, 129, 139, 145, 152–53, 165, 175, 178–79, 194, 196, 216–17, 221–23; concern about German policy, 35, 46–47, 47–48, 55, 84, 95, 111, 188

Far Eastern agreements, 19–20, 36–38, 41–45, 54, 71, 86, 89, 90, 117, 118–19, 120, 140–41, 149, 166–67, 190, 192, 197, 203, 204–5, 206, 210; alleged responsibility for Chiang Kai-shek's defeat, 1, 21, 79–82, 97–98, 110–11, 112, 122–26, 136, 156, 187, 188, 209; secrecy of, 20, 37, 41–45, 199. See also Yalta Conference

Farley, James, 92; and Roosevelt's health, 21, 128–29

Federal Bureau of Investigation (F.B.I.), 75, 76, 128, 168, 169, 170, 171

Federal Employee Loyalty Program, 68, 71, 76, 96, 221

Ferguson, Homer, 5n3, 82, 97, 99, 108n8, 132, 155, 156, 167, 168, 172, 186

Foreign policy: charges of past mistakes in, 4, 7, 57, 59, 60, 61, 63, 64, 65, 81, 84, 85–86, 98n23, 99, 105, 106n1, 110, 123, 125, 142–43, 146, 148, 151

Geneva Conference of 1955, 8, 9, 195, 213, 214–16; resolutions on, 215; political significance of, 216–17

George, Walter, 183, 200; and amendment to Bricker Amendment, 183, 184–85

Germany, 10, 11, 14, 15, 68–69, 86, 108, 116, 119; Yalta agreements on, 16, 17, 46–47, 78, 82, 84–85, 95, 188; and reparations, 16, 17, 46, 48–49, 95, 188; and unconditional surrender, 47–48, 95, 188; allegedly harsh treatment of, 29, 35, 53, 54, 55, 61, 61n11, 84–85, 95, 109, 111, 128, 143, 206

Great Britain, 24, 200, 206, 207, 209, 210; 1946 U.S. loan to, 50; charges of imperialism against, 25, 37. See also Churchill, Winston

Gwinn, Ralph, 91, 97

Hale, Robert, 5n4, 59, 99, 161, 196, 213; and resolution on Yalta, 90–91, 110–11, 114, 155, 156, 227–28

Halleck, Charles, 5n3, 63, 131

Harriman, W. Averell, 12, 38, 43, 44, 113, 150, 221; role at Yalta, 13

Hickenlooper, Bourke, 5n2, 160, 168, 174, 175

Hiss, Alger, 13, 73, 75, 77–78, 103, 115, 119, 122, 187, 189, 193, 214; role at Yalta, 13, 20, 73–74, 79, 91, 93, 99, 100, 110, 112, 123, 128, 130, 131, 136, 147, 148, 149, 151, 152, 155, 167, 175, 186, 194, 203, 206, 209, 210, 211, 213; perjury trial and conviction, 8, 9, 70, 71, 77, 86, 87, 91–92, 145, 222

Hoffman, Clare, 5n2, 28, 91, 101, 182

Hoover, Herbert, 5n3, 27, 64, 141, 190

Hopkins, Harry, 12, 103; criticisms of, 67, 93, 94, 102

Humphrey, Hubert, 156, 160, 184

Hurley, Patrick, 123, 124, 125; resignation as U.S. Ambassador, 36–37, 42; charges of disloyalty against, 37, 38, 127, 141–42

Ives, Irving, 5n4, 97, 132

Japanese peace treaty, 9, 105, 117–22, 147, 231; reservations to, 117–18, 120, 121, 133, 140; debate on, 120–21, 133

Jenner, William, 5n2, 82–83, 93, 95,

97, 98, 106, 108n8, 118n37, 121, 122, 126–27, 182–83, 214, 230–31; and reservations to Japanese peace treaty, 117–18; and resolution on Geneva Conference of 1955, 215

Jennings, John, 5n3, 50–51, 51n32

Jessup, Philip, 93; debate on nomination to UN, 111–13

Johnson, Lyndon: response to House Joint Resolution 200, 160

Johnson, Walter: and publication of the Yalta papers, 208

Judd, Walter, 38, 59, 95, 98, 111, 141, 161, 176; and demand for enforcement of Yalta terms, 46, 80; and contention that Chiang Kai-shek was betrayed at Yalta, 81–82, 97, 122

Keating, Kenneth, 5n4, 84, 99, 132

Kefauver, Estes, 181, 184

Kem, James, 5n3, 93, 98, 108, 108n8, 109n9, 121, 132; and resolution on Truman-Attlee conference, 102; and resolution on Department of State, 130

Kersten, Charles, 5n3, 145, 147, 162; and liberation resolutions, 116, 135–36, 229–30; and amendment to Mutual Security Act, 116, 135; and resolution to repudiate Yalta, 156n3, 232–33

Kilgore, Harley, 181, 184

Knowland, William, 5n3, 78, 79, 81–82, 91, 97, 124, 127, 132, 142, 166, 167, 171, 173, 199, 201, 214, 215–16; criticism of secrecy of executive policy, 101, 106, 185–86; criticism of Far Eastern policy, 103, 156–57, 197, 204

Korean Aid Act, 88; debate on, 88–89

Korean War, 9, 96, 103, 109, 122, 127, 138; responsibility for, 98, 126, 131, 137, 187, 188, 197; impact of, 8, 21, 87, 97, 222

Krock, Arthur, 5n3, 25, 44, 121, 126, 133, 163n22

Kurile Islands, 35–36, 41–45, 117–21, 231

Lane, Arthur Bliss, 5n3, 91, 134; role in campaigns, 147

Langer, William, 5n2, 50, 82, 84, 101, 108n8, 188, 214

Lawrence, David, 4n1, 5n2, 29, 36, 208; criticisms of Roosevelt and New Deal, 45, 185, 209–10; criticisms of German policy, 35

Lehman, Herbert, 113, 204

Lemke, William, 5n2, 59, 61, 83, 84, 95

Lend-lease, 146, 188

Lewis, Fulton, Jr., 4n1, 5n2, 126–27

Liberation policy, 109, 130, 135–36, 137, 145–46, 148, 149, 150, 153, 158, 162, 164, 189; resolutions advocating, 9, 110, 116, 135, 229–30

Lodge, Henry Cabot, 5n4, 71, 106n1, 132

Lodge, John Davis, 5n4, 54, 58, 84, 97, 98

Luce, Clare Boothe, 5n2, 29, 45, 63

MacArthur, Douglas, 103, 141, 142; dismissal of, 105, 122; and knowledge of Yalta agreements, 204–5, 214; hearings on dismissal of, 9, 123–27. See also Wake Island conference

McCardle, Carl, 191, 201

McCarran, Patrick, 5n2, 79, 85, 121, 169, 175, 221; and resolution on executive agreements, 130–31

McCarthy, Joseph, 5n2, 96, 102, 108, 121, 147, 154, 166, 189, 199, 201, 203–4, 214, 216, 220; charges by, 20, 84, 87, 93, 98, 100, 105, 126–28, 141, 142, 147, 177, 188, 206; and Bohlen nomination, 168, 169, 170, 171, 174, 175; impact on Republican strategy, 99, 101, 105, 129, 136, 142, 177; and resolution to repudiate Yalta, 196, 235–36; break with Administration, 169, 171, 194, 198–99, 215–16; and resolution on Geneva Conference of 1955, 215; censure of, 9, 195; and McCarthyism, 99, 101, 174, 177, 186-87, 221

Machrowicz, Thaddeus, 144, 161, 198; and Yalta resolutions, 114, 156, 196, 227–28, 229

McLeod, Scott, 166; and Bohlen's loyalty, 169, 170, 171, 172

McMahon, Brien, 96, 113, 114n28, 122

Malone, George, 5n2, 82, 90, 93, 94, 98, 103, 108n8, 109–10, 121, 127, 175

Manion, Clarence: dismissal of, 185; and formation of For America party, 185n12

Mansfield, Mike, 184, 190

Marshall, George, 12, 55, 82, 93, 103, 123, 124, 126, 205; and mission to China, 71, 80, 127; and nomination as Secretary of Defense, 94. See also Marshall Plan

Marshall Plan, 9, 56, 68, 81–82, 219; debate on, 60–61. See also Marshall, George

Martin, Edward, 93, 98, 120, 139–40

Martin, Joseph, 5n3, 45, 84, 101

Mason, Noah, 5n2, 98, 101, 103, 188
Merrow, Chester, 5n4, 26, 59, 63
Miller, Arthur, 5n2, 88, 98, 103, 127
Millikin, Eugene, 5n4, 48–49, 101, 132, 186
"Moderates": definition of, 5, 5n4, 6–7; criticisms of Yalta by, 6, 7, 84, 97–98, 139, 151; position on foreign policy, 6–7, 39, 55, 56, 57, 67, 84, 118, 136, 139, 152–53, 176, 180, 214–15; change in focus, 6, 7, 8, 9, 68, 70, 83–84, 88, 105, 179, 182–83, 221, 222–23
Moley, Raymond, 5n3, 36, 89, 98, 126
Morgenthau Plan, 48, 78
Morse, Wayne, 98n23, 106n1, 132, 156
Mundt, Karl, 5n3, 34–35, 45, 59, 60, 61, 90, 101, 108n8, 109n9, 154, 174, 175, 216; and development of loyalty issue, 20, 92–93, 206; and demand for publication of text of Yalta agreements, 57–58
Mutual Assistance Act, 82, 96, 108; debates on, 83, 109
Mutual Security Act of 1951, 109; Kersten amendment to, 116, 135, 145, 230

The Nation, 4n1, 26, 96, 125, 161
New Deal: criticisms of, 1–3, 20–21, 45, 51–52, 56, 59–60, 61, 63, 65, 73; use of Yalta to discredit, 3–4, 45, 47–48, 55, 63, 66, 70–71, 75, 77–78, 79, 81, 85, 88, 90, 91, 92–94, 95, 98, 99, 100–102, 107, 108, 109–10, 115, 122, 127–28, 131, 132, 133–34, 136–37, 139–40, 141–42, 151–52, 164–65, 175, 177, 178, 182, 185, 188, 192–93, 206–7, 209–10, 210n36, 221–22
New Republic, 5n1, 25, 26, 96, 113, 161
Newsweek, 4n1, 26, 36, 96, 121–22, 125, 133, 161, 177, 193–94, 197, 213; and Soviet involvement in Far East, 32, 44–45, 46, 125
The New York Times, 4n1, 5n4, 34, 84–85, 96, 113–14, 126, 170n37, 177, 183, 196, 201, 208–9, 211, 213; initial reaction to Yalta, 26–27, 36n40, 54; and Soviet involvement in Far East, 32, 44–45, 46; and repudiation of Yalta, 121–22, 143, 151, 162–63
Nixon, Richard, 5n3, 84, 146, 148, 196, 223; and development of loyalty issue, 20, 91, 144–45, 187
North Atlantic Treaty Organization (NATO), 62, 82–83, 84, 107, 116, 219

O'Konski, Alvin, 5n3, 28, 59; criticisms of Yalta agreements, 93–94, 161–62; campaign use of Yalta by, 53, 147

"Partisans": definition of, 5, 5n4, 6–7; criticisms of Yalta by, 6–7, 54, 56, 57, 58, 84–85, 95, 97–98, 130, 139, 175, 182, 188, 202, 206; position on foreign policy, 6–7, 8, 39, 56, 57, 60, 83–84, 87, 121, 131, 154, 180, 214, 215, 216–17; and loyalty issue, 91–92, 93, 103, 127–28, 129, 152–53, 195; change in focus, 6, 7, 8, 9, 70, 84, 87, 106, 129
Pegler, Westbrook, 4n1, 5n2, 84; criticisms of Roosevelt and New Deal, 63, 66, 79, 90, 91, 208, 209–10; and loyalty issue, 78, 79, 91, 107, 188
Polish-Americans, 4n1, 238–43: organizations of, 34, 53, 54, 114–15, 162, 199; appeals to, 28, 52–54, 66, 84, 98–99, 114–16, 146, 147–49, 187–88, 189, 198–99; issues involving, 21, 26–27, 145–46, 161–62; and anniversaries of events, 9, 84, 115, 134–35, 148, 197; criticisms of Yalta, 27–28, 34, 40–41, 52, 53, 84, 114, 115, 134–35, 136, 197
Potsdam Conference, 18, 34, 36, 44, 51, 54, 55, 58, 62, 68, 88, 96, 100, 102, 107, 111, 212, 216
Publication of Yalta papers, 8, 9, 155n3, 164, 191–93, 195, 199–204, 206–12; debate on, 202–4, 206, 208–11; rationale for, 202, 206–7; charges of censorship of, 177–78, 192, 195, 204, 210–11; uses of, 191. See also Yalta Conference

Rankin, John, 5n2, 45, 50, 73; and resolution on Truman-Churchill conference, 131; criticisms of German policy, 128
Rayburn, Sam, 178, 190
Recognition of Eastern European and Balkan governments, 39–40
Reece, B. Carroll, 5n3, 45, 51–52, 64–65, 106
Reed, Daniel, 5n2, 28, 162
Republican National Committee, 23, 39, 51, 64, 88, 97, 141; publications of, 4n1, 28, 44–45, 52, 64–65, 99, 136, 142–43, 146–48, 152, 187, 212–13
Republican National Convention: and campaign of 1948, 63–64; and campaign of 1952, 141–43, 223
Republican Senate Policy Committee,

44, 97, 99, 146, 212–13; and Yalta papers, 206–7

Republican strategy on foreign policy, 1, 2–3, 4–9, 18–19, 34–35, 39–40, 51–53, 55, 56, 60, 62–66, 67, 68–69, 70, 71–72, 87, 88, 97, 99–100, 105, 106, 107, 129, 130, 136–40, 141–43, 144–48, 152–53, 154–55, 156, 175, 187; and platform planks, 64, 142–43, 227; change after 1953, 178–79, 180, 186, 194, 195–96, 197, 212; emphasis on use of executive authority, 8, 19, 44–45

Repudiation of Yalta, 8, 9, 40, 59, 62, 63, 64, 84, 87, 105, 118–19, 121–22, 130, 134–35, 136, 137, 140, 142–43, 147–49, 148n48, 151–53, 154, 156, 157, 159, 161–62, 163–65, 174, 186, 187–88, 198–99; Democratic strategy on, 140–41, 143–44, 149–51, 178–79, 189–91, 197–98; resolutions demanding, 9, 90–91, 110–11, 114, 116, 121, 155–56, 158, 196, 227–30, 232–36. See also Yalta Conference

Richards, James, 57, 111, 200

Roosevelt, Franklin, 1, 2, 3, 4, 6, 10, 11, 24, 33, 40, 68, 216, 219; attempt to reach détente with Soviets, 3, 11, 23, 34, 47–48, 85, 187; decisions at Yalta, 3, 4, 6, 14–18, 27–28, 29, 32, 43; decision-making methods, 2, 3, 4, 19, 25, 29, 30, 42, 45, 48, 81, 102, 131, 185, 206, 209; address about Yalta to joint session of Congress, 19, 20, 26, 203; questions about health of, 20–21, 67, 92, 101, 128, 206, 210n36; and charges of being pro-Communist, 30, 45, 63, 66, 74n5, 77, 102, 193, 209, 210

Rozmarek, Charles, 4n1, 53; denunciations of Yalta, 199; support for Republican candidates, 66

Saltonstall, Leverett, 125, 183

The Saturday Evening Post, 4n1, 5n2, 25, 61, 89, 98, 100, 103, 126–27, 164n23, 176, 188, 209, 213; criticisms of New Deal, 80, 91, 109, 127, 175, 182, 185

Scott, Hugh, 5n4, 84, 93

Secret diplomacy: resolutions on and demands concerning, 106, 130, 131, 137, 146–47, 151, 186, 187, 191, 192–93. See also Yalta Conference

Security risks, 70–71, 77, 78, 79, 80, 91, 92, 93, 94, 99, 100, 102, 107, 112, 136 137, 151, 168, 169, 177, 186–87, 188, 193–94, 222

Shafer, Paul, 5n2, 28, 35, 98, 99, 127;

criticism of Soviet occupation of Kuriles, 35–36

Sheehan, Timothy, 5n3, 115–16, 176, 188

Sino-Soviet treaty of 1945, 32, 37, 43, 140, 141, 149

Smith, Frederick, 50, 59, 61

Smith, H. Alexander, 5n4, 78, 97–98, 112, 120, 124–25, 132, 167, 180, 183

Smith, Lawrence, 5n2, 28, 59, 93, 97, 106, 107, 132, 162, 165, 176, 185 188; and Yalta resolution, 111, 114, 155, 196, 228–29; criticism of German policy, 35, 85, 111, 155, 188

Sokolsky, George, 4n1, 5n2, 36, 50, 61, 82, 97, 107, 122, 126–27; criticisms of Roosevelt and New Deal, 29, 45, 63, 66, 79, 80, 90, 91, 127–28, 133, 134, 151, 152, 177, 188, 209–10; criticisms of German policy, 29, 35, 84, 85; response to Eisenhower, 138, 164, 176, 185, 208, 213

Southern Democrats: criticisms of Administration foreign policy, 89, 109, 133, 182, 183–84, 185. See also Bricker Amendment

Soviet Union, 1, 15, 16, 24, 29, 35, 41, 42, 165; U.S. relations with, 10–12, 14, 17, 21, 23, 25, 26–27, 30, 31–32, 33–34, 37, 39, 40, 43, 47, 49–50, 59, 64, 66, 68, 69, 90, 108, 117, 120, 126–27, 136, 155, 162, 175, 187, 218, 219; trustworthiness of, 3, 18, 62, 79, 82, 87, 88, 95, 99, 112, 114, 135, 144, 150, 158, 188, 196, 198, 212–13, 220; explosion of atomic bomb, 8, 70, 222; suspicions about objectives of, 28, 29, 32, 33, 46, 56–57, 71, 72, 85, 86, 129, 176, 177, 193, 195, 199, 209, 213–16, 221, 222. See also Stalin, Joseph

Stalin, Joseph, 10, 11, 21, 107, 137, 145, 164, 212. See also Soviet Union

Stassen, Harold, 5n4, 52, 112

Stettinius, Edward, Jr., 12, 20, 25, 44, 92–93, 167, 211; and Yalta secret agreements, 19, 31, 42, 43, 225–26; role at Yalta, 13, 101n32, 128

Stevenson, Adlai, 148; and campaign of 1952, 150–51; criticisms of Republican strategy, 150, 189

Taft, Robert, 5n2, 34–35, 61, 87, 95, 101n1, 109n9, 166; and campaign of 1952, 136–38, 139, 141–42, 144–45, 146, 151, 153; and House Joint Resolution 200, 160, 165; and Bohlen nomination, 168, 171–72; use of loyalty issue, 98, 101–2, 108, 109–10, 136–37, 138, 142, 151, 175

Teheran Conference, 10, 18, 48, 54, 55, 58, 66, 67, 96, 107, 110, 119, 125, 138, 143, 144, 188, 192, 212, 214

Thye, Edward, 5n4, 90, 108n7, 172, 216

Time, 4n1, 5n3, 100, 133–34, 172n43, 213; initial reaction to Yalta, 26–27, 30, 32, 36, 44–45, 46; emphasis on harmfulness of Yalta, 84, 89, 91, 126, 175, 188; repudiation of Yalta, 143, 163–64

Truman, Harry, 20, 33, 56, 63, 66, 67, 68, 71, 78, 117, 123, 131, 150, 179, 218, 219, 220; Administration of, 39, 40, 54, 57, 58, 64, 70, 72, 80, 81, 86, 89, 103, 118, 129; response to critics, 75, 76, 77, 113, 150; defense of Yalta, 4, 21, 62, 85, 95–96, 113; shift from Roosevelt's foreign policy, 4, 43, 44, 49, 56, 218–19, 220; dismissal of MacArthur, 122. *See also* Wake Island conference

Truman-Attlee conference, 102

Truman-Churchill conference, 131–33

Truman Doctrine, 9, 55, 56–60, 68, 82, 219, 221, 226–27

United Nations, 14, 16, 25, 29, 30, 78, 107, 111, 112, 113, 119, 143, 175, 182; Covenant on Human Rights, 133, 183; Yalta agreements concerning, 14, 16, 17–18, 19. *See also* Yalta Conference

U.S. Department of State, 13, 43, 47, 55, 58–59, 90, 95, 130, 131, 163, 166, 169, 173, 176, 177, 190, 202; nominations for posts in, 78, 79, 156, 165–68; appropriations for, 50, 109; charges of disloyalty in, 8, 20, 37, 38, 78, 81, 87, 93, 102, 127, 137, 187, 193–94; demands for purge of, 137, 153, 154; and publication of Yalta papers, 192, 200–201, 206, 211

U.S. House of Representatives: Committee on Foreign Affairs, 58, 110–11, 196, 212; and House Joint Resolution 200, 158–59, 160, 161–62

— Committee on Un-American Activities, 67, 76, 92, 145, 193; investigations by, 73–74, 75, 77

— House Joint Resolution 200, 8, 9, 158–65, 178, 180, 189, 190, 196, 197, 235; impact of, 166, 174, 186. *See also* Congressional debates

U.S. News and World Report, 4n1, 5n3, 172n43, 176, 185, 192–93; initial reaction to Yalta, 26, 30, 36, 44–

45, 46, 47; and harmfulness of Yalta, 89, 98, 151, 177–78, 188, 209–10; and repudiation of Yalta, 121–22, 163

U.S. Senate: debate on assignment of U.S. troops to Europe (1951), 107–8; and Wherry resolution, 107; and Senate Resolution 99, 108

— Committee on Foreign Relations, 25, 78, 99, 102, 112–13, 156, 170, 171, 185; hearings on Bohlen nomination, 166–68, 168–69, 171–72; hearings on Hurley resignation, 37–38, 42; hearings on Japanese peace treaty, 118–20; and House Joint Resolution 200, 160; hearings on Geneva Conference resolution, 216

— Committee on the Judiciary: and Bricker Amendment, 132–33, 180–81; and Internal Security Subcommittee, 131, 155. *See also* Congressional debates

Vandenberg, Arthur, 5n4, 24, 44, 48–49, 51, 54, 62, 63, 78, 84

Vorys, John, 5n4, 59, 88, 131; and House Joint Resolution 200, 158, 197, 235

Vursell, Charles, 5n2, 52, 59, 61, 127, 201

Wake Island conference, 103. *See also* MacArthur, Douglas; Truman, Harry

Watkins, Arthur, 5n3, 82, 83, 90, 109n9, 132, 172, 180, 188, 214; and reservation to Japanese peace treaty, 117–19, 120, 121, 140

Wedemeyer, Albert, 151; testimony during MacArthur hearings, 123, 124

Welker, Herman, 108n8, 121, 174, 175

Wherry, Kenneth, 5n2, 63, 78, 82, 90, 93, 97, 101, 108n8, 109n9, 128; and resolution on assignment of U.S. troops to Europe, 107–8

White, Wallace, 24, 26

Wiley, Alexander, 5n4, 98n23, 99, 119, 121, 124, 156, 165, 186, 192; initial reaction to Yalta, 26; and Bohlen nomination, 170, 172–73, 174; and Bricker Amendment, 132, 180, 181, 183

Wood, John, 5n2, 109, 139

Yalta Conference: Bohlen's role at, 13, 165, 167, 170, 172, 174; Byrnes's role at, 13, 19–20, 36, 42–44; Hiss's role at, 13, 20–21, 71, 73–74, 77, 78, 79, 81, 91–93, 99, 100, 110, 112, 119, 122, 128, 130, 131, 136, 147, 148, 149, 152, 155, 167, 186–87,

193–94, 203, 206, 207, 209, 210, 211, 213, 214; drinking at, 51, 51n32; communiqué of, 19, 25, 27; secret agreements of, 19–20, 29–31, 35–36, 37–38, 41–45, 47, 55, 88, 106, 177–78, 199–200, 206–7, 210–11; spirit of, 1, 21, 22, 33–34, 38, 87–88, 176–77, 178; and secret, personal diplomacy, 1, 3–4, 8, 19–20, 25, 29, 30, 35–37, 41–45, 46–47, 48–49, 53, 55, 58, 65–66, 67, 77, 81, 83, 85, 88, 90, 92, 94, 97–98, 99, 101, 102, 106, 107–8, 120–21, 123, 125, 126, 130–32, 133–34, 137, 140, 142–43, 148, 152, 154–55, 157, 162, 164–65, 177–78, 181–82, 185, 186, 187, 191, 192–93, 199–200, 203–4, 206–7, 209–11, 215–16; impact of Cold War on, 1, 3, 4, 9, 18, 21, 85–86, 97–98, 213–14, 219, 221; shift in criticisms of, 1, 3, 6, 7, 8, 9, 18, 85–86, 141–42, 218, 222. *See also* Curzon line agreement; Eastern European agreements; Far Eastern agreements; Publication of Yalta papers; Repudiation of Yalta; Secret diplomacy; United Nations